ACTA UNIVERSITATIS STOCKHOLMIENSIS
Stockholm Studies in Statistics 1

FREDRIK NYGÅRD ARNE SANDSTRÖM

MEASURING INCOME INEQUALITY

Almqvist & Wiksell International
Stockholm — Sweden

ISBN 91-22-00439-4

Printed in Finland by
Hangö Tryckeri Ab
Hangö, 1981

PREFACE

During the last decade the interest in the size distribution of income and the redistribution of incomes has increased substantially. One effect of this has been the discussion of relevant tools for comparing two or more size distributions of incomes with respect to their inequality. Despite the plenitude of papers on income distributions there is still a need for surveys on this topic.

More precisely, in this study our interest will be focused on one-component measures of income inequality. Basically the purpose is to sort out the seemingly abundant, and sometimes even confusing, suggestions regarding such measures which are found in the literature.

Two directions are easily recognized in the literature: one penetrating the fundamental conditions of inequality comparisons, without entering into any practical considerations to speak of, and another holding up some specific measure of inequality evaluation as the one and only appropriate one, disregarding more profound difficulties.

We attempt to show that these directions are not incompatible. In due course we hope to lay a basis for the discussion by considering the fundaments of inequality comparisons. On the basis of these contemplations a number of optional inequality measures are then exposed, both measures in general use as well as some more uncommon forms.

The exposition reflects at the same time the leading idea of a general family of inequality measures, to which most presented measures conform. In addition, a treatment of two particular topics of interest, viz. decomposition analysis and sampling properties, is undertaken.

After an introduction in chapter 1, in which some primary considerations are outlined, graphical descriptions of the size distribution of income are given in chapter 2.

Chapter 3 deals with the ranking of income distributions and different types of inequality comparisons.

Various criteria on the inequality ranking and on inequality measures are discussed and illustrated in chapter 4.

Functional forms of the size distribution of income are briefly reviewed in chapter 5 and

normative inequality measures based on social evaluation functions in chapter 6.
Chapter 7 deals with measures of inequality. In section 7.1 several fractile and level measures of inequality are surveyed. The Lorenz curve and related topics, e.g. the use of Lorenz curves to compare salary and tax policies, are discussed in section 7.2. Section 7.3 introduces a distribution comparative function, and in section 7.4 a general measure of inequality is defined. Various measures of income inequality that have been proposed in the literature are discussed in relation to the general measure.
Chapter 8, in turn, discusses practical calculations, and chapter 9 deals with decompositions of the measures.
Chapter 10 is devoted to the problems involved in measuring inequality on a sample basis.
A brief summary of the previous discussion is given in chapter 11, and an extension to simultaneous comparisons of income distributions is discussed in chapter 12.
Finally, an index is supplemented.

Co-authorship is a delicate and stimulating experience: You may compare notes but never rest assured that your opinions and manner of presentation cohere to those of your fellow writer. Moreover, co-authorship provides you with a tempting opportunity of having someone else to blame. We will however suppress this temptation for good by declaring that section 1.1, chapters 2—4, 6, and 10 are written by Nygård, and section 1.2, chapters 5, 7—9, and 12 by Sandström.

The study has emerged during the course of the collaborative research project, in which the Departments of Statistics at the University of Stockholm and Åbo Akademi (the Swedish University of Turku) participate.

The research has been supported by Svenska Handelsbankens forskningsstiftelse, Stockholm, Swedish Council for Research in the Humanities and Social Sciences, Stockholm, Sweden, the Academy of Finland, Helsinki, Osuuspankkijärjestön Tutkimussäätiö, Helsinki, and Åbo Akademis Jubileumsfond, Turku, Finland.

We greatfully acknowledge the financial support of Jan Wallanders forskningsstiftelse, Svenska Handelsbanken, Stockholm, Sweden, making the printing of this book possible.

We wish to express our special appreciation to Staffan Wahlén, who willingly undertook the unpleasant task of correcting our English, and to Siri Eriksson, Tina Hasselgren, Hulda Hjörleifsdottir, and Bibi Thunell for helping us with type-writing.

We are also deeply indebted to the staff of Stockholms Universitetsbibliotek and Åbo Akademis Bibliotek, especially to Ingmar Lundberg (ÅAB), for their efforts in providing us with reference literature from far and near.

Finally, we are grateful to Olivier Guilbaud, Sten Malmquist, Leif Nordberg, and Yrjö O. Vartia for helpful suggestions resulting from critical reading of earlier drafts.
Needless to say, we take full responsibility for all remaining errors, misprints, and other imperfections in the text; the only excuse being our frequent journeys between Finland and Sweden.

M/S Fennia, an evening in October, 1981

Fredrik Nygård
Åbo Akademi

Arne Sandström
University of Stockholm

CONTENTS

1. INTRODUCTION

The distribution of income, its shape in different countries and evolution over time, has since the turn of the century, and particularly in the last few decades, been the subject of numerous theoretical and empirical studies. This is not a manifestation of the prominence of income distributions per se; rather it falls back upon the close relationship between the distribution of income and major social topics of current interest. Among such topics we observe the following:

(A) 'The law of Nature' of the income distribution.

This classical issue concerns the determination of some specific theoretical distribution (e.g. the lognaormal or the Pareto distribution) according to which income is distributed irrespective of time and place. See e.g. Pareto [1897], Gini [1936], Gibrat [1931],[1957], Champernowne [1973].

(B) Theories of personal income formation.

Which individual qualities and/or other factors determine personal income ? See e.g. Ord [1975], Lydall [1976], Tinbergen [1977], Sahota [1978]. To what extent may income be attributed to remuneration of productive factors (labor, capital, etc) ? See e.g. Brown [1968], Brown [1976].

(C) The relationship income - welfare.

Income is frequently assumed to be of utmost importance with respect to individual utility and total social welfare. If this is the case, to what extent may welfare be raised by alterations in the income distribution, and may an optimal distribution of income be specified? See e.g. Dalton [1920], Lerner [1944], Atkinson [1970], Sen [1973].

(D) Social equity aspects.

An equal distribution of income may in itself be seen as a legitimate goal of society. To what extent has this goal been reached? Is there any correspondence between the actual income distribution and the aim of achieving equity? Do big income differences occur between individuals, and does inequality therefore prevail? Is the level of income the same between different groups of the population? See e.g. Sen [1973], Brown [1977], Tinbergen [1978], Varian [1979].

(E) The macroeconomic effects of the income distribution.

How are the income distribution and essential macroeconomic variates, such as consumption and saving, related? How does a change in the distribution of income affect these magnitudes? See e.g. Staehle [1937], Kravis [1962], Brown [1976], Musgrove [1980].

(F) The incidence of transfers.

How is the income distribution affected by governmental measures such as taxation and other transfers? Are the redistributional measures efficient? See e.g. Jakobsson and Normann [1974], Nicholson and Britton [1976], Krupp [1978], Stiglitz [1978].

In this book we confine our attention to only one aspect of the income distribution, viz. the distributional quality called 'inequality'. More precisely, the main objectives of the study are to

* *examine the notion of income inequality in general, and particularly the possibilities of using some kind of measuring-rod to give this notion an operational signification*

* *deal with the problems involved in comparisons of the inequality of*

two or more distributions, with special reference to the case of international comparisons

* *propose methods of attributing parts of an overall inequality to sources of different kinds.*

Consequently, we will concentrate on a more general discussion at the expense of the specific economic questions sketched above, thereby depriving ourselves of the means of a closer discussion of the relationship between these and the income distribution.
As inequality considerations nevertheless are common to several of these questions in that their treatment calls for an analysis of income inequality and its effects (e.g. in connection with (C)-(F) above), a general knowledge of different inequality traits is of vital importance to the further analysis. This broad view of income inequality forms the basis of the subsequent discussion.

The mere use of the word 'income inequality' suggests that our subject is to be approached with great caution. As pointed out by Sen [1978], [1980] there are at least three aspects of the notion 'inequality', and its antipole 'equality', that must be recognized.

Firstly, 'inequality' has a *descriptive* meaning: If two or more magnitudes are not all of exactly the same size inequality in its descriptive sense is demonstrated. It is precisely this kind of inequality that standard statistical measures of dispersion seek to capture. Accordingly we will also use the name 'income dispersion' when referring to descriptive income inequality.

Secondly , it must not be overlooked that 'inequality' and 'equality' allude to 'equity', a clearly *prescriptive* (normative) concept.

If the income distribution exhibits 'inequality' this will frequently make people (and perhaps especially policy-makers) uneasy as it may be taken as an indication that the distribution is inequitable. This prescriptive implication of income inequality falls back upon some idea of the shape of an equitable distribution.

In this context we also note that 'inequality' may be seen as a feature of the distribution of income among either individual income receiving units (subsequently abbreviated as i.r.u (sing.), i.r.u's (pl.)) - usually persons or households - or larger collectives of i.r.u's. This can be concluded from the following alternative definitions of the equitable distribution. See Alker [1970], Nicholson and Britton [1976], Tinbergen [1978]. The definitions readily bring out the prescriptive quality of our subject.

The minimum definition

An eqiutable income distribution is attained if each i.r.u can satisfy certain minimum needs.

Roughly speaking this definition postulates a lower bound for the equitable distribution, corresponding to a minimum subsistence level, but leaves all incomes above this bound out of consideration.

The communist definition

An equitable income distribution is attained if each i.r.u gets an income according to its need.

The egalitarian definition

An eqitable income distribution is attained if each i.r.u gets exactly the same income.

The liberalist definition

An equitable income distribution is attained if each i.r.u gets an income according to its productive contribution to society.

The grouping definition

An equitable income distribution is attained if representative i.r.u's of different population subgroups (e.g. socioeconomic groups) have the same income.

The (marginal) utilitarian definition

An equitable income distribution is attained if each i.r.u gets the same (marginal) utility out of its income.

It goes without saying that supplementary or competing definitions may well be put forward. For instance, it is sometimes argued that the appropriate thing to do is to distinguish between 'vertical' and 'horizontal' equality. It this context 'vertical' equality refers to the proposition that all i.r.u's with the same need should get the same income (cf the communist definition), while 'horizontal' equality means that the living standard of the i.r.u's should be the same irrespective of their need (cf the utilitarian definition).

Once the question of an appropriate definition of the equitable income distribution is settled the notion of prescriptive inequality may simply be defined as

Income inequality prevails if some i.r.u (or collective of i.r.u's) gets an actual income differing from its legitimate income according to the equitable distribution.

It may be noted that descriptive inequality can be viewed as a special case of this definition, viz. when the equitable distribution is taken as egalitarian.

Thirdly, the notion of inequality is sometimes given a chiefly *predictive* interpretation. Such instances may occur when the income distribution takes the (subordinate) position of an 'explanatory variable'.
For instance, if we consider the relationship between consumption expenditures and the income distribution it may be argued that the total consumption expidentures in an economy depend not only on the total income, as simple macroeconomic models suggest, but also on the distribution or 'inequality' of this income in such a way that a 'more equal' distribution raises the level of consumption.

It is not surprising that incompatible ways of evaluating income inequality may emanate from distinct principal considerations, depending on whether stress is laid on the descriptive, prescriptive, or predictive features of the inequality notion.
Our discussion will mainly be confined to descriptive and prescriptive aspects of income inequality. A predictive interpretation, originating from the relationship income - welfare, will, however, also be touched upon because of the attention it has attracted in the literature.

Two other questions at issue, closely related to the interpretation of inequality, are those of a proper definition of the basic concepts 'income' and 'income receiving unit'. As these problems have to be solved separately for each specific income distribution study only some broad outlines will be given here.

Turning to the first question we can distinguish between two types of income distribution studies.
Firstly, there are studies where income is interpreted in a restricted

sense. Studies of this type, e.g. (A),(B),(F) above, mainly deal with clear-cut income concepts, some of which are summarized in table 1.1. These studies often seek to capture descriptive inequality and we will give them the label '*positive*'. It should be noted that in positive studies no restrictions can a priori be laid on the magnitude of income: incomes may be positive (e.g. wages), zero, or even negative (e.g. taxes, some entrepreneurial incomes).

Secondly, there are studies where income is taken as a proxy for welfare or utility, usually originating in reasoning along the line 'welfare depends on consumption possibilities and these in turn on income'. These studies will ba named '*normative*'. In these cases the determination of an appropriate definition of income is less clear-cut. As individual welfare depends on received free services (subsidized public health, education, etc), as well as on available income, the income concept should be quite extensive. Moreover, as individual consumption is necessarily positive - mere survival requires at least some consumption - it seems reasonable to expect any well-conditioned income definition to raise positive values of the observed incomes.[1)] The translation of such a definition into operational terms is however not an easily solved problem. As a matter of fact we will in practice occasionally encounter cases, in which our expectation of positive incomes is violated (negative available incomes due to entrepreneurial losses, etc), manifestating an ill-conditioned income definition from the normative point of view. In the subsequent discussion we will assume that the ideal definition holds true and suppose that normative income is always positive. Yet we occasionally will allow incomes of magnitude zero, simply because seen as limiting cases these bring out many arguments sharply.

1) Pareto [1896] states (translation according to Brown [1976]): "We should observe that when researching into the distribution of income, we are not concerned with the sources of income. Even the poorest man must be ragarded as having sufficient income to keep him alive."

Table 1.1. Income concepts in official statistics.

1. PRIMARY INCOME

   (a) Compensation of employees

      (i) Wages and salaries

         a. In cash
         b. In kind

      (ii) Employers' contributions to social security and similar schemes

   (b) Income of members from producers' co-operatives

   (c) Gross entrepreneurial income of unincorporated enterprises

2. PROPERTY INCOME RECEIVED

   (a) Imputed rent of owner-occupied dwellings

   (b) Interest

   (c) Dividends

   (d) Rent

3. CURRENT TRANSFERS AND OTHER BENEFITS RECEIVED

   (a) Social security benefits

   (b) Pensions and life insurance annuity benefits

   (c) Other current transfers

4. TOTAL HOUSEHOLD INCOME (1 + 2 + 3)

5. DIRECT TAXES PAID

6. SOCIAL SECURITY AND PENSION FUND CONTRIBUTIONS

   (a) Social security

   (b) Pension fund

7. TOTAL AVAILABLE HOUSEHOLD INCOME (4 - (5 + 6))

Source: Provisional Guidelines on Statistics of the Distribution of Income, Consumption and Accumulation of Households.

Moreover, it must be pointed out that, besides the income concept in itself, the length of the time period during which the incomes are recorded is of fundamental importance when forming an idea about the shape of the income distribution.[1)] Owing to the lack of other data annual income is a commonly studied magnitude.

Many objections have been raised against this custom laying stress on the fact that the only adequate income magnitude is the lifetime income. See e.g. Paglin [1975], Stoikov [1975], Weizsäcker [1978]. We do not support this view, since we find it hard to accept that it does not really matter how a given income is distributed over the lifetime of an individual. Rather, we will argue that the prevailing custom of using annual income is acceptable, if it is not interpreted as revealing anything else than a static picture, a 'snapshot', of the income distribution. This snapshot should, whenever possible, be supplemented by a dynamic analysis, an income distribution 'movie', following individuals over the years and their movements up and down the income distribution. Despite the rareness of dynamic income data some attempts towards a dynamic analysis have been made. See e.g. Hart [1976], Shorrocks [1976], Creedy et al [1981].

The discussion in this study will mainly be confined to static aspects of income inequality and the construction of a good 'snapshot apparatus'. Dynamic problems will only partially be dealt with, chiefly in connection with the decomposition of an overall inequality.

Concerning the second definitional issue, viz. the determination of how the i.r.u's should be defined, we note that in positive studies this is a matter entirely depending on the scope of the study; it may be appropriate to record income per capita, per earner, per household, etc.

1) The length of the time period is basically part of the income definition. The occurrance of negative incomes may sometimes be due to the fact that incomes are recorded during too short a period.

In the case of normative studies we will however argue that the only appropriate i.r.u is the individual, "since it is human beings not households that have stomachs and feel the cold" (Wiles [1978]), and consequently the individual forms the natural basis of welfare considerations. Thus, in normative studies the income concept may be derived through some proper 'percaptilatisation'.

Let us conclude this section with a short glance at the factors contributing to the personal income. A number of theories of the personal income distribution have been presented in the literature; a penetrating review is given by Sahota [1978]. Most theories are partial, and only in the last few years have some efforts of amalgamation been made (see e.g. Blinder [1974]). Factors, which are commonly accepted as determining the personal income, can roughly be divided into four categories (cf Pen [1978]):

* Personal characteristics
* State of the market, scarcity, and marginal productivity
* Political, economic, and administrative power in the society
* Luck and other stochastic events.

The constituents of personal characteristics may partly be described as 'parameters', i.e. factors which are constant for the individual (such as race, sex, social background, genotype , etc) or can only gradually be changed (e.g. age, education, job experience, taste) , partly as 'variables', i.e. attributes which may be subject to relatively quick changes (place and amount of work, temporary illness, etc). The state of the market and the power situation in the society in turn determine the yield of these personal qualities.

In this context it may be noted that it is sometimes argued (cf e.g. Kurien [1977], Söderström [1981]) that the only reasonable way of handling income inequality is by a division of the existing income differences into compensatory (choice-related) and non-compensatory (opportunity-related) differences. The argument is that only non-compensatory income differences matter for equity purposes. It is however very hard to give these notions operational signification, and they will be ignored in the present study. Yet, if one succeeds in extracting non-compensatory income differences, most of the subsequent discussion may be applied to this new income magnitude.

1.2 SOME FREQUENTLY USED NOTATIONS AND DEFINITIONS

This section is devoted to some of the notations and definitions to be used in the book. The discussion is partly made in the continuous case (Riemann integrals) and partly in both the continuous and discrete cases (Riemann-Stieltjes integrals).

Let Y denote a random variate (income variate), defined at the interval $[0,\infty[$ if not otherwise stated, with the continuous and (at least once) differentiable cumulative distribution function (c.d.f.) $F(y)$. When integrating a function of y or a function of $F(y)$ over $F(y)$ we will at our convenience use a notation with or without the argument of F, i.e., when letting w be a function of $F(y)$, we write

$$\int_0^\infty w[F(y)]dF(y) = \int_0^1 w(F)dF$$

Both the cumulative distribution function (c.d.f.), $F(y)$, and the 1st moment distribution function[1)] (m.d.f.), $F_1(y)$, play an important role in the theory of inequality measurement. The j:th m.d.f. is defined by

$$F_j(y) = \mu_j^{-1} \int_0^y t^j \, dF(t), \quad j = 0,1,2,... \qquad (1.1)$$

where $\mu_j = \int_0^\infty y^j \, dF(y)$ is the j:th moment about zero, $j = 0,1,2,...$. The μ_j's are subsequently assumed to be finite and the expectation of Y, viz. μ_1, is denoted μ.[2)] The c.d.f. $F(y)$ is given by $F_o(y)$ in (1.1) and the 1st m.d.f.

1) $F_1(y)$ is labelled the incomplete first moment by Kendell and Stuart [1977 - p. 49].

2) The variance of the c.d.f. is defined by $\sigma_0^2 = \mu_2 - \mu_1^2 = \mu_2 - \mu^2$.

by $F_1(y)$. The j:th moment about zero of the 1st m.d.f. is denoted by γ_j and defined by

$$\gamma_j = \int_0^\infty y^j \, dF_1(y) = \frac{\mu_{j+1}}{\mu}\ .^{1)}$$

In empirical studies F(y) is the cumulative share of income receiving units (i.r.u.'s) with income $\leq$ y and $F_1(y)$ is the cumulative income share of these i.r.u.'s.

The j:th complementary m.d.f. $G_j(y)$ is defined by $G_j(y) = 1 - F_j(y)$, j = 0,1,2,..

It can be shown (cf. Piesch [1975]) that the frequency function ($\frac{dF(y)}{dy} = f(y)$, 'people curve') and the 1st moment-frequency function ($\frac{dF_1(y)}{dy} = f_1(y)$, 'income curve') intersect in $y = \mu = \int_0^\infty yf(y)dy$. This is illustrated in fig 1.1.

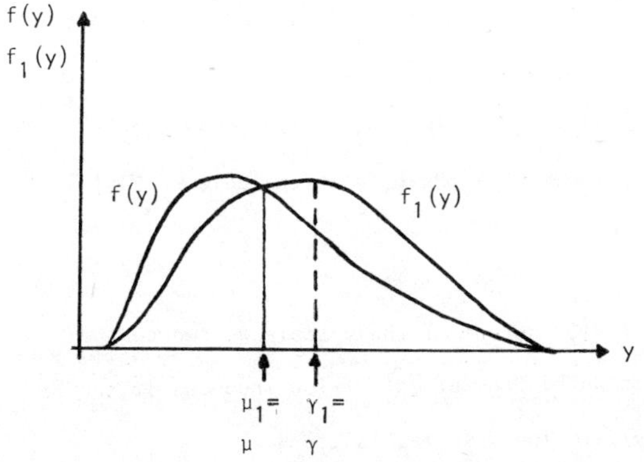

FIGURE 1.1 Illustration of a frequency function (f(y)) and the corresponding 1st moment-frequency function ($f_1(y)$). The intersection between f(y) and $f_1(y)$ at the point y = μ is depicted.

1) The arithmetic mean value of $F_1(y)$ equals $\gamma_1 = \frac{\mu_2}{\mu} = \frac{\sigma^2 + \mu^2}{\mu} = \mu(V^2+1)$ and the variance $\sigma_1^2 = \gamma_2 - \gamma_1^2 = \frac{\mu_3}{\mu_1} - (\frac{\mu_2}{\mu_1})^2$, where V^2 is the coefficient of variation.

It can be shown (cf.,e.g. Bortkiewicz [1930] and Piesch[1975]) that

$$(\forall y \in [0,\infty[)(F(y) \geq F_1(y)). \tag{1.2}$$

By the definition of $G_j(y)$ $(= 1 - F_j(y))$ and the relation (1.2) it is obvious that $G_1(y) \geq G(y)$ for $y \in [0,\infty[$. $F(y)$, $F_1(y)$, $G(y)$ and $G_1(y)$ are outlined in figures 1.2(a) and (b), respectively.

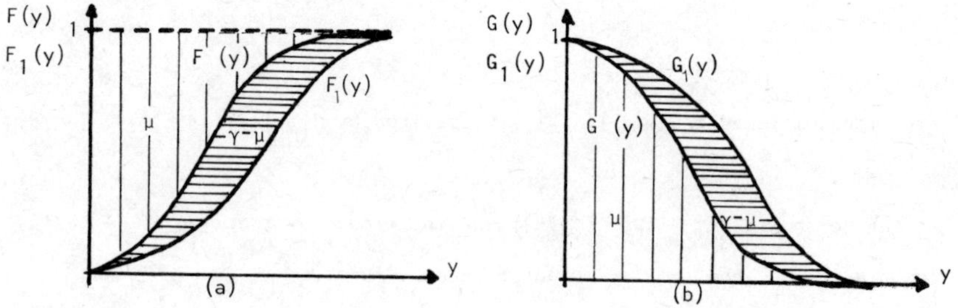

FIGURE 1.2 Illustration of $F(y)$ and $F_1(y)$ in (a) and $G(y)$ and $G_1(y)$ in (b).

It can also be seen that the arithmetic mean, $\int_0^\infty y \, dF_j(y)$, of the jth m.d.f. can be written as the area under $G_j(y)$, i.e. $\int_0^\infty G_j(y)\, dy$.
The area under $G(y)$ is thus equal to μ and the area under $G_1(y)$ equals $\mu(V^2+1)$[1] and hence the area between $G(y)$ and $G_1(y)$, i.e. between $F(y)$ and $F_1(y)$, equals μV^2.

By using a log y-scale, $y \in [1,\infty]$, instead of the y-scale we reduce the effect of high incomes and strengthen the effect of low incomes. It can be shown that the area under $G(y)$, in log y-scale, is

$$\int_1^\infty G(y) d \log y = \int_1^\infty \log y \, dF(y) = \log \mu_g ,$$

[1] This is the inequality measure proposed by Niehans [1955].

i.e. the logarithm of the geometrical mean and the area under $G_1(y)$ equals

$$\int_1^\infty G_1(y)d \log y = \int_1^\infty \log y \; dF_1(y) = \int_1^\infty \frac{y}{\mu} \log y \; dF(y) = \log \mu_{gw}$$

which can be interpreted as the logarithm of the geometrical mean of $F_1(y)$ or as the logarithm of a weighted geometrical mean. The area between $G_1(y)$ and $G(y)$ can thus be written as

$$\log \frac{\mu_{gw}}{\mu_g} = \log \frac{\mu_{gw}}{\mu} + \log \frac{\mu}{\mu_g} = T_1 + T_2,$$

where T_1 and T_2 are the two measures proposes by Theil [1967], cf. sec. 7.3.1 and sec. 7.4.

Abbreviations

c.d.f.	cumulative distribution function
cf.	confer
ch.	chapter
FIM	the international standard for 'Finnish Marks'
i.r.u.	income receiving unit
LC	Lorenz-curve
m.d.f.	moment distribution function
n.e.t.	non-egalitarian transfer
sec.	section
SEK	the international standard for 'Swedish Crowns'

2. A GRAPHICAL DESCRIPTION OF THE SIZE DISTRIBUTION OF INCOME

In this chapter we present some of the various methods used for depicting income distributions.
Presupposing that statistical data on incomes are available we wish to transform the data into an intelligible form. This can be done in a variety of ways, starting from standard techniques for graphical representation to more sophisticated methods especially designed for description of income data. The methods have one feature in common: they provide means of forming an idea about the shape of the distribution. Some graphical methods are however more pretentious and seek to go beyond sheer description and summarize essential characteristics of the distribution in one go. We return to a short discussion of this issue in section 2.6.

The illustrations in this chapter refer to the 'official' income distribution in Finland and Sweden 1971/72 . Data, based on the Finnish and Swedish surveys on relative income differences, are given in table 2.1.[1)]

1) Since the data originate from sample surveys the figures in table 2.1 should strictly speaking be interpreted as estimates.

Table 2.1. Available household incomes in Finland 1971 and Sweden 1972, decile groups.

FINLAND 1971

	Number of households			Incomes		
Income interval (FIM)	Absolute frequency	Population share (cumulative values within brackets)		Mean income (FIM)	Share of total income (cumulative values within brackets)	
(1)	(2)	(3)	(4)	(5)	(6)	(7)
- 5536	149548	0.10	(0.10)	4036	0.025	(0.025)
5537 - 7939	149548	0.10	(0.20)	6767	0.041	(0.066)
7940 - 10115	149548	0.10	(0.30)	9043	0.055	(0.121)
10116 - 12421	149548	0.10	(0.40)	11248	0.068	(0.189)
12422 - 14736	149548	0.10	(0.50)	13552	0.083	(0.272)
14737 - 17080	149548	0.10	(0.60)	15921	0.097	(0.369)
17081 - 19762	149548	0.10	(0.70)	18441	0.112	(0.481)
19763 - 23144	149548	0.10	(0.80)	21355	0.131	(0.612)
23145 - 28640	149548	0.10	(0.90)	25675	0.156	(0.768)
28641 -	149551	0.10	(1.00)	38150	0.232	(1.000)
Total	1495483			16419		

SWEDEN 1972

	Number of households			Incomes		
Income interval (SEK)	Absolute frequency	Population share (cumulative values within brackets)		Mean income (SEK)	Share of total income (cumulative values within brackets)	
(1)	(2)	(3)	(4)	(5)	(6)	(7)
- 9800	357636	0.10	(0.10)	6028	0.022	(0.022)
9801 - 13500	357636	0.10	(0.20)	11508	0.042	(0.064)
13501 - 17200	357636	0.10	(0.30)	15344	0.056	(0.120)
17201 - 20900	357636	0.10	(0.40)	19180	0.070	(0.190)
20901 - 24700	357636	0.10	(0.50)	22468	0.082	(0.272)
24701 - 29200	357636	0.10	(0.60)	26852	0.098	(0.370)
29201 - 33800	357636	0.10	(0.70)	31510	0.115	(0.485)
33801 - 39500	357636	0.10	(0.80)	36716	0.134	(0.619)
39501 - 48100	357636	0.10	(0.90)	43292	0.159	(0.778)
48101 -	357638	0.10	(1.00)	60554	0.222	(1.000)
Total	3576362			27345		

Source: Finnish survey on relative income differences 1971
Swedish survey on relative income differences 1972

2.1 PEN´S PARADE

To get a first impression of the shape of the income distribution Pen [1971] draws a parallel between the distribution and a parade of people. This illuminating interpretation starts out from the supposition that each i.r.u is given the image of a person - in the case of households we can use the head of each household as representatives - with height proportionate to income so that i.r.u's with average income appear as people of average height. These images are then instructed to form a parade according to height in such a way that the shortest persons are in the van and the tallest in the end of the parade. After this the parade marches by the spot , where we stand watching the procession, at uniform speed so that all marchers have gone by in, say, one hour.

We quote Pen [1971] in his suggestive narration of the personal (before tax) income distribution in the United Kingdom:

> "In the first seconds a remarkable thing already happens .. we see a number of people of negative height passing ... After this tragi-comic opening we see tiny gnomes pass by, the seize of a matchstick, a cigarette ... It takes almost fifteen minutes before the passing marchers reach the height of substantially more than four feet ... But a new suprise awaits us here. We keep on seeing dwarfs .. We know that the parade will last an hour, and perhaps we expected that after half-an-hour we would be able to look the marchers straight in the eye, but that is not so .. about twelve minutes before the end the average income recipients pass by ... After the average income recipients have passed, the scene changes rather quickly. The marchers´ height grows ... In the last few minutes giants sudenly loom up."

Pen´s parade may easily be converted into a graph by letting the horizontal axis in a diagram represent time and the vertical axis denote the height of the passing marchers. Equivalently the values along the horizontal axis can be taken as the cumulative proportion of i.r.u's, when ordered from the poorest (shortest) to the richest (tallest), and the vertical axis as the corresponding incomes relative to the mean income.

In figure 2.1 the Finnish and Swedish income parades are sketched. As might be expected - our data refer to incomes after tax and other redistributional measures - the processions are not as striking in their appearance as Pen´s UK parade. Note also that the data only determine ten points of the graphs exactly, and as the depicted parades are obtained by smoothening a curve through these points the charts are not necessarily fully accurate.

2.2 CHARTS BASED ON THE FREQUENCY DISTRIBUTION

Using the data of table 2.1 we may draw a histogram depicting the frequency distribution of income. This is done in figure 2.2. Both the Finnish and Swedish histogram exhibit a shape characteristic of income distributions in general: The frequency distribution is spread over a range of considerable width, and skewed to the right with a peak to the left of the mean income.

In figure 2.3 the distribution function of income, viz. the cumulative frequency distribution (the ogive), is drawn by joining the known coordinates by straight lines.[1)] The diagram is in fact equivalent to the chart of Pen´s parade (figure 2.1), since the parade may be converted into the ogive by

1) This representation is exact if the incomes within each bracket are uniformly distributed.

Figure 2.1 Pen´s parade: Available household incomes in Finland and Sweden 1971/72

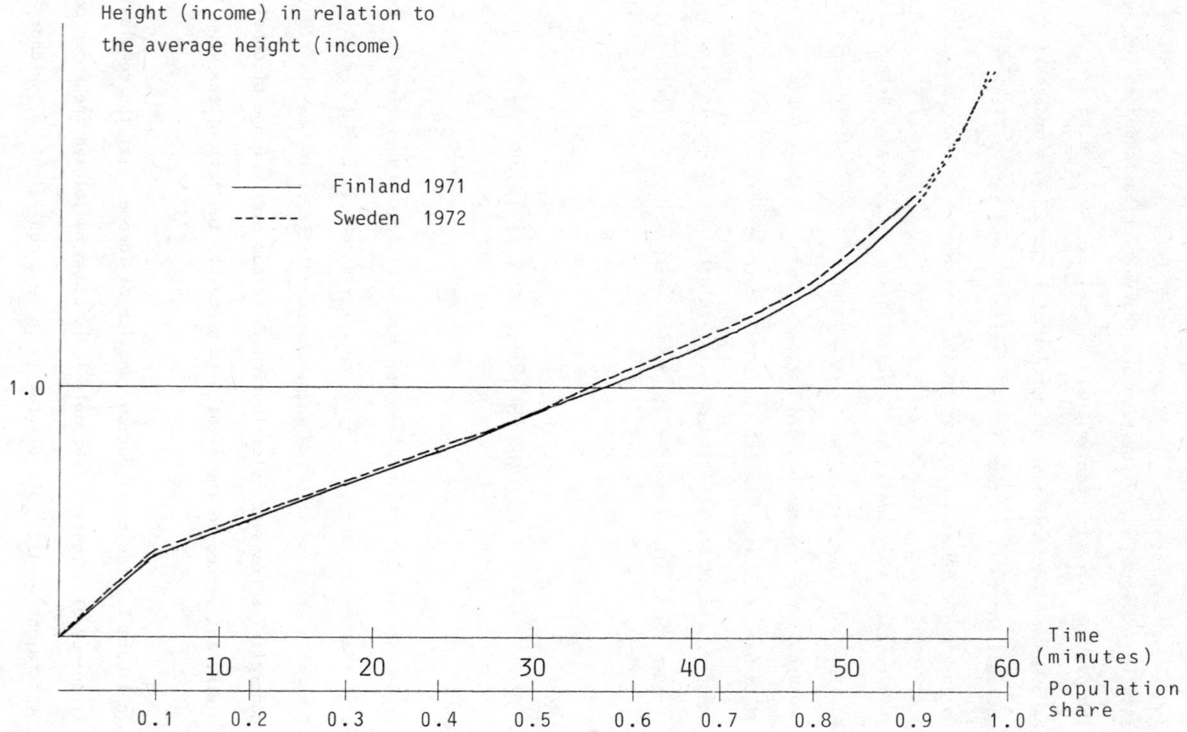

Figure 2.2 Frequency distribution histogram: Available household incomes in Finland and Sweden 1971/72

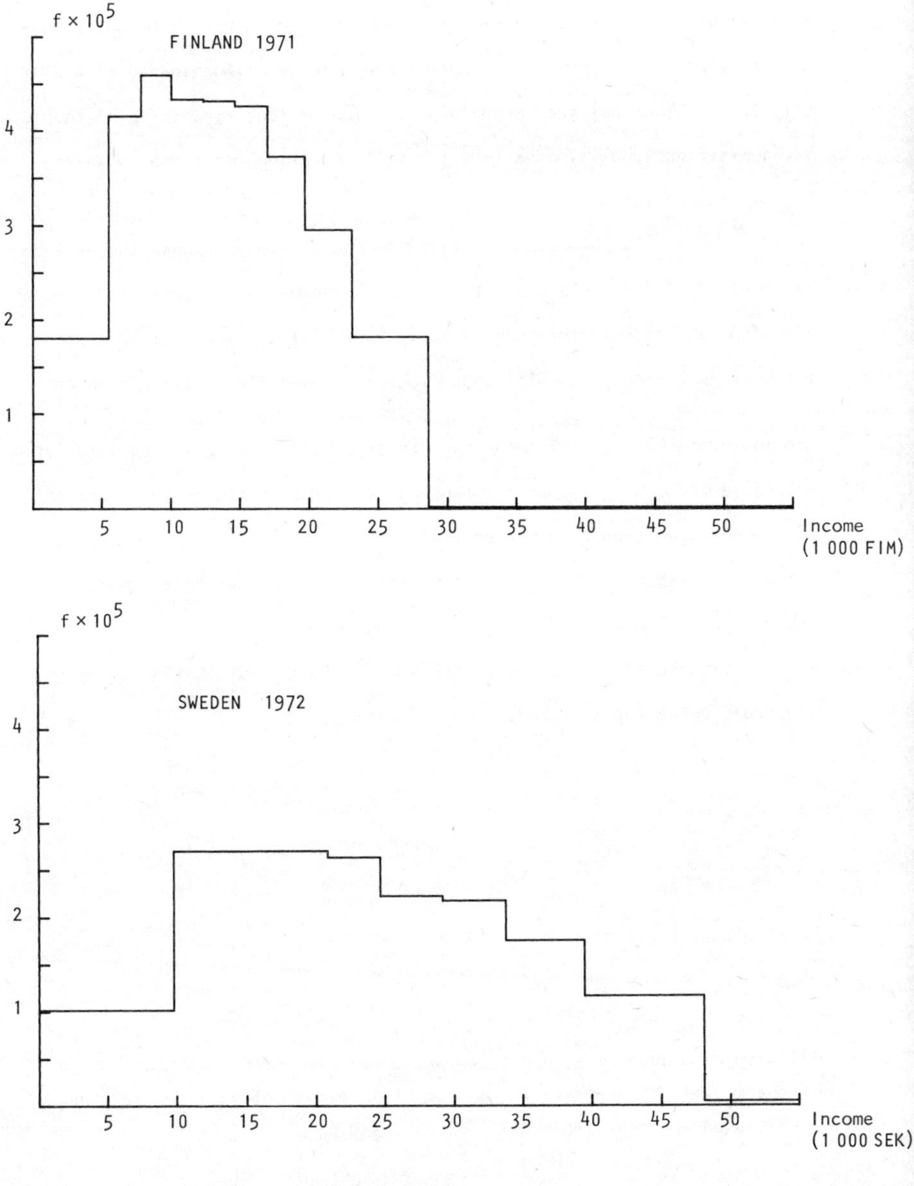

interchanging the horizontal and vertical axis and transforming the 'heights' (incomes relative to the mean income) into absolute incomes.

A number of hypotheses concerning the shape of the income distribution may be interpreted in terms of the logarithm of income.[1)] For instance, Gibrat [1931] suggested that the income distribution is lognormal (cf also chapter 5), a distributional hypothesis which still occasionally turns up in the literature.
In accordance with Champernowne [1973] we could name the logarithm of income "income-power" and a chart chart showing the number of i.r.u's in different income-power brackets the "people-curve". We will however instead prefer the self-explanatory denominations 'logincome' and 'logincome histogram'.

The logincome histogram for our data is given in figure 2.4. The logarithmic procedure reduces the numerical range of the distribution - the upper tail is brought down closer to the central part of the distribution - and in comparison with figure 2.2 the chart exhibits a somewhat more symmetrical shape with a peak close to the average logincome.
It is of course also possible to depict the income distribution using the logincome ogive (or a 'parade' of logincomes).

1) This presupposes that all incomes are positive (cf the discussion in chapter 1). If negative incomes occur in empirical data they are usually excluded when the logincome is considered.

Figure 2.3 Frequency distribution ogive: Available household incomes in Finland and Sweden 1971/72

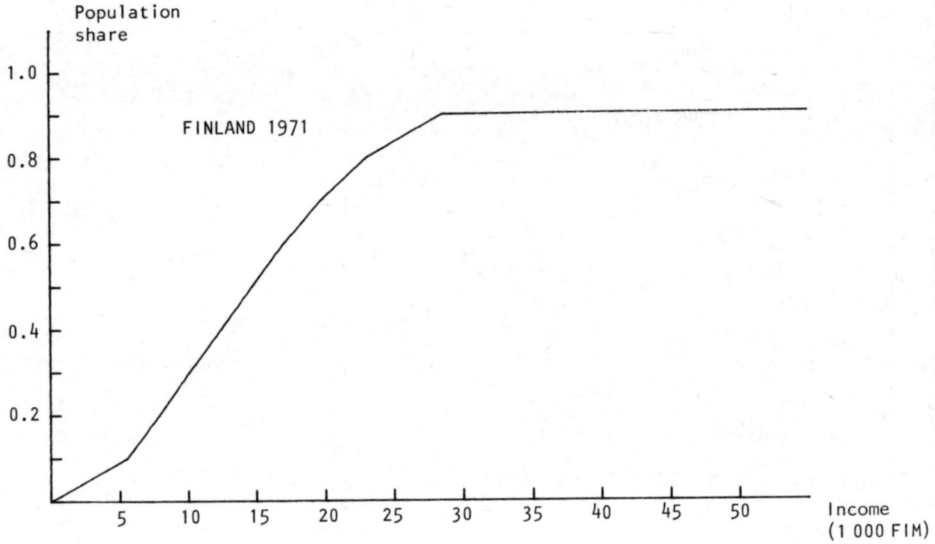

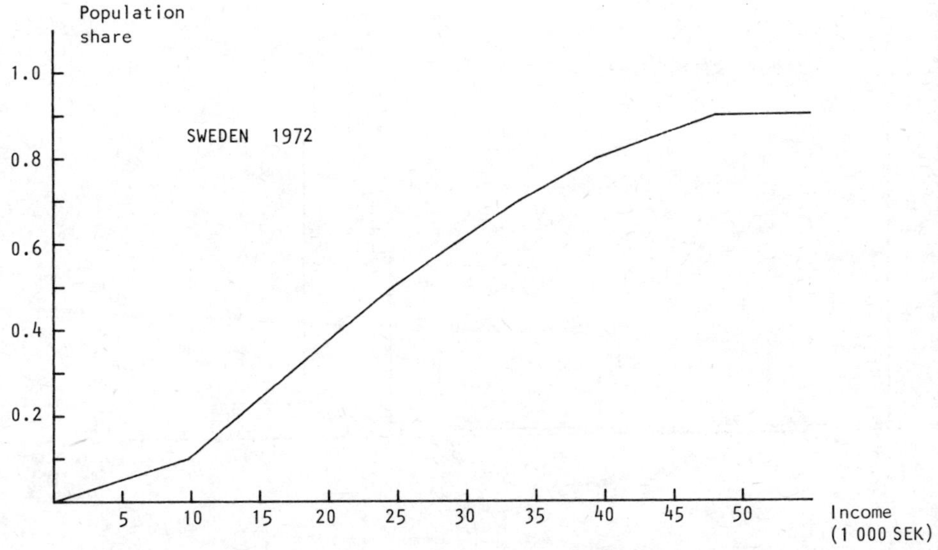

Figure 2.4 Logincome histogram: Available household incomes in Finland and Sweden 1971/72

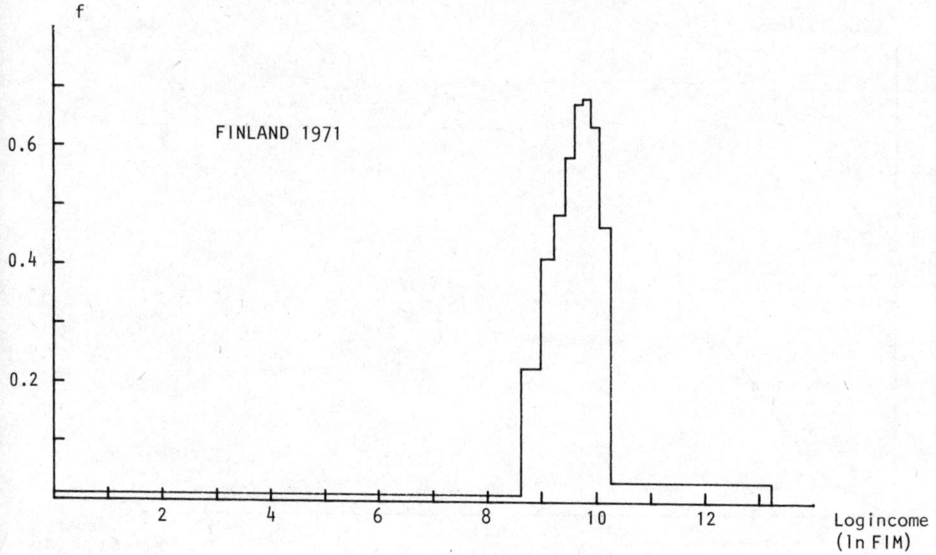

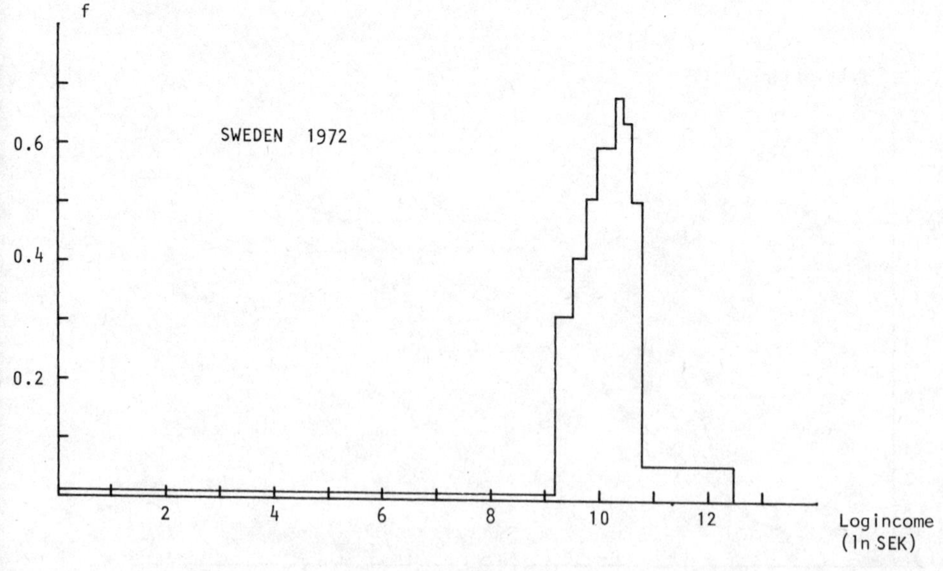

2.3 CHARTS BASED ON THE MOMENT DISTRIBUTION

The (first) moment distribution of income, whose distribution function gives the cumulative share of total income beneath different income levels (cf column (7) in table 2.1), holds a prominent position in income inequality analysis due to its close relationship to the Lorenz curve and the notion of Lorenz domination (see below and section 4.2).
In figure 2.5 the frequency distribution of the moment distribution, showing the amount of total income accruing to i.r.u's in the different income brackets, is given in the form of a histogram. Figure 2.6 in turn gives the ogive of the moment distribution. Similar charts may also be drawn on log-income basis.[1)]

2.4 THE LORENZ CURVE

Perhaps the most common method of describing an income distribution graphically is to use the Lorenz curve. This graphical method, which originates from Lorenz [1905], combines the ogive of the income distribution and its moment distribution in one diagram.
It is helpful to distinguish between two types of Lorenz graphs, viz. absolute and relative diagrams. In a relative Lorenz diagram the horizontal axis denotes the values of the relative distribution function, i.e. cumulative

1) The frequency distribution of the logincome moment distribution is the "income-curve" of Champernowne [1973].

Figure 2.5 Moment distribution histogram: Available household incomes in Finland and Sweden 1971/72

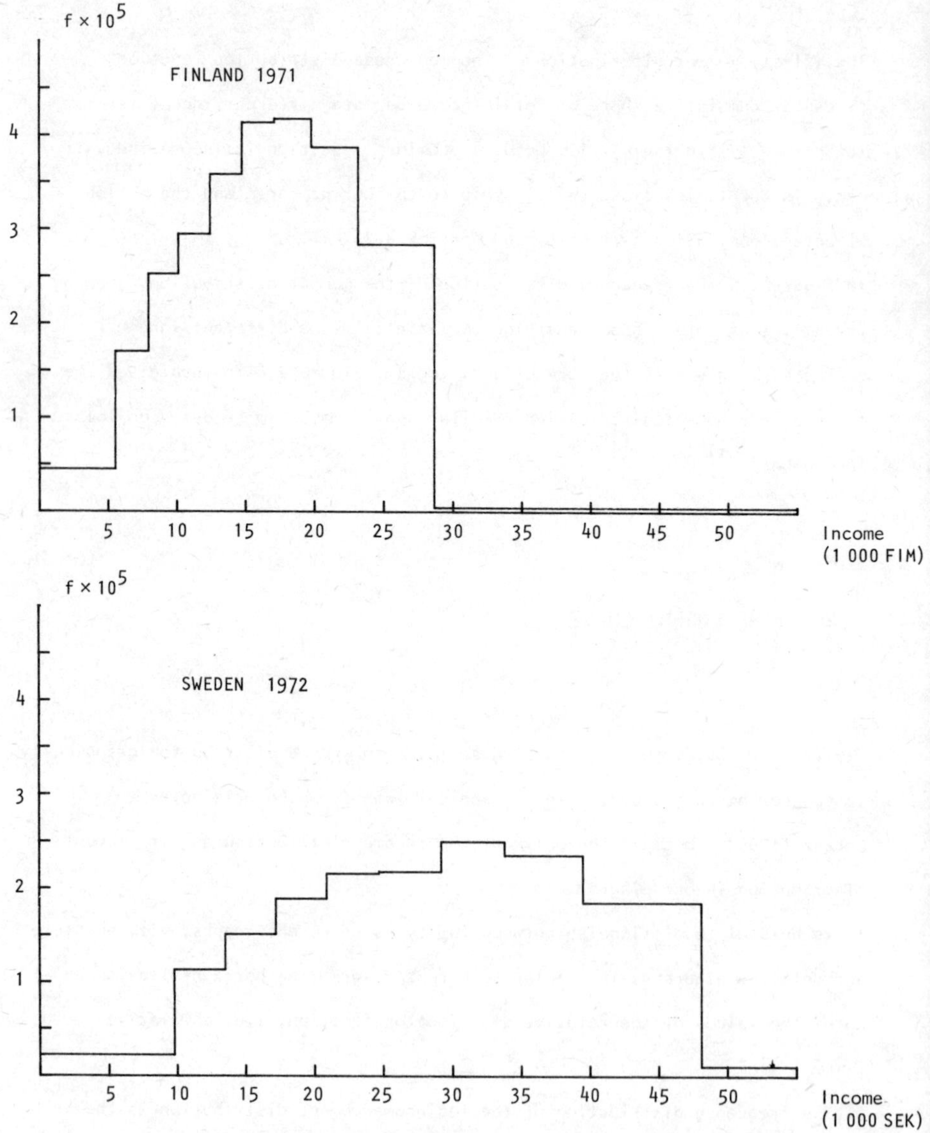

Figure 2.6 Moment distribution ogive: Available household incomes in Finland and Sweden 1971/72

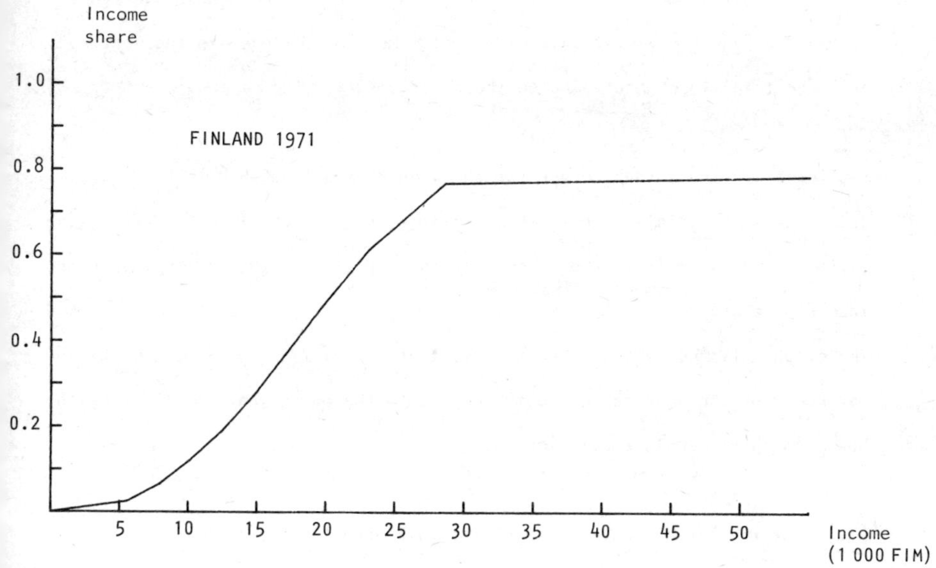

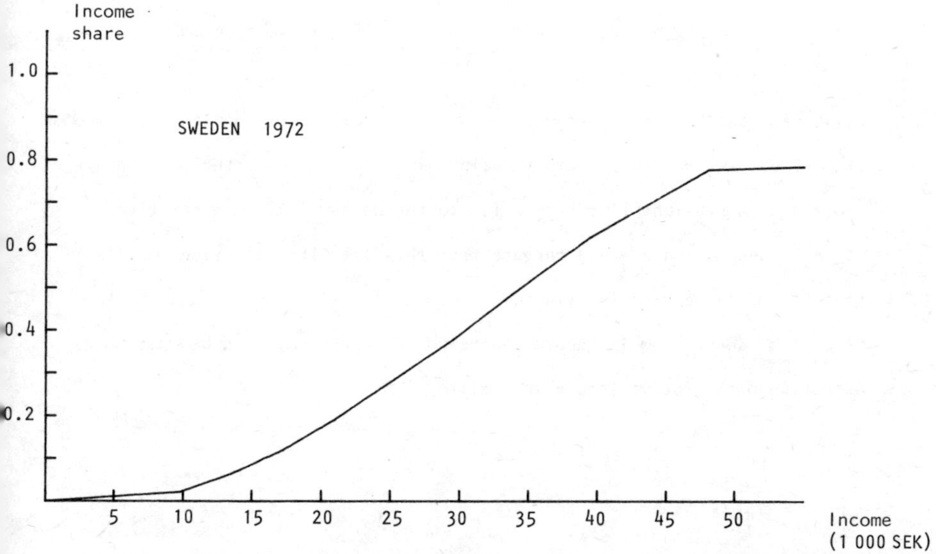

population shares, whereas the vertical axis represents the values of the relative moment distribution function, i.e. the corresponding income shares (cf columns (4) and (7) in table 2.1).
In an absolute diagram the relative shares are replaced with absolute magnitudes, i.e. the horizontal axis gives the number of i.r.u's and the vertical axis the total income accruing to these i.r.u's.

In figure 2.7 the Lorenz curves for the Finnish and Swedish data have been drawn; again by joining the known coordinates by straight lines - a representation which is exact if the incomes of the i.r.u's are the same within each income bracket.
The graph tells us, among other things, that in 1971/72 approximately 27 per cent of the aggregated income accrued to the poorer half of the Finnish and Swedish household population.

Note that the Lorenz curve is sensitive to changes in the number of income brackets and their boundaries. With shorter brackets the Lorenz curve will tend to stretch downwards. We return to this point in section 8.3.

As a graphical tool the Lorenz curve was originally used to visualize income dispersion; we note that a distribution giving all i.r.u's the same income appears as a straight line from origo to the point (1,1) in a relative Lorenz diagram, and every departure from this 'egalitarian' line implies that income dispersion is at hand.
As will be seen below in chapter 4 the Lorenz curve may also be used when assessing prescriptive income inequality.

Figure 2.7 Lorenz curve: Availabe household incomes in Finland and Sweden 1971/72

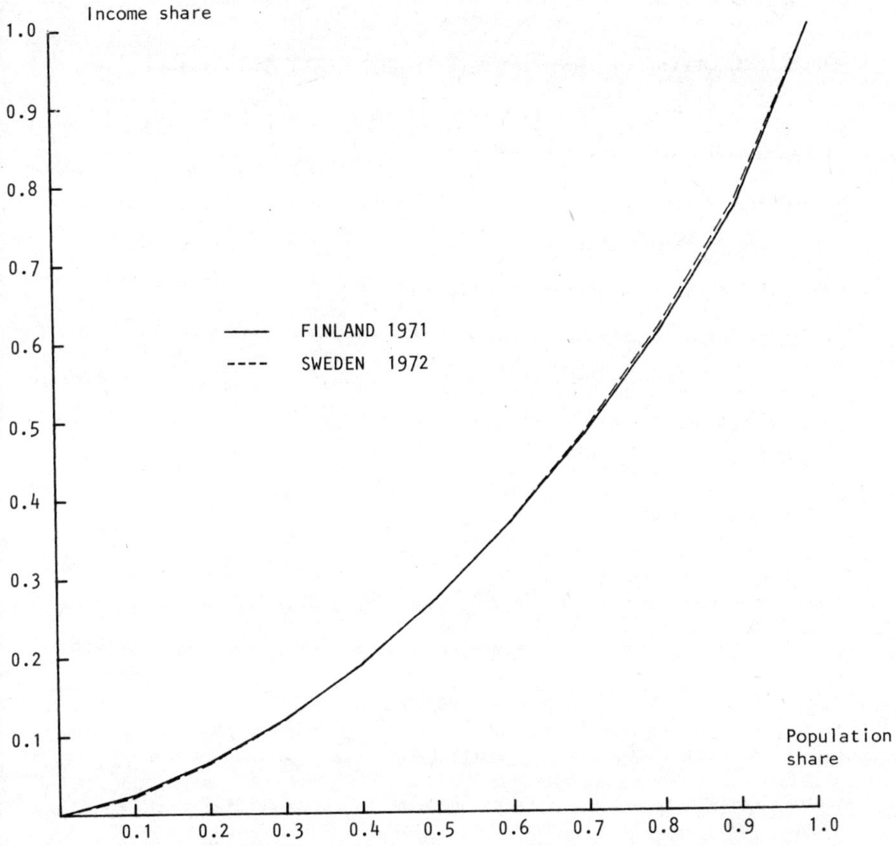

2.5 THE PARETO AND GINI CHARTS

The charts of Pareto- and Gini-type originate from two suggestions about the functional form of the income distribution (see also section 5.1).

Pareto [1897] stated that the income distribution may be described as $n_y = c\,y^{-\alpha}$ or $\log n_y = \log c - \alpha \log y$, where y denotes a given income, n_y is the number of i.r.u's with incomes exceeding y, and c and α are positive constants. It is easily seen that this distributional hypothesis is equivalent to the statement that the frequency distribution of income, f(y) is a member of the family of Pareto distributions, $f(y) = \alpha c^{\alpha} y^{-(\alpha+1)}$, $y \geq c$.
The Pareto chart is obtained if in a double-logarithmic diagram, where the horizontal axis denote the income, we plot the number of i.r.u's (in absolute amounts or as population shares) with incomes exceeding the level given by the horizontal axis. According to Pareto´s hypothesis this chart should describe a straight line.
In figure 2.8 the Pareto charts of our data are depicted. As can be seen the diagram does not support the hypothesis of Pareto distributed household incomes as a whole, even if the Pareto chart at higher income levels fairly well may be summarized by a straight line.

Gini [1909],[1936] proposed the modified form $\log n_y = \log d + \delta \log z_y$ of Pareto´s distributional hypothesis, where n_y as above denotes the number of i.r.u's with income exceeding y, z_y is the total income (or income share) accruing to these i.r.u's, and d and δ are positive constants. It is not difficult to see that this functional form, which we name Gini´s distributional hypothesis, holds exactly only if the incomes are Pareto distributed (with $\alpha = \delta/(\delta-1)$).

Figure 2.8 Pareto chart: Available household incomes in Finland and Sweden 1971/72

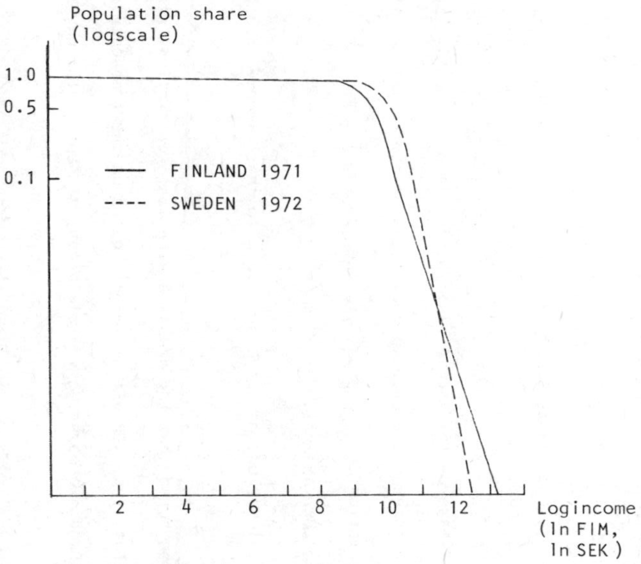

Figure 2.9 Gini chart: Available household incomes in Finland and Sweden 1971/72

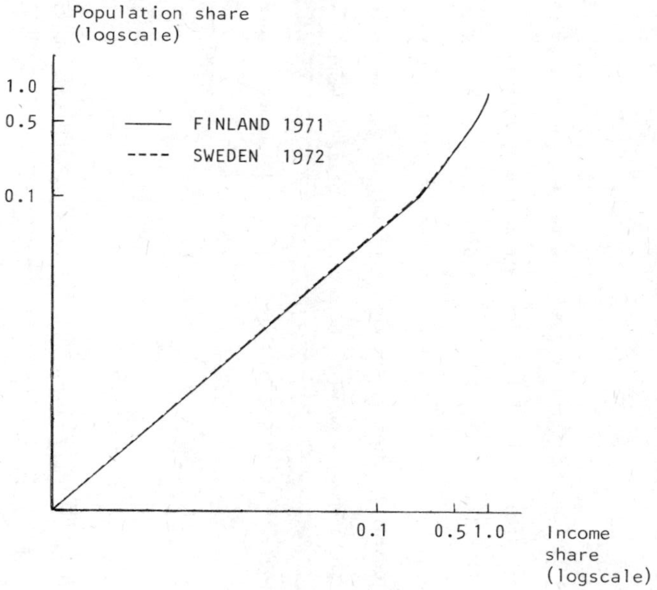

In figure 2.9 the points (z_y,n_y) are plotted for our data using a double-logarithmic diagram. If these points are joined by straight lines we obtain the so called Gini chart, which may also be interpreted as a chart of Lorenz type with the number of i.r.u's and incomes cumulated from the highest income bracket towards the lowest, and the coordinate axes interchanged (and made logarthmic) in comparison with the ordinary Lorenz diagram.

Pareto´s and Gini´s income hypotheses will be discussed in more detail in chapter 5.

2.6 A SHORT APPRAISAL OF DIFFERENT GRAPHICAL METHODS

The use of graphs in income distribution studies usually falls back upon some of the following reasons.

(A) Graphs are excellent, sometimes even indispensable, descriptive tools

(B) If the shape of the income distribution is only roughly known, graphical methods provide a good basis of approximations through interpolation or extrapolation; thereby facilitating the pursuit of a further analysis

(C) Graphical methods may be appropriate to chart income inequality.

It should be noted that the graphs of the last few sections are equivalent in the sense that they are all ultimately based on the frequency distribution of income, and, moreover, given one graphical representation, say the ogive, it is always possible in principle to draw any of the other diagrams. Hence, formally it makes very little difference which graphical method is used.

From the practical point of view there are however usually good reasons for preferring one graphical method to another; the principal rule being that the selected representation should accord as far as possible with the specific objective at hand.

If we only aim at description there is little sense in abandoning the familiar histogram and ogive (similar to Pen´s parade) of the frequency distribution. Particularly, the Pareto- and Gini-type charts usually furnish poor descriptive tools.

On the other hand, if our aim is to fit some continuous function to the data for purposes of interpolation or extrapolation, charts of Pareto or Gini type may indeed prove useful, at least for some income levels. The use of such approximations are often of direct interest in the case of studies based on official income statistics, since for many purposes the official figures in themselves (classified - sometimes truncated - data, unknown class limits, etc) fail to describe the income distribution with the desired accuracy.
In this context the leading course of action is to select such a representation of the distribution that some elementary function, e.g. a straight line or a simple polynomial, may be closely fitted to it. This implies that diagrams depicting the income distribution as a monotone curve are likely to prove advantageous (cf also Spiegel [1961; pp 30-31]). Hence, the ogive of the frequency or moment distribution, or some transformation of these (e.g. the Lorenz curve, the Pareto or Gini chart), possibly using a logincome scale,

may render an appropriate basis for this approach.[1)]

Concerning point (C) we note that, under the presupposition that income inequality depends only on the frequency distribution (cf chapter 3 and 4), the Lorenz curve representation is well suited to capture elements of inequality. The reasons for this will be made clear in chapters 4 and 7. The importance of the simple histogram and ogive of the frequency distribution as inequality indicators should not be overlooked either. And, of course, if the income is in fact Pareto distributed, the charts of the Pareto and Gini types may be used to illustrate income inequality, since in this case there is a one-to-one correspondence between the parameters of the distribution and the straight line of the charts.[2)]

1) A simple transformation of the ogive is, for instance, the logit-transformation $\log\{F(y)/(1-F(y))\}$, where $F(y)$ gives the values of the relative ogive, suggested by Vartia [1980] for purposes of interpolation by cubic spline functions.

2) In fact, Pareto and Gini suggested that the value of the parameters α and δ, respectively, may be used as inequality indicators (cf section 5.1).

3. THE INCOME VECTOR, THE INCOME DISTRIBUTION AND DIFFERENT TYPES OF INEQUALITY COMPARISONS

3.1 THE INCOME VECTOR AND THE INCOME DISTRIBUTION

Suppose that we consider a situation (community) involving N i.r.u's, say persons, denoted $a_1,a_2,..,a_N$. The income amount y_i which is given to person a_i can now be interpreted according to two distinct approaches.

Firstly, according to a deterministic approach it can be argued that y_i is to be seen as a fixed income attributed to a_i. The row vector $\vec{y} = (y_1,y_2,..y_N)$, a point in the N-dimensional space R^N, will be referred to as the *income vector*. The interpretation of the vector is clear-cut: Person a_i is given the income y_i, and any addition to or deprivation of this amount implies an altered income vector.

On the basis of the income vector we may form the *income distribution* by regarding the values y_i as observations on a common variate 'income', recording its different values, and counting the number of observations for each value. This procedure obviously involves loss of information as the income distribution no longer reveals which income is given to which i.r.u.[1] Evidently, the income distribution is discrete.

When the number, N, of i.r.u's involved in the distribution is large it is often convenient to group the incomes into brackets (cf ch 2) or even to approximate the distribution by fitting a continuous function to the data (cf

1) Note that according to this definition we have used the word 'income distribution' slightly inaccurately in chapter 1; in some passages, e.g. when discussing the equitable 'distribution', the proper term would have been the 'income vector'.

sec 2.6 and ch 5). Examples of curve-fitting are easily found in the literature (see e.g. Kloek and van Dijk 1977 , Maddala and Singh 1977 , Dagum 1977 , McDonald and Jensen 1979 , Baxter 1980 , Vartia and Vartia 1981).

Secondly, there is a randomised approach to the notion of income. According to this approach, which stems from the theories of personal income formation, the realized income of person a_i is to be seen as the outcome of a random process since a component of random variation is included in the income formation (cf p 10, ch 1). The *income vector* may in this case be defined as the row vector $\vec{Y} = (Y_1, Y_2, .., Y_N)$, where Y_i denotes the (continuous) random variable describing the income formation of person a_i. Any modification of the random variables Y_i results in a new income vector, whereas it would be undue to attribute alteration effects to spontaneous changes in realized incomes.
On the basis of the observed incomes we may as in the deterministic case - and with a similar loss of information - form the observed *income distribution*. Due to the stochastic elements involved this discrete distribution should be regarded as a sample of size N from an underlying probability distribution of income and the further analysis should be carried out with this probability distribution in mind.

In this study we start out from the deterministic interpretation of the income vector. As will be seen the information contained in this vector is under some general conditions equivalent to the information obtained from the relative frequency distribution of income. From this the analysis will be extended to include continuous income (probability) distributions, simply because continuous distributions are analytically tractable and notationally more convenient than their discrete analogues. A continuous distribution also provides an accurate and handy approximation of the discrete income distribution in empir-

ical studies where the number of i.r.u's usually amounts to hundreds of thousands.
The use of relative frequencies and continuous distributions must however clearly be kept apart from a genuine stochastic approach to income inequality. As the discussion in this study starts out from the deterministic approach, every attempt to interpret the results within the stochastic framework - although such an interpretation is formally possible - should be faced with the greatest scepticism.

3.2 THE RANKING OF INCOME VECTORS

3.2.1 THE INEQUALITY RELATION

Recall that the notion of income inequality is partly descriptive, partly prescriptive, and partly predictive. An analysis of only the income vector (or the income distribution) may be sufficient for descriptive or predictive purposes but at the same time quite superficial for prescriptive purposes, since inequality in the prescriptive sense may depend, besides on the income distribution, on several other features of the social situation.
To allow for a more general discussion of income inequality we introduce the concept of the *social state* of a community, defined as a complete account of the actual social conditions (including the income vector). To qoute Arrow 1951 :

"The most precise definition of a social state would be a complete description of the amount of each type of commodity in the hand of each individual, the amount of each productive resource invested in each type of productive activity, and the amounts of various types of collective activity."

A description of the distribution of personal characteristics may further well be included in the social state.

As in this book we confine ourselves to income inequality and its measurement several aspects of the social state may be neglected, but it should once more be observed that a restriction of the analysis to the distribution of merely one commodity, viz. income, may involve intricate losses of prescriptive information.

To explore some of the elements involved in the measurement of income inequality let us pay attention to its principal field of application, viz. the comparison and ranking of income distributions of different (alternative) social states.

Let Ω denote the set of all feasible income vectors of the social states. Our general objective is to impose an ordering on the elements of Ω. The aspiration of this ordering should be to take account of our inequality considerations.

Let R denote the binary relation, on which the ordering is based. R may be seen as a preference relation on Ω with respect to income inequality and it will consequently be referred to as the *inequality relation*. A natural minimal requirement on R is that it should generate a *quasi-ordering*, i.e. that the relation should have the properties:

R is *reflexive*

For any $\vec{y}$ in Ω is $\vec{y}R\vec{y}$, or in short

$(\forall\vec{y} \in \Omega)(\vec{y}R\vec{y})$.

R is *transitive*

For any $\vec{y}$, $\vec{z}$ and $\vec{w}$ in Ω holds that if $\vec{y}R\vec{z}$ and $\vec{z}R\vec{w}$ then $\vec{y}R\vec{w}$, or in short

$(\forall\ \vec{y},\vec{z},\vec{w}\ \varepsilon\ \Omega)\{(\vec{y}R\vec{z}\ \wedge\ \vec{z}R\vec{w}) \rightarrow (\vec{y}R\vec{w})\}$.

If $\vec{y}R\vec{z}$ we write $\vec{y}\leqq\vec{z}$ and read "$\vec{y}$ is not more unequal than $\vec{z}$" or "$\vec{z}$ is not more equal than $\vec{y}$". If $\vec{y}R\vec{z}$ and $\vec{z}R\vec{y}$ we write $\vec{y}\cong\vec{z}$ and read "$\vec{y}$ and $\vec{z}$ are equally unequal (or equally equal)". If $\vec{y}R\vec{z}$ but not $\vec{z}R\vec{y}$ we write $\vec{y}<\vec{z}$ and read "$\vec{z}$ is more unequal than $\vec{y}$" or "$\vec{y}$ is more equal than $\vec{z}$".

A quasi-ordering is a comparatively weak measure as it does not necessarily imply that all pairs of feasible income vectors are rankable vis-a-vis each other. A stronger measure is obtained by assuming that the inequality relation has the additional property that

R is *connected*

For any $\vec{y}$ and $\vec{z}$ in Ω holds $\vec{y}R\vec{z}$ or $\vec{z}R\vec{y}$ (or both), or in symbols

$(\forall\ \vec{y},\vec{z}\ \varepsilon\ \Omega)(\vec{y}R\vec{z}\ \vee\ \vec{z}R\vec{y})$.

This type of ordering will be named *complete*. It seems reasonable to aim at complete orderings in the first place, since with a complete ordering all feasible income vectors are comparable and a comparison of the inequality of alternative vectors is thus straightforward.

On the other hand it should be noted that the relevance of any complete ordering may be disputed. To quote Sen [1973]:

> "There are reasons to believe that our idea of inequality as a ranking relation may indeed be inherently incomplete. If so, to find a measure of inequality that involves a complete ordering may produce artificial problems, because a measure can hardly be more precise than the concept it represents."

If we accept this view but still consider a quasi-ordering as somewhat too weak a measure, we may strenghten the quasi-ordering by the assumption that

R is *antisymmetric*

For any $\vec{y}$ and $\vec{z}$ in Ω holds that if $\vec{y}R\vec{z}$ and $\vec{y}\neq\vec{z}$ then we can not have $\vec{z}R\vec{y}$, or in short $(\forall\ \vec{y},\vec{z} \in \Omega)\{(\vec{y}R\vec{z} \wedge \vec{y}\neq\vec{z}) \rightarrow \{\neg(\vec{z}R\vec{y})\}\}$.

Antisymmetry implies that if $\vec{z}$ and $\vec{y}$ are of the same degree of inequality, $\vec{y}\cong\vec{z}$, then $\vec{y}$ and $\vec{z}$ must be identical, $\vec{y}=\vec{z}$. It is obvious that this property in many cases may be too restrictive. An antisymmetric qusi-ordering will be named *partial*.

With the help of the inequality relation we may, for a given income vector $\vec{y}$, divide Ω into the subsets

$$E(\vec{y}) = \{\vec{z} \in \Omega | \vec{z} \leq \vec{y}\},$$
$$U(\vec{y}) = \{\vec{z} \in \Omega | \vec{y} \leq \vec{z}\}, \text{ and}$$
$$M(\vec{y}) = \Omega - \{E(\vec{y}) \cup U(\vec{y})\}.$$

The subset $E(\vec{y})$ consists of all income vectors that are not more unequal ('not worse') than $\vec{y}$, $U(\vec{y})$ includes all vectors that are not more equal ('not better') than $\vec{y}$, and $M(\vec{y})$ consists of vectors not rankable vis-a-vis $\vec{y}$.

If the inequality relation is transitive and $\vec{y}\leqq\vec{z}$ it is easily seen that $E(\vec{y}) \subseteq E(\vec{z})$ and $U(\vec{z}) \subseteq U(\vec{y})$. If the relation is reflexive and connected, we have $E(\vec{y}) \cup U(\vec{z}) = \Omega$ and $M(\vec{y}) = \emptyset$. An antisymmetric relation in turn implies that $E(\vec{y}) \cap U(\vec{y}) = \{\vec{y}\}$.

When we use the inequality relation to rank income vectors the following lemma is of fundamental importance.

Lemma.

If R is a quasi-ordering on Ω then for any $\vec{y},\vec{z},\vec{w} \in \Omega$ holds

(a) $(\vec{y} \cong \vec{z} \wedge \vec{z} \cong \vec{w}) \rightarrow (\vec{y} \cong \vec{w})$

(b) $(\vec{y} < \vec{z} \wedge \vec{z} \cong \vec{w}) \rightarrow (\vec{y} < \vec{w})$

(c) $(\vec{y} \cong \vec{z} \wedge \vec{z} < \vec{w}) \rightarrow (\vec{y} < \vec{w})$

(d) $(\vec{y} < \vec{z} \wedge \vec{z} < \vec{w}) \rightarrow (\vec{y} < \vec{w})$.

A simple proof is given in e.g. Sen 1970 .

Two inequality relations which have been suggested within the deterministic framework, in which case we have $\Omega \subseteq R^N$ are

Rawls' relation

$\vec{y} \leq_{RAWLS} \vec{z}$ if and only if $\min\{y_1,y_2,..,y_N\} \geq \min\{z_1,z_2,..,z_N\}$, and

Pareto's relation

$\vec{y} \leq_{PARETO} \vec{z}$ if and only if $y_i \geq z_i$ for every $i=1,2,..N$.

Here - and frequently in the sequel - we add a lower index to the notation "≦" of the inequality relation in order to distinguish between different relations.[1)] According to Rawls´ relation the income vector which gives the least favoured i.r.u a higher income is judged as more equal. If we compare two income vectors and each individual has no lower income according to the first than to the second, and at least one person is given a higher income by the first vector then this vector will be ranked as more equal by the Paretian relation.

It is easily seen that the Rawlsian inequality relation imposes a complete ordering on Ω, whereas the Paretian relation induces a quasi-ordering since e.g. in the case N=2 the vectors ($1,$2) and ($2,$1) will not be ranked. The Paretian relation is in fact partial. Another distinction between the two relations is that the Rawlsian may be applied even if only the income distributions are known and it may thus readily be translated into the case of continuous distributions (e.g. by replacing the minimum incomes with a suitably chosen quantile income), while this is not the case of the Paretian relation.

Alternative criteria to be imposed on a 'good' inequality relation are discussed at length in chapter 4. It may, however, be mentioned now that the construction of an adequate inequality ordering will prove a difficult task. It

1) This lower index also helps us make a notational distinction between the inequality relation "≦" (or indexed: " $\leq_R$") and the ordinary numerical interpretation of "≦".

should also be noted that there are many aspects involved in inequality ranking and a treatment of all comparisons of income vectors alike will no doubt run the risk of obscuring essential facts and thereby producing artificial problems.

Using the terms introduced by Sen [1979] we may distinguish two different types of comparisons of income distributions, viz. *situational* and *comprehensive* comparisons. The crucial difference is that situational studies deal with the evaluation of optional income distributions (social states) for a fixed group of individuals (i.r.u's) at a given point of time and a given place, whereas comprehensive comparisons employ the actual distributions (social states) in different populations, e.g. distributions at separate points of time and/or in different countries.

In addition we will consider a third type of comparisons, which may be seen as a compromise between situational and comprehensive studies. This will be named *quasi-comprehensive* (or *quasi-situational*).

3.2.2 THE ELEMENTS OF SITUATIONAL COMPARISONS

Situational comparisons form the elementary basis of the ranking of income vectors and distributions. In these comparisons we are met with a *ceteris paribus* framework: We consider a situation which involves N individuals (i.r.u's) and assume that all components of the social state, including the total income T, are given with the exception of the income vector. The set of feasible income distributions is in this case restricted to $\Omega(T,N)$

$= \{\vec{y} \in R^N \mid \sum_{i=1}^{N} y_i = T\}$ and for $\vec{y},\vec{z} \in \Omega(T,N)$ our objective is to tell whether $\vec{y}$ is a more unequal income vector than $\vec{z}$ or not. In other words, we wish to impose (at least) a quasi-ordering on the elements of $\Omega(T,N)$.

The standard method of situational comparisons of income inequality goes in fact one step further in that it is assumed that the inequality of the vector $\vec{y}$ may be summarized by some one-dimensional inequality measure or index. This measure may be written as a function $I = I(\vec{y})$, $I: \Omega(T,N) \rightarrow R$, and the function is usually designed in such a way that a higher numerical value is to be interpreted as revealing a higher degree of income inequality. Examples of measures of this type are the Gini coefficient and the maximum equalization ratio.

Further, for purposes of situational ranking we may use the function $C(\vec{y},\vec{z}) = I(\vec{y}) - I(\vec{z})$, $C: \Omega(T,N)\times\Omega(T,N) \rightarrow R$, with the interpretation that $\vec{y} \leqq_I \vec{z}$, i.e. $\vec{y}$ is not more unequal than $\vec{z}$, if and only if $C(\vec{y},\vec{z}) \leqq 0$ or $I(y) \leqq I(z)$.

The measures $I(\vec{y})$ are frequently assumed to be cardinal, independent of any permutation of incomes (which implies that the measures may be calculated from the income distribution) and continously differentiable. It is obvious that such inequality indexes generate complete orderings. It should also be observed that the measures $I(\vec{y})$, as well as the Rawlsian and Paretian relation, only depend on the income vector and our prescriptive aspirations may hence be badly distorted if these relations carelessly are applied to empirical income data.

The scope of situational comparisons is in practice resticted to purposes of planning or social choice.[1)] Despite this insuffiency the situational comparisons provide a proper theoretical basis of inequality judgement and a discussion of the situational case will prove of great methodological value. We will return to this in chapter 4.

1) It can be argued that the situational approach is insufficient also in cases of planning because of its demanding ceteris paribus assumptions. A change in the income vector may affect other factors of the social state than the income vector itself, even if the total income T is unchanged.

3.2.3 THE ELEMENTS OF COMPREHENSIVE COMPARISONS

The lack of attention attached to the primary conditions of comprehensive comparisons is highly striking in the literature as the most favoured topics among empirical investigators of income inequality seem to be the evolution of inequality over time and differences in the income inequality between countries, which are topics of a clearly comprehensive nature.

To faciliate a fairly general account of the difficulties involved in comprehensive comparisons we consider two communities with sets X_1 and X_2 , respectively, of feasible social states. Assume that the communities are enjoying $\vec{x}_1 \varepsilon X_1$ and $\vec{x}_2 \varepsilon X_2$ with the corresponding income vectors $\vec{y}_1 \varepsilon \Omega_1$ and $\vec{y}_2 \varepsilon \Omega_2$, respectively.

When comparing the income inequality in community 1 with the inequality in community 2 the comprehensive question to be answered can be put forward as:

"Is the income vector $\vec{y}_1$ of the social state $\vec{x}_1$ judged as more equal in community 1 than the vector $\vec{y}_2$ of the state $\vec{x}_2$ is in community 2?"

This seemingly straightforward framing of the question conceals several difficulties.

To start with we note that the inequality relation R, the rule according to which the inequality of the feasible income vectors is judged, may not be the same in the two communities. Indeed, as the inequality judgements should be related to some idea of an equitable (or optimal) distribution and such distributions may be defined in several ways, the identity of the inequality relations would be a very severe requirement. For instance, if community 1 confesses the minimum definition of an equitable income vector and community 2 the egalitarian definition there is little prescriptive sense in imposing the same inequality ranking on both communities, regardless of the explicit form of the

ranking. Consequently we have to admit the existence of two relations, R_1 and R_2, each ruling the inequality judgements of its own community.
The problem of comprehensive comparisons is however more profound since the approval of two relations R_1 and R_2 will not generally provide an answer to the comprehensive question even in the case when R_1 and R_2 reflects the same inequality preferences in the sense that $\vec{y}R_1\vec{z}$ if and only if $\vec{y}R_2\vec{z}$.
Toillustrate this assume that $\vec{y}_1$ is judged as more equitable than $\vec{y}_2$ in both communities. As the 'intensity' of the ranking may differ between the communities this assumption per se can not sustain any clear-cut judgement about comprehensive income inequality. Consider for instance two egalitarian communities and let $\vec{y}_1$ and $\vec{y}_2$ represent a minor and a slightly larger deviation, respectively, from the equitable income distribution (equal division of all income) in these communities. In community 1, crowded with radical egalitarians, even small disturbances of the equitable income vector are taken as significant losses of equity. Community 2, on the other hand, is populated by moderate egalitarians and not too concerned with minor deviations from the optimal vector. Thus, even if $\vec{y}_1$ is preferred to $\vec{y}_2$ in both communities, this does not guarantee that $\vec{y}_1$ from the radical view of community 1 is judged as more equal than $\vec{y}_2$ from the moderate view of community 2.
Further, assuming that some specific standard measure of inequality, say $I(\vec{y})$, reflects the preferences (but not the intensities of the preferences) of both communities, so that $I(\vec{y}_1) \leq I(\vec{y}_2)$ implies $\vec{y}_1R_1\vec{y}_2$ and $\vec{y}_1R_2\vec{y}_2$. It is clear from the discussion above that a comparison of $I(\vec{y}_1)$ and $I(\vec{y}_2)$ is not sufficient for answering the comprehensive question.

The mere identification of the inequality relations is thus insufficient for a comprehensive comparison. The plain fact of the matter is that genuine comprehensive comparisons can only be carried out accidentally when the preference relations R_1 and R_2 are exactly identical.

3.2.4 THE ELEMENTS OF QUASI-COMPREHENSIVE COMPARISONS

The general impractability of genuine comprehensive comparisons raises the question of how to deal with inequality comparisons between different communities.

A reasonable procedure is to use one of the communities involved as a standard of comparison - for the sake of simplicity the argument will consistently be pursued in terms of the characteristics of community 1.[1)] This means that we replace the comprehensive question with:

"Does community 1 judge the income vector $\vec{y}_1$ as more equal than it would have judged the occurance of the vector $\vec{y}_2$?"

The question calls for a comparison which we will name quasi-comprehensive (or quasi-situational). As opposed to genuine comprehensive comparisons, but in conformity with situational comparisons, a quasi-sitational comparison employs one specific inequality relation, viz. the relation of community 1. As opposed to situational comparisons - recall that the objective of situational comparisons is an evaluation of different alternatives for a given community - the quasi-comprehensive comparison involves the actual social states of two (or more) different communities.

The main problem of quasi-situational comparisons arises from the very fact that the social states, $\vec{x}_1$ and $\vec{x}_2$, and the corresponding income vectors, $\vec{y}_1$ and $\vec{y}_2$, owe their origin to different communities with different sets of feasible social states. Generally there is no immediate interpretation of $\vec{x}_2$ to community 1 as this specific state may not be feasible in community 1, i.e. $\vec{x}_2 \notin X_1$.

1) It is of course also possible to base the comparison on the characteristics of a suitably chosen hypothetical 'reference community'.

If we want to carry out the comparison of income inequality we must at least find a way of translating $\vec{y}_2$ out of Ω_2 into Ω_1. Given an appropriate procedure of translation we may then with some qualifications apply the methods of comparison developed within the situational framework.

Three facts must be considered when transforming $\vec{y}_2$ from Ω_2 to Ω_1.

(A) The incomes of Ω_1 and Ω_2 may not be directly comparable.

(B) The number of individuals (i.r.u's) may differ between the two communities.

(C) The individuals (i.r.u's) involved in the two communities are distinct.[1)]

These points appear markedly when income inequality is to be compared internationally.[2)] In these cases the income vectors $\vec{y}_1$ and $\vec{y}_2$ are given in different units of measurement, viz. the domestic currencies in question, and the comparison must be anticipated with a transformation of the currencies to some common standard. Principally, there are three alternative transformations: Firstly, we may transform the incomes to some standard currency, say US dollars, with the help of official exchange rates, although some objections may be raised against this method as the exchange rate between the domestic and the standard currency is subject to frequent fluctuations. Secondly, we may standardize the incomes through a division of each income with some domestic income standard, e.g. the mean income, the median income or the minimum income, and by this obtain relative incomes independent of the units of measurement. Thirdly, recognizing the argument that the notion of income inequality should be applied to real incomes, not nominal, we may seek a true cost-of-living index (or a 'true' exchange rate) and use this in converting the incomes into

1) As opposed to situational comparisons, where I always can recognize my own income according to the alternative income vectors, give quasi-situational comparisons rise to a situation in which there is no immediate interpretation of which income in the other community that accrues to me.

2) As a simple example the reader may consider the vectors (\$1,\$2) and (£2,£4, £6) of two different communities.

a common standard.[1] It should be noted that these three methods essentially transform the income vector $\vec{y} = (y_1,y_2,..,y_N)$ into $c\vec{y} = (cy_1,cy_2,..,cy_N)$, where c denotes a factor of proportionate change which is set equal to the exchange rate parity, the inverse of the domestic income standard, or the true cost-of-living index (under the assumption that the index is the same for all individuals in the community). As the choice of a specific c-factor always to some degree tends to be arbitrary it would be convenient if we could design an inequality ranking which is independent of any specific choice of the c-value. We will return to this qualification in the next chapter when discussing suitable criteria on the inequality relation, but it may be pointed out beforehand that many commonly used inequality relations fulfil the condition $\vec{y} \cong_R c\vec{y}$ of invariance to proportional changes in incomes.

The points (B) and (C) above will be dealt with in detail in chapter 4. In broad outline the problem of income vectors of different size will be handled through a replication procedure which transforms the vectors into two equi-sized vectors, whereas the treatment of point (C) will make use of a procedure that matches each i.r.u of community 2 with one i.r.u in community 1.

1) This argument is of substantial importance to normative studies, since an income of $100 does not represent the same consumption possibilities in for instance Finland and Sweden. The same argument is also valid in the case of intertemporal comparisons (an income of $100 today as compared to an income of $100 ten years ago).

3.3 POSITIVE VERSUS NORMATIVE STUDIES OF INEQUALITY

In chapter 1 we distinguished two alternative approaches to the measurement of income inequality, viz. a 'positive' and a 'normative' approach. In this section we will discuss these approaches in somewhat greater detail.

Positive studies and positive measures

The prefix 'positive' is attached to studies in which information on the individual incomes *directly* influences the distributional judgements. Inequality measures originating from this approach will accordingly be named positive measures. As these measures are directly related to the income vector may they generally be written in the form $I = I(\vec{y})$. This feature of the positive measures indicates that they may relatively easily be designed for purposes of measurement of income dispersion. Simple examples of such measures are the standard deviation, the mean deviation, and the mean difference of incomes. The incorporation of the prescriptive aspects of income inequality into positive measures is on the other hand less straighforward and requires that additional information about the social state is taken into account. We will return to this problem in subsequent chapters.

Normative studies and normative measures

Normative studies are based on the fundamental principle that each social state, with its inherent income vector, generates an individual welfare (or utility) vector and this in turn determines the community´s level of total welfare. This principle will be more closely discussed in chapter 6 and in this section we confine ourselves to a simplified discussion of the broad ouline of normative studies.

Let us assume that the community in question includes N individuals (i.r.u's) and that person a_i gets an amount of utility equal to $u_i = u_i(y_i)$ out of his income y_i, $u_i\colon R_+ \to R$, an assumption which calls for an extensive, non-negative, definition of income (recall the welfare chain: income - consumption possibilities - welfare). We moreover suppose that there exists a 'social welfare function' $w = w(u_1,u_2,..,u_N)$, $w\colon R^N \to R$, revealing the level of total welfare in the community.[1)] For given individual utility functions w may be written as $w = W(y_1,y_2,..,y_N) = W(\vec{y})$. Both individual utility and social welfare are assumed to be increasing functions of their arguments.

Now, according to the normative line of thought the level of social welfare increases as the income vector becomes less unequal and the equitable income vector is thus defined as the vector which maximizes social welfare. See e.g. Dalton 1920 , Atkinson 1970 . Any well-behaved measure of income inequality must consequently depend on the same factors which determine the social welfare, viz. the welfare functions and the income vector. Inequality measures of this type will be named normative. It may be noted that normative measures treat the income vector in another way than positive measures, since the income vector enters into the normative measures only indirectly through the welfare functions.[2)]

The normative index may formally be written as $I = I_W(\vec{y})$. Obviously, the obser-

1) This implies that normative studies are considerably more exacting than positive studies: while information on individual incomes is sufficient for positive studies a normative study requires supplementary details on the relationship between individual incomes and individual utility and between individual utility and social welfare.

2) If the argument is carried to extremes the income vector may be disputed any influence on the normative measure, which is apparently the case if we relax the assumption that individual utility increases with income and stipulate that all individual utility functions are constant.

vance of normative measures to our descriptive and prescriptive aspirations will basically depend on the explicit specification of the social welfare function $W(\vec{y})$. Moreover, as soon as this function is specified in detail we may use this information to 'solve' the inequality ranking in terms of the income vector alone and rewrite the normative index as an explicit function of the income vector, viz. $I = I(\vec{y})$ for given W. This implies that normative measures ultimately may be examined according to the same rules as positive measures. Conversely the normative implications of a positive measure $I = I(\vec{y})$ may be checked by seeking a function W such that the induced normative measure $I_W(\vec{y})$ yields exactly the function $I(\vec{y})$ when solved.

In this study primary importance will be attached to measures of the form $I(\vec{y})$. As a consequence of this the positive measures will hold a prominent position.

4. CRITERIA ON THE INEQUALITY RANKING

A favourable and widely adopted approach to the issue of inequality measurement is to set up a number of criteria which we wish the inequality relation to follow. The final choice of an appropriate inequality ranking will then be made from the set of inequality relations which fulfil the criteria. See e.g. Sen [1973], Champernowne [1974], Blackorby and Donaldson [1977], Fields and Fei [1978], Hart [1978], Bourguignon [1979], Cowell [1980].

In this chapter we discuss a number of criteria and their significance to situational and quasi-comprehensive comparisons. Most of the criteria to be discussed may be justified both within a positive and a normative framework. We will pay relatively little attention to this and chiefly concentrate on the consequences of the criteria and their practability.

4.1 NORMATIVE CRITERIA

Let us first consider some criteria explicitly stated in terms of the individual utility functions.

Suppose that individual utility $u_i(y)$ is an increasing function of income y for all individuals a_i, i=1,..,N. As mentioned in sec. 3.3 normative inequality measures are derived through the application of a social welfare function to the individual utilities and the equitable income vector is for a given total income, $\Sigma y_i = T$, taken as the distribution which maximizes social welfare. The maximization exercise is then trusted to support a basis for distributional judgements.

If the social welfare function is represented as $w = w(u_1(y_1), u_2(y_2), .., u_N(y_N)) = W(\vec{y})$ we may state the normative approach as

<u>The social welfare criterion (WEL)</u>

> The income vector $\vec{y}$ is not more unequal than the vector $\vec{z}$, $\vec{y} \leqq_{WEL} \vec{z}$, if $W(\vec{y}) \geqq W(\vec{z})$ for all welfare functions W in a specified set $\mathcal{W}$.

The implications of the WEL are obviously dependent on the explicit choice of the set $\mathcal{W}$ which may include one or more social welfare functions.

The welfare function is frequently assumed to be of the utilitarian form $W(\vec{y}) = \Sigma u_i(y_i)$, i.e. social welfare is taken as equal to the sum of the individual utilities. With this specification, however, situations may occur in which the WEL leads to violations of our descriptive understanding of inequality.[1)] See Sen [1973],[1978].

To directly incorporate equity considerations into the normative framework Sen [1973] proposed the following criterion.

1) The problem arises because the application of the WEL to the utilitarian function is not primarly concerned with the interpersonal distribution of incomes. In fact, this is not only an utilitarian problem but holds for any welfare function which is an increasing function of its arguments.

The weak equity axiom (WEA)

Let individual a_i have a lower utility level than individual a_j for each level of income, i.e. $(\forall\, y \in R_+)(u_i(y) < u_j(y))$. Then in distributing a given total income T among N individuals, the equitable income vector is in the set $\Omega_o(T,N) = \{\vec{y} \in R_+^N\colon y_i > y_j, \Sigma y_i = T\}$, i.e. the equitable vector is found among the vectors giving a_i a higher income than a_j.

A somewhat similar criterion, in the sense that it favours individuals at lower utility levels, is the following restatement of the Rawlsian inequality relation in utility terms.

Rawls' criterion (RAWLS)

The income vector $\vec{y}$ is not more unequal than the vector $\vec{z}$, $\vec{y} \leq_{RAWLS} \vec{z}$, if $\min\{u_1(y_1),u_2(y_2),..,u_N(y_N)\} \geqq \min\{u_1(z_1),u_2(z_2),..,u_N(z_N)\}$.

On the other hand, if we do not wish to favour any particular utility level we may adopt the Paretian relation in utility terms.

Pareto's criterion (PARETO)

The income vector $\vec{y}$ is not more unequal than the vector $\vec{z}$, $\vec{y} \leq_{PARETO} \vec{z}$, if $(\forall\, i=1,..,N)(u_i(y_i) \geqq u_i(z_i))$.

Although these criteria at first glance may seem reasonable their relevance may be called in question.
Concerning the WEA it should be noted that the axiom disregards all ranking aspirations as it merely gives a (partially inconclusive) definition of the equitable income vector. Given any income vector $\vec{y} \notin \Omega_o(T,N)$ the only thing that can be argued is that there exists another income vector $\vec{z} \in \Omega_o(T,N)$ which is not more unequal than $\vec{y}$ and, further, given any two income vectors $\vec{y}$ and $\vec{w}$ we have no means to decide whether $\vec{y} \leq_{WEA} \vec{w}$ or $\vec{w} \leq_{WEA} \vec{y}$. Moreover,

as the equitable vector $\vec{z} \in \Omega_o(T,N)$ is defined for a given total income the WEA must be modified if we wish to use it in connection with quasi-comprehensive comparisons.

The Rawlsian criterion in turn implies that the income vector $\vec{z}$, which gives all individuals the same utility level, is equitable in situational comparisons, in the sense that for any other income vector with the same total income $\vec{z} \leqq_{RAWLS} \vec{y}$ holds.[1] Applied to quasi-comprehensive comparisons, on the other hand, this criterion has some doubtful implications. For instance, the income vector which generates the utility vector (2,2,1000) will be judged as more equal than the income vector generating the utilities (1,1,1), although this is in sharp contrast to the usual descriptive understanding of inequality.

The Paretian relation again induces an incomplete ranking of the income vectors and has the additional drawback of regarding an increase in any individual income, the other incomes remaining constant, as an inequality decreasing event regardless of to whom the income increase is given.[2] Thus, for instance, the vector giving the utilities (1,1,1) will be regarded as more unequal than the income vector generating the utilities (1,1,1000). Again our descriptive understanding is violated.

Apart from the above objections the WEL, WEA, RAWLS, and PARETO suffer from the deficiency of failing a clear operational purport, since the application of these criteria requires close information about each individual utility function and in practice no such detailed information is available.[3] We are

1) This follows from the assumption that individual utility $u_i(y)$ is an increasing function of income.

2) When applied to situational comparisons the incompleteness of the Paretian relation is most fatal: For any income vectors $\vec{y}$ and $\vec{z}$ with the same total income the criterion is inconclusive as to whether $\vec{y} \leqq_{PARETO} \vec{z}$ or $\vec{z} \leqq_{PARETO} \vec{y}$, unless $\vec{z} = \vec{y}$, in which case the comparison is trivial.

3) In recent years some isolated attempts to identify individual utility functions have however been made. See Praag [1978].

thus frequently compelled to make the simplifying assumption of identical utility functions, i.e. $u_i(y) = u(y)$ for $i=1,..,N$, if we insist on a normative approach. It should be noted that with the assumption of identical utility functions the WEA loses all its relevance and the Rawlsian and Paretian criterion may be restated as $\vec{y} \leqq_{RAWLS} \vec{z}$ if $u(\min y_i) \geqq u(\min z_i)$ and $\vec{y} \leqq_{PARETO} \vec{z}$ if $(\forall\ i=1,..,N)(u(y_i) \geqq u(z_i))$.

The assumption of identical utility functions obviously does not exclude the possibility of descriptive shortcomings and we will consequently not consider the RAWLS or PARETO as desirable properties of an inequality ranking.

4.2 SITUATIONAL COMPARISONS

The assumption of identical utility functions is similar to a requirement that all i.r.u's should a priori be treated as equals. A natural consequence of an aspiration of this kind is that the inequality judgement should not be affected by the specific allocation of N given incomes among N i.r.u's.

In order to facilitate a more formal discussion of this issue we introduce a N×N permutation matrix $P = \{p_{ij}\}_{i=1,..,N}^{j=1,..,N}$. To qualify as a permutation matrix one of its elements p_{ij} in each row and column should be equal to 1 and all remaining elements be zero, i.e. $p_{ij} = 0$ or 1 and $\sum_i p_{ij} = \sum_j p_{ij} = 1$. Further, let P_N denote the set of all permutation matrixes of size N×N. The result of post-multiplying $\vec{y} = (y_1, y_2, .., y_N) \in \Omega(T,N)$ by $P \in P_N$ is thus another N-vector $\vec{z} = \vec{y}P$, in which the elements are permutated in comparison with $\vec{y}$. We may now state the following criterion.

<u>The symmetry criterion (SYM)</u>

> Let P denote any permutation matrix of size N×N. If $\vec{z} = \vec{y}P$, where $\vec{y} \in \Omega(T,N)$, i.e. if the vector $\vec{z}$ can be represented as a permutation of the elements of $\vec{y}$, then $\vec{y}$ and $\vec{z}$ have the same degree of inequality, $\vec{y} \cong_{SYM} \vec{z}$, or in short
>
> $(\forall P \in P_N)(\vec{y} \cong_{SYM} \vec{y}P)$.

This criterion is sometimes also referred to as the anonymity or permutation criterion, and simply states that the inequality judgement is independent of which income is given to which i.r.u. Accordingly the SYM judges for instance the vectors (\$1,\$2,\$3), (\$1,\$3,\$2), (\$2,\$1,\$3), (\$2,\$3,\$1), (\$3,\$1,\$2), and (\$3,\$2,\$1) of Ω(\$6,3) as equally unequal and, generally, given any income vector $\vec{y} \in \Omega(T,N)$ we may settle N!-1 other vectors with the same degree of inequality by going through all permutations of the elements of $\vec{y}$. This implies

that the distinction between the income vector and the income distribution, spelled out in section 3.1, loses its meaning and the inequality judgement can be based on knowledge of the income distribution only.
A second consequence of the SYM to be noted is that the criterion ensures the reflexivity of the inequality relation, i.e. that $\vec{y} \cong \vec{y}$, which is easily seen by choosing the N×N permutation matrix as the identity matrix I.
Moreover, when the SYM holds, we may always rearrange the individual incomes in non-descending order, $y_i \leqq y_{i+1}$, i=1,..,N-1, without affecting the inequality. This rearrangement is for notational convenience assumed to be carried out in the sequel whenever the SYM is appropriate and mostly we will use the word 'income distribution' when referring to this ordered income vector.

The SYM property, which is commonly accepted in the literature (see e.g. Atkinson [1970], Kolm [1976], Cowell [1977], Fields and Fei [1978]) is exceedingly convenient if we are faced with a situation in which the income distribution, but not the income vector, is known. This is for instance usually the case with the income data of official assessment statistics. Indeed, under these circumstances a rejection of the SYM would deprive us of all means of judging inequality.
On the other hand it must be realized that the SYM is, sometimes excessively, homogenizing in its treatment of all i.r.u's alike. Although the criterion no doubt may be appropriate when income dispersion is examined, it may badly distort our prescriptive views. Consider, for instance, a community of two i.r.u's taken as households. In household 1 there are five persons and in household 2 two persons. When comparing the alternative vectors ($1000,$2000) and ($2000,$1000) we may for prescriptive reasons judge the income vector ($1000,$2000), giving the smaller household the higher income, as the more unequal income vector. The use of the SYM in this case would clearly be a mistake as the SYM judges the income vectors as equally unequal.

The example illustrates the fact that the SYM can not be taken as a self-sufficient criterion and that it by no means should be applied carelessly to inequality studies, It is obvious that particularly the definition of the i.r.u's is of vital importance in order to avoid fatal prescriptive shortcomings. Strictly speaking the SYM is justified only if there are no prescriptive objections against a treatment of all i.r.u's alike.

The basic idea of the SYM may alternatively be put forward in a more general form (cf. Cowell [1980]) by assuming that the available information about the social state provides means of stratifying the N i.r.u's exhaustively into k mutually exclusive, homogeneous, groups.
Let N_j denote the number of i.r.u's belonging to group j, j=1,..,k, $\Sigma N_j = N$, and suppose for notational convenience that the i.r.u's originally are given the subscripts 1 to N in such a way that subscripts 1 to N_1 indicate the members of group 1, N_1+1 to N_1+N_2 the members of group 2, and, generally, the subscripts $N_1+N_2+..+N_{j-1}+1$ to $N_1+N_2+..+N_j$ the members of group j. With this convention accrue the first N_1 incomes of the distribution $\vec{y} = (y_1,y_2,..,y_N)$ $\varepsilon\ \Omega(T,N)$ to the i.r.u's of group 1, the following N_2 incomes to the i.r.u's of group 2, etc. Further, let P_1, P_2, .., P_k denote permuation matrixes of size $N_1 \times N_1$, $N_2 \times N_2$, .., $N_k \times N_k$, respectively, define a constrained N×N permutation matrix as

$$P^C = \begin{pmatrix} P_1 & 0 & . & . & 0 \\ 0 & P_2 & . & . & 0 \\ . & . & . & . & . \\ 0 & 0 & . & . & P_k \end{pmatrix},$$

and let $\mathcal{P}^C_{N_1+N_2+..+N_k}$ denote the set of all such constrained matrixes. We may now state the following criterion.

<u>The partial symmetry criterion (PARSYM)</u>

Let $P_j \varepsilon P_{N_j}$, j=1,..,k, denote any series of permutation matrixes of size $N_j \times N_j$, respectively, and P^C be the corresponding constrained permutation matrix of size N×N. If $\vec{z} = \vec{y}P^C$, where $\vec{y} \varepsilon \Omega(T,N)$, i.e. if the vector $\vec{z}$ can be represented as a constrained permutation of the elements of $\vec{y}$, then $\vec{y}$ and $\vec{z}$ have the same degree of inequality, $\vec{y} \cong_{PARSYM} \vec{z}$, or in short-hand $(\forall\ P^C \ \varepsilon\ P^C_{N_1+N_2+..+N_k})(\vec{y} \cong_{PARSYM} \vec{y}P^C)$.

The PARSYM simply states that any reallocation of the given incomes within each of the k subgroups should not affect the inequality judgement and implies that this judgement may be based directly on the income distribution in these k groups of i.r.u's. The incomes within each subgroup may thus be assumed to be given in non-descending order.

Consider for instance a community of four households, two five-person and two two-person households, with the income vector $\vec{y}$ = (\$1000,\$2000,\$3000,\$4000) ε Ω(\$10000,4), where the incomes \$1000 and \$2000 accrue to the two-person and the incomes \$3000 and \$4000 to the five-person households. Now, if the i.r.u's are stratified into groups according to household size and the PARSYM is applied (with k=2, N_1=N_2=2) we will conclude that the original vector $\vec{y}$ is equally unequal as the alternative vectors (\$1000,\$2000,\$4000,\$3000), (\$2000, \$1000,\$3000,\$4000), and (\$2000,\$1000,\$4000,\$3000). On the other hand a comparison of the inequality of $\vec{y}$ and, say, the vector (\$3000,\$2000,\$1000,\$4000) is outside the scope of the PARSYM.

As the set of constrained N N permutation matrixes is included in the set of all N N ordinary permutation matrixes, $P^C_{N_1+N_2+..+N_k} \subseteq P_N$, an inequality ranking obeying the SYM will also follow the PARSYM.[1)] If there is only one population group (k=1, N=N_1) the PARSYM is obviously equivalent to the SYM. An in-

1) It may be noted that there are $N_1!N_2!..N_k!$ elements in the set $P^C_{N_1+N_2+..+N_k}$, whereas the set P_N includes $N! = (N_1+N_2+..+N_k)!$ elements.

equality relation following PARSYM is, as in the case of the SYM, easily seen to be reflexive.

The PARSYM will prove useful in connection with the decomposition of income inequality. It should also be noted that the PARSYM is in line with most definitions of an equitable income vector, as the definitions can often be made operational using a division of the population into homogeneous subgroups (e.g. i.r.u's with 'identical utility functions', 'equal needs', or 'equal productivity'). For the moment, and mostly in the sequel, we will however assume that the SYM is a proper criterion to meet our purposes.[1)]

A condition on the inequality ranking of general approval is known as 'the principle of transfers' or 'the Pigou-Dalton criterion' (cf. Dalton [1920], Atkinson [1970], Sen [1973], Fields and Fei [1978]).

Consider the income vector $\vec{y} \in \Omega(T,N)$. Let y_p and y_r be any two individual incomes with $y_p \leq y_r$. We introduce a transformation $h(\vec{y})$, $h: \Omega(T,N) \rightarrow \Omega(T,N)$, of the vector $\vec{y}$ by defining

$$\vec{z} = h(\vec{y}) \text{ if } z_i = y_i \text{ for } i \neq p,r,$$
$$z_p = y_p - t, \qquad t > 0. \qquad (4.1)$$
$$z_r = y_r + t,$$

The transformation obviously leaves the total income T unchanged. If the income vector $\vec{z}$ can be obtained from $\vec{y}$ through a transformation of type (4.1) we will say that $\vec{z}$ differs from $\vec{y}$ by a *non-egalitarian transfer* (*n.e.t*). With the convention that the incomes are given in non-descending order, $y_1 \leq y_2 \leq .. \leq y_N$, the transformation may be written as

$$\vec{z} = h(\vec{y}) = \vec{y} + \vec{s} = (y_1, y_2, .., y_p, .., y_r, .., y_N) + (0, 0, .., -t, .., t, .., 0).$$

The non-egalitarian transfer operates according to the principle 'taking from the poor, giving to the rich' and thus in an obvious sense increases income

1) Alternatively we may in line with the PARSYM interpret the subsequent discussion as concerning one of the k homogeneous population subgroups.

inequality.[1)]

Further we will say that $\vec{z} = H(\vec{y})$ differs from $\vec{y}$ by a finite number of n.e.t's if there exists a sequence $h_1, h_2, .., h_k$ of transformations of type (4.1) with $\vec{z} = H(\vec{y}) = h_k(..h_2(h_1(\vec{y}))..)$, and by $\mathcal{H}$ we denote the set of all finite n.e.t-sequences. We may now state

The principle of transfers (TRANSF)[2)]

The income vector $\vec{y} \in \Omega(T,N)$ is more equal than the distribution $\vec{z} \in \Omega(T,N)$, $\vec{y} <_{TRANSF} \vec{z}$, if $\vec{z}$ differs from $\vec{y}$ by a finite number of non-egalitarian transfers, i.e. if $\vec{z}$ can be written as $\vec{z} = H(\vec{y})$ where H denotes a sequence $h_1, h_2, .., h_k$ of transformations of type (4.1), or $(\forall\ H \in \mathcal{H})(\vec{y} <_{TRANSF} H(\vec{y}))$.

We note that the inequality relation implied by the TRANSF is transitive. Assuming that negative incomes are non-feasible we may now consider an arbitrary income vector $\vec{y} \in \Omega(T,N)$. Let $\vec{z}_e = (\mu, \mu, .., \mu)$, $\mu = T/N$, denote the income vector which distributes the total income T equally among the N i.r.u's and $\vec{z}_u = (0,0,..,0,T)$ be the income vector which gives all income to the richest i.r.u, for convenience assumed to be a_N, in the original vector $\vec{y}$ and no income to the other N-1 i.r.u's. It can easily be seen that if $\vec{y} \neq \vec{z}_e$ and $\vec{y} \neq \vec{z}_u$ then there

1) The inequality increase may also be justified from a normative standpoint assuming, say, that social welfare is determined by the utilitarian function $w = \Sigma u(y_i)$. If utility increases with income at a decreasing rate the result of an n.e.t is a lower level of social welfare and consequently a higher degree of inequality.

2) The principle is usually stated the other way around in terms of 'egaltarian transfers', i.e. transfers which diminish the incomes of relatively rich persons and augment the incomes of relatively poor persons. See e.g. Fields and Fei [1978].
Note also that our formulation gives a strong version of the TRANSF. A less demanding condition (the weak principle of transfers, WEAKTRANSF) would be obtained by stipulating that an n.e.t-sequence should not diminish inequality i.e. $(\forall\ H \in \mathcal{H})(\vec{y} \leq_{WEAKTRANSF} H(\vec{y}))$.

exist sequences H_e and H_u of n.e.t's such that $\vec{y} = H_e(\vec{z}_e)$ and $\vec{z}_u = H_u(\vec{y})$.[1)] According to the TRANSF it follows $\vec{z}_e <_{TRANSF} \vec{y} <_{TRANSF} \vec{z}_u$. More generally we may define subsets $E(\vec{y};T,N)$, $U(\vec{y};T,N)$, and $M(\vec{y};T,N)$ of $\Omega(T,N)$ as

$$E(\vec{y};T,N) = \{\vec{z} \in \Omega(T,N) \mid \vec{y} = H(\vec{z}) \text{ for some n.e.t-sequence } H \in \mathcal{H}\},$$

$$U(\vec{y};T,N) = \{\vec{z} \in \Omega(T,N) \mid \vec{z} = H(\vec{y}) \text{ for some n.e.t-sequence } H \in \mathcal{H}\},$$

$$M(\vec{y};T,N) = \Omega(T,N) - (E(\vec{y};T,N) \cup U(\vec{y};t,N)).$$

According to the TRANSF $E(\vec{y};T,N)$ consists of all vectors $\vec{z}$ with $\vec{z} <_{TRANSF} \vec{y}$ (for instance, $\vec{z}_e \in E(\vec{y};T,N)$ if $\vec{y} \neq \vec{z}_e$), $U(\vec{y};T,N)$ includes all vectors $\vec{z}$ with $\vec{y} <_{TRANSF} \vec{z}$ (for instance $\vec{z}_u \in U(\vec{y};T,N)$ if $\vec{y} \neq \vec{z}_u$), and $M(\vec{y};T,N)$ is the set of income vectors not comparable vis-a-vis $\vec{y}$. As it is easily seen that the set $M(\vec{y};T,N)$ is not empty - for instance, given $\vec{y} = (\$0,\$4,\$6) \in \Omega(\$10,3)$, we have $\vec{z} = (\$1,\$2,\$7) \notin E(\vec{y};\$10,3)$ and $\vec{z} \notin U(\vec{y},\$10,3)$ - the inequality relation of the TRANSF is not connected och hence incomplete. Moreover, it is clear that the TRANSF provides no means of comparing income vectors involving different total incomes.

It should also be noted that the inequality relation according to our definition of the TRANSF is not reflexive. As we will shortly see an application of the TRANSF presupposes that the SYM is accepted and the reflexive property of the inequality relation will thus be inherited from the SYM.

The fact that the TRANSF designates two income vectors, viz. $\vec{z}_e$ and $\vec{z}_u$, as extreme is a point that may not merely be passed over. The extremeness of these vectors may in fact be taken as criteria on the inequality relation.

<u>The egalitarian criterion (EGAL)</u>[2)]

If a total amount T of income is to be distributed among N i.r.u's the egalitarian income vector $z_e = (\mu,\mu,..,\mu)$, $\mu = T/N$, is more equal than

1) The existence of H_e is proved in Hardy et al. [1934; lemma 2, p. 47]. The proof is in fact more general: it shows that any distribution which Lorenz dominates $\vec{y}$ (see page 68) can be transformed to $\vec{y}$ by a finite sequence of n.e.t's. H_u in turn simply consists of the sequence $h_1,..,h_{N-1}$, where h_i transfers the income from the ith poorest i.r.u to the richest.

2) See note 1 on the next page.

any other income vector, i.e. for all $\vec{y} \in \Omega(T,N)$, $\vec{y} \neq \vec{z}_e$, holds $\vec{z}_e <_{EGAL} \vec{y}$.

The criterion of immense concentration (CON)[1]

If a total amount T of income is to be distributed among N i.r.u's the income vector $\vec{z}_u = (0,0,..,0,T,0,..,0)$, giving all income to only one i.r.u, is more unequal than any other income vector, i.e. for all $\vec{y} \in \Omega(T,N)$, $\vec{y} \neq \vec{z}_u$, $\vec{y} <_{CON} \vec{z}_u$ holds.

As we have seen the EGAL and the CON follow from the TRANSF, but the converse is evidently not true. While the extreme inequality of $\vec{z}_u$ and consequently the suitability of the CON as a criterion at first glance seems indisputable, several objections may be raised against a treatment of $\vec{z}_e$ as the most equal distribution. Only if there are no prescriptive reasons for not treating all i.r.u's alike, is there a rationale for this procedure. It follows that a rejection of the SYM together with an approval of the TRANSF (or merely the EGAL) would indicate a very dubious standpoint. The fact is that any reasonable application of the EGAL or the TRANSF presupposes that the SYM is justified.[2] Since the inequality ranking may be based on the income distribution when the SYM is an appropriate criterion, it seems practicable to restate the TRANSF to meet the notion of a continuous income distribution.

Consider the non-negative income variate Y characterized by the c.d.f. F(y) and the density function f(y). Let A*, A, B, and B* denote the real intervals $a < y < a+1$, $a+d < y < a+d+1$, $b < y < b+1$, and $b+e < y < b+e+1$, respectively, where $0 \leqq a < a+1 \leqq a+d < a+d+1 \leqq b < b+1 \leqq b+e < b+e+1$. The intervals may

1) In line with the weak principle of transfers it is also possible to state weak versions of the EGAL and the CON, viz. $(\forall \vec{y} \in \Omega(T,N))(\vec{z}_e \leq_{WEAKEGAL} \vec{y})$ and $(\forall \vec{y} \in \Omega(T,N))(\vec{y} \leq_{WEAKCON} \vec{z}_u)$

2) The same is true also for the CON, since if there are prescriptive arguments in favour of a differentiated treatment of i.r.u's we may for instance have the inequality ranking $(T,0,..,0) < (0,0,..,T)$.

thus be interpreted as (disjoint) income brackets.

Alluding to the notion of a 'mean preserving spread' (cf. Rothschild and Stiglitz [1970], Atkinson [1970]) we introduce a step function defined by

$$s(y) = \begin{cases} \alpha & \text{for } y \in A^*, \\ -\alpha & \text{for } y \in A, \\ -\beta & \text{for } y \in B, \\ \beta & \text{for } y \in B^*, \end{cases} \tag{4.2}$$

where α and β are positive constants with $\alpha d = \beta e$. It is easily seen that $\int_0^\infty s(y)dy = 0$ and $\int_0^\infty ys(y)dy = 0$. Defining a function h as

$$h(y) = f(y) + s(y)$$

we have $\int_0^\infty h(y)dy = 1$ and $\int_0^\infty yh(y)dy = \int_0^\infty yf(y)dy$. It follows that h may be interpreted as a density function having the same mean as f, if $h(y) \geqq 0$ for all y, i.e. if $f(y) \geqq \alpha$ for $y \in A$ and $f(y) \geqq \beta$ for $y \in B$. The functions f(y), s(y), and h(y) are illustrated in figure 4.1.

A step function which fulfills (4.2) will be named a non-egalitarian transfer. The verbal interpretation runs as follows:

Consider the relatively poor i.r.u's with incomes in the interval A and the relatively rich i.r.u's in the income bracket B. According to the density function f(y) there are $F(a+d+l) - F(a+d)$ i.r.u's in the income bracket A and $F(b+l) - F(b)$ i.r.u's in the interval B. From αl i.r.u's in A we now transfer an income amount equal to $t = \alpha l d$ to βl i.r.u's in B. As a consequence of this transfer the αl transfer payers, originally situated in A, will find themselves in the lower income bracket A*. The transfer amount t is then distributed among the βl transfer receivers and this moves them up from the old income bracket B to the new bracket B*.

Further, if the density function h may be written as

$$h(y) = f(y) + \sum_{i=1}^{k} s_i(y),$$

Figure 4.1 The functions f(y), s(y) and h(y) involved in a non-egalitarian transfer.

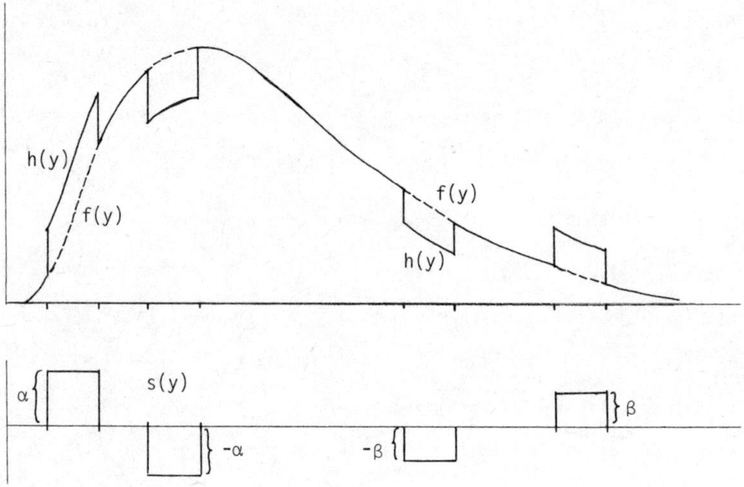

where each of the functions $s_1(y), s_2(y), .., s_k(y)$ is of type (4.2), we will say that the c.d.f. $H(y) = \int_0^y h(x)dx$ differs from F(y) by a finite number of non-egalitarian transfers.

Assuming that there exists an upper income bound, say y_m, which no feasible income can exceed, it is easily seen that if H(y) differs from F(y) by a finite n.e.t-sequence we have

$$\int_0^{y_m} \{H(y)-F(y)\}dy = 0, \text{ and}$$

$$\int_0^{y} \{H(x)-F(x)\}dx \geq 0 \text{ for every } y,\ 0 \leq y < y_m, \qquad (4.3)$$
$$> 0 \text{ for some } y,\ 0 < y < y_m,$$

where $H(y) = \int_0^y h(x)dx.$ 1)

Conversely, if (4.3) holds for two c.d.f's H(y) and F(y) it can be shown that H(y) could have been obtained from F(y) by a sequence of non-egalitarian transfers.[2] This allows us to state a continuous analogue to the TRANSF.

<u>The integral condition (INTEGRAL)</u>

Let Y and Z denote two income variates bounded in the interval $[0, y_m]$ with c.d.f's $F_Y(y)$ and $F_Z(y)$, respectively. If

$$\int_0^y \{F_Z(x)-F_Y(x)\}dx \begin{cases} \geqq 0 \text{ for every } y,\ 0 \leqq y < y_m, \\ > 0 \text{ for some } y,\ 0 < y < y_m, \text{ and} \\ = 0 \text{ for } y = y_m, \end{cases}$$

then the income variate Y is less unequally distributed then the variate Z. This will be denoted $Y <_{INTEGRAL} Z$.

As in the case of the TRANSF the inequality relation of the INTEGRAL is not necessarily reflexive. To ensure reflexivity we simply postulate that $Y \cong Y$ holds for any continuous income variate Y.[3]

1) The assumption of a finite maximum income, y_m, is necessary to allow for a direct application of the results of Rothschild and Stiglitz [1970]. The assumption is not very limiting as far as the present discussion is concerned.

2) Strictly speaking: If (4.3) holds there exist sequences $\{H_n\}$ and $\{F_n\}$ converging weakly to H and F, respectively, such that for all n H_n could have been obtained from F_n by a finite number of n.e.t's. See Rothschild and Stiglitz [1970].

3) Another method of ensuring reflixivity - in line with Rothschild and Stiglitz 1970 - would be to allow the magnitude $\alpha = 0$ (or $1 = 0$) in the n.e.t-definition (4.2) and stipulate that this leaves inequality unchanged.

Let us now turn to a consideration of the cumulative incomes in the vector $\vec{y}$. As above we assume that the SYM holds and that the individual incomes are arrayed in non-descending order. Let $Q_j(\vec{y})$ denote the cumulated incomes of the j poorest i.r.u's in $\vec{y}$, $Q_j(\vec{y}) = \sum_{i=1}^{j} y_i$. Then coordinates $(j, Q_j(\vec{y}))$, j=1,.. ..,N, when joined by straight lines, describe a Lorenz-type curve with incomes and i.r.u's cumulated in absolute amounts, rather than relative to the totals as in section 2. . Using this notation we may define

Lorenz domination[1)]

> If $\vec{y}$ and $\vec{z}$ represents two distributions of a given total income T among N i.r.u's and $Q_j(\vec{y}) \geq Q_j(\vec{z})$ for every j=1,..,N, then the distribution $\vec{y}$ is said to Lorenz dominate the distribution $\vec{z}$. The Lorenz domination is strict if $\vec{y}$ Lorenz dominates $\vec{z}$ and $Q_j(\vec{y}) > Q_j(\vec{z})$ for some j=1,..,N.

If the distributions $\vec{y}$ and $\vec{z}$ are plotted in a Lorenz-type diagram a Lorenz domination of $\vec{y}$ over $\vec{z}$ will imply that the Lorenz curve of the distribution $\vec{y}$ is situated inside, i.e. nowhere below, the Lorenz curve of $\vec{z}$. This is illustrated in figure 4.2.

Lorenz domination may well be used as a criterion of the inequality ranking:

The criterion of Lorenz domination (LDOM)

> The income distribution $\vec{y}$ is not more unequal than the distribution $\vec{z}$, $\vec{y} \leq_{LDOM} \vec{z}$, if $\vec{y}$ Lorenz dominates $\vec{z}$ and more equal than $\vec{z}$, $\vec{y} <_{LDOM} \vec{z}$, if the Lorenz domination is strict, or in short
>
> $\{(\forall\ j=1,..,N)(Q_j(\vec{y}) \geq Q_j(\vec{z})\} \rightarrow (\vec{y} \leq_{LDOM} \vec{z})$, and
>
> $\{(\vec{y} \leq_{LDOM} \vec{z}) \wedge (\exists\ j=1,..,N)(Q_j(\vec{y}) > Q_j(\vec{z})\} \rightarrow (\vec{y} <_{LDOM} \vec{z})$.

1) In the case of a continuous income variate the definition of Lorenz domination may be stated as: Let Y and Z represent two income variates bounded in the interval $[0, y_m]$ with c.d.f's $F_Y(y)$ and $F_Z(y)$, respectively. If $\int_0^{y_m} t dF_Y(t) = \int_0^{y_m} t dF_Z(t)$ and $\int_0^{y} t dF_Y(t) \geq \int_0^{z} t dF_Z(t)$ for every $0 \leq F = F_Y(y) = F_Z(z) \leq 1$, then the variate Y is said to Lorenz dominate the variate Z.

Figure 4.2 Lorenz domination: Distribution $\vec{y}$ dominates distribution $\vec{z}$

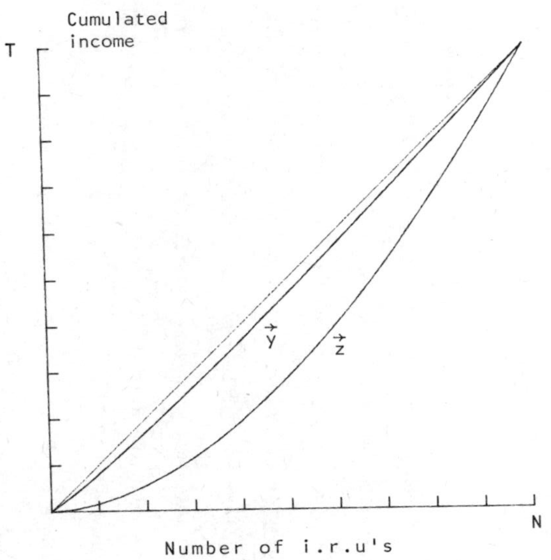

Figure 4.3 Lorenz domination: The extreme distributions $\vec{z}_e$ and $\vec{z}_u$

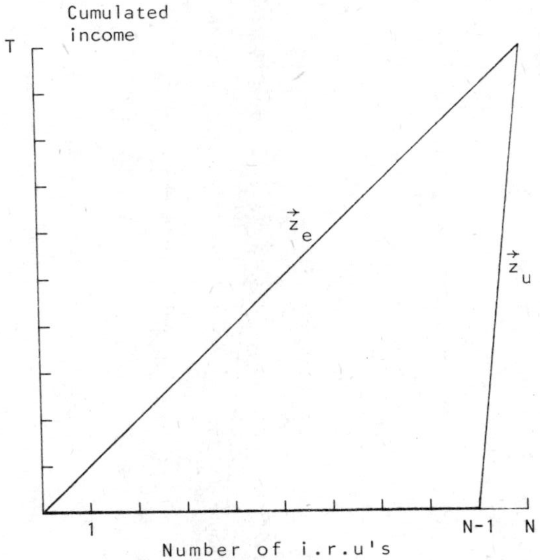

It is readily seen that the egalitarian distribution $\vec{z}_e = (\mu,\mu,..,\mu)$ Lorenz dominates any other distribution of the same total income. As $Q_j(\vec{z}_e) = \frac{T}{N}j$ the egalitarian distribution may be plotted in a Lorenz-type diagram as a straight line from origo with slope T/N (see figure 4.3). It may also be seen that the extreme distribution $\vec{z}_u = (0,0,..,T)$ is Lorenz dominated by any other distribution of the same total income. It follows that the LDOM shares the property of the TRANSF of implying the EGAL and the CON. This is not a mere coincidence - in fact it may be shown that under symmetry, i.e. if the SYM holds, the TRANSF is equivalent to the LDOM. See Hardy et al. [1934], Rothschild and Stiglitz [1970], Atkinson [1970], Jakobsson and Normann [1974], Fields and Fei [1978]. In addition it is readily seen that the LDOM (and the TRANSF) imposes a partial inequality ranking on $\Omega(T,N)$ (cf. Rothschild and Stiglitz [1970]).

The advantage of the LDOM over the TRANSF is its suitability for practical handling: Given two income distributions $\vec{y}$ and $\vec{z}$ in $\Omega(T,N)$ it may prove a laborious exercise to use the TRANSF in determining whether $\vec{y} <_{TRANSF} \vec{z}$ or $\vec{z} <_{TRANSF} \vec{y}$ as this requires that we find out the n.e.t-sequence, if any, by which the distributions differ. The LDOM on the other hand is quite easily applicable as there are no difficulties involved in plotting the Lorenz curves of the distributions and examining whether one of the distributions Lorenz dominates the other strictly. From the equivalence between the LDOM and the TRANSF it then follows that $\vec{y} \in E(\vec{z};T,N)$, i.e. there exists an n.e.t-sequence by which $\vec{z}$ differs from $\vec{y}$, if $\vec{y}$ Lorenz dominates $\vec{z}$ strictly. Further, if the Lorenz curves intersect we have $\vec{y} \in M(\vec{z};T,N)$, stating that there is no sequence of n.e.t's by which the distributions differ.

The significance of the LDOM is reinforced by a result, originally stated by Atkinson 1970 and later refined by Dasgupta et al 1973 , and Rothschild and Stiglitz 1973 . According to this result, it can be demonstrated that the LDOM and the WEL are equivalent criteria, if the welfare functions of the WEL are defined as the set of symmetric and 'equality preferring' functions, i.e. functions such that for every $\vec{y} \in \Omega(T,N)$ hold

$W(\vec{y}) = W(\vec{y}P)$ for every permutation matrix $P \in \mathcal{P}_N$, and

$W(\vec{y}) < W(\vec{z})$ if $z_i = y_i$ for $i \neq p,r$

$$z_p = y_p + \tfrac{1}{2}\alpha(y_r - y_p), \qquad 0 < \alpha \leq 1, \quad y_p \neq y_r.$$
$$z_r = y_r - \tfrac{1}{2}\alpha(y_r - y_p),$$

Moreover, if the LDOM implies the WEL, then W must be a symmetric, equality preferring function (cf. Rothschild and Stiglitz [1973]).

The notion of an equality preferring function (e.p.f) may seem somewhat abstruse and by way of explanation we note that the function is defined in terms of what could be called an 'egalitarian' transfer. If $y_p < y_r$, which for symmetry reasons we may assume, a transfer amount $t = \frac{1}{2}\alpha(y_r - y_p)$, at most equal to half the income difference between the i.r.u's a_r and a_p, is taken from the income y_r of the richer i.r.u and given to the poorer i.r.u a_p. The social welfare function is of the equality preferring type if this transfer results in a higher level of social welfare. Examples of e.p.f's are

the class of utilitarian social welfare functions, $w = \Sigma u(y_i)$, where $u(y)$ is increasing and concave,

the class of social welfare functions, $w = w(u(y_1),\ldots,u(y_N))$, which are increasing, symmetric, and strictly quasi-concave in individual utilities and where the utility function u is increasing and concave,

the class of social welfare functions, $w = W(\vec{y})$, which are symmetric and strictly quasi-concave,

the class of social welfare functions, $w = W(\vec{y})$, which are strictly S-concave.[1)]

The equivalence between the WEL and the LDOM (or the TRANSF) is a highly prac-

1) A function $W(\vec{y})$ is quasi-concave if $\min\{W(\vec{y}),W(\vec{z})\} \leq W(\alpha\vec{y} + (1-\alpha)\vec{z})$, where $0 \leq \alpha \leq 1$, holds for all pairs of vectors $\vec{y}$ and $\vec{z}$ in $\Omega(T,N)$.
A function $W(\vec{y})$ is S-concave if $W(\vec{y}) \leq W(\vec{y}B)$ for each vector $\vec{y}$ in $\Omega(T,N)$ and every bistochastic matrix B of size N×N.

ticable, since it allows us to state that the social welfare of the income distribution $\vec{y}$ is higher than the welfare of any other distribution $\vec{z}$ which it strictly Lorenz dominates, provided that social welfare is an e.p.f, and consequently the distribution $\vec{y}$ is more equal (in terms of the WEL) than any of the distributions $\vec{z}$. The appealing point in this reasoning is that welfare judgements can be made without excessive assumptions on the functional form of the social e.p.f.

From the equivalence between the LDOM and the WEL it also follows that if we wish to adopt the WEL, but reject the LDOM (or the TRANSF), we must have reason to believe that the W-function is not an e.p.f.

4.3 EXTENDED SITUATIONAL COMPARISONS: VARIATIONS IN THE TOTAL INCOME

The domain of the SYM, the TRANSF, and the LDOM is clearly restricted to situational comparisons with a given set of i.r.u's and a given total income.
To make a first step towards quasi-comprehensive comparisons we now consider the case of a slightly extended situational comparison, in which the ceteris paribus assumption of a fix total income is relaxed, viz. the problem of ranking $\vec{y} \varepsilon \Omega(T_1,N)$ and $\vec{z} \varepsilon \Omega(T_2,N)$ with respect to income inequality. The same set of i.r.u's $\{a_1,a_2,..,a_N\}$ is assumed to be involved in both distributions, i.e. y_i and z_i denote the incomes of the same i.r.u according to the alternative vectors in question. Now, if we can put forward a reasonable procedure of translation between $\Omega(T_1,N)$ and $\Omega(T_2,N)$ with inherent inequality implications - for instance a translation which leaves inequality unchanged - we may use this to shift $\vec{z} \varepsilon \Omega(T_2,N)$ into $\vec{z}* \varepsilon \Omega(T_1,N)$ and proceed with a situational comparison of $\vec{y}$ and $\vec{z}*$. In the first place it seems reasonable to examine translations which shift all individual incomes in the same way, say by a constant or percentage addition to each income.

The case of equal constant additions to incomes may formally be written as a transformation $\vec{z} = \vec{y} + b\vec{e}$, where $\vec{y} \varepsilon \Omega(T,N)$, b is a constant, and $\vec{e}$ denotes the N-dimensional unit vector $\vec{e} = (1,1,..,1)$. The transformation adds a 'bonus' b to each income in the original distribution and for the resulting income vector $\vec{z}$ holds $\vec{z} \varepsilon \Omega(T+bN,N)$. How does this affect income inequality ? According to Dalton 1920 :

> " .. equal additions to all incomes diminish inequality and equal subtractions increase it",

which implies that $\vec{z} < \vec{y}$ if $b > 0$, and $\vec{y} < \vec{z}$ if $b < 0$. Kolm 1976a writes in turn

"And I have found many people who feel that it is an equal absolute increase in all incomes which does not augment inequality",

and suggests that the transformation leaves inequality unchanged, $\vec{z} \cong \vec{y}$. Independence of equal additions to all observations is also a basic idea of some standard statistical measures of dispersion, e.g. the range and the variance. This principle may be taken as a criterion of the inequality ranking.

Independence of equal additions to incomes (ADD)

If $\vec{e} = (1,1,..,1)$ denotes the N-dimensional unit vector, b is a real-valued constant, and $\vec{y} \in \Omega(T,N)$, then $\vec{z} = \vec{y} + b\vec{e} \in \Omega(T+bN,N)$ and $\vec{y}$ are equally unequal, $\vec{z} \cong_{ADD} \vec{y}$, or in short $(\forall\ b \in R)(\vec{y} \cong_{ADD} \vec{y}+b\vec{e})$.[1)]

If instead of equal additions to incomes we consider equal proportional increments, we may adopt a transformation of type $\vec{z} = c\vec{y}$, where $\vec{y} \in \Omega(T,N)$ and c is a positive constant. Obviously, $\vec{z} \in \Omega(cT,N)$. The analougue to the ADD would in this case be

Independence of proportional changes in incomes (PROPORTION)

If c is any positive constant, $c > 0$, and $\vec{y} \in \Omega(T,N)$, then $\vec{z} = c\vec{y} \in \Omega(cT,N)$ and $\vec{y}$ are equally unequal, $\vec{z} \cong_{PROPORTION} \vec{y}$, or in short $(\forall\ c \in R_+)(\vec{y} \cong_{PROPORTION} c\vec{y})$.

The PROPORTION essentially states that the inequality is not directly influenced by the nominal level of individual incomes, but rather by the individual income shares, i.e. the proportion of total income accruing to each of the N i.r.u's, a fact which is readily seen by choosing the factor c of proportional

1) Sometimes the constant b of the ADD is restricted to some certain area of variation: According to Kolm [1976a] the ADD holds for $b > 0$, and if only positive incomes are feasible we must adopt the restriction $b > -\min(y_i)$. Other limitations on b are of course also possible.

change as $c = 1/T$.[1)]

Neither the ADD nor the PROPORTION may be taken as self-sufficient criteria - the ADD contradicts for instance the position taken by Dalton quoted above. When it comes to the PROPORTION we note that the criterion is supported by the opinion that a proportionate income tax, viz. a proportional change with $c < 1$, is distributionally neutral (cf. Jakobsson and Normann [1974]). On the other hand it is often argued that a proportional income increase, $c > 1$, over the whole income range increases distributional inequality - this is roughly the opinion of many trade unions (cf. Kolm [1976a]) - a position inconsistent with the PROPORTION.[2)]

To illustrate the implications of the ADD and the PROPORTION we may contrast the criteria under the assumption that the LDOM holds. Consider for instance the three income vectors $\vec{y}_1 = (\$2,\$2,\$2)$, $\vec{y}_2 = (\$1,\$2,\$3)$, and $\vec{y}_3 = (\$0,\$0,\$6)$ of $\Omega(\$6,3)$ and the five vectors $\vec{z}_1 = (\$200,\$200,\$200)$, $\vec{z}_2 = (\$199,\$200,\$201)$, $\vec{z}_3 = (\$198,\$198,\$204)$, $\vec{z}_4 = (\$100,\$200,\$300)$, and $\vec{z}_5 = (\$0,\$0,\$600)$ of $\Omega(\$600,3)$. According to the LDOM we have $\vec{y}_1 <_{LDOM} \vec{y}_2 <_{LDOM} \vec{y}_3$ and $\vec{z}_1 <_{LDOM} \vec{z}_2 <_{LDOM} \vec{z}_3 <_{LDOM} \vec{z}_4 <_{LDOM} \vec{z}_5$. Now, the income vectors of $\Omega(\$6,3)$ may be compared to the vectors of $\Omega(\$600,3)$ relying on the ADD with the transformation $\vec{z} = \vec{y} + 198\vec{e}$, or the PROPORTION with the transformation $\vec{z} = 100\vec{y}$. According to the ADD we get the ranking $(\vec{y}_1 \cong_{ADD} \vec{z}_1) <_{LDOM} (\vec{y}_2 \cong_{ADD} \vec{z}_2) <_{LDOM} (\vec{y}_3 \cong_{ADD} \vec{z}_3) <_{LDOM} \vec{z}_4$

1) The PROPORTION is sometimes erroneously interpreted as merely requiring that inequality should be independent of the income unit, so that inequality is the same wheteher individual incomes are recorded in dollars or cents. This property, which formally may be stated "if $\vec{y}$ and $\vec{z}$ are commensurable income vectors with $\vec{y} \leqq \vec{z}$ and c is a positive constant, then $c\vec{y} \leqq c\vec{z}$", obviously follows from the PROPORTION. The PROPORTION in itself is however much more demanding.

2) Dalton [1920] in turn takes the opposite position: "It appears, rather, that proportionate additions to all incomes diminish inequality, and that proportionate subtractions increase it."

Figure 4.4. Lognormal distributions illustrating the PROPORTION and the ADD.

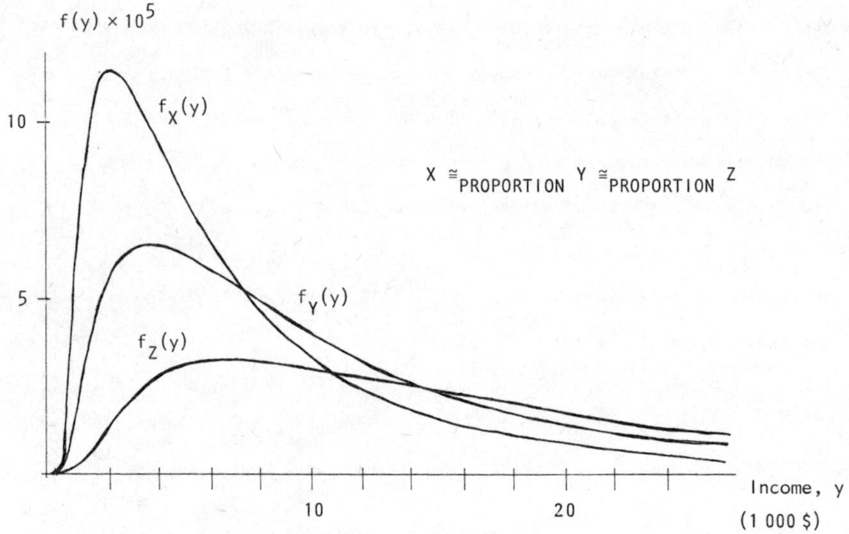

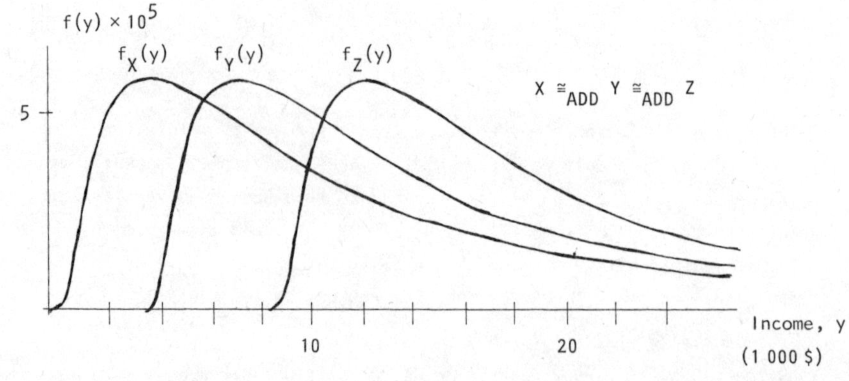

$<_{LDOM} \vec{z}_5$, while the PROPORTION results in the ranking $(\vec{y}_1 \cong_{PROPORTION} \vec{z}_1) <_{LDOM} \vec{z}_2 <_{LDOM} \vec{z}_3 <_{LDOM} (\vec{y}_2 \cong_{PROPORTION} \vec{z}_4) <_{LDOM} (\vec{y}_3 \cong_{PROPORTION} \vec{z}_5)$. $\vec{y}_1 \cong \vec{z}_1$ is common to both rankings and, generally, it is readily seen that both under the ADD and the PROPORTION the egalitarian distribution of any total income is judged as equally unequal as the egalitarian distribution of any other total income. Now, compare the distribution $\vec{y}_3$ = (\$0,\$0,\$6), representing the case of immense concentration in Ω(\$6,3), with the income vector $\vec{z}_3$ = (\$198,\$198, \$204). As $\vec{z}_3$ in no respect represents a distribution of extreme inequality in Ω(\$600,3) - on the contrary it may be argued that $\vec{z}_3$ is the result of a minor disturbance of the egalitarian distribution $\vec{z}_1$ = (\$200,\$200,\$200) and thus represents a fairly equal distribution - we might like to judge $\vec{z}_3 < \vec{y}_3$. This is consistent with the PROPORTION, but not with the ADD suggesting $\vec{z}_3 \cong \vec{y}_3$. On the other hand, it could be argued that $\vec{z}_5$ = (\$0,\$0,\$600) is more unequal than $\vec{y}_3$ = (\$0,\$0,\$6), since the already wealthy i.r.u a_3 of $\vec{y}_3$ is even better off in $\vec{z}_5$. This view is in turn consistent with the ADD, but inconsistent with the PROPORTION.

The difference between the ADD and the PROPORTION can also be interpreted directly in terms of the income distribution function. The income of the distribution $\vec{y} \in \Omega(T_1,N)$ may be interpreted as a variate Y with the frequency (density) function $f_Y(y)$. With this distribution we compare $\vec{z} \in \Omega(T_2,N)$ represented as a variate Z with frequency function $f_Z(y)$. It may easily be shown that if $f_Z(y) = f_Y(y-\mu_2+\mu_1)$, where $\mu_1 = T_1/N$ and $\mu_2 = T_2/N$ denote the mean incomes of the distributions, then $\vec{y}$ and $\vec{z}$ are equally unequal according to the ADD. On the other hand, if $f_Z(y) = \mu_1\mu_2^{-1} f_Y(\mu_1\mu_2^{-1}y)$, then we have $\vec{y} \cong \vec{z}$ according to the PROPORTION.[1)] In figure 4.4 a number of lognormal distributions with same degree of inequality according to the ADD and the PROPORTION are depicted.

1) See also Schaich [1971].

Obviously, the acceptance or rejection of the ADD or the PROPORTION is in the end a matter of prescriptive position. The attitude among many current writers on the subject of income inequality is that the PROPORTION is to be preferred to the ADD, an attitude which in most cases seems to be based on the tacit assumption that whereas inequality per se depends only on the relative income shares the social implications (or the 'perception') of a given inequality level may well vary with the total or mean income. See e.g. Sen 1973; pp 72-73 .

It should be noted that both the ADD and the PROPORTION may be taken as special cases of a more general transformation leaving inequality unchanged.

The genaralized independence criterion (ADD-PROPORTION)

For a given vector $\vec{w} = w\vec{e} = (w,w,..,w) \in \Omega(Nw,N)$ and any positive constant c, the vector $\vec{z} = c(\vec{y} - \vec{w}) + \vec{w}$, where $\vec{y} \in \Omega(T,N)$, and $\vec{y}$ are equally unequal, $\vec{z} \cong_{ADD\text{-}PROPORTION} \vec{y}$, or
$(\forall\, c \in R_+)(\vec{y} \cong_{ADD\text{-}PROPORTION} c(\vec{y}-\vec{w})+\vec{w})$.

If $\vec{w}$, named "the center of transformation" by Kolm [1976a], is taken as the origin, $\vec{w} = 0\vec{e}$, then the transformation reduces to $\vec{z} = c\vec{y}$ or the transformation involved in the PROPORTION. If $\vec{w}$ tends to infinity in the direction of $-\vec{e}$ we may for any number b choose $c = 1 - w^{-1}b$ and it is easily seen that at the limit we have $\vec{z} = \vec{y} + b\vec{e}$,or the transformation of the ADD. The general transformation shifts egalitarian distributions into egalitarian distributions and for small negative values of w inequality is judged approximately as according to the PROPORTION. When w tends towards minus infinity the inequality ranking will more and more tend towards the ranking of the ADD. For instance, with $\vec{y} = (\$0,\$0,\$6) \in \Omega(\$6,3)$ and $\vec{z} \in \Omega(\$600,3)$ we have - remember that $\vec{y} \cong_{PROPORTION}$ (\$0,\$0,\$600) and $\vec{y} \cong_{ADD}$ (\$198,\$198,\$204) - $\vec{y} \cong_{ADD\text{-}PROPORTION}$ (\$2,\$2,\$596) for $w = -1/49$, $\vec{y} \cong_{ADD\text{-}PROPORTION}$ (\$66,\$66,\$468) for $w = -1$, and $\vec{y} \cong_{ADD\text{-}PROPORTION}$ (\$195,\$195,\$210) for $w = -130$.

Another way of passing from one level of total income to another was suggested by Rothschild and Stiglitz [1973]. The procedure is based on a modification of the TRANSF. Consider $\vec{y} \in \Omega(T,N)$ with individual incomes arrayed in non-descending order. The distribution $\vec{z} \in \Omega(T - (1-\alpha)t,N)$ is said to differ from $\vec{y}$ by an *inefficient* non-egalitarian transfer if $\vec{z}$ results from a redistribution of the incomes in $\vec{y}$ involving one individual, say a_p, giving up t of his income y_p and, provided that $p \neq N$, another richer i.r.u, say a_r $(r > p)$, receiving a bonus at most equal to t. The bonus may be denoted αt, $0 \leqq \alpha \leqq 1$. In accordance with the TRANSF we now may state

The principle of inefficient transfers (INTRANSF)

> The income distribution $\vec{y}$ is less unequal than the distribution $\vec{z}$, $\vec{y} <_{\text{INTRANSF}} \vec{z}$, if $\vec{z}$ differs from $\vec{y}$ by a finite sequence of inefficient transfers.

Obviously, if $\vec{y} \in \Omega(T,N)$ and $\vec{z}$ differs from $\vec{y}$ by a number k of inefficient transfers, then $\vec{z} \in \Omega(T - \sum_{i=1}^{k} (1-\alpha_i)t_i,N)$, where $(1-\alpha_i)t_i$ denotes the non-redistributed amount, 'the transfer cost' , of the ith inefficient transfer.

As shown by Rothschild and Stiglitz [1973] the INTRANSF is equivalent to the LDOM - with incomes cumulated in absolute amounts - and to the WEL with the feasible social welfare functions taken as the set of symmetric and monotone increasing e.p.f's.

Although this is a remarkable result, it should be noted that the ranking imposed by the INTRANSF suffers from the deficiency of being one-sidedly incomplete, as given any distributions $\vec{y} \in \Omega(T_1,N)$ and $\vec{z} \in \Omega(T_2,N)$, where $T_1 > T_2$, the INTRANSF (or equivalently the LDOM or the WEL) will rank $\vec{y} < \vec{z}$ whenever a ranking is possible. To put it in another way, a distribution $\vec{y}$ representing a higher total income will never be ranked as equally or more unequal than a distribution $\vec{z}$ of a lower total income, since $\vec{y}$ and $\vec{z}$ are either incomparable or $\vec{y} < \vec{z}$ according to the INTRANSF. As a consequence of this we have, for instance, (\$0,\$0,\$600) $<_{INTRANSF}$ (\$0,\$0,\$6), (\$200,\$200,\$200) $<_{INTRANSF}$ (\$2,\$2,\$2) and (\$2,\$2,\$596) $<_{INTRANSF}$ (\$2,\$2,\$2). Evidently the INTRANSF is likely to violate any descriptive aspiration.[1)]

We are now supplied with four alternative procedures of shifting the level of total income, viz. the ADD, the PROPORTION, the ADD-PROPORTION, and the INTRANSF, each corresponding to a specific prescriptive position and each yielding an inequality ranking of its own. Although the final choice of an appropriate translation procedure should take prescriptive considerations into account, we may not totally ignore the descriptive features and the practicability of the procedure. In this respect the PROPORTION holds a favourable position since the transformation involved is extremely simple - it suffices to express the individual incomes as shares of the total income - and the descriptive qualities of the PROPORTION are quite reasonable.[2)]

To sum up the discussion of this section: Given a relevant procedure of translation we may carry out the extended situational comparison either directly (the case of the INTRANSF) or indirectly through a transformation of the income

1) This also illustrates the main shortcoming of the WEL. While it may be quite justified to conclude that (\$0,\$0,\$600) represents a higher level of social welfare than (\$0,\$0,\$6), it is a different matter to state that (\$0,\$0,\$600) is a more equal distribution than (\$0,\$0,\$6). The deficiency of the WEL arises from the definitional correspondence between higher social welfare and less inequality. Whereas social welfare clearly should respond to inequality, the converse may not be granted.

2) The somewhat anomalous judgement (\$0,\$0,\$6) $\cong_{PROPORTION}$ (\$0,\$0,\$600) is alleviated by recalling that normative incomes are, by way of definition, always positive so that the PROPORTION in fact states (\$ε,\$ε,\$6-2ε) $\cong_{PROPORTION}$ (\$100ε,\$100ε,\$600-200ε), where ε is a small income amount, and thus (\$ε,\$ε,\$6-2ε) $<_{LDOM}$ (\$ε,\$ε,\$600-2ε).

vectors involved to a common total income followed by a comparison of the transformed vectors using the tools of situational ranking (the case of the ADD, the PROPORTION, and the ADD-PROPORTION).

4.4 DIFFERENT I.R.U-GROUPS OF IDENTICAL SIZE

The method of ranking spelled out in the last section may be extended to the case of a simplified quasi-situational comparison.

Consider a community consisting of 2N i.r.u's. The population is now divided into two equisized subgroups, each comprising N i.r.u's. The two groups may be interpreted as two different miniature communities and a comparision of the corresponding income vectors $\vec{y} \in \Omega(T_1,N)$ and $\vec{z} \in \Omega(T_2,N)$ inherits the ceteris paribus features of the extended situational comparison, except for the fact that the income vectors now apply to two different sets of i.r.u's. Let $\{a_{11}, a_{12},..,a_{1N}\}$ denote the set of i.r.u's in community 1 and $\{a_{21},a_{22},..,a_{2N}\}$ be the set of i.r.u's involved in community 2.

In order to make $\vec{z}$ rankable vis-a-vis $\vec{y}$ we must find a way of making the vector $\vec{z} \in \Omega(T_2,N)$ of community 2 interpretable to the members of community 1. If we succeed in this we may then compare the inequality of the 'translated' vector $\vec{z}$ with $\vec{y}$ using the inequality relation R of community 1. A natural way of reinterpreting $\vec{z}$ in community 1 is by means of a matching procedure: Each of the N i.r.u's of community 2 is matched to one (and only one) i.r.u in community 1. If a match occurs between individual a_{2j} of community 2 and individual a_{1i} of community 1, this may be taken as indicating that the income z_j of a_{2j} is to be attributed to a_{1i} and compared with his income y_i in $\vec{y}$. The matching process thus results in a new income vector $\vec{z}^*$ which formally may be written as $\vec{z}^* = \vec{z}P$, where $P \in \mathcal{P}_N$ is a permutation matrix with elements $p_{ij} = 1$ if the i.r.u's a_{2j} and a_{1i} are matched and $p_{ij} = 0$ otherwise. If $\vec{z}^*$ lies within the set of feasible income distributions in community 1 we may use its inequality relation to rank the income vectors $\vec{z}^*$ and $\vec{y}$.

As there are N! different permutation matrixes of size N×N, or equivalently

N! alternative sets of matchings, the final inequality may rest on one of the following approaches (see Sen [1976]):

The existential approach

$\vec{y}$ is not more unequal than $\vec{z}$, $\vec{y} \leqq_E \vec{z}$, if there exists a permutation matrix P with $\vec{y} \leqq_R \vec{z}P$, or in short $\{(\exists\ P \in \mathcal{P}_N)(\vec{y} \leqq_R \vec{z}P)\} \leftrightarrow (\vec{y} \leqq_E \vec{z})$.

The distinguished approach

$\vec{y}$ is not more unequal than $\vec{z}$, $\vec{y} \leqq_D \vec{z}$, if $\vec{y} \leqq_R \vec{z}P^*$ for a specific $P^* \in \mathcal{P}_N$, $(\vec{y} \leqq_R \vec{z}P^*) \leftrightarrow (\vec{y} \leqq_D \vec{z})$.

The universal approach

$\vec{y}$ is not more unequal than $\vec{z}$, $\vec{y} \leqq_U \vec{z}$, if $\vec{y} \leqq_R \vec{z}P$ for every permutation matrix P, $\{(\forall\ P \in \mathcal{P}_N)(\vec{y} \leqq_R \vec{z}P)\} \leftrightarrow (\vec{y} \leqq_U \vec{z})$.

The problem of choosing between these three approaches is made obsolete by noting the fundamental result (see Sen [1976; p. 27]) that the approaches coincide if the inequality relation R of the reference community, i.e. community 1, is transitive and symmetric. This is the case if the inequality relation follows the SYM and the LDOM, a fact which strongly supports the use of these criteria. From the above it follows that we may compare the inequality of the vectors $\vec{y}$ and $\vec{z}$ in the same way as in the case of extended situational comparisons, provided that the inequality relation is symmetric and transitive, since we may, without loss of generality, assume that the matching is carried out according to the distinguished approach using $P^* = I$, the N×N identity matrix. This conclusion serves as the basis of quasi-situational comparisons.

4.5 VARIATIONS IN THE PRICE STRUCTURE

Turning to monetarily (or temporally) distinct communities gives the inequality comparison some new features which should properly be dealt with. The main difference from the type of comparison discussed above is that the accounting unit for income (the domestic currency) is not necessarily the same in both communities.

Formally, retaining the assumption of equisized communities, the comparison involves two communities with income vectors $\vec{y} \in \Omega(T_1,N)$ and $\vec{z} \in \Omega(T_2,N)$, respectively. For ease of exposition we assume throughout this section that the individual money incomes of $\vec{y}$ and the total income T_1 of community 1 are calculated in dollars, while the money incomes of $\vec{z}$ and the total income T_2 of community 2 are calculated in pounds.

If we are interested only in income dispersion and accept the PROPORTION as a suitable base for inequality comparison the case may be handled as in section 4.4, since we may convert the vectors to some standard currency (cf. sec. 3.2.4) e.g. US dollar, by the use of official exchange rates, or to dimensionless vectors by division by some domestic income standard without affecting the inequality. The case of the ADD is more complex, since the inequality ranking is not independent of the specific conversion rate used as will be seen below. Moreover, in order to incorporate normative considerations into our analysis some of the rigid ceteris paribus assumptions of the previous sections must be relaxed. This applies particularly to the tacit assumption of a fixed price structure.

In this section a method for handling price variations and their effects on income inequality within a normative framework will be given in broad outline. The method is based on the notion of a constant-utility exchange rate (price index) and the matching procedure of section 4.4.[1]

Suppose that the commodity prices in community 1 are given by the dollar vector $\vec{p}_1$ and that the pound prices $\vec{p}_2$ rule in community 2. The utility function $u_{ij}(.)$ of individual a_{ij}, i=1,2, j=1,..,N, has in this case not only the individual´s income, but also the ruling prices, as an argument. His utility may thus formally be written as $u_{ij} = u_{ij}(y,\vec{p})$, where y is his income and $\vec{p}$ is the commodity price vector.[2] Under the assumption that the comparison is to be carried out in terms of the characteristics of community 1 the utility functions $u_{1i}(.)$ are of primary importance. We note that the current social state in community 1 gives rise to the individual utilities $u^1_{1i} = u_{1i}(y_i,\vec{p}_1)$ and a matching, as described in the last section, is now carried out.

Suppose that a match occurs between a_{2j} of community 2 and a_{1i} of community 1. The match is in this case interpreted as giving a_{1i} the money income $z^*_i = z_j$ pounds at the associated prices p_2, and the matched utility will thus be $u^2_{1i} = u_{1i}(z^*_i,\vec{p}_2) = u_{1i}(z_j,\vec{p}_2)$. The *dollar equivalent income* z^{**}_i at current prices $\vec{p}_1$ is now defined as the dollar income amount satisfying $u_{1i}(z^{**}_i,\vec{p}_1) = u^2_{1i} = u_{1i}(z^*_i,\vec{p}_2)$ or, to put it in another way, as the cost required for individual a_{1i} to reach the utility level u^2_{1i} at prices $\vec{p}_1$. The ratio $r_i = z^{**}_i/z^*_i$, which may be seen as a function $r_i = r_i(z^*_i)$ of the matched pound income, constitutes a constant-utility exchange rate, that is the conversion rate to be used when converting the matched pound income z^*_i into dollars in order to offset the effect on a_{1i}´s utility of the price change from $\vec{p}_2$ to $\vec{p}_1$. The exchange rate

1) A more detailed discussion of the construction of a constant-utility price index and the problems involved in this falls beyond the scope of this book. The reader is referred to standard textbooks on microeconomic theory and index numbers (e.g. Samuelson and Swamy [1974], Theil [1975], Allen [1975]).

2) In the literature the utility function is frequently written in the form $u_{ij}(\vec{q})$, where $\vec{q}$ denotes the commodity quantities purchased by individual a_{ij} subject to the budget constraint $y = \vec{p}\vec{q}^T$. We prefer the alternative form $u_{ij}(y,\vec{p})$, or the 'indirect utility function' (Theil [1975]), for ease of exposition.

obviously depends both on how the individuals are matched and on the level of the matched pound income.

When all matched pound incomes z_i^*, i=1,..,N, are converted into dollar equivalent incomes according to the exchange rates $r_i(z_i^*)$ we get the *dollar equivalent income vector* $\vec{z}^{**} = (r_1(z_1^*)z_1^*, r_2(z_2^*)z_2^*, .., r_N(z_N^*)z_N^*) = (z_1^{**}, z_2^{**}, .., z_N^{**})$ to the matched pound vector $\vec{z}^* = \vec{z}P$, where $P \varepsilon \mathcal{P}_N$ denotes the permutation matrix involved in the matching (cf. sec. 4.4).

Under the assumption of identical individual utility functions in community 1, $u_{1i}(y,\vec{p}) = u(y,\vec{p})$ for i=1,..,N, implying that the exchange rate only depends on the level of the attributed pound income and not on the outcome of the matching process per se, it is easily seen that every matching procedure results in the same dollar equivalent income vector, except for possible permutations of incomes. Hence, given a transitive and symmetric inequality relation in the reference community, the quasi-comprehensive comparison of $\vec{y}$ and $\vec{z}$ may be carried out through a ranking of $\vec{z}^{**} = (r(z_1)z_1, r(z_2)z_2, .., r(z_N)z_N)$, corresponding to the distinguished matching $\vec{z}^* = \vec{z}I$, and $\vec{y}$, where $r(z_i)$ denotes the level dependent constant-utility exchange rate. This means that the comparison of $\vec{y} \varepsilon \Omega(T_1,N)$ at prices $\vec{p}_1$ and $\vec{z} \varepsilon \Omega(T_2,N)$ at prices $\vec{p}_2$ has been transformed into a similar comparison of $\vec{y} \varepsilon \Omega(T_1,N)$ and $\vec{z}^{**} \varepsilon \Omega(\Sigma r(z_i)z_i,N)$, both at prices $\vec{p}_1$, which can be handled according to the methods of the extended situational comparison of section 4.3.

The analysis is further simplified if in addition it is appropriate to assume that the exchange rate is independent of the level of attributed income, i.e. if $r(z_1) = r(z_2) = .. = r(z_N) = r$.[1)] With this assumption the comparison is essentially reduced to an extended situational ranking of $\vec{y} \varepsilon \Omega(T_1,N)$ and $\vec{z}^{**} = (rz_1,...,rz_N) = r\vec{z} \varepsilon \Omega(rT_2,N)$.

1) Under the assumption of utility maximizing individuals this implies that the preferences must be homothetic (see e.g. Samuelson and Swamy [1974]).

From the above it follows that, in general, much stress should be laid on the use of the correct constant-utility exchange rate (or the price index, in the case of temporally distinct communities), since an inaccurate exchange rate may badly distort the inequality ranking.

Suppose for instance that community 1, enjoying the income vector $\vec{y}$ = (\$0,\$5, \$7) ε Ω(\$12,3) at prices $\vec{p}_1$, judges inequality according to the LDOM and the ADD and intends to compare the current inequality with the inequality of the income vector $\vec{z}$ = (£2,£4,£6) ε Ω(£12,3) of community 2, in which the prices are given by $\vec{p}_2$. The exchange rate is known to be level-independent, but its true value is unknown to community 1. As an approximation the value r = 1.5 is used, i.e. in order to compensate for the price differences 1 pound should be converted to 1½ dollars, whereas the true constant-utility exchange rate in fact is r = 2.[1)] Community 1 then compares the vector $\vec{z}$** = (\$3,\$6,\$9) ε Ω(\$18,3), which is believed to be the dollar equivalent to $\vec{z}$, with $\vec{y}$ and finds $\vec{z}$** $\cong_{ADD}$ (\$1,\$4,\$7) $<_{LDOM}$ $\vec{y}$. A conversion according to the true exchange rate r = 2 would however yield the reversed ranking $\vec{z}$** = (\$4,\$8,\$12) $\cong_{ADD}$ (\$0,\$4,\$8) $>_{LDOM}$ $\vec{y}$.

Provided an level independent exchange rate the PROPORTION once again proves to advantage , since under the PROPORTION the ranking will not be affected by the particular exchange rate chosen - in fact it suffices to express the money incomes as proportions of the total incomes. Accordingly, if the PROPORTION is prescriptively accepted in community 1 the ranking of $\vec{y}$ ε $\Omega(T_1,N)$ at prices $\vec{p}_1$ and $\vec{z}$ ε $\Omega(T_2,N)$ at prices $\vec{p}_2$ is straightforward since the comparison can be made as if there were no price differences.

1) This example also illustrates the crucial role of the conversion rate in connection with the ADD even if we are only interested in income dispersion without any normative considerations.

It should however also be noted that a rejection of the PROPORTION in favour of some competing criterion, say the ADD, is not bound to make an inequality ranking impossible in cases when the true value of the exchange rate is unknown. Since it is frequently possible to restrict the set of feasible exchange rates to some set A we may rank the vectors $\vec{y}$ and $\vec{z}$ according to the rule:

$\vec{y}$ is not more unequal than $\vec{z}$ if $\vec{y} \leqq_R \vec{z}^{**} = r\vec{z}$ for all feasible exchange rates $r \varepsilon A$.[1)]

Now then, what are the consequences of the above discussion for empirical studies of income inequality?
We are supplied with a relatively simple theoretical model of comparison, but we still have to resolve some of the usual hardships when applying theoretical models in practice: We have to obtain empirical counterparts to the magnitudes of the model. The main problem in the construction of an empirical research strategy for quasi-comprehensive income inequality lies in the calculation of the constant-utility exchange rates, as this requires information on the individual utility functions.[2)] In practice we are frequently faced with situations in which no sufficiently detailed information on utility functions is available. In these circumstances the commonly adopted research strategy is to disregard price variations or to proceed as if only income dispersion were studied, i.e. the incomes are converted to a standard currency or ex-

1) This rule may easily be extended to the case of (unknown) level dependent exchange rates. See also Sen [1973; pp. 65-69].

2) This is a well-known index number problem. Under some conditions the true constant-utility exchange rate may be approximated with exchange rates (price indexes) of the Laspeyres and Paasche types (see e.g. Samuelson and Swamy [1974]). If these approximations are sufficiently accurate for income inequality comparisons is a question which requires careful consideration in each specific case.

pressed as ratios to some domestic income standard.[1] Here we can learn a lesson from the theoretical discussion: If the resulting inequality ranking is taken to reveal normative considerations, then the tacit assumptions are that the reference community judges inequality according to the PROPORTION, that all individuals in the reference community have (approximately) the same utility function, and, very important, that the exchange rate is level independent. This almost surely implies that a reference switch has been made, viz. instead of using community 1 as a reference we have passed over to a hypothetical reference community where the PROPORTION and a level independent exchange rate are ruling.[2] It is obvious that this switch can be most damaging when it comes to interpretation of an obtained inequality ranking, since there is not much sense in using a hypothetical reference community if it is remote from reality.

1) The reason for neglecting price differences is usually, besides cases of pure ignorance, found in the argument that the total inequality can be split into two components, one due to variations in the total real income, and one due to differences in the distribution of that income (cf. the discussion of variations in the total income, sec. 4.3). Price differences affect the first component, whereas the second is assumed to be handleable as in the case when no price differences exist (see also Sen [1973]).

2) Whereas the hypothesis of identical utility functions is hard to test in practice (".. an act of faith rather than an application of economic theory", Allen [1975; p. 47]), there is empirical evidence against the assumption of a level independent exchange rate.
The reference switch may of course also be due to the rejection of the PROPORTION.

4.6 VARIATIONS IN THE POPULATION SIZE

In order to relax the assumption of equisized communities we finally introduce the following criterion.

Independence of replications of incomes (REPLIC)

Let A_{ik} denote the N×k matrix in which the elements of the ith row all equal 1 and the remaining (N-1)k elements are zero.

If $\vec{y} \in \Omega(T,N)$ and $A_k = [A_{1k}\ A_{2k}\ ..\ A_{Nk}]$ is the N×kN matrix formed by the matrixes A_{ik}, i=1,..,N, then $\vec{z} = \vec{y}A_k \in \Omega(kT,kN)$ and $\vec{y}$ are equally unequal, $\vec{y} \cong_{REPLIC} \vec{z}$, for every positive integer k, or

$(\forall\ k \in Z_+)(\vec{y} \cong_{REPLIC} \vec{y}A_k)$.

Since each A_{ik}, when premultiplied with $\vec{y}$, replicates the income y_i of i.r.u a_i k-fold, the incomes in the vector $\vec{z}$ of the REPLIC may be written as

$$z_{k(i-1)+1} = z_{k(i-1)+2} = \dots = z_{ki} = y_i, \quad i = 1,..,N.$$

Accordingly, the criterion simply states that if we study an income vector of size kN, in which each income is replicated k times in comparison with the vector $\vec{y}$, then the vectors should be judged as equally unequal. If the inequality relation follows the SYM, which we have assumed, it is readily seen that the REPLIC implies that the inequality ranking can be based solely on the relative frequency distribution of income. Hence, the REPLIC forms in a way the base for an interpretation of the income as a variate described by a (continuous) density function.

The REPLIC - also known as independence of proportional population changes - has been suggested by Dalton [1920], Yntema [1933], Sen [1973], and Champernowne [1974], among others. Although this criterion, or a substitute, is of vital importance to practical inequality rankings, it seems to have escaped criticism.[1)] The propriety of the REPLIC is usually ascribed to the fact that if two or more communities, identical in every respect, are merged, it seems reasonable to expect the income inequality in the combined community to be exactly the same as in each one of the merged communities.[2)] Yet it can be argued that if, for instance, the distributions ($1,$2) and ($1,$2) are merged into ($1,$1,$2,$2), this will not keep the inequality unchanged. As no single i.r.u in the combined distribution has a dominating income, in the sense that his income exceeds the sum of the incomes of the other i.r.u's, the income inequality could be judged as lower than in the original distribution ($1,$2). But since no straightforward alternative to the REPLIC seems to be available we will subsequently adopt this criterion.

In this context it should also be noted that the REPLIC frequently will imply that the maximum degree of inequality rises with the population size, i.e. a distribution involving a larger number of i.r.u's may represent such a high degree of inequality that it is impossible to find an equally unequal distribution involving a smaller number of i.r.u's. For instance, it is easily seen that according to the REPLIC, the LDOM, and the PROPORTION holds $\vec{y} < \vec{z} = (0,0,0,T) \in \Omega(T,4)$ for any $\vec{y} \in \Omega(T,2)$, since $\vec{z} \cong_{PROPORTION} (0,0,0,2T) >_{LDOM} (0,0,T,T) \cong_{REPLIC} (0,T) \geq_{LDOM} \vec{y}$.

1) Some traces of scepticism toward the REPLIC are, however, evident in Sen 1976 and Cowell 1977 .

2) The REPLIC may also be interpreted in terms of social welfare. See Sen [1973], Dasgupta et al [1973].

4.7 QUASI-COMPREHENSIVE COMPARISONS, SUMMARY

To sum up the handling of quasi-comprehensive comparisons we outline the ranking procedure step by step:

Let $\vec{y} \in \Omega(T_1,N_1)$ and $\vec{p}_1$ denote the current income vector and the price structure in community 1, and let $\vec{z} \in \Omega(T_2,N_2)$ denote the income vector in community 2, in which prices are given by $\vec{p}_2$. We assume that community 1, which is taken as the reference base of the inequality ranking, judges situational inequality according to a symmetric and transitive inequality relation (the SYM and the LDOM, for instance). The comparison of $\vec{y}$ and $\vec{z}$ may be divided into five steps.

(1) Use the REPLIC to transform $\vec{y}$ and $\vec{z}$ into two equisized vectors. This can always be accomplished by an N_2-fold replication of $\vec{y}$ followed by an N_1-fold replication of $\vec{z}$, resulting in $\vec{y}^* \in \Omega(T_1^*,N)$, $\vec{y}^* \cong_{REPLIC} \vec{y}$ at prices $\vec{p}_1$, and $\vec{z}^* \in \Omega(T_2^*,N)$, $\vec{z}^* \cong_{REPLIC} \vec{z}$ at prices $\vec{p}_2$, where $T_1^* = N_2T_1$, $T_2^* = N_1T_2$, and $N = N_1N_2$.

(2) Provided that the exchange rate (price index) is the same for all i.r.u's in community 1 and level independent, establish the exchange rate r which offsets the inequality effect of the price change from $\vec{p}_2$ to $\vec{p}_1$ if $\vec{z}^*$ is interpreted as a feasible income distribution in community 1.

(3) Use the exchange rate r to transform the distribution $\vec{z}^*$ at prices $\vec{p}_2$ to $\vec{z}^{**} = r\vec{z}^* \in \Omega(T_2^{**},N)$ at prices $\vec{p}_1$, where $T_2^{**} = rT_2^*$.

(4) Transform $\vec{y}^* \in \Omega(T^*,N)$ and $\vec{z}^{**} \in \Omega(T^{**},N)$ into distributions involving a common total income T without changes in the inherent income inequalities. This gives us $\vec{y}^{**} \in \Omega(T,N)$, $\vec{y}^{**} \cong \vec{y}^*$, and $\vec{z}^{***} \in \Omega(T,N)$, $\vec{z}^{***} \cong \vec{z}^{**}$.

(5) Rank $\vec{y}^{**}$ and $\vec{z}^{***}$ according to the situational inequality relation. If $\vec{y}^{**} \leqq_R \vec{z}^{***}$ we conclude that $\vec{y}$ does not represent a more unequal distribution than $\vec{z}$, $\vec{y} \leqq \vec{z}$, to community 1.

This step-by-step procedure may in each specific case be subject to some modifications - e.g. if the INTRANSF is accepted, or the exchange rate is unknown but restricted to $r \in A$.

We would once again like to point out two crucial points in the comparison: the determination of the exchange rate(s) and the relevant transformation involved in passing from one level of total income to another, and with these the possibility of unintended reference switches.

Among the different ways of changing the total income the PROPORTION is, as we have earlier noted, perhaps the most practicable. This property is reinforced by the REPLIC, since it is easily seen that distributions which according to the REPLIC and the PROPORTION are equally unequal give rise to identical ordinary Lorenz curves, with incomes and numbers of i.r.u's cumulated in relative amounts, and conversely.

To conclude this section the relations between different criteria are summed up in figure 4.5.

Figure 4.5 Logical and rational implications between different criteria on the inequality relation.

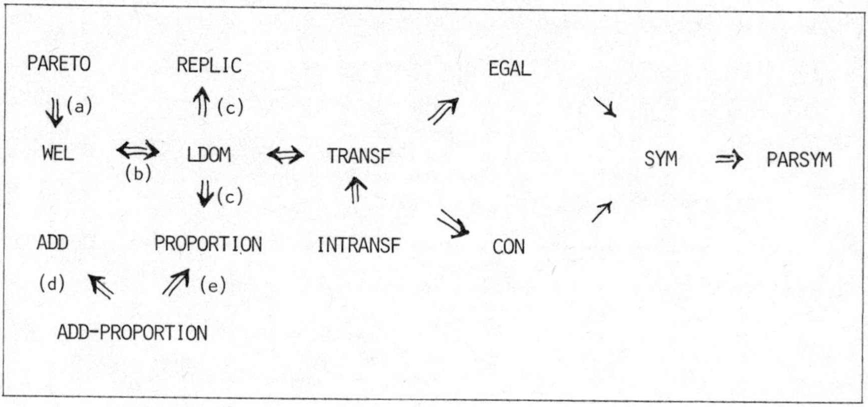

$A \Rightarrow B$ Logical implication, i.e. B is logically a necessary condition for A

$A \rightarrow B$ Rational implication, i.e. B is rationally a necessary condition for A

(a) The Pareto criterion given in terms of incomes (cf. p.41). Provided that the function $w = W(\vec{y})$ is increasing.

(b) Provided that the set $\mathcal{W}$ of feasible social welfare functions consists of symmetric and equality preferring functions.

(c) Provided that Lorenz domination is interpreted in relative terms, i.e. the incomes and number of i.r.u's are cumulated as ratios of their totals.

(d) Provided that the center of transformation is located to minus infinity.

(e) Provided that the center of transformation is located to origo.

4.8 NUMERICAL MEASURES OF INEQUALITY

Inequality comparisons can, as we incidentally noted in section 3.2, be built on an ordinal or a cardinal basis. The ordinal approach results in a ranking, while the cardinal approach gives rise to numerical inequality measures. Current practice in choosing between the approaches is by Fields and Fei [1978] described as follows:

> "Check for Lorenz domination in the hope of making an unambigous comparison; if Lorenz domination fails, calculate one or more cardinal measures." 1)

In this section we will discuss the general properties of numerical inequality measures and present a number of criteria on this type of cardinal inequality ranking. Our objective is to construct an appropriate function $I(\vec{y})$, $I: \Omega \to R$, such that $I(\vec{y}) \leq I(\vec{z})$ corresponds to the ordinal ranking $\vec{y} \leq_R \vec{z}$, or, to put it in another way, to construct a comparison function $C(\vec{y},\vec{z}) = I(\vec{y}) - I(\vec{z})$, $C: \Omega\times\Omega \to R$, with the property $C(\vec{y},\vec{z}) \leq 0$ whenever $\vec{y} \leq_R \vec{z}$. It must be recognized that the inequality function $I(.)$ may be given a double-edged interpretation. Firstly, the inequality measure $I(.)$ should be designed so that an ordinal ranking $\vec{y} \leq_R \vec{z}$ is reflected by the measure as $I(\vec{y}) \leq I(\vec{z})$.[2] Secondly, even

1) Lorenz domination here refers to domination in relative terms. As this rests on the PROPORTION, as well as on the SYM, the REPLIC, and the LDOM, the claim of "unambigous" comparisons may to some extent be disputed.

2) In the first place it may seem trivial to represent an ordering $\vec{y} \leq_R \vec{z}$ numerically: We assign real numbers $I(\vec{y})$ to the vectors $\vec{y} \in \Omega$ in such a way that $\vec{y} \leq_R \vec{z}$ implies $I(\vec{y}) \leq I(\vec{z})$. If the number of feasible income vectors is infinite this may however be impossible, since the set of real numbers may be too small to admit the desired representation. See Debreu [1959], Sen [1973]. This possible difficulty is however neglected in the present discussion.

if the ordinal inequality relation underlying the inequality measure $I(.)$ is inherently incomplete, which, for instance, is the case of the rankings of the preceding sections, there will principally be no difficulties involved in calculating the measures $I(\vec{y})$ and $I(\vec{z})$ for <u>any</u> two income vectors. To avoid ordinally misleading interpretations of an observed numerical comparison $C(\vec{y},\vec{z}) = I(\vec{y}) - I(\vec{z})$ we may either restrict the domain of the function $C(\vec{y},\vec{z})$ to the subset $S_R = \{(\vec{y},\vec{z}) \in \Omega\times\Omega \mid \vec{y} \leqq_R \vec{z} \vee \vec{z} \leqq_R \vec{y}\}$, including only the vectors which are comparable according to the inequality relation in question, or take action to ensure that the inequality measure $I(.)$ results in warranted numerical values, so that $I(\vec{y}) \leq I(\vec{z})$ reveals that $\vec{y}$ is not more unequal than $\vec{z}$, also in the case when the underlying inequality relation fails to tell whether $\vec{y} \leqq_R \vec{z}$ or $\vec{z} \leqq_R \vec{y}$. We return to this second point later in this section.

To begin with we restate the criteria of the preceding sections to meet the notion of a real-valued inequality index. To stress that the measure depends on the population size we use the notation $I(\vec{y},N)$. It should be observed that the criteria only assure that the inequality measure reacts in unanimity with the ordinal inequality relation $\leqq_R$ within the set S_R.

<u>The social welfare criterion (WEL)</u>[1)]

If $W(\vec{y},N) \geqq W(\vec{z},N)$ for all welfare functions $W \in \mathcal{W}$, i.e. if $\vec{y} \leqq_{WEL} \vec{z}$, then $I(\vec{y},N) \leqq I(\vec{z},N)$.

<u>The symmetry criterion (SYM)</u>

Let $P \in \mathcal{P}_N$ denote any permutation matrix of size N×N. If $\vec{z} = \vec{y}P$, where $\vec{y} \in \Omega(T,N)$, i.e. if $\vec{y} \cong_{SYM} \vec{z}$, then $I(\vec{y},N) = I(\vec{z},N)$.

<u>The partial symmetry criterion (PARSYM)</u>

Let $P^C \in \mathcal{P}^C_{N_1+N_2+..+N_k}$ be any constrained permutation matrix of size N×N.

1) In conformity with the notation $I(\vec{y},N)$ we also add the argument N to the social welfare function.

If $\vec{z} = \vec{y}P^C$, where $\vec{y} \in \Omega(T,N)$, i.e. if $\vec{y} \cong_{PARSYM} \vec{z}$, then $I(\vec{y},N) = I(\vec{z},N)$.

The principle of transfers (TRANSF)

If $\vec{z}$ differs from $\vec{y}$ by a finite number of non-egalitarian transfers, $\vec{z} = H(\vec{y})$ where $\vec{y} \in \Omega(T,N)$ and H denotes a sequence of transformations of type (4.1), i.e. if $\vec{y} <_{TRANSF} \vec{z}$, then $I(\vec{y},N) < I(\vec{z},N)$.

The egalitarian criterion (EGAL)

Let $\vec{z}_e = (\mu,\mu,..,\mu)$, $\mu = T/N$, denote the egalitarian income vector. If $\vec{y} \in \Omega(T,N)$ and $\vec{y} \neq \vec{z}_e$, i.e. if $\vec{z}_e <_{EGAL} \vec{y}$, then $I(\vec{z}_e,N) < I(\vec{y},N)$.

The criterion of immense concentration (CON)

Let $\vec{z}_u = (0,0,..,0,T,0,..,0)$ denote the N-vector giving all income to only one i.r.u. If $\vec{y} \in \Omega(T,N)$ and $\vec{y} \neq \vec{z}_u$, i.e. if $\vec{y} <_{CON} \vec{z}_u$, then $I(\vec{y},N) < I(\vec{z}_u,N)$.

The criterion of Lorenz domination (LDOM)

If $\vec{y} \in \Omega(T,N)$ Lorenz dominates $\vec{z} \in \Omega(T,N)$, i.e. if $\vec{y} \leq_{LDOM} \vec{z}$, then $I(\vec{y},N) \leq I(\vec{z},N)$, and if the domination is strict, $\vec{y} <_{LDOM} \vec{z}$, then $I(\vec{y},N) < I(\vec{z},N)$.

Independence of equal additions to incomes (ADD)

Let $\vec{e} = (1,1,..,1)$ denote the N-dimensional unit vector and b be a real-valued constant. If $\vec{z} = \vec{y} + b\vec{e}$, where $\vec{y} \in \Omega(T,N)$, i.e. if $\vec{y} \cong_{ADD} \vec{z}$, then $I(\vec{y},N) = I(\vec{z},N)$.

Independence of proportional changes in incomes (PROPORTION)

Let c be any positive constant, c > 0. If $\vec{z} = c\vec{y}$, where $\vec{y} \in \Omega(T,N)$, i.e. if $\vec{y} \cong_{PROPORTION} \vec{z}$, then $I(\vec{y},N) = I(\vec{z},N)$.

The generalized independence criterion (ADD-PROPORTION)

Let $\vec{w} = w\vec{e} = (w,w,..,w)$ be a given center of transformation and c denote any positive constant. If $\vec{z} = c(\vec{y}-\vec{w}) + \vec{w}$, where $\vec{y} \in \Omega(T,N)$, i.e. if $\vec{y} \cong_{ADD\text{-}PROPORTION} \vec{z}$, then $I(\vec{y},N) = I(\vec{z},N)$.

Independence of replications of incomes (REPLIC)

If $\vec{z} \in \Omega(kT,kN)$ can be interpreted as a k-fold replication of $\vec{y} \in \Omega(T,N)$ for some positive integer k, i.e. if $\vec{y} \cong_{REPLIC} \vec{z}$, then $I(\vec{y},N) = I(\vec{z},kN)$.

In this context we take the opportunity to comment on some features of numerical inequality measures. A first fundamental point to be noted is that for income vectors $\vec{y}$ and $\vec{z}$ in S_R the inequality measure, according to the criteria above, is nothing but a bare translation of the inequality ordering between the vectors into real numbers. From this it follows that measurement of normative income inequality with an inequality index is justified only if the same qualifications as those which apply to the underlying inequality relation are fulfilled. An immediate consequence is that the income vectors whose inequality is to be compared through measurement must be expressed in terms of comparable income magnitudes (real incomes). Further, it is readily seen that the links between the different criteria of the inequality relation is passed over to the inequality measures. Hence, a measure which obeys the LDOM will also have the properties EGAL and CON and fulfil the TRANSF. Conversely, if an inequality measure follows the TRANSF this implies that the LDOM is satisfied.

Turning to a closer inspection of the criteria, we note that according to the WEL the inverse $\{W(\vec{y},N)\}^{-1}$ of the social welfare function may for instance serve as an inequality measure.[1)]

The SYM (or the PARSYM) is not very demanding with respect to the construction of inequality measures; on the contrary functions with the (PAR)SYM-property are quite easily found; for instance, any function of the additive form $I(\vec{y},N) = \sum_{i=1}^{N} d(y_i)$ (or $I(\vec{y},N) = \sum_{j=1}^{k} \sum_{i=1}^{N_j} d_j(y_i)$ in the case of the PARSYM) will do.

Moreover, as it is desirable that the inequality measure should respond smoothly to changes in the income vector, we will assume that the measure the following property.

The condition of continuity (CONT)

$\lim_{\vec{y} \to \vec{y}_0} I(\vec{y},N) = I(\vec{y}_0,N)$ holds for any $\vec{y}_0 \in \Omega(T,N)$.

Further, it is usually presumed that the measure is continuously differentiable with respect to each individual income y_i, which gives us

The condition of first-order partial derivatives (DERIV)

The measure $I(\vec{y},N)$ has continuous first-order derivatives $\frac{dI}{dy_i}$, $i=1,..,N$.

The TRANSF (the LDOM) which is a fundamental criterion in our measurement ambitions, since it forms the basis of strict inequality judgements ("more equal than"), may now be subject to a closer inspection.

Let $\vec{z}$ differ from $\vec{y} \in \Omega(T,N)$ by a non-egalitarian transfer so that $\vec{z} = (y_1,..$ $..,y_i-t,..,y_j+t,..,y_N)$ where $y_i < y_j$. According to the TRANSF we have $I(\vec{z},N) - I(\vec{y},N) > 0$. The Taylor expansion of the difference $I(\vec{z},N) - I(\vec{y},N)$ may be written on the form $I(\vec{z},N) - I(\vec{y},N) = -t\frac{dI}{dy_i} + t\frac{dI}{dy_j} + r(t)$, where $r(t)/t \to 0$ when $t \to 0$. From this we get the expression

1) This once again points out the definiency of the WEL: the definitional correspondence between higher social welfare and less income inequality.

$\frac{dI}{dy_i} < \frac{dI}{dy_j}$ for sufficiently small values of the transfer amount t. Hence,

$$\frac{dI}{dy_j} - \frac{dI}{dy_i} > 0 \text{ , for } y_i < y_j,$$

forms a necessary condition on the measure $I(\vec{y},N)$ if we require it to satisfy the TRANSF.

According to the TRANSF (or merely the EGAL) the egalitarian distribution results in a minimum value of the inequality measure. It seems natural to normalize the measure in such a way that this minimum is zero.[1] This gives us the following criterion.

<u>The criterion of minimum normalized measures (MINNORM)</u>

If $\vec{z}_e = (\mu,\mu,..,\mu) \in \Omega(T,N)$ represents the egalitarian distribution, then $I(\vec{z}_e,N) = 0$.

Depending on how the measure reacts on different transformations of incomes we may distinguish several types of measures. Among these the ralative-invariant and absolute-invariant measures hold an important position, due to their ease of interpretation. An *absolute-invariant* measure is defined as an inequality measure which reacts according to the ADD, whereas a *relative-invariant* measure is in accordance with the PROPORTION.[2] Obviously, relative-invariant and absolute-invariant measures will generally not result in the same inequality conclusions.

Regarding the relative-invariant measures it is usually assumed that the maximum value of inequality is 1.[1] More specifically we use the following criterion (cf. the CON and the discussion on page 91).

1) Criticism of the general approval of normalized measures is found in Cowell [1977].

2) See also section 7.4.

The criterion of maximum normalized measures (MAXNORM)

$I(\vec{y},N) \leq 1$ holds for any vector $\vec{y} \in \Omega(T,N)$, and if $\vec{z}_u$ denotes the vector of immense concentration, $\vec{z}_u = (0,..,0,T,0,..,0) \in \Omega(T,N)$, then

$\lim_{N \to \infty} I(\vec{z}_u,N) = 1.$

The MINNORM and the MAXNORM may be summed up as

The range criterion (RANGE)

If the inequality measure $I(\vec{y},N)$ follows both the MINNORM and the MAXNORM, then the RANGE is satisfied.

The RANGE obviously implies that $0 \leq I(\vec{y},N) \leq 1$ for any vector $\vec{y} \in \Omega(T,N)$.

As long as we confine the inequality measurement to the domain S_R of an underlying inequality relation (e.g. a relation satisfying the LDOM and the ADD) the comparison of any two obtained numerical inequality values is clear-cut. If we do not wish to press the cardinal properties of the used inequality measure, it can be argued that the obtained inequality values is of very little use, since the comparison could as well have been based directly on the inequality relation.
Turning to the more puzzling issue of inequality measurement outside the set S_R (e.g. the case of intersecting Lorenz curves), we note that numerical inequality measures nevertheless may be computed and any specific measure may thus be taken to induce a complete ordering on Ω. That is, if $I(\vec{y},N) \leq I(\vec{z},N)$ for the inequality measure chosen, we interpret this as "$\vec{y}$ is not a more unequal distribution than $\vec{z}$", which we may denote $\vec{y} \leq_I \vec{z}$ where the subscript I refers to the inequality measure in question. The extension of the inequality measure to a complete ordering is clearly a delicate task which

requires careful consideration, particularly as it runs the risk of producing exorbitant inequality conclusions (cf. the passage, quoted from Sen [1973], page 39).

It should also be noted that the measure criteria SYM, TRANSF, REPLIC, and PROPORTION (or ADD) do not determine any unique inequality measure. On the contrary there exist a vast number of measures which satisfy these criteria. If two inequality measures, I_1 and I_2, result in the same complete ordering, i.e. if $I_1(\vec{y}) \leqq I_1(\vec{z})$ implies $I_2(\vec{y}) \leqq I_2(\vec{z})$ and conversely, they are said to be *ordinally equivalent*. A requirement of normalized measures (the MINNORM, the MAXNORM) does not reduce the number of possible inequality measures to any great extent.[1)]

To restrain the inequality measures more effectively we must consider their cardinal properties. An investigation of the cardinal properties also forms the analytical basis when discussing the significance of obtained numerical values (within or outside the set S_R) or the relevance of the complete orderings induced by different inequality measures.

One possible way of taking the cardinal qualities of the inequality measure into account is to strenghten the principle of transfers. This has been discussed by e.g. Kolm [1976b], Love and Wolfson [1976], Mehran [1976], and Cowell [1977]. The basic idea is to postulate how the inequality measure should respond to different types of non-egalitarian transfers.

Using the approach of Kolm [1976b] we consider transfers between i.r.u's with a given income difference. It seems reasonable to stipulate that the inequality should increase more if an n.e.t takes place between relatively poor i.r.u's than if the transfer involves richer i.r.u's. Thus, the inequality index

1) Given, for instance, a relative-invariant measure we may always construct a "new", ordinally equivalent, measure by using a monotone increasing transformation with range [0,1] of the given inequality measure. An example of such a transformation is the function $f(x) = (1 - e^x)/(1 - e)$.

should increase less as a result of a transfer of, say, \$1 from a person with income \$900 to a person with \$1000 than as a result of transferrring the same income amount from an individual with \$100 to another with income \$200. Formally, let both $\vec{z}$ and $\vec{w}$ differ from $\vec{y} \in \Omega(T,N)$ by a single non-egalitarian transfer, so that $\vec{z} = (y_1,..,y_i-t,..,y_j+t,..,y_N)$, $y_i < y_j$, and $\vec{w} = (y_1,..,y_k-t,..,y_l+t,..,y_N)$, $y_k < y_l$, where $y_k > y_i$ and the transfer distance is the same in both cases, $y_j - y_i = y_l - y_k = h$.[1] According to our discussion the following inequality should now hold:

$$I(\vec{z},N) - I(\vec{y},N) > I(\vec{w},N) - I(\vec{y},N)$$

or

$$I(\vec{z},N) > I(\vec{w},N).$$

This property will be named <u>the principle of diminishing transfers (DIMTRANSF)</u>. As above we may use a Taylor expansion to derive the necessary condition

$$\frac{dI}{dy_j} - \frac{dI}{dy_i} > \frac{dI}{dy_l} - \frac{dI}{dy_k}, \quad y_i < y_k, \; y_l - y_k = y_j - y_i = h,$$

of the DIMTRANSF. The magnitude $dI/dy_j - dI/dy_i$, seen as a function of the income y of the transfer giver and the transfer distance h, viz.

$$\left.\frac{dI}{dy_j}\right|_{y_j=y+h} - \left.\frac{dI}{dy_i}\right|_{y_i=y},$$

may be called 'the strength of transfer' (cf Love and Wolfson 1976).

Cowell [1977] uses a slightly different approach when stating his 'strong principle of transfers'.[2] This notion rests on a distance metric,

$d = g(y_j/T) - g(y_i/T)$,

reflecting the difference in income position between the i.r.u's involved in the non-egalitarian transfer, and stipulates that the amount of inequality increase depends, besides on the transfer size, only on d, the distance

1) Note that the vectors $\vec{z}$ and $\vec{w}$ may be represented as intersecting Lorenz curves, which implies that the inequality comparison can not be based on the TRANSF only.

2) See also sec. 7.4.

between the two individuals involved in the transfer.[1] Now, given a specific distance metric it is possible to derive unique measures of inequality by treating the strong principle of transfers as a basic property of the measure.[2] Depending on the choice of d, the derived inequality measure may, or may not, fulfil the DIMTRANSF.[3]

The cardinal properties of the inequality measure are of great consequence when considering decompositions of an overall inequality into 'subinequalities' between and within constituent parts (e.g. socio-economic groups) of a population or components (e.g. wages and entrepreneurial incomes) of a total income.

If we require an overall inequality to be decomposable in a simple way, say as a weighted sum of 'within' and 'between' inequalities, this effectively cuts down the set of optional inequality measures. A closer discussion of this issue will be deferred to chapter 9.

Another issue which is closely related to the cardinal qualities of the inequality measures is the question of the statistical properties of a measure. Since inequality measures are frequently in practice calculated on the basis of sample data it would be very useful to have some means of testing whether the observed numerical difference between the inequality of two or more distributions may be attributed to sampling errors. In this context hausen [1939] writes:

"The sampling distribution of measures of income inequality can no

1) As g-functions of the distance metric Cowell suggests the family $g(x)=\frac{-1}{\beta} x^{\beta}$.

2) See Cowell [1977].

3) Note that the approach of Cowell also suggests an immediate generalization of the DIMTRANSF using some other measure of the transfer distance than the absolute difference in incomes. This will be discussed in sec. 7.4 below.

longer be neglected, as it has been it the past",

but still - surprisingly enough - this is an issue which has attracted very little attention in the vast literature on inequality measurement. This aspect of inequality measures will be dealt with in chapter 10 below.

Dalton [1920] and Champernowne [1974] consider a good inequality measure to be mathematically tractable and easy to compute, e.g. from grouped data. Although this is an appealing property, it lost much of its significance with the accessibility of electronical computers. Consequently we will not stress this property.

Yntema [1933] states that

> "a true coefficient must characterize each distribution by a single definite value which will lead to an unambiguous conclusion when the extent of inequality between different distributions is being compared."

In our opinion this reflects an attitude towards inequality measurement which is troughly mistaken, and we will consequently not pursue any 'best' inequality measure. Instead we seize upon the fact that there are several aspects of income inequality and that some measures are suited to reflect one aspect and some another. See also Champernowne [1974], Wiles [1978]. Concerning our final inequality judgements a consideration of how alternative inequality measures reflect the incomes in different parts of the distribution may particularly prove useful. In this context Champernowne 1974 points out three aspects of inequality of which at least one should be detected by the measure: Inequality due to extreme wealth, inequality due to less extreme incomes, and inequality due to extreme poverty.

To sum up: The construction of an inequality index measure is in many respects a technical issue. Nevertheless, one must not overlook the fundamental fact that an inequality index should always be "in harmony with the connotation implied in the word inequality" (Yntema [1933]).[1] This point is of the greatest importance.

1) See also Sen [1978].

5. FUNCTIONAL FORMS OF SIZE DISTRIBUTIONS OF INCOMES

A size distribution of personal income is frequently skewed. Several attempts have been made either to explain this skewness or, because of the observed stability and regularity of these distribution, to fit functional forms.

The main schools of explaining the skewness are reviewed in Bjerke [1970] and can be summarized as

(1) the stochastic school
'income formation is regarded as a product of certain stochastic processes'

(2) the sociological school
'income formation at any time is a result of a historical process, and the shape of a size distribution of income may be changed when the relative importance of different institutional factors is changed'.

However, no functional form of general approval has emerged from these theoretical considerations and the many attempts of fitting c.d.f.'s to empirical data reflect this unavailingness.

Other grounds for fitting c.d.f.'s can also easily be found, e.g. for extrapolating (and interpolating) purposes since the extreme parts of a distribution of income are frequently unknown (cf. e.g. Linders [1929]) because data may only be given above certain lower income bound or in grouped data the upper class may be open.

certain lower income bound and in grouped data the upper class is open.

The information given by data can be summarized with a continuous density function (d.f.) and its characteristics, i.e. the mean, the standard deviation, the skewness etc. This will make it possible to study differences between two distributions. But a measured difference between two distributions (or a measured difference of the inequality of the distributions) will on the other hand be affected by the chosen d.f.

It can also be stated (see Hart [1978]) that for some fitted d.f's the relatio between different measures of inequality are easy to establish, but this must not be seen as a reason for fitting d.f.'s.

Moreover, an assumption of the specific form of the income distribution may be profitable when considering the sample properties of alternative inequality measures.

The two most commonly used d.f.'s are the Pareto and the lognormal functions. The Pareto d.f. is said to give a good fit in the upper tail of the income distribution and the lognormal is usually used to fit in the mid-range of the income scale.

The purpose of this chapter is to briefly review the stochastic school and to give references to papers discussing this and the fit of functional forms. In sec. 5.1 we will briefly discuss the Pareto and related distributions.

The stochastic school

The stochastic school mainly rests on the law of proportional effect. This law is stated in Aitchison and Brown [1957 - p.22] as:

> *"a variate subject to a process of change is said to obey the law of proportional effect if the change in the variate at any step of the process is a random proportion of the previous value of the variate".*

Let the income be y_o at a certain date. The income in period t, Y_t, will by the law of porportionate effects be generated iteratively according to $Y_t = Y_{t-1}(1 + \varepsilon_t)$, where ε_t represents a 'random shock' which is independent of the value Y_{t-1}. We can rewrite the income generating process as $\log Y_t = \log y_o + \log(1 + \varepsilon_1) + \log(1 + \varepsilon_2) + \dots + \log(1 + \varepsilon_t)$ which under standard assumptions yield a lognormal variate according to the central limit theorem.

Gibrat [1931 and 1957] proposed that the income formation relies this law. If we write $Z_i = \log Y_i$, $i = 0,1,2, \dots ,t$, and $u_i = \log(1 + \varepsilon_i)$, $i = 1,2,\dots, t$, we have $Z_t = z_o + \sum_{i=1}^{t} u_i$. The variance of Z_t, $Var(Z_t)$, equals the sum of the variances $Var(u_i)$, where the random variable u_i's are identically distributed with finite variance. As time t increases the variance of the logarithmic incomes increases. This fact led Kalecki [1945][1)]

1) Kalecki said ([1945 - page 162]): "... for a priori reasons it is clear that changes in the standard deviation of the logarithm of a given variate are to a great extent determined by economic forces. It follows therefore that the standard deviation of the variate log Y is fully or partly constrained and as a result the random changes are not independent of the values of the variate log Y that are subject to them."

to reformulate Gibrat's process to a variance stabilizing process defined by $Y_t = A\,Y_{t-1}^{\beta}(1 + \varepsilon_t)$ or in logarithmic terms $Z_t = \alpha + \beta Z_{t-1} + u_t$, which yields $Z_t = \alpha(\frac{1 - \beta^t}{1 - \beta}) + \beta^t Y_o + \sum_{i=1}^{t} \beta^{t-i} u_i$, where $0 < \beta < 1$. Kalecki showed, under some conditions, that in this case, too, Z_t tends towards a normal distribution. The variance of Z_t, in this case, becomes equal to $(\frac{1 - \beta^{2t}}{1 - \beta^2})\mathrm{Var}(u)$ and in the limit $(t \rightarrow \infty)$ $(1 - \beta^2)^{-1}\mathrm{Var}(u)$. See also Klein [1962 - pp. 161-163] and Shorrocks' discussion of Brown's [1976] paper.

The lognormal distribution has been discussed in a number of papers and the interested reader is referred to e.g. the book of Aitchison and Brown [1957 - especially ch. 11]. In the lognormal process there are three underlying assumptions:

(i) the process is first-order Markov,

(ii) the law of proportional effects holds and

(iii) the process is time homogeneous.

In the general discussions on stochastic income processes it is assumed that, given an initial income distribution and certain assumptions concerning the process, it will converge towards a certain skewed d.f. (equilibrium distribution).One of the used conditions for the convergence is that the transition probabilities, i.e. the probability of moving from a given income interval to the next is independent of the initial distribution and only depends on the income before (interval i) and that after (interval j) the transition.

If some restrictions are imposed on the transition probabilities, cf. e.g. Bjerke [1970 - pp. 238-240] and Klein [1962 - pp. 169-171], then the process tends towards certain d.f.'s.

Denote by $p_{ij}(t)$ the probability that a person at time t has moved from income interval i to income interval j and by $P_i(t)$ the probability that at time t a person is in interval i. Then $\sum_{j=1}^{\infty} P_{ij}(t) = 1$ and the transition equation is $P_j(t + 1) = \sum_{i=1}^{\infty} P_{ij}(t)P_i(t)$.

Champernowne [1953], [1973][1)] assumed an infinite number of income intervals (Y_{i-1}, Y_i), $i = 1,2,\ldots$ (with minimum income y_o) to be of geometrical length with $y_i = ky_{i-1} = k^i y_o$, $k > 1$, i.e. $y_i - y_{i-1} = (k - 1)y_{i-1} = (k - 1)k^{i-1}y_o$. For $j \neq 1$ the transition probability is assumed to be a function of t and j-i only and we write $p_{ij}(t) = q_t(j - i)$, $j \neq 1$, $i = 1,2,\ldots$. $p_{i1}(t)$ equals by this $1 - \sum_{j=2}^{\infty} q_t(j - i)$ and hence the transition equation becomes $P_j(t + 1) = \sum_{j=1}^{\infty} P_i(t)\, q_t(j - i)$, $j \neq 1$, and $P_1(t + 1) = \sum_{i=1}^{\infty} (1 - \sum_{j=2}^{\infty} q_t(j - i))P_i(t)$. With this model and certain other assumptions Champernowne showed that the resulting equilibrium distribution is of Pareto-type.See also Aitchison and Brown [1954 - pp. 92-93], [1957 - p.109], Klein [1966 - p.169], Bjerke [1970 - p. 238], Cramer [1971 - pp.60-64] and Ord [1975 - p. 153].

Aitchison and Brown [1954], [1957] assumed intervals of arithmetic length and that the income range is between zero and infinity. The intervals (y_{i-1}, y_i) were defined to be of equal length by $y_o = 0$ and $y_i = y_{i-1} + h = ih$. For $j \neq 1$ the transition probabilities are assumed to be functions of t and the ratio j/i only and we write $p_{ij}(t) = q_t(j/i)$, $j \neq 1$, $i = 1,2,\ldots$ and $p_{i1}(t) = 1 - \sum_{j=2}^{\infty} q_t(j/i)$.

[1)] Champernowne's paper from 1953 is reprinted in appendix 6 in his book of 1973.

Hence the transition equation becomes $P_j(t + 1) = \sum_{i=1}^{\infty} P_i(t)q_t(j/i), j \neq 1$, and $P_1(t + 1) = \sum_{i=1}^{\infty} (1 - \sum_{j=2}^{\infty} q(j/i))P_i(t)$. Aitchison and Brown assumed the intervals to be of infinitesimal length [1954 - pp. 94-] and showed that under certain assumptions the equilibrium distribution tends towards the lognormal.

Both these models assume a constant population of i.r.u.'s. As a cause of this Rutherford [1955] introduced a birth and death process to the income formation. He assumed that every year there were entrants of the same age and that their incomes were normal (lognormal). For mortality Rutherford [1955 - p.200] used life tables. By these assumptions and some others Rutherford showed that the equilibrium distribution of the process was the Gram-Charlier Type A. Birth and death income processes are also discussed by Cramer [1971 - pp. 64-68].

For reviews on stochastic income processes see e.g. Bjerke [1970], Brown [1976] Sahota [1978 - pp. 7-9] and Ord [1975]. Stochastic processes are also discussed by e.g. Mandelbrot [1960], Singh and Maddala [1975] and Ord [1975]. Markov chains are used by Esberger and Malmquist [1972] to describe and analyze the income growth in Sweden.

Fitting of functional forms

Contrary to the authors of the stochastic school, who try to explain the income formation, there are others who only fit functional forms to empirical data. Functional forms that have been proposed are e.g. Pareto type I, II and III-, Weibull-, $sech^2$-, Beta-, Gamma-, exponential-, Yule-, Burr-, scaled F- and Champernowne's distribution.

For papers discussing the pros and cons of one or more specific funtional forms to fit income distributions, the reader is referred to e.g.

Davies [1941]: Pareto, Gamma, Champernowne's, lognormal and Davies suggestion,

Champernowne [1937], [1952], [1973][1]: his own functional form,

Fisk [1961]: Champernowne's and a special case of this, the $sech^2$-distribution,

Klein [1962]: Pareto, lognormal, Pearson Type III, Champernowne's,

Cramer [1971]: Pareto, lognormal,

Salem and Mount [1974]: Gamma,

Singh and Maddala [1976]: Burr distribution, with special cases Pareto I and II, Weibull, exponential and $sech^2$ (see also Cronin [1979])

Maddala and Singh [1977]: Pareto I, II and III, Champernowne's, $Sech^2$, Dagum's suggestions, Beta, Gamma, Burr,

Bartels [1977][2]: three- and two-parameter Gamma, Weibull, lognormal, four-parameter inverse hyperbolic sine normal, $sech^2$, log logistic, Champernowne's, three-parameter log Student, Box-Cox-Champernowne, Beta, log Pearson IV (see also Hart [1981]),

Cowell [1977]: Pareto I, II, III, lognormal, Weibull, exponential, $sech^2$, Burr, Champernowne's, Yule, Beta, Gamma,

Dagum [1977]: his own functional form,

Kakwani [1980b]: Pareto, Burr, Beta, Champernowne, lognormal, Gamma,

Vartia and Vartia [1981]: scaled F.

This list could be extended but we only want the reader to see the immense suggestions that have been made on functional forms to fit income distributions. It also gives a picture of the complexity of the income distributions. Since we do not intend to use any functional forms when measuring income inequality we leave this discussion and do not look at problems such as aggregating.

1) Ord [1971 - p. 156] justified Champernowne's distribution by a stochastic model.

2) Bartels and Vries [1977] transformed incomes by logarithmic, inverse hyperbolic sine- and Box Cox transformations and applied these to symmetrical density functions.

5.1 PARETO AND RELATED DISTRIBUTIONS

We assume that the income, Y, is a continuous variable. If $f(y)dy$ is the proportion of individuals with income in the interval $[y,y+dy]$,we may approxima $f(y)$ with constants in short interval of the y-axis. With this starting-point Pareto [1897] suggested a measure of equality of a distribution of income (or wealth). In a rectangular co-ordinate system on a double-logarithmic paper he took the income (Y) as the abscissa and n_y, the number of individuals having an income greater than y, as the ordinate, see figure 5.1.

The minimum income that the individuals receive is denoted by y_o and the total number of individuals with incomes exceeding y_o is denoted by n_{yo} (= N). Let $\tan \omega = \alpha$, where ω is the angle between the two straight lines $\overline{AC}$ and $\overline{CB}$ in figure 5.1, and $\alpha > 0$.

After empirical studies Pareto assumed the following relation to hold for an arbitrary $y > y_o$:

$$\{\log n_{yo} - \log n_y\} = \{\log y - \log y_o\}\alpha \tag{5.1}$$

or

$$n_y/n_{yo} = \{y_o/y\}^{\alpha} \tag{5.2}$$

The left hand side of (5.2) is equal to the proportion of individuals having an income greater than y. If $F(y) = P(Y \leq y)$, then we can write (5.2) as

$$F(y) = 1 - y_o^{\alpha} y^{-\alpha} = 1 - \{1 - F_1(y)\}^{\alpha/(\alpha-1)}, \text{ for } \alpha > 1 \qquad (5.3)^{1)}$$

where $(1 - F_1(y))$ is the proportion of the total income received by the individuals having an income greater than y and $F_1(y)$ is the 1st m.d.f..

Pareto observed that (5.3) or the transformation

$$\log\{1 - F(y)\} = k - \alpha \log y \qquad (5.4)$$

fitted empirical data quite well. He regarded (5.4) as a 'natural law' (see, e.g., Ord [1975]) and the constant α as a measure of equality. This 'natural law' is the so called 'Pareto law'. Pareto also found α to be equal to 1.5 [2)] for the countries that he studied.

Ord [1975 - p.152] stated that "α has, ..., a natural interpretation as a measure of inequality ...". Bortkiewicz [1930] gave a comprehensive discussion of the Pareto distribution and the meaning of α (e.g., that α is a measure of equality and related to some well-known measures of inequality). Moreover, he discussed the conflict between empirical data and the Pareto law. It is accepted, in most of the literature, that at least the upper tail of the income distribution can be approximated by (5.4). However, there are some contradictory studies. Gastwirth [1972], for example, said: "It appears that the Pareto fit was not bad as late as 1955 but is no longer appropriate" (on U.S. income data).

1) This is the c.d.f. labelled Pareto Type I. Pareto Type III is written as $F_{III}(y) = 1 - e^{-ky}\{\gamma + \delta y\}^{-\alpha}$. Pareto Type II is given by letting $k = 0$ and Pareto Type I by letting $k = \gamma = 0$ and $\delta = y_o^{-1}$.

2) Creedy [1977a] suggested that there may be errors in Pareto's computations.

How should we interpret the measure α? Pareto himself said that the greater the equality of the distribution of income is, the less is α. This interpretation is however mistaken, cf. Bortkiewicz [1930], and may be due to the fact that Pareto gave two contradictory definitions of 'inequality' (Bortkiewcz [1930], Gibrat [1931 and 1957]).

As noted above the Pareto distribution is frequently used to fit the upper tail of an income distribution. For this reason α can not be used as a measure of equality for the <u>entire</u> distribution. The argument is as follows: If all individuals have the same income, μ, the Pareto-curve for incomes less than μ depicts a horizontal straight line (see figure 5.2) and in the point μ ($\log \mu$) on the abscissa the Pareto curve is a vertical straight line. For the part above the arithmetic mean income it is true that the greater α is (the slope of the Pareto-curve), the greater is the equality of the distribution.

For the lower part of the income distribution ($< \mu$) the argument has to be reversed: the greater the equality is, the lower is α (cf. Bowman [1945]). Criticism of α as a measure of inequality is e.g. given by Yntema [1933] and Gini [1936]. For estimates of α the reader is referred to the work of Bortkiewicz [1930].

Figure 5.1

A geomterical interpretation of the Pareto Distribution (On double-logarithmic paper)

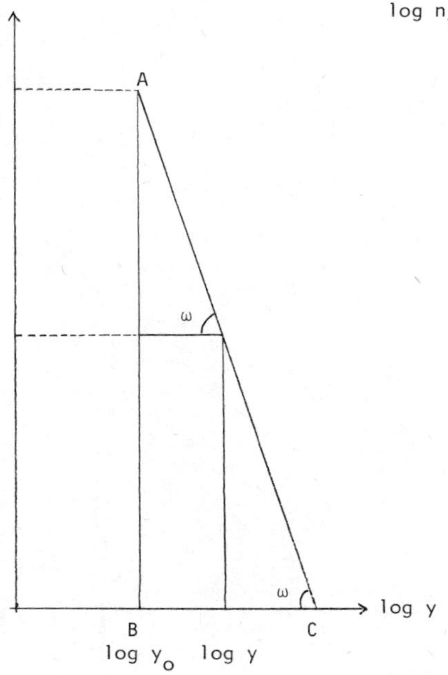

Figure 5.2

The Pareto curve of an income distribution of complete equality and the Pareto curve of an income distribution of non-complete equality.

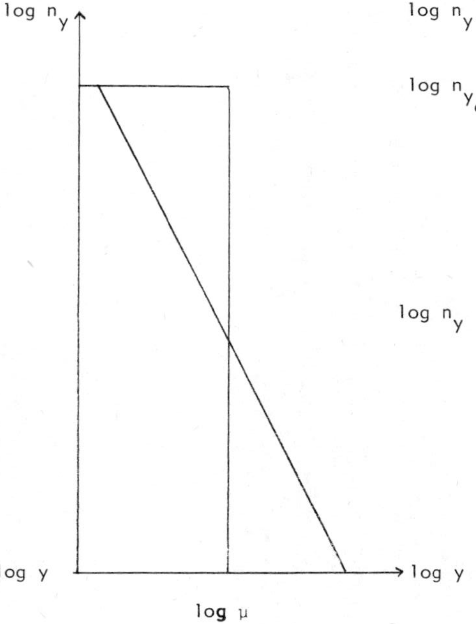

Figure 5.3

A geometrical interpretation of the Gini Distribution (On double-logarithmic paper)

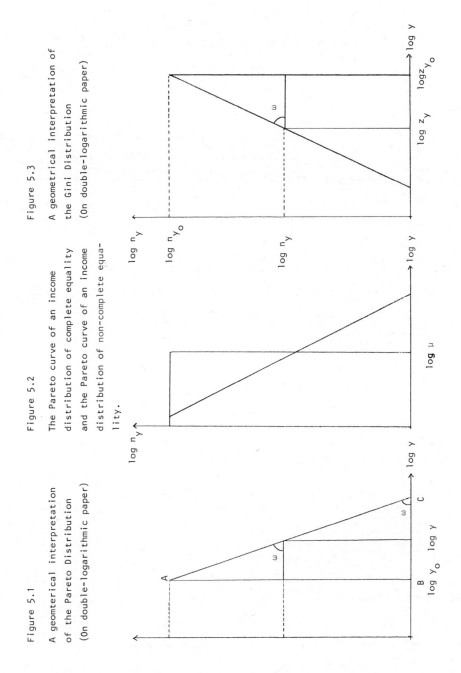

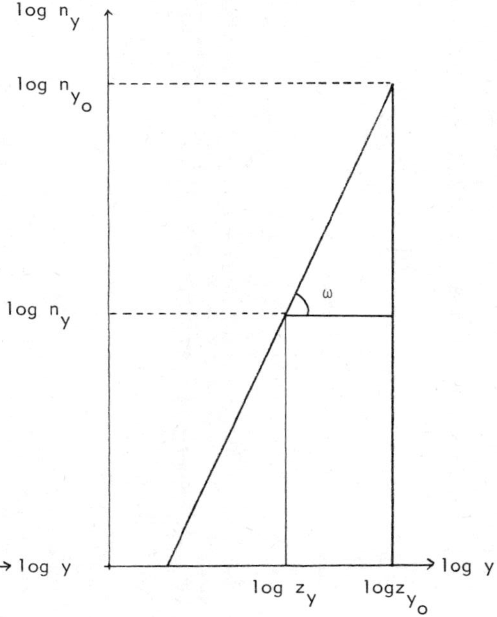

For $\alpha > 1$ the arithmetic mean of the Pareto distribution is finite and given by $\frac{\alpha}{\alpha-1} y_o$ (see e.g. Cramér [1946]) and the mean above a chosen value y is $\frac{\alpha}{\alpha-1} y$. The variance of the Pareto distribution is only defined for $\alpha > 2$.

The Gini distribution, Gini [1909], is identical to the Pareto distribution, but in contrast to Pareto, Gini worked with the aggregate of incomes, z_y, which is received by the number of individuals, n_y, above a given income level y.

If we let y_o be the minimum income, then z_{yo} is the total aggregated income of all the individuals receiving income, n_{yo}. On a double-logarithmic paper we let the aggregate of incomes exceeding y, z_y, be the abscissa and the aggregate of the individuals, n_y, having an income exceeding y be the ordinate, see figure 5.3.

For an arbitrary $y > y_o$ we get (cf. 5.1)

$$\{\log n_{yo} - \log n_y\} = \delta\{\log z_{yo} - \log z_y\} \tag{5.5}$$

where δ is equal to $\tan \omega \geq 1$.

(5.5) can be written as

$$(n_y/n_{yo}) = (z_y/z_{yo})^{\delta}. \tag{5.6}$$

The left hand side is equal to the proportion of the individuals having an income greater than y and the factor within brackets on the right-hand side is the proportion of the aggregated incomes of these individuals and we can write (5.6) as

$$F(y) = 1 - \{1 - F_1(y)\}^{\delta} \tag{5.7}$$

Comparison of (5.3) and (5.7) shows that the Pareto and the Gini c.d.f.'s are identical with $\delta = \frac{\alpha}{\alpha-1}$, for $\alpha > 1$.

A transformation of (5.5) gives the formula that Gini worked with:

$$\log n_y = p + \delta \log z_y \tag{5.8}$$

where p is a constant, for a given distribution, and equals $\log(z_{yo}^{-\delta}\, n_{yo})$.

δ is Gini's measure of inequality or 'index of concentration' and (5.8) is a straight line.

Since a distribution where all individuals have the same income μ, will yield a Gini-curve which is a straight line with the angle 45°, and a Gini-curve fitted to empirical data will never lie above the 45 degree line, we can state that the less the value of δ is the more equal the distribution is, a fact which follows immediately from the relation between δ and α, (for $\alpha > 1$).

This relation also explains why the Gini measure is more 'sensitive' to inequality than the Pareto measure (cf. Bortkiewicz [1930 - p. 98]).

Bowman [1945] analyzed the *reversed Gini-curve*, i.e. instead of aggregating from the top she aggregated incomes starting from the lower parts of the distribution. The reversed Gini-curve (or Bowman-curve) will now lie on the opposite side of the 45°-line in comparison with the Gini-curve. The formula for the reversed Gini-curve is

$$F(y) = \{F_1(y)\}^{\beta} \tag{5.9}$$

or

$$\log n'_y = q + \beta \log z'_y, \tag{5.10}$$

where n'_y is the number of individuals receiving incomes less than or equal to y and z'_y is the aggregated incomes of these individuals. The constant q is equal to $\log(n'_{y_m} \; z'^{-\beta}_{y_m})$, where y_m is the maximum income, and the measure β $(0 \leq \beta \leq 1)$ gets higher the more equal the distribution is, i.e. β is an equality measure.

As can be seen from the earlier discussion the distribution functions of Pareto and Gini are identical, with $\delta = \frac{\alpha}{\alpha - 1}$, for $\alpha > 1$, and we will now compare them to the Bowman (or reversed Gini) distribution function.

The two distributions (Gini and Bowman) stress different parts of the distribution, a fact which can be seen from the relations between the c.d.f. F(y) and the 1st m.d.f. $F_1(y)$:

$$\text{Gini:} \quad 1 - F(y) = (1 - F_1(y))^{\delta} \tag{5.11}$$

$$\text{Bowman:} \quad F(y) = F_1(y)^{\beta} \tag{5.12}$$

where $\delta \geq 1$ and $0 \leq \beta \leq 1$. Before we proceed we have to make some assumptions regarding the range of the income variable Y. Firstly we recall that income is nonnegative. In the case of the Gini distribution we are studying the upper tail of the distribution and make reference to a minimum income $y_o > 0$ and in the case of the Bowman distribution the situation is reversed, i.e. we are studying the lower tail with reference to a maximum income $y_m < \infty$. This means that the income ranges from y_o to infinity in the Gini-case and from zero to y_m in the Bowman-case. It is also possible to plot the two c.d.f.'s in a Lorenz diagram (cf. sec. 7.2) with F(y) as the abscissa and $F_1(y)$ as the ordinate. The Lorenz area, i.e. the area between the Lorenz curve (LC), (points $(F(y), F_1(y))$) and the diagonal, can, for the Gini distribution function, be set equal to that of the Bowman distrbution function. This Lorenz area realtion gives $\delta = 1/\beta$. The LC's are now reversed, i.e. the LC_B (B stands for Bowman) is pressed down in the lower parts and the LC_G is pressed upwards.

The Gini distribution function can be interpreted as a more 'equalizing' distribution in the lower tail than the Bowman distribution function, given the above mentioned Lorenz relation. The arithmetic means of the two distributions are $\mu_G = \delta y_o$ and $\mu_B = \beta y_m$.

Since, if the total income and the number of individuals are known, the measures α, δ and β are based on assumed laws according to which the distributions are uniquely determined, we will not investigate how the criteria in chapter 4 are fulfilled (cf. Dalton [1920]).

The advantage of the three distributions, or transformations of them, lies in their readable graphical interpretation and capability of featuring different parts of the distributions.

6. NORMATIVE MEASURES OF INEQUALITY

6.1 THE CONCEPT OF A SOCIAL EVALUATION (WELFARE) FUNCTION

We start out by considering the set X of alternative social states (cf. section 3.2) in a community with N individuals. Each individual is assumed to rank the social states $\vec{x} \in X$ according to a function $u_i = u_i(\vec{x})$, $i=1,..,N$, revealing the individual utility of the state $\vec{x}$. We can now define a social welfare function as $w(\vec{x}) = w(u_1(\vec{x}),..,u_N(\vec{x}))$ according to which society ranks the alternative states $\vec{x} \in X$.[1)]

The properties of the social welfare function will largely depend on the assumed measurability-comparability framework of the individual utility functions. Sen [1977] separates between five alternative framings of which the ordinal non-comparability framework seems to be only one of general approval. According to this individuals are assumed to be able to give a complete ordinal ranking ('better', indifferent', or 'worse') of the social states. The ranking can be represented numerically so that a state $\vec{x}$, which individual a_i prefers to the state $\vec{z}$, is assigned a higher numerical value, $u_i(\vec{x}) > u_i(\vec{z})$. Moreover, this framework provides no means of making interpersonal comparisons of utility, as a consequence of which criteria of the WEA- or RAWLS-type can not be applied. Social welfare in turn is assumed to behave in accordance with the Pareto criterion so that welfare increases when-

1) This may be seen as a generalization of the welfare function presented in chapter 3 by allowing the individual utility to depend on other features of the social state than merely the individual´s own income.

ever at least one utility is augmented while none is reduced.
In welfare economics the set X of social states is frequently restricted to the set Ω of feasible income distributions, i.e. individual utility is taken as a function of the income vector only.

As shown by Arrow [1963] there exists no logically consistent social welfare function satisfying four "conditions of correspondence" which a priori appear reasonable (see also Sen [1977],[1979]). We will not go into the extensive discussion of Arrow´s impossibility theorem, but rather follow the somewhat different approach adopted by Little [1952] and Kondor [1975], among others, and simply assume that someone has consistent preferences regarding the elements of Ω. That is to say that there exists a function $w = W(\vec{y})$, $W: \Omega \to R$, which we name 'the social evaluation function' (or the 'master-ordering'). The individual (or institution) whose preferences are described by $W(.)$ is called 'the client' in accordance with Kondor [1975] - Arrow would probably prefer the term 'dictator'. Compared with the general case above we simply take the idividual utility function of the client to represent social evaluation, i.e. $W(\vec{y}) = u_C(\vec{y})$, where C stands for client. The function $W(\vec{y}) = W(y_1,..,y_N)$ is further assumed to be symmetric and the income distribution (instead of the income vector) may hence be used as an argument.

The social evaluation function may be contrasted to the, superficially tantamount, 'social welfare function' of section 3.3. The latter was obtained by letting $u_i(\vec{y}) = u_i(y_i)$ in the general welfare function $w(u_i(\vec{y}),..,u_i(\vec{y}))$ and then expressing it in terms of the y_i's alone.[1)] The imposed supposition of utilities depending only on the individual´s own income is apparently very

1) This presupposes in general the existence of cardinal utility functions.

restrictive. The symmetry of the social welfare function may be assured through the additional requirement of identical individual utility functions, $u_i(y) = u(y)$, $i=1,..,N$. The advantage, if any, of this approach is that it allows us to retain the concept of a function revealing general social welfare.

The present approach is conceptually distinct in that it individualizes 'social welfare' by attributing the evaluation function to a specific client. Although this feature may be disputed, the approach allows the client´s utility to be influenced by other incomes than his own. In fact, the symmetry assumption forces the client to treat every income alike.

Given an ordinal social evaluation function W_1 we may easily construct another evaluation function W_2 with the property that $W_1(\vec{y}) > W_1(\vec{z})$ implies and is implied by $W_2(\vec{y}) > W_2(\vec{z})$.[1] Such functions are said to be ordinally equivalent. Even in the case of cardinal evaluation functions it is hard to advocate the assumption of a fully determined function. Rather, it seems appropriate to take the view that if $W(\vec{y})$ is regarded as a reasonable function then at least some of the ordinal equivalents to W should also be considered as sound alternatives. As a consequence of this we will basically consider the evaluation function W to be given as unique only up to a monotone transformation.

1) We can define the ordinal equivalent to W_1 by $W_2(\vec{y}) = \phi(W_1(\vec{y}))$, where ϕ is a monotone increasing function.

6.2 CARDINALITY AND THE DALTON-ATKINSON APPROACH

We are now supplied with a social evaluation function, which orders the distributions of Ω according to $W(\vec{y}) > W(\vec{z})$ whenever the client prefers the distribution $\vec{y}$ to the distribution $\vec{z}$. We further assume that $W(\vec{y}) > 0$ for every $\vec{y} \in \Omega$.

Essentially we have gained nothing so far by the introduction of the evaluation function, since we could as well express the ordering with the help of a preference relation of the type discussed in section 3.2.

We now assume that the evaluation function possesses cardinal properties by letting W be continuous, increasing and S-concave.[1)] However, we will not adopt the assumption implied by the WEL, i.e. that W increases along the ray of equality, due to its close relationship with the Pareto criterion and its descriptive shortcomings demonstrated in section 4.3. Instead we will use a standardization procedure and construct an index of inequality from the evaluation function.

Let $\vec{z}^* \in \Omega(T,N)$ denote the optimal distribution which, for a given amount T of total income, maximizes the social evaluation function in the sense that $W(\vec{z}^*) \geqq W(\vec{y})$ for every $\vec{y} \in \Omega(T,N)$. In general there may, for a given evaluation function, exist one or more optimal distributions.

The level of inequality of an income distribution $\vec{y} \in \Omega(T,N)$ can now be assessed in two distinct ways (see Sen [1978]).

(A) According to Dalton's [1920] method we compare the socially evaluated value, $W(\vec{y})$, of $\vec{y}$ with the value $W(\vec{z}^*)$ of the evaluation function which

1) The assumption of S-concavity is made for illustrative reasons and may well be relaxed in a more general treatment.

would be obtained if the same total income were optimally distributed.

(B) According to Atkinson's [1970] method we compare the total income T of $\vec{y}$ with the minimum total income needed to generate the same value of the evaluation function.[1)]

Since W is assumed to be S-concave we have $W(\vec{z}_e) \geq W(\vec{y})$, where $\vec{z}_e = (T/N,..,T/N)$, for any $\vec{y} \in \Omega(T,N)$. Thus, the optimal distribution is for any total income given by the egalitarian distribution of that income. The S-concavity also implies that $W(\vec{z}_u) \leq W(\vec{y})$, where $\vec{z}_u = (0,0,..,T)$, for any $\vec{y} \in \Omega(T,N)$.

Using Dalton's method we derive from the social evaluation function the following inequality measure, satisfying the RANGE-criterion,

$$I(\vec{y}) = 1 - \frac{W(\vec{y})}{W(\vec{z}_e)} . \qquad (6.1)$$

The ratio $W(\vec{y})/W(\vec{z}_e)$ may in itself be seen as an 'equality' measure (anticipating the notions of the next chapter).

Obviously, monotone transformations of the evaluation function do not leave the index (6.1) unchanged and consequently not much can be said about its properties without rigorous assumptions on the form of the evaluation function. This makes the index unappealing, since there are rarely any good reasons for posing strong cardinal assumptions on the W-function.

Turning to comparisons of the Atkinson type we note that, for any given $\vec{y} \in \Omega(T,N)$, the income distribution yielding the same value $w=W(\vec{y})$ of the evaluation function as $\vec{y}$ with a minimum of total income is of the egalitarian type $\vec{\mu}_e = (\mu_e,\mu_e,..,\mu_e) \in \Omega(N\mu_e,N)$. The inequality measure should hence be based on a comparison of $T = N\mu$ and $T_e = N\mu_e$ (or μ and μ_e).

Atkinson suggested the index

1) Basically this method may be applied even if the evaluation function is ordinal (see e.g. Blackorby and Donaldson [1976]).

$$I(\vec{y}) = 1 - T_e/T = 1 - \mu_e/\mu \quad , \quad \mu = T/N \ , \qquad (6.2)$$

where μ_e is called "the equally distributed equivalent income" (Atkinson 1970). Again, the second term of the expression represents an 'equality' measure. The index (6.2) has the straightforward and appealing interpretation of the proportion of total income wasted on inequality. Thus, an index value $I(y) = 0.4$ tells us that the actual level of 'social welfare' could be attained with only $100(1 - 0.4) = 60$ per cent of the total income by a transition to an egalitarian distribution.[1)]

As an illustration of (6.2) we consider Atkinson's [1970] original application of this measure with the social evaluation function given by

$$w = W(\vec{y}) \; = \; \begin{cases} \Sigma(a + b\frac{1}{1-\varepsilon}y_i^{1-\varepsilon}) \ , & \varepsilon \neq 1 \\ \Sigma(a + b \ln y_i) \ , & \varepsilon = 1 \ , \end{cases} \qquad (6.3)$$

where a, b, and ε are real constants, $b > 0$, $\varepsilon > 0$.[2)] This function originates from the field of decision-making under uncertainty (see e.g. Nygård and Sandström [1980]) and the parameter ε may be considered as a measure of 'risk aversion'. By solving the equation $W(\vec{\mu}_e) = W(\vec{y})$ for μ_e we easily obtain

$$\mu_e \; = \; \begin{cases} (\frac{1}{N}\Sigma y_i^{1-\varepsilon})^{1/(1-\varepsilon)} \ , & \varepsilon \neq 1 \\ \mu_g \ , & \varepsilon = 1 \ , \end{cases} \qquad (6.4)$$

where μ_g denotes the geometric mean income, and Atkinson's inequality index (6.2) may hence be written as

1) In the same way the Dalton index (6.1) can be interpreted as the proportion of optimally attainable 'social welfare' suppressed by the actual distribution, i.e. as an 'efficiency measure'.

2) Atkinson only required $\varepsilon \geqq 0$. As Sen [1978] pointed out the value $\varepsilon = 0$ has however some very doubtful implications.

$$I(\vec{y}) = 1 - \left[\frac{1}{N}\Sigma\left(\frac{y_i}{\mu}\right)^{1-\varepsilon}\right]^{1/(1-\varepsilon)} , \quad \varepsilon \neq 1 \tag{6.5}$$

$$1 - \frac{\mu_g}{\mu} , \quad \varepsilon = 1 .$$

The measure is readily seen to be relative invariant and ranging between zero and one.

A general discussion of the properties of the index (6.2) is given by Blackorby et al [1978]. Following this we rewrite the evaluation function as

$$w = W(\vec{y}) = \phi(W^*(\vec{y})) ,$$

where ϕ is increasing. It can be shown - this and the following assertions are proved in Blackorby et al [1978] - that (6.2) yields a relative invariant measure if and only if W^* is positively linearly homogeneous, i.e. if $W^*(c\vec{y}) = c\,W^*(\vec{y})$ for $c > 0$, implying homotheticity of W. In this case the equally distributed equivalent income is given by

$$\mu_e = W^*(\vec{y})/W^*(\vec{e}) ,$$

where $\vec{e}$ denotes the N-dimensional unit vector. Further, given a relative index $I(\vec{y})$, an ordinal equivalent to the corresponding evaluation function W may be derived as

$$W^{**}(\vec{y}) = \mu_e = \mu(1 - I(\vec{y})). \text{[1)]} \tag{6.6}$$

In the case of the Atkinson index (6.5) this function is given by (6.4), the generalized mean of order $1-\varepsilon$, and the index itself may be derived not only from (6.3) but from any evaluation function ordinally equivalent to (6.4).

1) Note that this is an intuitively quite appealing form of the evaluation function. See note on page 80 and Sen [1976].

Multiplying (6.2) by μ gives us Atkinson's 'μ-modified' measure (cf. Kolm [1976]),

$$I(\vec{y}) \;=\; \mu - \mu_e \,, \qquad (6.7)$$

which is absolute invariant if and only if the W*-function is unit-translatable, i.e. if $W^*(\vec{y}+b\vec{e}) = W^*(\vec{y}) + b$. The equally distributed equivalent income is now given by

$$\mu_e \;=\; W^*(\vec{y}) \;-\; W^*(0\vec{e}).$$

Conversly, given an absolute invariant measure $I(\vec{y})$ may an ordinally equivalent to the implied evaluation function be constructed as

$$W^{**}(\vec{y}) \;=\; \mu_e \;=\; \mu - I(\vec{y}). \qquad (6.8)$$

6.3 OTHER NORMATIVE MEASURES

Assuming that a representative client judges utility according to the function $u = u(y)$, $u\colon R_+ \to R$, which is cardinal, twice differentiable and unique up to a positive linear transformation, we can base the inequality measure directly on a comparison of the utilities $u(y_1)$, $u(y_2)$,.., $u(y_N)$.[1)] Most traditional statistical measures of dispersion can be employed in this case.

1) Note that this approach slightly differs from the one previously adopted in this chapter: the present approach is based on a comparison of the $u(y_i)$'s, whereas the previous one rests on a simultaneous evaluation of $w = W(\vec{y})$.

Praag [1978] proposed the measure

$$I(\vec{y}) = \frac{1}{N}\left(\Sigma \{\ln u'(y_i)\}^2 - \frac{\{\Sigma \ln u'(y_i)\}^2}{N} \right), \qquad (6.9)$$

where u'(y) is the marginal utility of income level y. The measure is thus simply the log-variance of marginal utility. The formula seems to originate from a partial equilibrium analysis, where the equitable income distribution is set equal to the equilibrium distribution with respect to marginal utility.

Michal [1978] proposed the use of a marginal-utility-weighted Gini coefficient (see section 7.4 and 8.1)

$$I(\vec{y}) = \frac{\Sigma\Sigma |u'(y_i)\, y_i - u'(y_j)\, y_j|}{2N^2 \dfrac{\Sigma u'(y_i)\, y_i}{N}} . \qquad (6.10)$$

It should be noted that these measures are strongly related to the notion of a social welfare function $w = w(u(y_1),u(y_2),..,u(y_N))$ and the WEL (cf. section 4.2).

6.4 THE NORMATIVE APPROACH CONCLUDED

Now then, what are the gains of the incorporation of a social evaluation function into inequality considerations?

Backed up by the above discussion we are inclined to conclude that the indirect way of obtaining inequality indicators through evaluation functions is not associated with any significant advantages from the practical point of view. The evaluation function provides some theoretical insight in what inequality measurement is all about and, indeed, if we were supplied with information on the exact form of the evaluation (or utility) function it would of course be reasonable to use the approach of Dalton or Atkinson in deriving inequality indexes (or simply use indexes of type (6.9) or (6.10)). But as we have previously noted no sufficiently detailed information enabling us to use (6.1) (or (6.9), (6.10)) is available in practice. Even an attempt to apply (6.2) or (6.7), which in principle is less demanding, will fail due to informational constraints. Consequently, the use of normative measures is bound to involve arbitrary assumptions to some extent. A possible way of judging the 'realism' of these imposed assumptions is by means of the properties of the generated inequality index. But why then at all bother about some social evaluation function, when we can as well concentrate our attention directly to the properties of different inequality measures ?

Since we will subsequently mainly deal with absolute and relative invariant inequality indexes the corresponding evaluation functions may be found ad hoc using (6.6) or (6.9) if we insist on a normative approach. It will require a great deal of self-confidence to reject any of the evaluation functions derived in this way.

7. THE LORENZ CURVE AND MEASURES OF INEQUALITY

If we are able to define an explicit functional form of the social welfare function, a form that in the view of the society reflects an acceptable ranking (on cardinal level) between actual distributions of incomes, then we could design inequality measures according to the discussion in ch. 6. As we have seen, on the other hand, there are few reasons for accepting or rejecting any functional form of the welfare function.What to do then? We could instead try to define one or more measures according to the discussion in sec. 1.1, i.e. by measuring the departure of the actual distribution from an equitable income distribution (reference distribution), and formalize these measures using the criteria of ch. 4.A definition of an inequality measure could then be formulated as (cf. Bartels[1977 - p. 12]):

> *An income inequality measure is a condensed quantitative indication of how and to what extent a certain income distribution differs from a reference distribution (equitable distribution) in which differences have been weighted according to specific normative distributional preferences.*

This quite general definition implies both the choice of an explicit reference distribution and the choice of a weight function reflecting normative distributional preferences. An axiomatic use of the criteria in ch. 4 will limit the possible weight functions. According to sec. 1.1 a reference distribution is defined as an equitable distribution or as a desired distribution in accordance with our normative preferences when constructing an inequality measure.

Our reference distribution could on the other hand be defined as an unequitable distribution, a definition which would imply 'a measure of equality'. The two extreme distributions are:

(i) the EGAL distribution,
i.e. a degenerated distribution, where all incomes are equally distributed. This is the egalitarian definition of an equitable distribution (cf. criterion EGAL of sec. 4.2). (Absolute equality.)

(ii) the CON distribution,
i.e. a binomial distribution where one i.r.u. receives all incomes and the remaining i.r.u.'s receive zero income (cf. criterion CON of sec. 4.2). (Absolute inequality.)

Between these extremes there may be an infinite number of possible reference distributions, which depend on our normative preferences.Note that the use of the EGAL and CON distributions implies that one is accepting the SYM criterion (sec.4.2). The definition of a reference distribution is connected with the income accountance period. If the EGAL-distribution is used as a reference distribution and the accountance period is lifetime the reference distribution during a specific year (cross-section study) will not be the EGAL-distribution above.

In some situations, cf. Bartels [1977 - p. 34], we cannot use the CON-distribution as a reference, but we can let one i.r.u. receive all incomes minus $\varepsilon > 0$ and let the remaining i.r.u.'s receive one equal part of ε.

There are also measures that are intended to reveal to what extent an actual distribution deviates from a symmetrical reference distribution (e.g. from a normal distribution): proposed measures of inequality are coefficients of skewness and the kurtosis (see e.g. Bartels [1977]). Since we do not see any reason for choosing such reference distributions for our purpose we will not discuss them further (cf. Sen [1973 - p. 31]).

In this chapter we will define a general measure of inequality (or equality), whose members in one way or another reflect prescriptive inequality or equality on cardinal (interval-scale) level according to the above definition of a measure (or to some transformation). The definition is thus made without any explicitly defined social welfare function. Although some authors vindicate that all 'statistical measures', i.e. measures not defended by any social welfare theory, "incorporate implicitly a definition of the marginal social values of the incomes of individuals and the implicit definition is frequently difficult to defend on rational economic grounds" (Johnson [1973 - p. 210], cf. Dalton [1920] and Atkinson [1970]), we will incorporate both 'statistical measures' and the social welfare based measures of ch. 6 in the general family.

Sec. 7.1 is devoted to measures of functions of level parameters and includes fractile measures and mean-value functions. The complementary c.d.f. and the complementary 1st m.d.f., discussed in sec. 7.1, lead to a definition of the Lorenz curve, discussed in sec. 7.2, and to the distribution comparative function defined in sec. 7.3.

The general measure of inequality (or equality) is defined in sec. 7.4. In that section we go through the most common measures, found in the literature, and we will see whether some criteria from ch. 4 are fulfilled or not.

The main purpose of the discussion in this chapter is to show that most inequality measures, suggested and used in the literature, formally can be seen as special cases of a general family of measures.

7.1 DEFINITIONS, FRACTILE AND LEVEL MEASURES OF INEQUALITY

This section begins with a treatment of some fundamental definitions, such as the mean-value theorem and the general family of means.
From the cumulative distribution function (c.d.f.) and the 1st moment distribution function (m.d.f.) depicted in figure 7.1 (cf. sec. 1.2) we may derive the values $F(y)$ and $F_1(y)$, respectively, for any income y.
From these we can obtain (i) fractile measures of inequality, i.e. measures that use information from the c.d.f. and the 1st m.d.f. only partially, and (ii) level measures of inequality, defined as functions of $F(y)$ and $F_1(y)$ (and means).
Finally we will define the complementary c.d.f. and the complementary 1st m.d.f.

A *standardized* (or relative) measure may be obtained by dividing a measure by an appropriate parameter (e.g. the arithmetic mean, μ) and a measure can be *normalized* into the [0,1]-interval, where zero stands for the inequality of the EGAL distribution and one for the inequality of the CON distribution. The EGAL and the CON distributions are defined in the introduction of this chapter.

7.1.1 SOME FUNDAMENTAL DEFINITIONS

In sec. 1.2 we defined the jth moment distribution function, (m.d.f.) $F_j(y)$, as

$$F_j(y) = \int_0^y \frac{t^j}{\mu_j} dF_0(t) \quad , \quad j = 0,1,\dots, \tag{7.1}$$

where μ_j is the jth moment about zero which is assumed to exist and to be nonzero. For j = 0 we have the cumulative distribution function, $F(y) = F_0(y)$. The distribution of the random variable Y (e.g. income) is concentrated over the non-negative set $[0,\infty[$ 1). The jth m.d.f. of Y is assumed to be continuously differentiable. The jth moment density function is

$$f_j(y) = \frac{dF_j(y)}{dy} = \frac{y^j}{\mu_j} f_o(y), \tag{7.2}$$

where $f_0(y) = f(y)$ is the density function of Y $(dF(y) = f(y)dy)$. Above, and in sec. 1.2, the definitions are written with argument y.

Let us define the inverse c.d.f. $F^{-1}(p)$ and the inverse 1st m.d.f. $F_1^{-1}(p)$ as

$$F^{-1}(p) = \inf_y\{y|F(y) \geq p\}$$

and $\qquad 0 < p \leq 1 \qquad (7.3)$

$$F_1^{-1}(p) = \inf_y\{y|F_1(y) \geq p\}$$

respectively. For p = 0 we define $F^{-1}(0) = \inf_y\{y|F(y) > 0\}$ and $F_1^{-1}(0) = \inf_y\{y|F_1(y) > 0\}$.

1) The set could be extended to $]-\infty,\infty[$. In some cases we will assume that the lower bound of Y is greater than 0 (e.g. 1) and/or that the upper bound of Y is finite.

Using (7.3) we have

$$p = F[F^{-1}(p)] = \int_0^p du \qquad 0 \leq p \leq 1 \tag{7.4}$$

and

$$L(p) = F_1[F^{-1}(p)] = \int_0^p \frac{F^{-1}(u)}{\mu}\, du = \int_0^p \tau(u)du \quad 0 \leq p \leq 1 \tag{7.5}$$

$\tau(p) = \dfrac{F^{-1}(p)}{\mu} = \dfrac{dL(p)}{dp}$ is called the standardized inverse distribution function (the "relative income").

Since the first moment about zero of the c.d.f. is assumed to exist and to be non-zero we have

$$\mu = \int_0^1 F^{-1}(p)dp \Rightarrow \int_0^1 \tau(p)dp = 1. \tag{7.6}$$

The Mean-value theorem (cf. e.g. Piesch [1975 - p.44]):

If the function u is continuous in the closed interval a and b there exists a number ξ, $a \leq \xi \leq b$, such that

$$\int_a^b u(x)dx = (b-a)u(\xi) \tag{7.7}$$

$u(\xi) = \bar{u}$ is the mean value of $u(x)$ in $[a,b]$.

The extended mean-value theorem:

If u and v are continuous in the closed interval $[a,b]$ and $v(x) \geq 0$ there exists a number ξ, $a \leq \xi \leq b$, such that

$$\int_a^b u(x)v(x)dx = u(\xi) \int_a^b v(x)dx \tag{7.8}$$

$u(\xi) = \bar{u}$ is the mean value of $u(x)$ with respect to $v(x)$ in $[a,b]$.

If $\dfrac{v(x)}{\int_a^b v(x)dx} = f(x)$, then we can interpret $f(x)$ as a density function and

if $u(x) = x$, then we have $u(\xi) = \bar{u} = \mu$ (the first moment about zero).

The lower and upper arithmetic mean

A density function, defined in $[F^{-1}(0), F^{-1}(1)]$, may be separated into a lower density function and an upper density function by a dividing point $F^{-1}(p)$, $F^{-1}(0) \leq F^{-1}(p) \leq F^{-1}(1)$.

The lower arithmetic mean, $\mu_L(p)$, can by (7.8) be defined as

$$\mu_L(p) = \frac{\int_0^p F^{-1}(u)du}{\int_0^p du} = \mu \frac{L(p)}{p} \tag{7.9}$$

and the upper arithmetic mean, $\mu_U(p)$, as

$$\mu_U(p) = \frac{\int_p^1 F^{-1}(u)du}{\int_p^1 du} = \mu \frac{[(1-L(p)]}{1-p} \tag{7.10}$$

$\mu_L(p)$ is monotonously increasing from $\mu_L(0) = F^{-1}(0)$ to $\mu_L(1) = \mu$ and $\mu_U(p)$ from $\mu_U(0) = \mu$ to $\mu_U(1) = F^{-1}(1)$.

The arithmetic mean of a c.d.f. can be written as a weighted mean of the lower and upper arithmetic means:

$$\mu = p\mu_L(p) + (1-p)\mu_U(p).$$

The first moment about zero of the 1st m.d.f. is defined by

$$\gamma = \int_0^1 F^{-1}(p)\tau(p)\,dp = \mu^{-1}[\sigma^2 + \mu^2] = \mu[V^2 + 1]$$

Where σ^2 is the variance and V the coefficient of variation.

Definition 7.1 The general mean family of the c.d.f. is defined by

$$\mu(r,q,p) = \left\{ \int_{F^{-1}(q)}^{F^{-1}(p)} (t^r/(p-q))\,dF(t) \right\}^{1/r} \quad , \; 0 \leq q < p \leq 1 \qquad (7.11)$$

and that of the 1st m.d.f. by

$$\gamma(r,q,p) = \left\{ \int_{F^{-1}(q)}^{F^{-1}(p)} (t^r/(p-q))\frac{t}{\mu}\,dF(t) \right\}^{1/r} \quad , \; 0 \leq q < p \leq 1 \qquad (7.12)$$

where $\mu = \mu(1,q,p)$ of (7.11).

From the relations between $\mu(r,q,p)$ and $\gamma(r,q,p)$ it is easily seen that

$$\gamma(r,q,p) = \left\{ \mu^{-1}[\mu(r+1,q,p)]^{r+1} \right\}^{1/r} .$$

Some members of the mean families, defined by (7.11) and (7.12), are given in table 7.1. Note that the lower and upper arithmetic means (7.9) and (7.10) are given by $\mu(1,0,p)$ and $\mu(1,p,1)$.

The median of the c.d.f. is denoted by $\tilde{\mu}$ and defined by $\tilde{\mu} = F^{-1}(0.5)$ and that of the 1st m.d.f. by $\tilde{\gamma} = F_1^{-1}(0.5)$. The latter was named 'the equatorial income' by Mendershausen [1939].

Table 7.1 Some members of the mean families defined by Definition 7.1

q	p	r	$\mu(r,q,p)$	name	$\gamma(r,q,p)$	name
0	1	$r \to -\infty$	$F^{-1}(0)$	"the minimum value"		
0	1	-1	$\mu(-1,0,1) = \mu_h^{-1}$	μ_h = the harmonic mean	$\gamma(-1,0,1) = \mu$	the arithmetic mean of the c.d.f.
0	1	$r \to 0$	$\lim_{r\to 0}(r,0,1) = \log \mu_g$	μ_g = the geometrical mean	$\lim_{r\to 0}\gamma(r,0,1) = \gamma_g = \log \mu_{gw}$	γ_g = the geometrical mean of the 1st m.d.f. $\log\mu_{gw} = \int_0^1 \tau(p) \ln F^{-1}(p)dp$; μ_{gw} = the weighted geometrical mean of the c.d.f.
0	1	1	$\mu(1,0,1) = \mu$	μ = the arithmetic mean	$\gamma(1,0,1) = \gamma = \mu(V^2+1)$	γ = the arithmetic mean of the 1st m.d.f.
0	1	$r \to +\infty$	$F^{-1}(1)$	"the maximum value"		
0	p	+1	$\mu_L(p)$	"the lower arithmetic mean" of the c.d.f.	$\gamma_L(p)$	"the lower arithmetic mean" of the 1st m.d.f.
q	1	+1	$\mu_U(q)$	"the upper arithmetic mean" of the c.d.f.	$\gamma_U(q)$	"the upper arithmetic mean" of the 1st m.d.f.

7.1.2 FRACTILE MEASURES OF INEQUALITY

For a fixed income y, $F(y) \geq F_1(y)$. This inequality is depicted in figure 7.1.

Two simple measures of inequality would be, for a fixed p, the difference between $F_1^{-1}(p)$ and $F^{-1}(p)$, the fractiles of the 1st m.d.f. and the c.d.f., i.e.

$$I_1(p) = F_1^{-1}(p) - F^{-1}(p) = D(p), \quad 0 \leq p \leq 1 \tag{7.13}$$

or the ratio

$$I_2(p) = F^{-1}(p)/F_1^{-1}(p) \qquad , 0 < p \leq 1. \tag{7.14}$$

It is obvious that these fractile measures are meaningful only if we compare $I_j(p)$, j = 1,2, between at least two countries or when comparing the values between different years within a country.

Figure 7.1 Illustration of obtaining fractile measures and level measures.

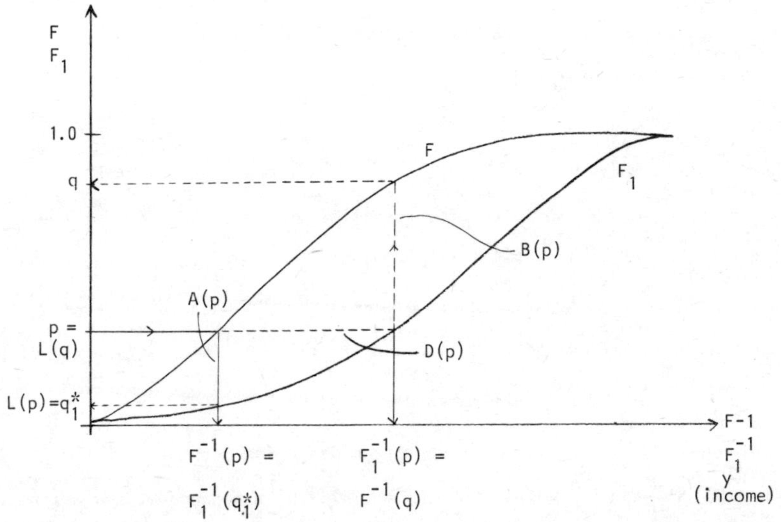

Holme's measure (see,e.g. Lorenz [1905] and Bortkiewicz [1930]) is defined by (7.13) by letting $p = 0.5$, i.e.

$$I_1(0.5) = \tilde{\gamma} - \tilde{\mu},$$

the difference between 'the equatorial income' (the median of the 1st m.d.f) and the median of the the c.d.f.. Bortkiewicz stated that this measure has nothing to do with the concentration but that it rather varies with total welfare (Bortkiewicz [1930 - pp 96 - 97]). $I_1(0.5)$ ranges between zero (the EGAL distribution, cf. the introduction to this chapter) and the total income of the society (in limit: infinity). Bortkiewicz proposed the *standardized Holme's measure* as the ratio between $I_1(0.5)$ and μ: $I_1(0.5)/\mu$.

A *normalized Holme's measure* was introduced as a 'new' measure by Mendershausen (cf. e.g.[1939] and Staehle [1937]) as the ratio $I_1(0.5)/\tilde{\gamma} = 1-\tilde{\mu}/\tilde{\gamma} = 1 - I_2(0.5)$. It varies between zero and one. Zero is obtained when all incomes are equal (the EGAL distribution) and one when 50% of the i.r.u. have no income at all (nothing is said about the other 50% of the i.r.u.'s). One interesting thing about Menderhausen's paper [1939] is that he discussed the sampling error of the normalized Holme's measure and also gave a formula for the standard error.

Other measures that have been proposed are functions of fractiles (quantiles), especially functions of percentiles of the c.d.f. (and of the 1st m.d.f.). The *range*, i.e. $F^{-1}(1) - F^{-1}(0) = F_1^{-1}(1) - F_1^{-1}(0)$, is one such function. Associated measures are the *standardized range* and the *normalized range* defined by $(F^{-1}(1) - F^{-1}(0))/\mu$ and $(F^{-1}(1) - F^{-1}(0))/F^{-1}(1)$, respectively. If $F^{-1}(0) \neq 0$ we can define the *max-min ratio* by $F^{-1}(1)/F^{-1}(0)$.

The standardized range is sensitive to incomes between the two extreme incomes $F^{-1}(0)$ and $F^{-1}(1)$ through the division of the range by the arithmetic mean μ. The range of the last four measures are as follows:

the range $\in [0,\infty[$

the standardized range $\in [0,\infty[$

the normalized range $\in [0,1]$

the max-min ratio $\in [1,\infty[$

The *interquartile distance*, $F^{-1}(0.75) - F^{-1}(0.25)$, and its standardized equivalents $(F^{-1}(0.75)- F^{-1}(0.25))/\mu$ or $(F^{-1}(0.75) - F^{-1}(0.25))/\tilde{\mu}$ are also proposed measures of inequality. A normalized interquartile distance is *Bowley's measure*, $[F^{-1}(0.75) - F^{-1}(0.25)]/[F^{-1}(0.75) + F^{-1}(0.25)]$. An alternative to Bowley's measure was proposed by Bortkiewicz [1930 - p.100] as $[F_1^{-1}(0.75) - F_1^{-1}(0.25)]/[F_1^{-1}(0.75) + F_1^{-1}(0.25)]$.

Other measures, e.g. ratios of percentiles, are given by e.g. Bartels [1977 - appendix 2B].

All these ratio measures are independent of proportionate addition to incomes (criterion PROPORTION of sec. 4.3) and the difference measures are independent of equal addition to incomes (criterion ADD of sec 4.3). The criterion TRANSF is only fulfilled when the transfer involves movements of the fractiles (cf. Dalton [1920]). For a discussion of TRANSF for the standarized range (relative range) see Sen [1973 - pp. 24-25].

Most writers agree that these measures are not preferable measures of inequality, since only "partial information" is used. On the other hand some writers (cf. e.g., Wiles [1978]) prefer these rough "measures of inequality" on the grounds that there may be lack of data.

7.1.3 LEVEL MEASURES OF INEQUALITY

The measures, considered in the last section, were functions of fractiles, i.e. for a fixed p, $0 \leq p \leq 1$, we examined $F^{-1}(p)$ and $F_1^{-1}(p)$.
We could, of course, also "go the other way around", i.e. for a fixed income we determine p, the proportion of i.r.u.'s, with income less than or equal to $F^{-1}(p)$, and q_1^* the income proportion of the i.r.u.'s, with income less than or equal to $F_1^{-1}(q_1^*)$, such that $F^{-1}(p) = F_1^{-1}(q_1^*)$, $0 \leq q_1^* \leq p \leq 1$.
This is illustrated in figure 7.1. Two possible measures would then be the difference, $p - q_1^*$ and the ratio q_1^*/p:

$$I_3(F^{-1}) = p-q_1^* = F[F^{-1}(p)] - F_1[F^{-1}(p)] = p - L(p) = A(p) \qquad (7.14)$$

and

$$I_4(F^{-1}) = q_1^*/p = \frac{F_1[F^{-1}(p)]}{F[F^{-1}(p)]} = \frac{L(p)}{p} = \frac{\mu_L(p)}{\mu}, \qquad (7.15)$$

where the last equality in (7.15) is obtained by using (7.10) and $F^{-1} = F^{-1}[p] = F_1^{-1}[q_1^*]$.

Let $F^{-1}(p_\mu) = F_1^{-1}(q_\mu)$ be the arithmetic mean, μ.
The difference measure (7.14) is then

$$I_3(\mu) = F(\mu) - F_1(\mu), \qquad (7.16)$$

or the well-known *maximum equalization ratio* (MER), a measure that will be discussed at length in sec.7.4.4. Taking $2\mu I_3(\mu)$ gives us the absolute mean deviation (see sec. 7.4.4), a measure that was proposed by Bortkiewicz in

1898 (see Bortkiewicz [1930 - p. 16] for reference).

The ratio $I_4(\mu) = \frac{F_1(\mu)}{F(\mu)} = \frac{\mu_L(p_\mu)}{\mu}$ is one of three measures proposed by Eltetö and Frigyes [1968] as "new measures of inequality".
The other two measures are

$$\frac{1-F(\mu)}{1-F_1(\mu)} = \frac{\mu}{\mu_U(p_\mu)} \quad \text{and} \quad \frac{F_1(\mu)[1-F_1(\mu)]}{F(\mu)[1-F(\mu)]} = \frac{\mu_L(p_\mu)}{\mu_U(p_\mu)} .$$

It is easily seen that the combination

$$(\frac{\mu_L(p_\mu)}{\mu} - 1)(\frac{\mu}{\mu_U(p_\mu)} - 1)/(1 - \mu_L(p_\mu)/\mu_U(p_\mu))$$

of the three ratios equals $F(\mu) - F_1(\mu)$, i.e. the MER (cf. Martić [1970], Kondor [1971] and Piesch [1975 - p. 62]).

If society has defined a "minimum income of subsistence" or a "poverty-line", e.g. $F^{-1}(p) = F_1^{-1}(q_1^*)$, then $p = F[F^{-1}(p)]$ is the "head-count ratio", a poverty measure that has been widely used (cf. Sen [1976 - p. 219] and Kakwani [1980c - p. 437]). In the same way we may use $L(p) = F_1[F^{-1}(p)]$ as an "income-poverty measure".

The identities between ratios of values of the c.d.f. and the 1st m.d.f. lead us to consider ratios (and/or differences) between mean values defined by the general mean family (7.11) (and (7.12)). One such example is a measure proposed by Champernowne [1973]: the difference between the arithmetic mean, μ, and the geometrical mean, μ_g, normalized (and standardized) by μ, i.e.

$$1 - \mu_g/\mu,$$

and because Y is assumed non-negative, $\mu_h \leq \mu_g \leq \mu$, μ_g equals zero when the CON distribution is at hand and $\mu_g = \mu$ when all incomes are equal (the EGAL distribution), the range of the measure is [0,1].

Two other measures, originating from information theory, are Theil's measures [1967]:

$$T_1 = \log \frac{\gamma_g}{\mu} = \log \frac{\mu_{gw}}{\mu}$$

and

$$T_2 = \log \frac{\mu}{\mu_g} \ .$$

These measures will be discussed at length in sec. 7.4.

Measures that are functions of lower and upper means are given e.g. in Piesch [1975 - p. 125].

7.1.4 THE COMPLEMENTARY C.D.F. AND THE COMPLEMENTARY 1ST M.D.F.

Frequently there is lack of information about i.r.u.'s with low incomes. This shortcoming has led economists and statisticians to count i.r.u.'s and incomes from the top, i.e. from the richest i.r.u and down.[1)] There may be other reasons for doing this: firstly, we have the trace from the Pareto tradition (cf. ch. 5), which implies that one considers the proportion of i.r.u.'s over some lower income $F_y^{-1}(p_0)$, $0 \leq p_0 \leq 1$, and secondly the simple interpretations of the areas under the complementary c.d.f. and the complementary 1st m.d.f. (cf. sec. 1.2) defined below. The complementary c.d.f. and the complementary 1st m.d.f. (cf. sec. 1.2) are denoted by

$$G(y) = 1 - F(y) \quad \text{and} \quad G_1(y) = 1 - F_1(y).$$

$G(y)$ equals the proportion of i.r.u.'s with incomes "more than" y, and $G_1(y)$ is the income proportion of these i.r.u.'s.

$G(y)$ has been used by e.g. Brittain [1962], Malmquist [1970], Esberger and Malmquist [1972] and Cowell [1977].

Notice that an integration of $G(y)$ and $G_1(y)$, with respect to y, gives the arithmetic means, μ and γ respectively. $G(y)$ and $G_1(y)$ are depicted in figure 7.2.

1) "The unorthodox "more-than" cumulative has been used ... because of the usual scarcity of data on low incomes and the consequent emphasis in the literature on the share of top groups." (Brittain [1962 - p. 99]).

Figure 7.2 The complementary c.d.f., $G(y) = 1-F(y)$, and the complementary 1st m.d.f., $G_1(y) = 1-F_1(y)$, $0 \leq q' \leq p' \leq q_1^* \leq 1$ and $p' = 1-p$, $q' = 1-q$, $q_1^* = 1-L(p)$, where q, p and q_1^* are given in figure 7.1.

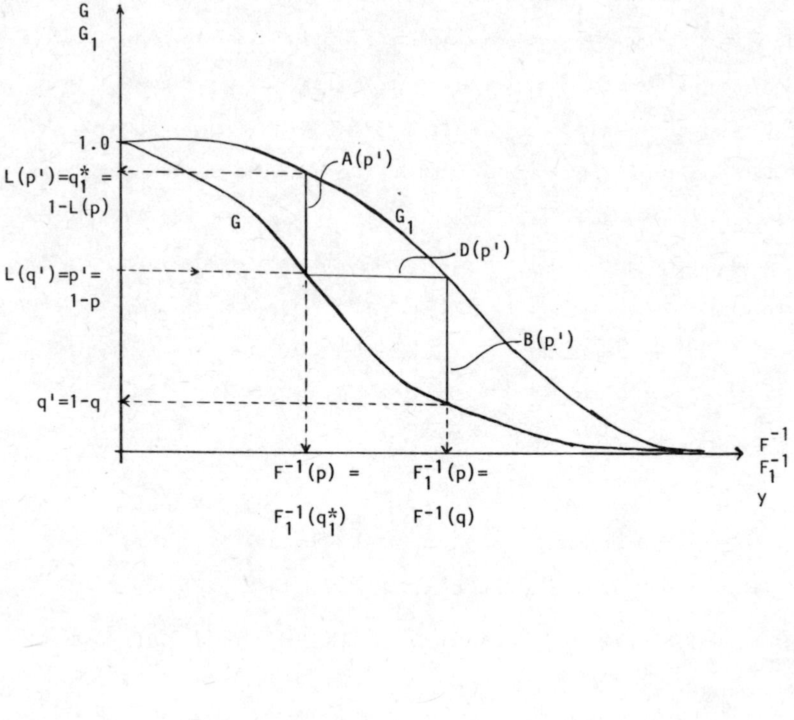

Since $F[F^{-1}(p)] \geq F_1[F^{-1}(p)]$, $0 \leq p \leq 1$, we have the reversed inequality for G and G_1, i.e. $G_1[F^{-1}(p')] \geq G[F^{-1}(p')]$, $0 \leq p' \leq 1$ and $p' = 1 - p$ (cf. figure 7.1). The ratio between $G[F^{-1}(p')]$ and $G_1[F^{-1}(p')]$ is by (7.10) $\mu/\mu_U(p)$, which is less than or equal to one.

For a fixed $p' = G[F^{-1}(p)] = G_1[F_1^{-1}(p)]$ (see figure 7.2) and we obtain three functions[1] $A(p')$, $D(p')$ and $B(p')$. They are equal to

$$A(p') = F[F^{-1}(p)] - F_1[F^{-1}(p)] = A(p) \qquad (7.17a)$$

$$B(p') = F[F^{-1}(q)] - F_1[F^{-1}(q)] = B(q) \qquad (7.17b)$$

and $D(p') = F_1^{-1}(p) - F^{-1}(p) = F^{-1}(q) - F_1^{-1}(q_1{*}) = F^{-1}(q) - F^{-1}(p) = D(p)$, (7.17c)

where $A(p)$, $B(q)$ and $D(p)$ are the corresponding functions in figure 7.1, and $p = 1 - p' \leq q = 1 - q'$.

By the definition of $L(p)$ in (7.5) we can write $A(p')$ and $B(p')$ as

$$A(p') = A(p) = p - L(p), \qquad (7.18a)$$

$$B(p') = B(q) = q - L(q) = q - p, \qquad (7.18b)$$

where $L(q) = p$, cf. figure 7.4, and using $\tau(p) = F^{-1}(p)/\mu = dL(p)/dp$ we write $D(p')$ as

$$D(p') = D(p) = \mu[\tau(q) - \tau(p)] = \mu\{dL(q)/dq - dL(p)/dp\} =$$
$$= \mu(L'(q) - L'(p)). \qquad (7.18c)$$

As we will see in the next section (sec. 7.2) the difference functions $A(p')$ and $B(p')$ can be used to define the *Lorenz Curve*, and the distance function $D(p')$ is in sec. 7.3 defined as the *distribution comparative function*.

1) These functions could of course also be obtained from figure 7.1.

7.2 THE LORENZ CURVE

"Plot along one axis cumulated per cents. of the population from poorest to richest, and along the other the per cent. of the total wealth held by these per cents. of the population." This is the discription given by Lorenz [1905 - p. 217] of how to plot the graphical curve that we nowadays know as the Lorenz Curve (cf. ch. 2). This graphical curve has ever since Lorenz' paper was published been the most used tool when analyzing income inequality. The horizontal axis in figure 7.3 indicates the aggregate of population proportion, F(y), and the vertical axis the aggregate of income proportion. In figure 7.3 we see that the 30% poorest i.r.u.'s receive only 6% of the income-cake.

If we have the EGAL distribution, the Lorenz Curve (LC) will be the diagonal line between (0,0) and (1,1). Thus the area between the diagonal line and the LC of the actual distribution indicates to what extent there is "inequality" within the examined society.

This area will be zero if the society is in absolut equality (the EGAL distribution). On the other hand, if the society is in absolute inequality (the CON distribution) the LC will follow the horizontal axis from (0,0) to (1,0) and then the vertical axis from (1,0) to (1,1), i.e. the area will equal 1/2.

Figure 7.3 The Lorenz Curve

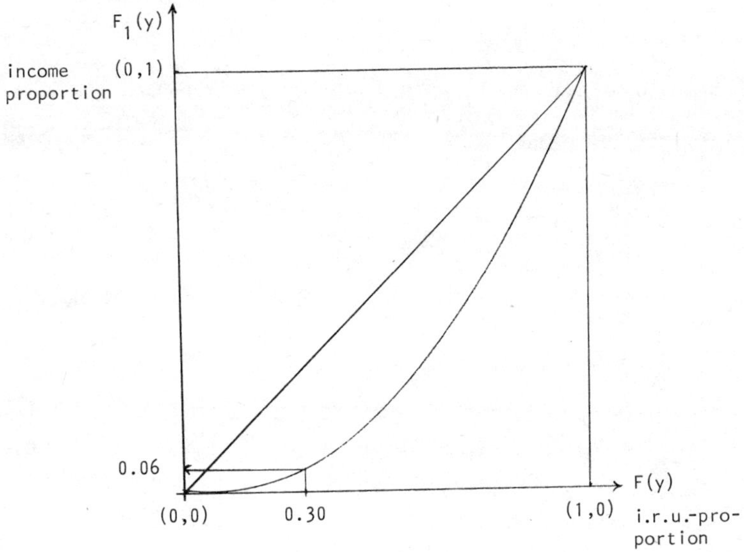

This section reviews the fundamental properties of the Lorenz Curve (LC) and the associated Lorenz area (LA).The LC and the LA are defined in sec. 7.2.1. Alternative ways of expressing the LA are given in table 7.2. Sec. 7.2.2 reviews various interpretations and definitions pertaining to the LC and the LA.Generalized LC's and the associated LA's are briefly discussed in sec 7.2.3 and the LC's and the LA's of truncated distributions are reviewed in sev 7.2.4.Sec. 7.2.5 deals with the LC's from transformed variables and the theory is applied to salary and tax policies in the last section (7.2.6).

7.2.1 DEFINITION OF THE LORENZ CURVE AND THE LORENZ AREA

The definition of a Lorenz Curve[1] (LC) is usually made in two equations: the curve whose ordinate and abscissa are F_1 and F, defined for the argument y as (cf. sec 7.1.1)

$$F(y) = \int_0^y dF(t) \quad \text{and} \quad F_1(y) = \int_0^y \frac{t}{\mu}\, dF(t),$$

is called the Lorenz Curve.

The formal definition of the LC will now be made in one equation (cf Gastwirth [1971a] and Piesch [1975 - p. 23[3]]).

Definition 7.2:[2] The Lorenz Curve (LC) corresponding to a non-negative random variable Y with c.d.f. F(y) and finite non-zero mean μ is defined by

$$L(p) = \int_0^p \tau(u)du, \quad 0 \leq p \leq 1,$$

(given in (7.5)), and where $\mu\tau(p) = F^{-1}(p)$ is the inverse distribution function (7.3).

L(p) is the proportion of the total income received by the lowest 100p% of the i.r.u.'s, in particular L(0)=0 and L(1)=1. The LC, L(p), is depicted in figure 7.4.

1) Labelled concentration curve by some authors
2) The definition is made for non-negative arguments ($y \in [0,\infty]$). The definition will in some cases (e.g. in sec.7.2.5, sec.7.2.6 and 9.2) be extended to all real-valued arguments ($y \in [-\infty,\infty]$), cf. e.g. Mehran [1976]. As pointed out by Wold [1935], the LC in this case will not generally be bounded by the p=F(y) - axis, and thus the Lorenz area defined by (7.20) will not have the upper bound 1/2. If the argument is non-positive then the LC will behave as an ordinary LC since $\tau(p) \geq o$.
3) Piesch gives references to authors who have used this one equation definition: it was introduced in the Italian school by Pietra in 1915.

Figure 7.4 The Lorenz Diagram and the Lorenz Curve $L(p)$

For a fixed p we can determine the difference functions $A(p)$, $B(p)$ and the slope of the tangent to the Lorenz Curve in the point $(p,L(p))$ i.e. $\tau(p) = F^{-1}(p)/\mu$ ("a relative income"). $\tau(p_\mu)$ is the slope of the tangent to $L(p)$ through the point $(p_\mu, L(p_\mu))$, and equals $1 (p_\mu = F(\mu))$

$A(p_\mu) = P_\mu - L(p_\mu)$ is equal to the maximum equalization ratio (MER).

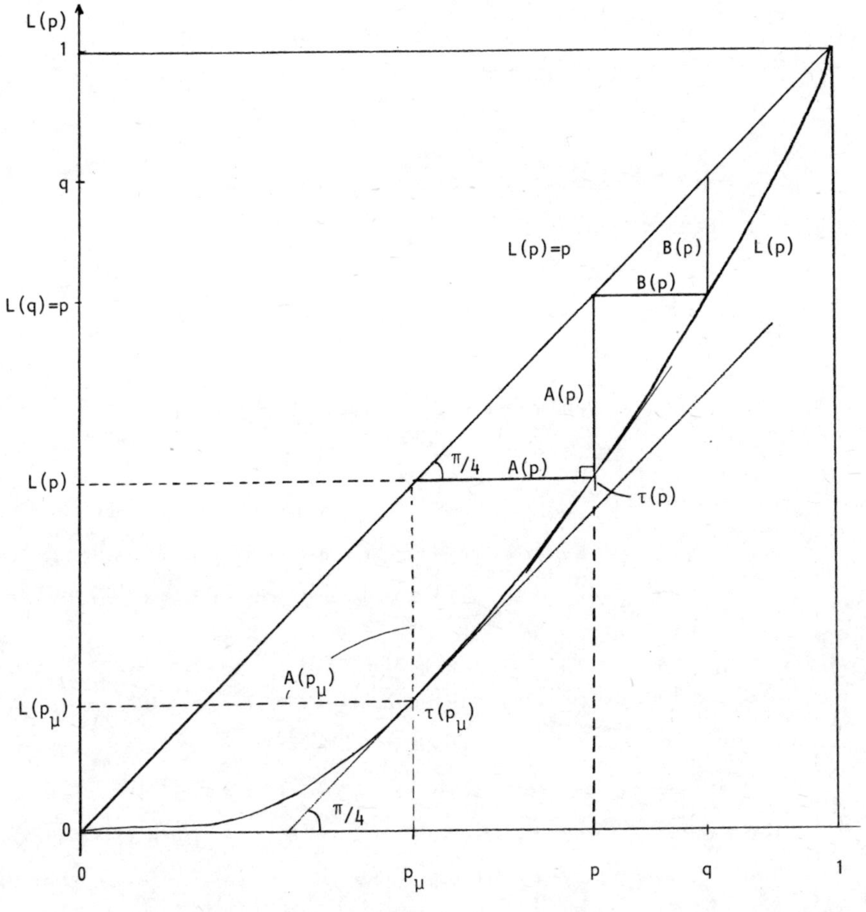

$F^{-1}(p)$ is strictly increasing (sometimes assumed in the weaker form: increasing) and L(p) is strictly convex (convex) and the first and second derivatives of L(p) with respect to p are

$$L'(p) = \frac{dF_1}{dF} = \tau(p) = \frac{F^{-1}(p)}{\mu} > 0 \tag{7.19a}$$

and

$$L''(p) = \frac{d^2F_1}{dF^2} = \frac{1}{\mu f[F^{-1}(p)]} > 0. \tag{7.19b}$$

From (7.19a) it follows that the slope of the tangent to the LC in $F^{-1}(p_\mu) = \mu$ equals one, i.e. $L'(p_\mu) = \tau(p_\mu) = 1$, see figure 7.4.

If two density functions $f_x(x)$ and $f_y(y)$ give the same LC then from (7.19 a-b) it follows that

$$f_y(y) = cf_x(x) = cf_x(cy),$$

where $c = \mu_x/\mu_y$, $\mu_y \neq 0$, (see sec. 4.3 and Schaich [1971]).

Lemma 7.1: The LC, L(p), is uniquely determined by its derivative, $\tau(p)$, the slope of the tangent to the curve. $\tau(p)$ increases strictly from $\tau(0) = 0$ to $\tau(1) = \infty$ and equals one for $p = p_\mu$.

The LC could now be compared with the egalitarian reference distribution, obtained by the EGAL distribution , with $F^{-1}(p) = \mu$, $0 \leq p \leq 1$. This distribution has the LC equal to the 'egalitarian line' (the diagonal line in the Lorenz diagram), i.e. $L(p) = p$ and $L'(p) = \tau(p) = 1$, $0 \leq p \leq 1$. The area between the LC and the egalitarian line is called the Lorenz area, or the area of concentration, and is used as a "measure" of inequality[1].

Definition 7.3: The Lorenz area (LA), or the concentration area, is the area between the LC, $L(p)$, and the egalitarian line, p, and is obtained by

$$LA = \int_0^1 (p - L(p))\,dp \qquad (7.20)$$

Partial integration of (7.20) and the fact that $dL(p) = \tau(p)dp$ give us alternative expressions for writing the Lorenz area:

$$LA = \frac{1}{2} - \int_0^1 L(p)\,dp = \int_0^1 p\,dL(p) - \frac{1}{2} = \int_0^1 (p - \frac{1}{2})\tau(p)\,dp, \qquad (7.21)$$

i.e. the LA could be expressed as a weighted function of $\tau(p)$, the slope of the tangent to the LC, with weight $(p - \frac{1}{2})$.

The LA could also be expressed as the covariance between the c.d.f. and the slope of the tangent to the LC, i.e.

$$LA = \int_0^1 p\tau(p)\,dp - (\int_0^1 p\,dp)(\int_0^1 \tau(p)\,dp) = \int_0^1 p\tau(p)\,dp - \frac{1}{2} = Cov(p,\tau(p)). \qquad (7.22)$$

The difference functions $A(p') = A(p)$ and $B(p') = B(p)$ from sec. 7.1.4 (cf. figure 7.1 and 7.2) will for different p, $0 < p < 1$, give the LC ($A(0) = B(0) = A(1) = B(1) = 0$), and the intrinsic correspondence[2]

1) This definition of the Lorenz area gives a relative measure according to the discussion in ch. 4.

2) A graduation schedule for the construction of the LC from a density function is given by e.g. Piesch [1975 - p. 24].

between on the one hand the c.d.f. and the 1st m.d.f. and on the other hand the LC is immediate. Using the difference function A(p) we can express the Lorenz area as $\int_0^1 A(p)dp$, see fig. 7.4.

As L(p) is strictly convex, A(p) = p - L(p) is strictly concave and vanishes at p = 0 and 1. It is easily seen that A(p) has its maximum for $p = p_\mu$, i.e. $A(p_\mu) = p_\mu - L(p_\mu) = F(\mu) - F_1(\mu)$. $A(p_\mu)$ is thus the MER, cf. sec. 7.1.3 and 7.4.4.

Some alternative expressions for the Lorenz area are given in table 7.2. Notice the last expression of part B in the table: multiplying the expression with 2 gives the "rank-order weighted mean difference" introduced by Bartels [1977 - pp. 23-24].

Table 7.2 Alternative ways of expressing the Lorenz area

A. Using, p,L(p) and τ(p):	
$LA = \int_0^1 (p-L(p))dp = \int_0^1 A(p)dp$	A(p) see sec. 7.1.4
$= \frac{1}{2} - \int_0^1 L(p)dp = \int_0^1 p\,d\,L(p) - \frac{1}{2}$	
$= \int_0^1 (p-\frac{1}{2})\,\tau(p)\,dp =$	a weighted function of τ(p)'s
$= \int_0^1 [1 - \frac{\mu_L(p)}{\mu}]p\,dp =$	$\mu_L(p)$ and
	$\mu_U(p)$ see (7.9)
$= \int_0^1 [\frac{\mu_U(p)}{\mu} - 1](1-p)dp =$	and (7.10) of sec.7.1.1
$= Cov(p,\tau(p))$	
B. Using the argument y	
$LA = \int_0^\infty (F(y) - F_1(y))dF(y) =$	Cf. A. above
$= \frac{1}{2\mu}\int_0^\infty F(y)[1-F(y)]dy = \frac{1}{2\mu}\int_0^\infty F(y)G(y)dy =$	partial integration
$= \frac{1}{2\mu}\int_0^\infty (1-F^2(y))\,dy =$	cf. Dorfman [1979]
$= \frac{1}{4\mu}\int_0^\infty\int_0^\infty \|y-x\|dF(x)dF(y) =$	
$= \frac{1}{2\mu}\int_0^\infty\int_0^\infty \|y-x\| \cdot \|F(y) - F(x)\|dF(x)dF(y)$	

7.2.2 VARIOUS INTERPRETATIONS AND DEFINITIONS

Figure 7.5 Interpretation of the lower and upper means in a Lorenz diagram

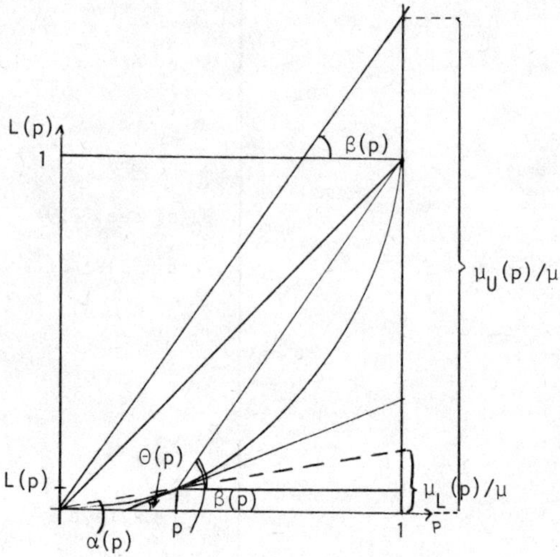

The lower and upper means (7.9) and (7.10) can be interpreted in the Lorenz diagram. For a fix p, $0 < p < 1$, we have the angles α and β as in figure 7.5. α is the angle between the p-axis and the secant through (0,0) and (p,L(p)) and β is the angle between the p-axis and the secant through (p,L(p)) and (1,1). This gives us

$$\mu_L(p) = \mu \frac{L(p)}{p} = \mu \tan \alpha(p)$$

and

$$\mu_U(p) = \mu \cdot \frac{1-L(p)}{1-p} = \mu \tan \beta(p)$$

where $\alpha(p) < \beta(p)$, $0 < p < 1$ (follows from the strict convexity of $L(p)$). The angle between the p-axis and the tangent to the LC in the point $(p,L(p))$ is $\Theta(p)$ and thus $\tan \Theta(p) = \tau(p)$ (or $\Theta(p) = \arctan \tau(p)$).

Elasticities

As pointed out by Belletini[1] [1954 - p.267] and Piesch [1975 - p.48] we could express elasticities of the LC as

$$\varepsilon_L(p) = \frac{dL(p)}{dp} \cdot \frac{p}{L(p)} = \frac{\tau(p)}{\tan \alpha(p)} = \frac{\tau(p)\mu}{\mu_L(p)} = \frac{\tan \Theta(p)}{\tan \alpha(p)}$$

and

$$\varepsilon_{1-L}(1-p) = \frac{d(1-L(p))}{d(1-p)} \cdot \frac{(1-p)}{(1-L(p))} = \frac{\tau(p)}{\tan\beta(p)} = \frac{\tau(p)\mu}{\mu_U(p)} = \frac{\tan \Theta(p)}{\tan \beta(p)} .$$

Regression-estimation of $\tau(p)$ and $F[F^{-1}(p)]$

The relationship between $\tau(p)$ and $F[F^{-1}(p)]$ can under a linear assumption be estimated by regression analysis using the method of least squares:

$$\hat{\tau}(p) = a_1 + b_1 F[F^{-1}(p)]$$

or

$$\hat{F}[F^{-1}(p)] = a_2 + b_2\, \tau(p),$$

1) Belletini does not use the term elasticity.

where $a_1 = (1 - 6LA)$

$b_1 = 12LA$

and $a_2 = (\frac{1}{2} - \frac{LA}{V^2})$

$b_2 = \frac{LA}{V^2}$,

where LA is the Lorenz area and V the coefficient of variation (cf. Piesch [1975 - pp. 104-105]).

The coefficient of correlation between $\tau(p)$ and $F[F^{-1}(p)]$, r, can be written as the square root of the product $b_1 b_2$ we have

$$r = \frac{2LA}{V} \sqrt{3} ,$$

where LA and V are defined above. From this we have the inequality of Glasser [1961 - p. 177], viz.

$$LA \leq \frac{V}{2\sqrt{3}} ,$$

(Glasser's inequality was in terms of the GINI coefficient, R, and written as

$$R \leq \frac{V}{\sqrt{3}}).$$

The Kakwani-Podder functional form for the LC

Kakwani and Podder [1976] proposed the following functional form for the LC:

$$\eta = k(\pi),$$

where η and π are, cf. figure 7.6,

$$\eta = \frac{p-L(p)}{\sqrt{2}} = \frac{A(p)}{\sqrt{2}} \geq 0 \qquad , 0 \leq \eta < A(p_\mu)/\sqrt{2}$$

$$\pi = \frac{p+L(p)}{\sqrt{2}} = \frac{A(p)}{\sqrt{2}} + \sqrt{2}L(p) \geq 0, \qquad 0 \leq \pi \leq \sqrt{2}$$

Since the η-function is used to estimate inequality measures from grouped observations it is left to the interested reader (cf. also Rasche et al [1980] and Kakwani [1980a],[1980b]). See also the discussion of LC-symmetry below.

Figure 7.6 The illustration of the Kakwani and Podder function $\eta = k(\pi)$

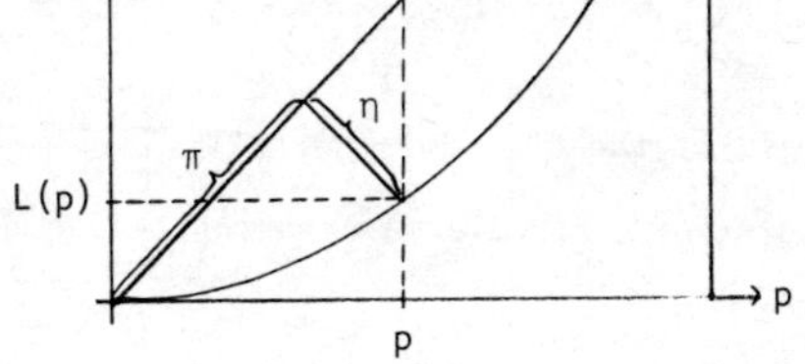

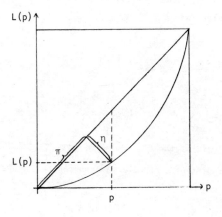

Indications of the LC

Taguchi [1968] defined location, dispersion, skewness and sharpness parameters of the LC (pp. 112-113). They are (cf. Piesch [1975 - pp. 99-104])

location parameter

$p_\mu = F(\mu)$

dispersion parameter

twice the Lorenzarea, i.e. $R = 2 \int_0^1 (p-L(p))dp, 0 \leq R \leq 1$, which is the Gini coefficient (cf. sec 7.4.1). Another dispersion measure proposed by Taguchi [1968 - p.112] and Piesch [1975 - pp. 99-100] is the length of the LC, λ, defined by $\lambda = \int_0^1 \sqrt{\tau(p)^2 + 1}\, dp$. Since $\lambda \in [\sqrt{2},2]$ it can be normalized as $\lambda^* = (\lambda - \sqrt{2})/(2 - \sqrt{2})$, i.e. $\lambda^* \in [0,1]$.

skewness parameter

$S = \cos 2\Theta_s = (1-\tau^2(p_s))/(1+\tau^2(p_s)), \qquad -1 \leq S \leq 1,$

where Θ_s is the angle of the tangent at $(p_s, L(p_s))$, and p_s is the saturation value, giving the maximum curvature ρ_s^{-1} of the LC; cf figure 7.7 and the sharpness parameter

sharpness parameter

ρ_s,

ρ_s is a measure of kurtosis of the LC and is normalized as $1-\rho_s/r$, where r expresses the radius of a circular arc having the same dispersion (R) as the given LC; $0 \leq 1 - \rho_s/r \leq 1$.

For a comprehensive discussion of Θ_s and ρ_s see Taguchi [1968] and

Piesch [1975].

The definitions of skewness and sharpness direct our attention to symmetrical and non-symmetrical LC's. Symmetrical LC's are discussed at length in Taguchi [1968 - pp. 113-115] and Piesch [1975 - pp. 87-98], who distinguish three types of symmetry, viz.

(i) self-symmetrical curves, i.e. LC's that are symmetrical with respect to the diagonal, drawn perpendicular to the eqalitarian line[1],

(ii) L-symmetry, i.e. $A(p) = A(1-p)$, $0 \leq p \leq 1$

(iii) p-symmetry, i.e. for a fixed $L(q)$ we define $c(L(q)) = q - L(q)$ and p-symmetry is present if $A(p) = A(\tilde{p})$ where p and $\tilde{p}$ are determined by the relation $L(p) + L(\tilde{p}) = 1$.

Figure 7.7 - The skewness and kurtosis of the LC.

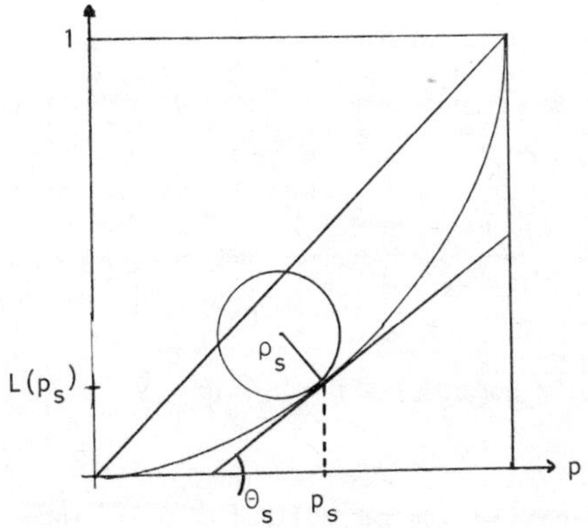

[1] See also Kakwani and Podder [1976]. They discuss symmetry by using their functional form $\eta = k(\pi)$, see the text above. As an example they assume that the LC has the equation $\eta = a\pi^{\alpha}[\sqrt{2} - \pi]^{\beta}$, $a > 0$, $\alpha > 0$, $\beta > 0$. If self-symmetry is at hand then $\alpha = \beta$, if $\beta > \alpha$ then the LC is skewed towards (1,1) and otherwise towards (0,0). Musgrove [1980] used the Kakwani and Podder equation, and related LC-symmetry to consumption behaviour. See also Kakwani [1980b].

7.2.3 THE GENERALIZED LORENZ CURVES $L_j(p)$

The LC defined and discussed in the previous sections can be considered as an ordinary LC: it is defined in the two equations case by the c.d.f. and the 1st m.d.f., i.e. by $F(y)$ and $F_1(y)$, or by $L(p)$ in the one equation case. Let $F_j(y)$ be the jth m.d.f., cf. sec. 1.3, defined by

$$F_j(y) = \int_0^y \frac{t^j}{\mu_j}\, dF(t), \tag{7.23}$$

where μ_j is the jth moment about zero, i.e. $\mu_j = \int_0^1 [F^{-1}(p)]^j dp < \infty$.

We define the generalized Lorenz Curve as

Definition 7.4 A generalized Lorenz Curve of order j corresponding to a non-negative random variable Y with c.d.f. F(y) and finite non-zero jth moment about zero, μ_j, is defined by ($j \geq 1$)

$$L_j(p) = \int_0^p \frac{\{F^{-1}(u)\}^j}{\mu_j}\, du = \frac{\int_0^p [F^{-1}(u)]^j du}{\int_0^1 [F^{-1}(u)]^j du}, \quad 0 \leq p \leq 1 \tag{7.24}$$

where $L_j(0) = 0$ and $L_j(1) = 1$.

The ordinary LC is a special case of the generalized LC, viz. when $j = 1$. We assume $L_j(p)$ to be at least twice continuously differentiable. Since

$$dL_j(p)/dp = [F^{-1}(p)]^j/\mu_j > 0 \text{ and } d^2L_j(p)/dp^2 = \frac{j[F^{-1}(p)]^{j-1}}{\mu_j}\,\frac{dF^{-1}(p)}{dp} > 0$$

the generalized LC is monotone and convex to the p-axis.

By comparison of two generalized LC's of the order (j+1) and j respectively, we have the fundamental inequality[1)]

$$L_{j+1}(p) < L_j(p), \qquad 0 < p < 1. \tag{7.25}$$

Moreover,

$L_{j+1}(0) = L_j(0) = 0$ and $L_{j+1}(1) = L_j(1) = 1$. The inequality (7.25) is depicted in figure 7.8.

Figure 7.8 Illustration of generalized Lorenz Curves

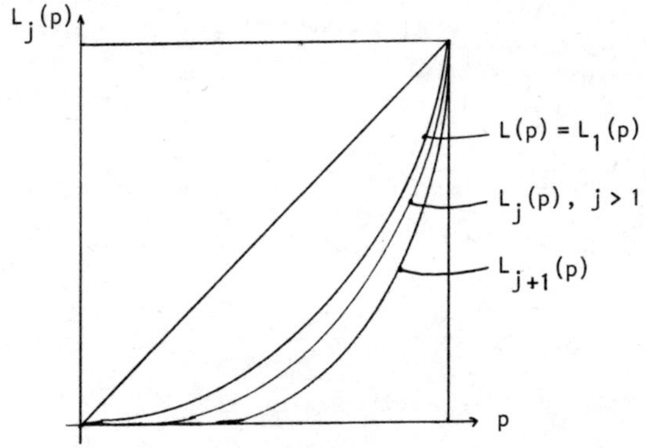

The generalization can be extended. Instead of considering the curve obtained by $F(y)$ and $F_j(y)$, we could consider another generalization, viz. the curve obtained by $F_j(y)$ as abscissa and $F_{j+1}(y)$ as ordinate. This curve also reminds us of an ordinary LC (cf. Piesch [1975 - p. 110]).

1) The inequality is proved by using the last term in (7.24) and the extended mean-value theorem (7.8).

Other LC-similar Curves

In the literature we can find other curves, similar to the Lorenz Curve. Kakwani [1977] proposed a generalized curve which he named *concentration curve*[1]: let $\rho(y)$ be a continuous function of y such that $\rho(y) \geq 0$ and its first derivative exist. Let the mean $\mu_\rho = E[\rho(y)] \neq 0$ exist and define the 1st m.d.f. about $\rho(y)$ as

$$F_{1\rho}(y) = \int_0^y \frac{\rho(t)}{\mu_\rho} dF(t).$$

$F_{1\rho}(y)$ is monotonically increasing and $F_{1\rho}[F_y^{-1}(0)] = 0$ and $F_{1\rho}[F_y^{-1}(1)] = 1$. The curve obtained by $F_{1\rho}(y)$ and $F(y)$ is now called the concentration curve (CC) of $\rho(y)$. The LC is of course, a special case of the CC when $\rho(y) = y$. The effects of the transformation $\rho(y)$ is discussed in sec. 7.2.5.

If $\rho^*(y)$ is another continuous function of y then Kakwani [1977 - p. 720] defines the graph of $F_{1\rho}(y)$ versus $F_{1\rho^*}(y)$ as the *relative concentration curve* of $\rho(y)$ with respect to $\rho^*(y)$.

Hainsworth [1964] discussed curves similar to the LC[2], e.g. he gave a picture of a nation's (nation A) trading balance through defining

$$\tau_i = \frac{\text{(export from A to nation i)}}{\text{(import from i to A)}},$$

and ordered the τ_i,s in ascending order. The X-axis in a coordinate system measures nation A:s import and the Y-axis the export from nation A. By plotting a polygongraph where the lines have slope τ_i, i=1, 2, ..., k, respectively, we have an LC-similar curve. For nations with $\tau_i > 1$ nation A has a trading surplus and for nations with $\tau_i < 1$ nation A has a trading deficit. If t = (nation A:s total import)/(nation A:s total export) and

1) Sometimes the name concentration curve is used for the ordinary LC (cf.sec.7.2.1).

2) "... all relationships between pairs of variables can be illustrated by means of an L-curve, ..." (Hainsworth [1964 - p. 431.]).

$\tau_i^* = t.\tau_i$ we have an LC with axes defined at [0,1]. Hainsworth also made applications of the LC to household budget analysis.

The ordinary LC was defined by Definition 7.2 (sec. 7.2.1) as

$$L(p) = \int_0^p \tau(u)du, \quad 0 < p < 1$$

where p is defined for an income variable Y such that $p = F_Y(y)$.

If, loosely speaking, we rerank the i.r.u's according to a second variable X and define an indicator variable $I\{A\} = \begin{cases} 1 \text{ if the event A occurs} \\ 0 \text{ otherwise} \end{cases}$

we can define a generalized LC as

$$L_S^*(p) = E[\,Y \cdot I\{X \leq F_X^{-1}(p)\}]/\mu_y \;.$$

The ordinary LC is in a similar way defined as $L(p) = E[\,Y \cdot I\{Y \leq F_Y^{-1}(p)\}]/\mu_y$.

$L_S^*(p)$ was introduced as the correlation curve by Blitz and Brittain [1964] and is labelled the pseudo LC by e.g. Fei, Ranis and Kuo [1978 - p. 45], [1979 - pp. 334-337]. The Lorenz area corresponding to $L_S^*(p)$ equals by definition

$$LA_S = \int_0^1 p dL_S^*(p) - \frac{1}{2} = \frac{1}{2} - \int_0^1 L_S^*(p)dp.$$

This area is labelled the concentration area and will be denoted $Ca(\frac{Y}{X})$.

By definition $Ca(\frac{Y}{X}) = LA_S = Cov\,(p_X, \tau_y(p_X))$ (see table 7.2) and the following properties hold:

(*i*) $Ca(\frac{Y}{X}) = LA$ — if the ranking in X is identical to the ranking in Y

(*ii*) $Ca(\frac{Y}{X}) = -LA$ — if the ranking in X is completely reversed to that in Y, i.e. if $F_x(x) = 1 - F_y(y)$

(*iii*) $-LA < Ca(\frac{Y}{X}) < LA$ — if the ranking in X diverges from the two extremes above.

The ordinary Lorenz area is, of course, obtained by $Ca(\frac{Y}{X}) = Cov\ (p_y, \tau_y(p_y))$. Taking two times the concentration area, $C(\frac{Y}{X}) = 2Ca(\frac{Y}{X})$, gives us what Kakwani [1977] labels the concentration index (for $X=\rho(y)$, a function of y), what Pyatt, Chen and Fei [1980] label the concentration ratio and what others (e.g. Fei, Ranis and Kuo [1978], [1979] and Shorrocks [1980b]) label the pseudo Gini coefficient.

Dividing $Ca(\frac{Y}{X})$ by the ordinary Lorenz area (or $C(\frac{Y}{X})$ by twice the Lorenz area, i.e. the Gini coefficient, R) we have

$$C = \frac{Ca(\frac{Y}{X})}{Ca(\frac{Y}{Y})} = \frac{C(\frac{Y}{X})}{C(\frac{Y}{Y})} = \frac{R^*}{R},$$

where $R = C(\frac{Y}{Y}) = 2LA$ is the ordinary Gini coefficient and $R^* = C(\frac{Y}{X})$ is the pseudo-Gini coefficient (or the concentration ratio).

C was introduced as a measure of correlation by Blitz and Brittain [1964].

Using (*i*) - (*iii*) above we see that

$$-1 \leq C \leq 1.$$

This result was also given by Rao [1969 - p.422].

C can be rewritten as $Cov\ (p_x, \tau_y(p_x)) \ / \ Cov(p_y, \tau_y(p_y))$ which equals

$$C = \frac{\rho(p_x, \tau_y(p_x))}{\rho(p_y, \tau_y(p_y))} = \frac{Cov(p_x, \tau_y(p_x))/\sigma_{px}\ \sigma_\tau}{Cov(p_y, \tau_y(p_y))/\sigma_{py}\ \sigma_\tau},$$

i.e. the ratio between two correlation coefficients (ρ)[1] where $\sigma_{px} = \sigma_{py}$, $\sigma_{\tau_{y(px)}} = \sigma_{\tau_{y(py)}} = \sigma_{\tau}$, $p_x = F_x(x)$ and $p_y = F_y(y)$. The numerator equals the correlation coefficient between the 'relative incomes' $\tau_y(p_x)$, i.e. $\frac{y}{\mu}$, and the 'relative ranks', p_x, according to variable X and the denominator equals the correlation coefficient between the 'relative incomes' $\tau_y(p_y)$, i.e. $\frac{y}{\mu}$, and the 'relative ranks', p_y, according to the income variable Y.[2] C is also labelled the relative correlation coefficient by Fields [1979a - p.440], [1979b - p.328]. See also the discussion by Fei, Ranis and Kuo [1979 - pp. 348-350].

In sec. 9.2 we will use C as a tool when decomposing the Gini coefficient (R=2LA) of total income by income sources.

1) The correlation coefficient ρ is not to be confused with the continuous function of y by Kakwani [1977].

2) Cf. Stuart [1954] and Kendall [1955 - pp. 124-126 and pp. 132-135].

7.2.4 TRUNCATED DISTRIBUTIONS

Information about low income receivers is often not available, e.g. in Sweden individuals with incomes below a given level need not fill in their tax assessment forms. Since income studies are frequently based on official assessment statistics this leads us to consider the size distribution of incomes truncated from below.

In this section we will study the effect on the Lorenz Curve (LC) when the income distribution is i) lower truncated, ii) upper truncated and iii) double truncated.

We begin with

Upper truncated c.d.f.

Let the c.d.f. be upper truncated (ut) in $y_m = F^{-1}(\xi)$, i.e. $\xi = F(y_m)$, see figure 7.9. The ut. c.d.f. is defined in $[0,F^{-1}(\xi)]$ as

$$F_{ut}(y) = \frac{F(y)}{F(y_m)} = \frac{F(y)}{\xi}, \quad y \in [0,F^{-1}(\xi)],$$

and the inverse c.d.f. as $F_{ut}^{-1}(p) = F^{-1}(\xi p), \quad 0 \leq \xi \leq 1.$

The arithmetic mean of the random variable Y in $[0,F^{-1}(\xi)]$ is, by using (7.9), equal to

$$\mu_L(\xi) = \mu\frac{L(\xi)}{\xi}. \tag{7.26}$$

The ut. LC is now

$$L_{ut}(p, \xi) = \frac{1}{\mu_L(\xi)} \int_0^p F_{ut}^{-1}(u)\,du = \frac{1}{\xi\mu_L(\xi)} \int_0^{\xi p} F^{-1}(t)\,dt = \frac{L(\xi p)\mu}{\xi\mu_L(\xi)} ,$$

i.e. by using (7.26)

$$L_{ut}(p; \xi) = \frac{L(\xi p)}{L(\xi)} = \frac{L(\xi p)}{L(\xi)L(p)} \cdot L(p) , \tag{7.27}$$

cf. Taguchi [1968 - p. 116] and Piesch [1975 - p. 77].

The LC is unchanged by upper truncation if $L(\xi p) = L(\xi) \cdot L(p)$.

Figure 7.9 Upper and lower truncated LC. The shaded area is the Lorenz area of the upper and lower truncated c.d.f., respectively.

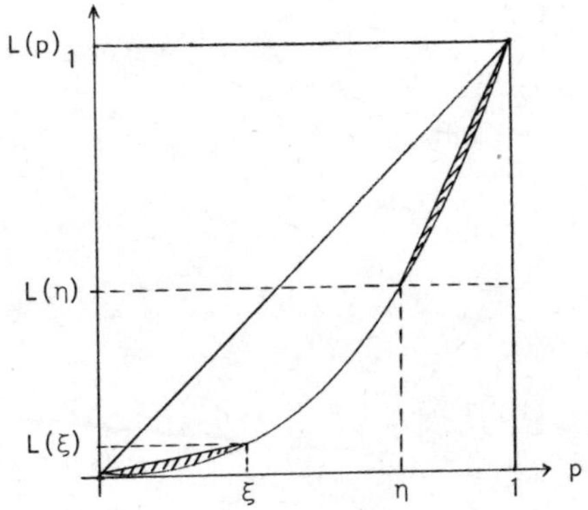

The Lorenz area of the upper truncated c.d.f. is

$$LA_{ut}(\xi) = \frac{1/2\,\xi\,L(\xi) - \int_0^{\xi} L(p)\,dp}{\xi L(\xi)} = \frac{1}{2} - \int_0^{\xi} \frac{L(p)}{\xi L(\xi)}\,dp.$$

As shown by Taguchi [1968 - theorem 4, p. 116] and Piesch [1975 - p. 79][1), the LC L(p) of any continuous c.d.f. is expressible as

$$L(p) = \frac{1/2 - LA}{p[1-LA(p)]}\exp\left\{-\int_p^1 \frac{d\xi}{\xi[1/2-LA(\xi)]}\right\}$$

where LA is the Lorenz area and LA(p) is the Lorenz area from the origo to p, i.e. LA = LA(1).

A necessary and sufficient condition for an arbitrary upper truncation to leave the LC unchanged, $L_{ut}(p;\xi) = L(p)$ (cf. (7.27)), is that the continuous density function f(y) is given by the form $f(y) = \frac{A}{y^k}$,

$$k < 1,\ \infty > y \geq a \begin{cases} \geq 0 & \text{for } k \leq 0 \\ > 0 & \text{for } 0 < k < 1 \end{cases}.$$

This form of the continuous density function is a necessary and sufficient condition for $L(p)L(\xi) = L(\xi p)$ to hold, $0 \leq p < \xi \leq 1$ (Taguchi [1968 - p. 116-117]).

Lower truncated c.d.f.

The c.d.f. is lower truncated (lt.) in $y_1 = F^{-1}(\eta)$, i.e. $\eta = F^{-1}(y_1)$ (see figure 7.9). The lt. c.d.f. is defined in $[F^{-1}(\eta),\infty[$ as

$$F_{lt}(y) = 1 - \frac{1-F(y)}{1-F(y_1)} = \frac{F(y) - \eta}{1 - \eta}, \quad y \in [F^{-1}(\eta),\infty[,$$

and the inverse c.d.f. as $F_{lt}^{-1}(p) = F^{-1}[1-(1-\eta)(1-p)]$.

1) Taguchi and Piesch express L(p) in terms of twice the Lorenz area (the Gini coefficient) instead of the Lorenz area LA above.

The arithmetic mean in the interval $[F^{-1}(\eta),\infty[$ is by (7.10) equal to

$$\mu_U(\eta) = \mu\frac{1-L(\eta)}{1-\eta} . \qquad (7.28)$$

and the lt. LC is

$$L_{lt}(p;\eta) = \frac{1}{\mu_U(\eta)}\int_p^1 F_{lt}^{-1}(u)\,du = \frac{1}{\mu_U(\eta)}\int_p^1 F^{-1}[1-(1-\eta)(1-u)]du =$$

$$= \frac{\mu}{\mu_U(\eta)}\cdot\left\{\frac{L[(1-\eta)p+\eta] - L(\eta)}{1-\eta}\right\}$$

or (using (7.28))

$$L_{lt}(p;\eta) = \frac{L[(1-\eta)p+\eta]-L(\eta)}{1-L(\eta)} = \frac{L[(1-\eta)p+\eta]-L(\eta)}{\{1-L(\eta)\}L(p)}\cdot L(p) \qquad (7.29)$$

The Lorenz area of the lower truncated c.d.f. is (cf. figure 7.9)

$$LA_{lt}(\eta) = \frac{\frac{1}{2}(1-\eta)(1-L(\eta)) - \int_\eta^1 [L(p) - L(\eta)]dp}{(1-\eta)(1-L(\eta))} .$$

By theorem 5 in Taguchi [1968 - p.117] and the corresponding theorem in Piesch [1975 - p.80] the LC L(p) of any continuous c.d.f. is expressible as

$$1-L(p) = \frac{\frac{1}{2}+LA}{(1-p)[\frac{1}{2}+LA(p)]}\exp\left\{-\int_0^p\frac{d\eta}{(1-\eta)[\frac{1}{2}+LA(\eta)]}\right\}.$$

A necessary and sufficient condition for $L_{lt}(p;\eta) = L(p)$, i.e. for an arbitrary lower truncation to leave the LC unchanged, is that the continuous density function has the Pareto form with $\alpha > 1$. This was proved independently by V. Schelling in 1934 and by Bhattacharya in 1963 (see Piesch [1975- p. 81] for reference, cf. also Taguchi [1968 - p.117-118]).

Figure 7.10 Double truncated LC.

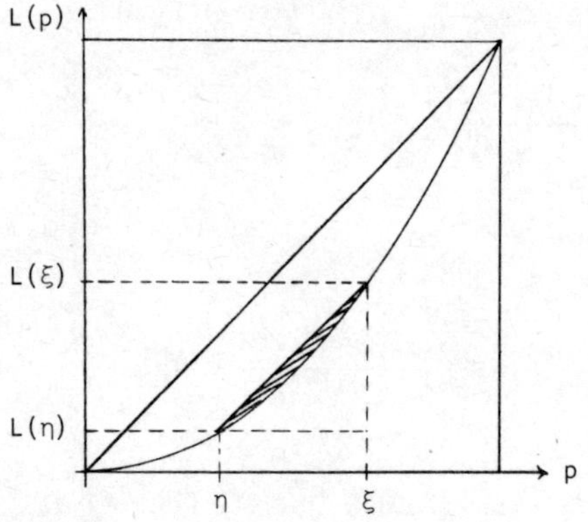

Double truncated c.d.f.

Consider a double truncated (dt) c.d.f., i.e. a c.d.f. that is both lower and upper truncated. Let the truncation-points be $F^{-1}(\eta)$ and $F^{-1}(\xi)$, $0 < F^{-1}(\eta) < F^{-1}(\xi) < \infty$. The dt c.d.f. is then defined by

$$F_{dt}(y;\eta,\xi) = \frac{F(y) - \eta}{\xi - \eta}$$

and the inverse c.d.f. $F_{dt}^{-1}(p) = F^{-1}[\eta + (\xi-\eta)p]$

The arithmetic mean of dt. c.d.f. is

$$\mu_{dt}(\xi,\eta) = \mu \frac{L(\xi) - L(\eta)}{\xi - \eta}$$

and the dt LC is

$$L_{dt}(p;\eta,\xi) = \frac{L(\eta + (\xi-\eta)p) - L(\eta)}{L(\xi) - L(\eta)}$$

The Lorenz area of the double truncated c.d.f. is (cf. figure 7.10)

$$LA_{dt}(\eta,\xi) = \frac{1}{2} - \frac{1}{[L(\xi)-L(\eta)][\xi-\eta]} \int_{\eta}^{\xi} [L(p)-L(\eta)]dp.$$

Letting $\eta = 0$ in the formulas above we obtain the upper truncated case and with $\xi = 1$ we have the lower truncated case.

Taguchi [1968 - p.119-121] extends the discussion to include the joint Lorenz curve of n ($n \geq 2$) double truncated c.d.f.'s.

7.2.5 LORENZ CURVES FROM TRANSFORMED VARIABLES

What would the effects be on income inequality of various salary increase policies or of various taxation policies? If we consider Lorenz domination (cf. ch. 4) as a mark of less inequality we could study the effects of various policies in a Lorenz diagram. In this section we will study the effects of transformations of the income and these effects are illustrated in sec. 7.2.6 by some simple salary increase policies and taxation policies.

The continuous random variable $y \in [0, \infty[$ has the c.d.f. $F_y(y)$, the inverse c.d.f. $F_y^{-1}(p)$ and the LC $L_y(p)$. Consider a continuous monotone transformation

$$z = \rho(y) \qquad \text{with } \rho(y) \geq 0 \text{ in } [0,\infty[.$$

Among the different kinds of transformations two simple types can be distinguished, viz.

i) $\frac{d\rho(y)}{dy} > 0$ in $[0,\infty[$, i.e. a monotone increasing transformation and

ii) $\frac{d\rho(y)}{dy} < 0$ in $[0,\infty[$, i.e. a monotone decreasing transformation.

To begin with we will give the general forms of the LC's of these two kinds of transformations[1] and the formulas for their Lorenz areas.

1) Kakwani [1977] denominates these curves concentration curves, see sec. 7.2.3.

i) monotone increasing transformation: $\frac{d\rho(y)}{dy} > 0$ in $[0,\infty[$.

The c.d.f. of the transformed variable is $F_z(z)$ and its inverse c.d.f. is $F_z^{-1}(p)$:

$$F_y(y) = F_z(\rho(y)) \quad \text{and} \quad F_z^{-1}(p) = \rho[F_y^{-1}(p)].$$

The LC of this transformed variable is

$$L_z(p) = \frac{1}{\mu_z}\int_0^p \rho[F_y^{-1}(u)]du = \frac{\int_0^p \rho[F_y^{-1}(u)]du}{\int_0^1 \rho[F_y^{-1}(u)]du} \tag{7.30}$$

and the Lorenz area becomes

$$LA_z = \frac{1}{2} - \int_0^1 L_z(p)dp = \frac{1}{2} - \frac{\int_0^1\int_0^p \rho[F_y^{-1}(u)]du\, dp}{\int_0^1 \rho[F_y^{-1}(u)]du}. \tag{7.31}$$

ii) monotone decreasing transformation: $\frac{d\rho(y)}{dy} < 0$ in $[0,\infty[$.

For a monotone decreasing transformation the c.d.f. $F_z(z)$ equals $1 - F_y[\rho^{-1}(z)]$ and its inverse c.d.f. is $F_z^{-1}(p)$.
The 'pseudo Lorenz Curve'[1)] $L_{Sz}(p) = F_{1z}(F_y^{-1}(p))$ is now concave and located over the egalitarian line (the diagonal) and as before the 'Lorenz area' is the area between the pseudo LC and the diagonal (with negative sign) :

1) Cf. sec. 7.2.3 where the pseudo LC is denoted $L_S^*(p)$

$$L_{Sz}(p) = \frac{1}{\mu_z} \int_{1-p}^{1} \rho[F_y^{-1}(u)]du = \frac{\int_{1-p}^{1} \rho[F_y^{-1}(u)]du}{\int_{0}^{1} \rho[F_y^{-1}(u)]du} \tag{7.32}$$

and by the definition of the Lorenz area

$$LA_{Sz} = \frac{1}{2} - \int_0^1 L_z(p)dp = \frac{1}{2} - \frac{\int_0^1 \int_{1-p}^{1} \rho[F_y^{-1}(u)]du\, dp}{\int_0^1 \rho[F_y^{-1}(u)]du}, \tag{7.33}$$

it becomes clear that this 'area' will have a negative sign.

LINEAR TRANSFORMATIONS

Consider a linear transformation $F_z^{-1}(p) = \rho[F_y^{-1}(p)] = \alpha + \beta F_y^{-1}(p)$, with $\beta \geq 0$ and existing non-zero mean $\mu_z = \alpha + \beta\mu_y$. The LC $L_z(p)$ can be written as

$$L_z(p) = wL_y(p) + (1-w)p, \tag{7.34}$$

where

$$w = \beta\mu_y/(\alpha + \beta\mu_y), \tag{7.35}$$

and the corresponding Lorenz area, LA_z as

$$LA_z = wLA_y = \left(\frac{\beta\mu_y}{\alpha+\beta\mu_y}\right)LA_y$$

$\alpha \geq 0,\ \beta \geq 0$

If we assume both parameters, α and β, to be non-negative, the weight (7.35) will be in the [0,1]-interval and thus

$$L_y(p) \leq L_z(p) \leq p,$$

cf. (7.34), i.e. inequality measured by the Lorenz area will not increase.

Letting $\alpha = 0$ ($\beta > 0$) we obtain $w = 1$ and this proportional transformation, $F_z^{-1}(p) = \beta F_y^{-1}(p)$, will equalize the LC's ($L_z(p) = L_y(p)$). With $\alpha > 0$ and $\beta = 1$ we have a "constant transformation", $F_z^{-1}(p) = \alpha + F_y^{-1}(p)$, and by (7.34) we see that the LC L_z will Lorenz dominate (LDOM, see ch. 4) the LC L_y, i.e. $L_y(p) < L_z(p) < p$, and inequality decreases, (letting $\alpha > 0$ and $\beta = 0$, the LC L_z will equal the egalitarian line, $L_z(p) = p$).

$\alpha < 0,\ \beta \geq 0$

If α is assumed negative we can distinguish two cases of transformations, viz., i) $\alpha + \beta\mu_y > 0$ and ii) $\alpha + \beta\mu_y < 0$. The assumption of a positive transformation is relaxed here and hence L_z' is a generalized LC[1].
In the first case the weight w will be greater than one ($w > 1$) and by a simple algebraical exercise we obtain the following relation:

$$L_y(p) = w'L_z(p) + (1-w')p \tag{7.36}$$

where

$$w' = w^{-1} = (\alpha + \beta\mu_y)/\beta\mu_y, \quad 0 < w' < 1.$$

1) Cf. footnote 2 to Definition 7.2

By (7.40) and $0 < w' < 1$ we have

$$L_z(p) < L_y(p) < p,$$

and thus the LC L_y will Lorenz dominate the LC L_z. Inequality, measured by the Lorenz area, will increase: $LA_y = w' LA_z$

In the second case the weight w will be negative ($w < 0$) and by a similar exercise to the one above we receive the relation

$$p = w'' L_z(p) + (1 - w')L_y(p), \qquad (7.37)$$

where

$$w'' = (1 - w)^{-1} = (\alpha + \beta\mu_y)/\alpha, \quad 0 < w'' < 1.$$

The LC of the transformed variable, L_z, will in this case be situated above the egalitarian line ($L = p$). The Lorenz area LA_z is by the definition of the area (7.21) negative and is equal to

$$LA_z = wLA_y,$$

where $w = \beta\mu_y/(\alpha + \beta\mu_y) < 0$.

The effects of various increasing linear transformations are given in table 7.3.

Table 7.3 The effect of an increasing linear transformation,

$F_z^{-1}(p) = \alpha + \beta F_y^{-1}(p)$, $\beta \geq 0$.

α	β	$\mu_z = \alpha + \beta\mu_y$	LC-relation	Lorenzarea
0	> 0	$\beta\mu_y$	$L_z(p) = L_y(p)$ proportional addition	$LA_z = LA_y$
> 0	0	α	$L_z(p) = p$ "absolute equality"	$LA_z = 0$
> 0	1	$\alpha + \mu_y$	$L_y(p) < L_z(p) < p$ absolute addition	$LA_z = wLA_y$ $0 < w < 1$, $w = \frac{\mu_y}{\alpha+\mu_y}$
< 0	> 0	> 0	$L_z(p) < L_y(p) < p$	$LA_z = wLA_y$ $w = \beta\mu_y/(\alpha + \beta\mu_y) > 1$
< 0	> 0	< 0	$L_y(p) < p < L_z(p)$	$LA_z = wLA_y$ $w = \beta\mu_y/(\alpha + \beta\mu_y) < 0$

For a monotone decreasing linear function, $F_z^{-1}(p) = \alpha + \beta F_y^{-1}(p) \geq 0$ with $\beta < 0$ and $\alpha > 0$ and $\mu_z = \alpha + \beta\mu_y > 0$, we have by using (7.32)

$$L_z(p) = w[1-L_y(1-p)] + (1-w)p, \tag{7.38}$$

with $w = \beta\mu_y/(\alpha + \beta\mu_y) < 0$. The LC L_z can be situated below or above the LC $L_y(p)$ and the Lorenz area is

$$LA_z = -wLA_y$$

and since $w < 0$ we can write (cf. Piesch [1975 - p.69])

$$LA_z = |w| \cdot LA_y = \left| \frac{\beta\mu_y}{\alpha+\beta\mu_y} \right| LA_y$$

The inequality measured by the Lorenz area will, for $\beta < 0$,

decrease if $-\beta < \frac{\alpha}{2\mu_y}$

and

increase if $-\beta > \frac{\alpha}{2\mu_y}$.

$L_z(p)$ is in this case situated below the egalitarian line. This fact can be seen if we rewrite (7.38) as

$$p = w'' L_z(p) + (1-w'')[1-L_y(1-p)], \tag{7.39}$$

where $0 < w'' = \frac{\alpha+\beta\mu_y}{\alpha} < 1$.

Since the LC $L_y(p)$, our original LC, is situated below the diagonal line, the LC $1-L_y(1-p)$ is situated above and p must be between $L_z(p)$ and $1-L_y(1-p)$. Thus $L_z(p)$ is situated below the diagonal line.

The main condition, except the case resulting in (7.37), has been that $F_z^{-1}(p) = \alpha + \beta F_y^{-1}(p) \geq 0$. If this inequality is reversed, i.e. $F_z^{-1}(p) = \alpha + \beta F_y^{-1}(p) < 0$, the resulting LC will be identical with the corresponding LC's obtained earlier. If we write $\alpha + \beta F_y^{-1}(p)$ as $-(\alpha' + \beta' F_y^{-1}(p))$ and treat $\alpha' + \beta' F_y^{-1}(p)$ as before, with $\mu_z = -(\alpha' + \beta'\mu_y)$, the result is immediate.

The Lorenz curves of the transformed variable $F_z^{-1}(p) = \rho[F_y^{-1}(p)]$ has for linear transformations been treated as regards its own c.d.f. $p = F_z[F_z^{-1}(p)]$. We could instead consider the pseudo Lorenz curve $L_{Sz}(p) = F_{1z}(F_y^{-1}(p))$, cf also the introduction to sec. 7.2.5.

For a monotonically increasing transformation the "new" LC as regards the original c.d.f. (named Concentration Curve by Kakwani [1977] - cf. sec. 7.2.3) will be situated as before, but a new situation will arise when the transformation is monotonically decreasing (cf. the first part of this section) viz. the LC will be concave and situated above the diagonal line.

General criteria for the position of the LC $L_z(p)$

As we have seen the LC of a linearly transformed variable **z**, $L_z(p)$ can be situated over or below p and over or below $L_y(p)$. This is also true in the non-linear case. The shape of $L_z(p)$ is dependent on i) the transformation $z = \rho(y)$ and ii) whether the LC is plotted as regards the c.d.f. of y or the c.d.f. of z (the Lorenz area can be written as $Cov[p_y, \tau_z(p_z)]$ or $Cov[p_z, \tau(p_z)]$, cf. table 7.2).

To get a general condition for $L_z(p) > L_y(p)$ or $L_y(p) > L_z(p)$ consider figure 7.11. The difference function $D(p) = L_z(p) - L_y(p)$ can be written as

$$D(p) = \int_0^p \left[\frac{F_z^{-1}(u)}{\mu_z} - \frac{F_y^{-1}(u)}{\mu_y} \right] du = \tag{7.40a}$$

$$= \int_0^p \frac{F_y^{-1}(u)}{\mu_z} \left[\frac{F_z^{-1}(u)}{F_y^{-1}(u)} - \frac{\mu_z}{\mu_y} \right] du, \tag{7.40b}$$

where $F_z^{-1}(p) = \rho[F_y^{-1}(p)]$ and $D(0) = D(1) = 0$.

Figure 7.11 The shape of the difference function $D(p) = L_z(p) - L_y(p)$.

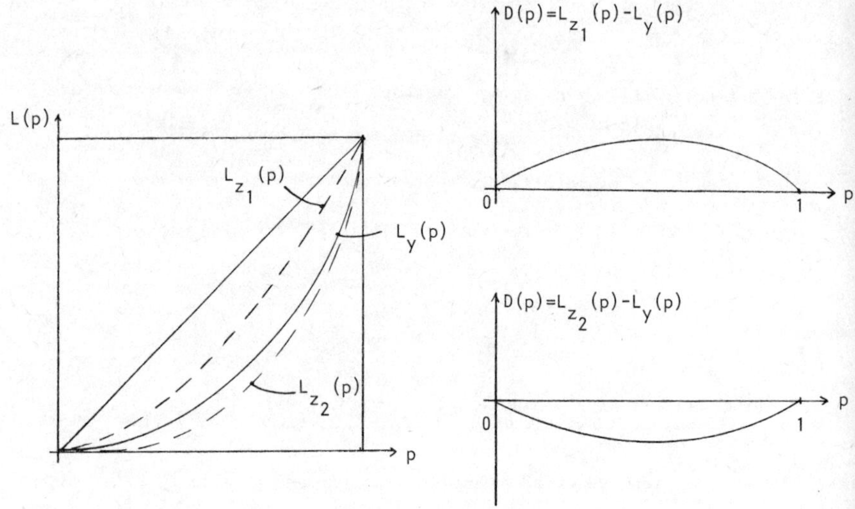

As shown by Fellman [1976, 1980], for a monotonically increasing transformation, we can consider the ratio $F_z^{-1}(p)/F_y^{-1}(p) = \rho[F_y^{-1}(p)]/F_y^{-1}(p) = t(p)$ in (7.40b)[1]. The following holds:

$t(p)$ is monotonically decreasing	$\Rightarrow$	$L_z(p) > L_y(p)$
$t(p)$ is constant	$\Rightarrow$	$L_z(p) = L_y(p)$
$t(p)$ is monotonically increasing	$\Rightarrow$	$L_z(p) < L_y(p)$

1) With regard to taxation, where $F_y^{-1}(p)$ is income before tax and $\rho[F_y^{-1}(p)]$ describes the tax function, the ratio $t(p)$ is the average tax rate (cf. e.g. Jakobsson[1976]).

A more general criterion will be obtained if we do as follows: consider once again figure 7.11. If $D(p)$ is convex from below then $D(p) < 0$, $0 < p < 1$, and $L_z(p) < L_y(p)$, $[D''(p) > 0]$. On the other hand, if $D(p)$ is concave from below then $D(p) > 0$, $0 < p < 1$, and $L_z(p) > L_y(p)$, $[D''(p) < 0]$. Using (7.40a) and differentiating twice we obtain

$$D''(p) = \frac{dF_y^{-1}(p)}{dp} \cdot \frac{1}{\mu_z} \left\{ \frac{d\rho[F_y^{-1}(p)]}{dF_y^{-1}(p)} - \frac{\mu_z}{\mu_y} \right\}, \tag{7.41}$$

where $dF_y^{-1}(p)/dp$ and μ_y is always positive. For positive $\mu_z = \rho(\mu_y)$, the sign of $D''(p)$ depends on the expression within brackets in (7.41). For positive transformations $(\rho[F_y^{-1}(p)] > 0)$ with $d\rho[F_y^{-1}(p)]/dF_y^{-1}(p) = M[F_y^{-1}(p)]$[1)] less than or greater then zero (cf. the beginning of this section) we have the following criterion by Piesch [1975 - p.71, satz 23]:

$$\text{if } \left| \frac{d\rho[F_y^{-1}(p)]}{dF_y^{-1}(p)} \right| \gtrless \frac{\mu_z}{\mu_y} \text{ then } L_z(p) \lessgtr L_y(p). \tag{7.42}$$

In the special case of a linear transformation, $F_z^{-1}(p) = \alpha + \beta F_y^{-1}(p) > 0$, the criterion can be stated as

$$\text{if } \left| \frac{d\rho[F_y^{-1}(p)]}{dF_y^{-1}(p)} \right| \gtrless \beta + \frac{\alpha}{\mu_y} \quad \text{then } L_z(p) \lessgtr L_y(p).$$

1) Regarding taxation, $M[F_y^{-1}(p)] = d\rho[F_y^{-1}(p)]/dF_y^{-1}(p)$ is the marginal tax rate (cf. e.g. Jakobsson [1976]).

A similar criterion for a positive transformation, $F_z^{-1}(p) = \rho[F_y^{-1}(p)] \geq 0$, is proposed by Kakwani [1977][1]. Define the elasticity of the transformed income by

$$\eta_\rho[F_y^{-1}(p)] = \frac{d\rho[F_y^{-1}(p)]}{dF_y^{-1}(p)} \cdot \frac{F_y^{-1}(p)}{\rho[F_y^{-1}(p)]} .$$

The criterion by Kakwani [1977 - corallary 2, p.721] is[2]

$$\boxed{\eta_\rho[F_y^{-1}(p)] \lesseqgtr 1, \text{ for every } F_y^{-1}(p) \geq 0 \Rightarrow L_z(p) \gtreqless L_y(p)^{3)}} \qquad (7.43)$$

A second criterion by Kakwani [1977 - corollary 1, p.720] states whether $L_z(p)$ is above or below the egalitarian line:

$$\boxed{\eta_\rho[F_y^{-1}(p)] \lesseqgtr 0, \text{ for every } F_y^{-1}(p) \geq 0 \Rightarrow L_z(p) \gtreqless p.^{4)}} \qquad (7.44)$$

1) See also Kakwani [1980b].

2) To show this, consider the generalized LC (the relative concentration curve, according to Kakwani [1977], cf. sec. 7.2.3) of $L_z(p)$ with respect to $L_y(p)$. The sign of the second derivative implies the stated criterion.

3) If $\eta_\rho = 1$ then $L_z(p) = L_y(p)$

4) If $\eta_\rho = 0$ then $L_z(p) = p$

7.2.6 ON THE USE OF LC's TO COMPARE SALARY OR TAX POLICIES

We may now use the previous discussion of LC's from transformed variables to compare the effects on inequality of various salary increasing policies (cf. e.g. Fellman [1976],[1980]) and various tax policies (cf. Jakobsson [1976], Fellman [1976],[1980] and Kakwani [1977]). In doing this we will assume that the inequality judgements follow the LDOM and the PROPORTION (cf. sec. 4.2-4.3) --- simil[illegible]ations may of course also be based on the ADD or some other criteria.

To do this we rewrite the LC (7.30) of a monotonically increasing transformation as

$$L_z(p) = \frac{\mu_y}{\mu_z} L_y(p) + \frac{1}{\mu_z} \int_0^p \{\rho[F_y^{-1}(u)] - F_y^{-1}(u)\}du. \tag{7.45}$$

As we shall see below, we may consider $\rho[F_y^{-1}(p)] - F_y^{-1}(p)$ or $F_y^{-1}(p) - \rho[F_y^{-1}(p)]$ as the inverse c.d.f.'s of a new variate X:

$$F_x^{-1}(p) = \begin{cases} \rho[F_y^{-1}(p)] - F_y^{-1}(p) \quad \text{if } \rho[F_y^{-1}(p)] \geq F_y^{-1}(p) \text{ and } d\rho/dF_y^{-1} \geq 1 & (7.46a) \\ F_y^{-1}(p) - \rho[F_y^{-1}(p)] \quad \text{if } \rho[F_y^{-1}(p)] \leq F_y^{-1}(p) \text{ and } d\rho/dF_y^{-1} \leq 1 & (7.46b) \end{cases}$$

Using (7.46a), with $F_z^{-1}(p) = F_y^{-1}(p) + F_x^{-1}(p)$ and $\mu_z = \mu_y + \mu_x$, we have

$$L_z(p) = wL_y(p) + (1-w)L_x(p), \tag{7.47a}$$

with $w = \mu_y/(\mu_y + \mu_x)$, $0 \leq w \leq 1$ and in this case the LC L_z is situated between the LC's L_y and L_x.

In the case of the second situation, i.e. (7.46b), with $F_y^{-1}(p) = F_z^{-1}(p) + F_x^{-1}(p)$ and using the fact that $F_y^{-1}(p) \geq F_z^{-1}(p) = \rho[F_y^{-1}(p)]$, $\mu_y = \mu_z + \mu_x$, we have

$$L_y(p) = w^* L_z(p) + (1-w^*) L_x(p), \qquad (7.47b)$$

with $w^* = \mu_z/(\mu_z + \mu_x)$, $0 \leq w^* \leq 1$. In this case the LC L_y will be situated between the LC's L_z and L_x.

The first approach, (7.47a), could be used when analyzing salary increasing policies and the second, (7.47b), when analyzing taxation policies, using the following definitions:

inverse c.d.f.	salary increase policy (7.47a)	taxation policy (7.47b)
$F_y^{-1}(p)$	income before salary increase	gross income
$F_z^{-1}(p)$	income after salary increase	tax
$F_x^{-1}(p)$	salary increase	net income

<u>Salary increase policies</u>

If, as stated above, we use $F_y^{-1}(p)$ in (7.46a) as the income <u>before</u> a salary increase has been realized and $F_z^{-1}(p) = \rho[F_y^{-1}(p)]$ as the income <u>afterwards</u> then $F_x^{-1}(p) = \rho[F_y^{-1}(p)] - F_y^{-1}(p)$ measures the salary increase.

By (7.47a) we can make the following statement, using (7.46a),

"The Lorenz Curve of the income after a salary increase is situated between the LC's of the income before the salary increase and the salary increase",

i.e. $L_y(p) \leq L_z(p) \leq L_x(p)$ or $L_x(p) \leq L_z(p) \leq L_y(p)$.

Some illustrating examples:

i) the increase in salary is of the same size regardless of previous salary, $F_z^{-1}(p) = F_y^{-1}(p) + \alpha, \quad \alpha > 0$

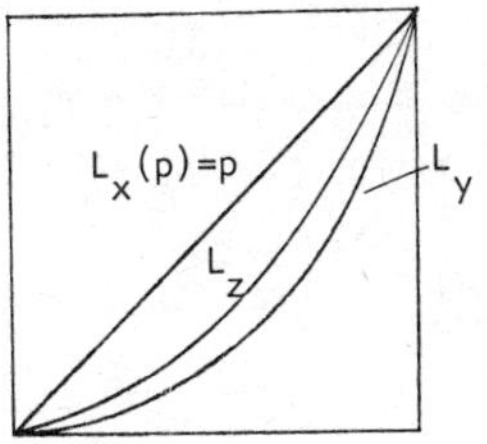

Inequality decreases, since

$$L_y(p) \leq L_z(p) < L_x(p) = p.$$

(cf. Fellman [1976, 1980]).

ii) the increase in salary is strictly proportional, $F_z^{-1}(p) = \beta F_y^{-1}(p)$, $\beta > 1$

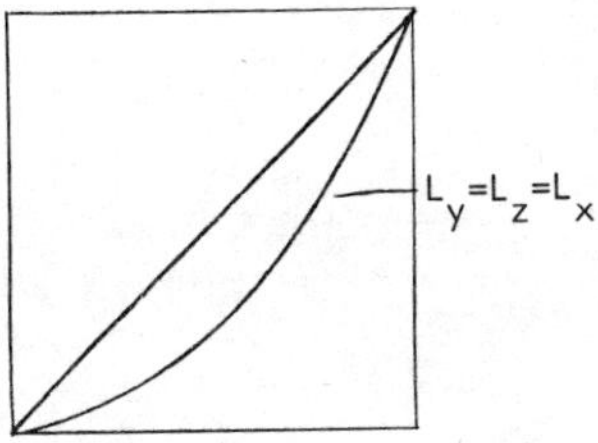

Inequality is unchanged, since

$$L_y(p) = L_z(p) = L_x(p)$$

(cf. Levine and Singer [1970] and Fellman [1980]).

Taxation policie

Let $F_z^{-1}(p) = \rho[F_y^{-}$] be a tax function, $F_y^{-1}(p)$ the gross income (income before tax) and F_x^{-} the net income (income after tax). By (7.46b), i.e. $F_y^{-1}(p) \geq F_z^{-1}(p) = \rho[F_y^{-1}(p)]$, and letting $0 \leq \frac{d\rho[F_y^{-1}(p)]}{dF_y^{-1}(p)} \leq 1$ and using (7.47b) we can make the following statement (a theorem by Piesch [1975 - p. 67, Satz 21], using (7.46b),

> "For every income distribution, the LC of the gross income is situated between the LC of the net income and that of the taxation",

i.e. $L_z(p) \leq L_y(p) \leq L_x(p)$ or $L_x(p) \leq L_y(p) \leq L_z(p)$.

In terms of the criterion (7.43) the two relations will be fulfilled if the tax elasticity $\eta_\rho[F_y^{-1}(p)]$ (the liability progression; cf. Jakobsson [1976]) is greater or less than one, since

$$\text{if } \eta_\rho[F_y^{-1}(p)] > 1 \Rightarrow L_z(p) < L_y(p) \Rightarrow L_z(p) < L_y(p) < L_x(p)$$

and

$$\text{if } \eta_\rho[F_y^{-1}(p)] < 1 \Rightarrow L_y(p) < L_z(p) \Rightarrow L_x(p) < L_y(p) < L_z(p).$$

If the tax function, $F_z^{-1}(p) = \rho[F_y^{-1}(p)]$, is such that the average tax rate $\frac{\rho[F_y^{-1}(p)]}{F_y^{-1}(p)}$, is monotonically increasing, then it follows by the criterion of Fellman [1976, 1980], cf. sec. 7.2.5, that $L_z(p) < L_y(p)$ and thus the first relation above is at hand. The same result, i.e. that income after tax will be more equally distributed than income before tax, is also proved by Kakwani [1977 - p.723] and Jakobsson [1976].

The income redistribution could also be measured by the elasticity of income after tax (the residual progression, cf. Jakobsson [1976]) denoted by $a[F_y^{-1}(p)]$

$$a[F_y^{-1}(p)] = \frac{dF_x^{-1}(p)}{dF_y^{-1}(p)} \cdot \frac{F_y^{-1}(p)}{F_x^{-1}(p)} .$$

Consider $L_x(p)$ as a function of $L_y(p)$. If L_x Lorenz dominates L_y then the second derivative of L_x with respect to L_y would be negative, i.e. $d^2L_x(p)/dL_y^2(p) < 0$. On the other hand L_y would Lorenz dominate L_x if the second derivative is positive. If L_x coincides with L_y (proportional tax) then the second derivative equals zero. The sign of the second derivative is determined by the sign of $\frac{dF_x^{-1}(p)}{dF_y^{-1}(p)} - \frac{F_x^{-1}(p)}{F_y^{-1}(p)}$, i.e.

$$\frac{dF_x^{-1}(p)}{dF_y^{-1}(p)} - \frac{F_x^{-1}(p)}{F_y^{-1}(p)} \gtreqless 0 \Longleftrightarrow a[F_y^{-1}(p)] = \frac{dF_x^{-1}(p)}{dF_y^{-1}(p)} \frac{F_y^{-1}(p)}{F_x^{-1}(p)} \gtreqless 1.$$

By the elasticity of income after tax, $a[F_y^{-1}(p)]$, we have the following criterion

$$\text{if } a[F_y^{-1}(p)] \gtrless 1 \text{ then } L_x \lessgtr L_y$$ [1)]

and thus the two relations above hold.

1) if $a[F_y^{-1}(p)] = 1$ then $L_x(p) = L_y(p)$.

By a proportional tax the elasticity of income after tax will consequently be one and by a progressive tax the elasticity will be less than one (cf. Jakobsson and Normann [1975]).

If we compare two progressive tax schemes working on the same income distribution, a necessary condition for $L_{x_2}(p)$ to Lorenz dominate $L_{x_1}(p)$ is that $a_2[F_y^{-1}(p)] < a_1[F_y^{-1}(p)]$ for every p. This was proved by Jakobsson [1976 - p.165] and is easily seen by considering $L_{x_2}(p)$ as a function of $L_{x_1}(p)$. The result follows from the negative sign of the second derivative $d^2L_{x_2}(p)/dL^2_{x_1}(p)$.

Jakobsson [1976] uses the elasticity of income after tax as a measure of tax progressivity. Another measure of tax progressivity was proposed by Suits [1977]: Consider the generalized LC

$$L_{Sz}(p) = F_{1z}(F_y^{-1}(p))$$

(cf.sec. 7.2.3). The measure of tax progressivity proposed by Suits is the double "pseudo-Lorenz area" (the pseudo Gini coefficient). If the tax schedule is regressive (for every p) the generalized LC will be above the diagonal line and the measure will be negative. A proportional tax will give the value zero and a progressive tax schedule (for every p) will yield a generalized LC below the diagonal line thus giving a positive value. The measure is defined in the interval [-1,1], where -1 is obtained in the limit case of regressivity and +1 in the limit case of progressivity. This generalized LC is defined in accordance with the correlation curve of Blitz and Brittain [1964 - cf.sec. 7.2.3]. A similar method will be used in sec. 9.2. to decompose the Gini coefficient by income components.

Suits also discusses a measure of tax progressivity when two or more individual tax systems are considered simultaneously (cf. the decomposition by income components, sec. 9.2). For a discussion of 'Suits measure' see also Davies [1980], Kienzle [1980] and Suits [1980].

Some illustrating examples:

i) If the "minimum income" is $F_y^{-1}(0) = Y_0 > 0$, $Y \in [y_0, \infty[$ and we let the i.r.u.'s have an equal taxation, i.e. $F_z^{-1}(p) = c$, constant, and $c < y_0$, then the LC $L_z(p)$ equals the diagonal line and the LC of the net income, $L_x(p)$, will be located below the LC of the gross income, $L_y(p)$. Thus inequality increases, since

$$L_x(p) < L_y(p) < L_z(p) = p.$$

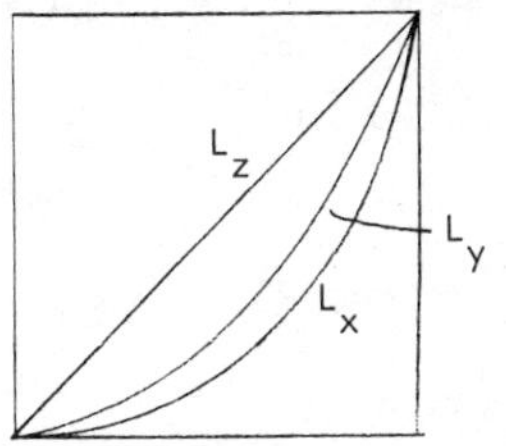

This can also be seen using tax elasticity, η_ρ, which in this case equals zero. By the footnote of (7.42) it follows that $L_z(p) > L_y(p)$. Since the elasticity of income after tax is greater than one it also follows immediately that tax $L_x(p) < L_y(p)$.

ii) By a proportional tax, i.e.

$F_z^{-1}(p) = \beta F_y^{-1}(p)$, $0 < \beta < 1$,

the three LC's coincide.

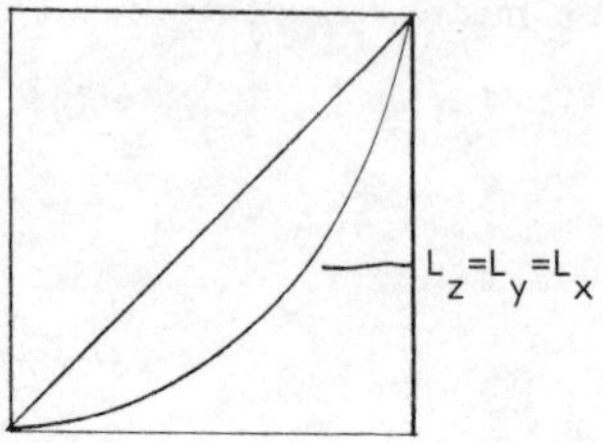

Inequality is unchanged,

since $L_z(p) = L_y(p) = L_z(p)$. Since the tax elasticity $\eta_\rho = 1$ it follows by the footnote of (7.43) that $L_z(p) = L_y(p)$ and thus the identity follows immediately. (The same result is also obtained by the fact that the elasticity of income after tax equals one, i.e. $a[F_y^{-1}(p)] = 1$).

iii) An example of a regressive tax function, cf. Piesch [1975 - p. 70], is

$$F_z^{-1}(p) = \rho[F_y^{-1}(p)] = F_y^{-1}(p) - \frac{F_y^{-1}(1)}{2\lambda}\left[\frac{F_y^{-1}(p)}{F_y^{-1}(1)}\right]^\lambda \quad \lambda > 1^{1)},$$

where λ is a constant, and using the inequality (7.25) of the generalized LC's (sec.7.2.3), we obtain the relation $L_x(p) < L_y(p)$, between the gross income and the net income.

1) A necessary condition for the tax elasticity to be less than one is that $\lambda > 1$ (not equal to one as in Piesch [1975- p. 70]).

From the statement above it follows that

$$L_x(p) < L_y(p) < L_z(p)$$

and thus inequality is increased.

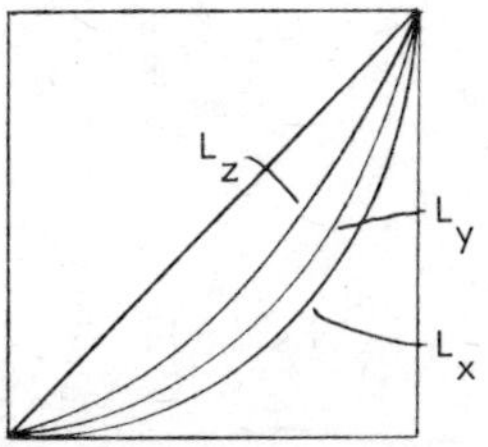

When the tax elasticity is less than one and the elasticity of income is greater than one, then the result is established through elasticities. Since $\eta_\rho > 0$ it follows by (7.44) that $L_z(p) < p$.

iv) A progressive tax function, i.e. $F_z^{-1}(p) = \frac{F_y^{-1}(1)}{2\lambda}\left[\frac{F_y^{-1}(p)}{F_y^{-1}(1)}\right]^\lambda \quad \lambda > 1$[1],

where λ is a constant, will decrease income inequality. The illustrated tax function above (cf. Piesch [1975 - p.70]) will by using the generalized LC's in sec.7.2.3, as above, give the relation $L_z(p) < L_y(p)$ and thus

$$L_z(p) < L_y(p) < L_x(p),$$

i.e. inequality is decreased.

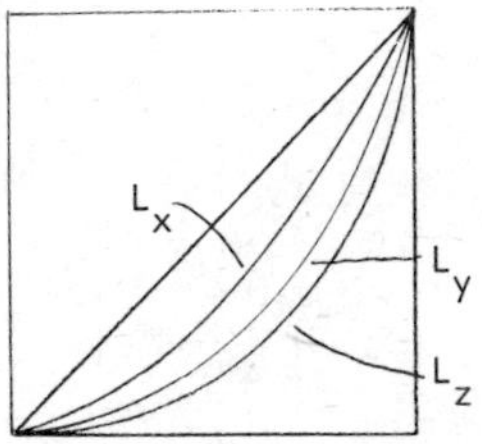

The tax elasticity (7.43) is $\eta_\rho[F_y^{-1}(p)] = \lambda > 1$ and by the criterion of Kakwani it implies that $L_z(p) < L_y(p)$ and thus the result above is established. The elasticity of income after tax is less than one (cf. iii) above).

1) A necessary condition for the elasticity of income after tax to be less than one is that λ is greater than one (not equal to one as in Piesch [1975 - p.70]).

7.3. THE DISTRIBUTION COMPARATIVE FUNCTION

7.3.1 DEFINITION

In section 7.1.4 we defined the complementary c.d.f. and the complementary 1st m.d.f. as

$$G(y) = 1 - F(y) \qquad \text{and} \qquad G_1(y) = 1 - F_1(y)$$

(see figures 7.2 and 7.12(a)).

For a fixed p', $0 \leq p' = 1 - p < 1$, where p is associated with the c.d.f. and the 1st m.d.f. we also defined the *distribution comparative function* as (cf. (7.18c))

$$D(p') = D(p) = \mu[\tau(q) - \tau(p)] = \mu\{L'(q) - L'(p)\} =$$

$$= F^{-1}(q) - F^{-1}(p) = F_1^{-1}(p) - F^{-1}(p) = G_1^{-1}(p')-G^{-1}(p'), \quad (7.48)$$

where $q > p$ is chosen so that $F^{-1}(q) = F_1^{-1}(p)$.
The distribution comparative function $D(p') = D(p)$ is non-negative and depicted in figure 7.12(b). Since the area $I(y)$ under $D(p') = D(p)$, $p' = 1 - p$, is zero for the EGAL distribution and growing as the distribution tends to a "more unequal distribution" (growing to infinity in the limit) it, or its standardized equivalent, could be used as a measure of inequality.

Frequently the y-scale for measuring income is changed to a logarithmic scale (base e and $y \geq 1$) to reduce the effect of high incomes, cf. e.g. Malmquist [1970]. The distribution comparative function in logy-scale could be written as

$$D_{\log}(p') = D_{\log}(p) = \log F_1^{-1}(p) - \log F^{-1}(p) = \log \{\frac{F_1^{-1}(p)}{F^{-1}(p)}\} \qquad (7.49)$$

Figure 7.12 Description of G(y) and $G_1(y)$ of an income distribution and its distribution comparative function $D(p') = D(p)$.

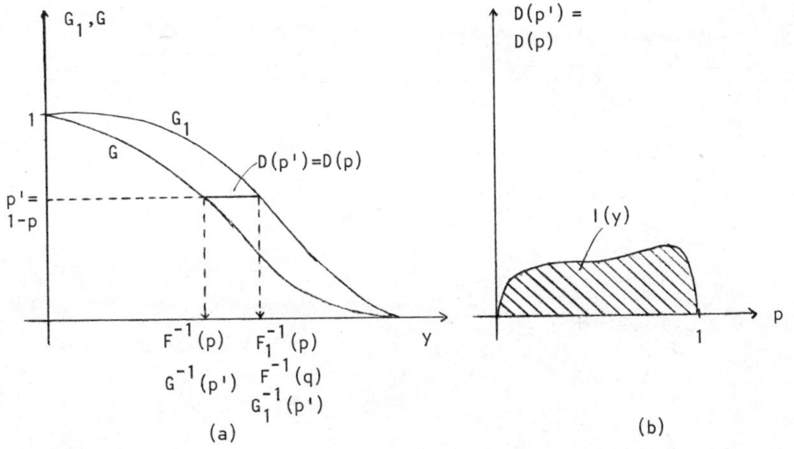

The measures of inequality, according to the discussion above, would be, cf. sec. 1.2,

(i) y-scale: $I(y) = V^2$ (7.50a)

where V is the coefficient of variation,

and

$$\text{(ii) log y-scale: } I_{\log}(y) = \log \frac{\mu_{gw}}{\mu_g} = \log \frac{\mu_{gw}}{\mu_g} + \log \frac{\mu}{\mu_g} = T_1 + T_2, \quad (7.50b)$$

where T_1 and T_2 are the measures proposed by Theil [1967] cf.sec.7.4.1.(see also sec. 1.2).

7.3.2 DECOMPOSITION BY THE EGAL DISTRIBUTION

$D(p') = D(p)$ can be decomposed into the difference of two functions,

$$D(p') = E_1(p') - E(p'), \tag{7.51}$$

describing the departure from the EGAL distribution, i.e. the distance between the incomes (log-incomes) and μ ($\log\mu$[1]).

$E_1(p')$ and $E(p')$ of (7.51) are defined by

(i) y-scale:

$$E_1(p') = F_1^{-1}(p) - \mu = \mu[\tau(q) - 1] \qquad q > p \tag{7.52a}$$

$$E(p') = F^{-1}(p) - \mu = \mu[\tau(p) - 1] \tag{7.52b}$$

and

(ii) log y-scale:

$$E_1(p') = \log F_1^{-1}(p) - \log\mu = \log\tau(q) \qquad q > p \tag{7.53a}$$

$$E(p') = \log F^{-1}(p) - \log\mu = \log\tau(p), \tag{7.53b}$$

where q is defined as in (7.48). Using the y-scale and integrating $E_1(p')$ and $E(p')$ shows that the measure $1(y) = \int_0^1 D(p')dp' = \int_0^1 E_1(p')dp'$, since the integral of $E(p)$ vanishes.

[1] By the EGAL distribution is $\mu = \mu_g$.

In the case of log y-scale the integral of $E_1(p')$, as regards dp' of the 1st m.d.f., equals $T_1 = \log \frac{\mu_{gw}}{\mu}$ and the integral of $E(p')$, as regards dp' of the c.d.f., equals $T_2 = \log \frac{\mu}{\mu_g}$ [1)].

Figure 7.13 Illustration of the function $E_1(p')$ in the y-scale.

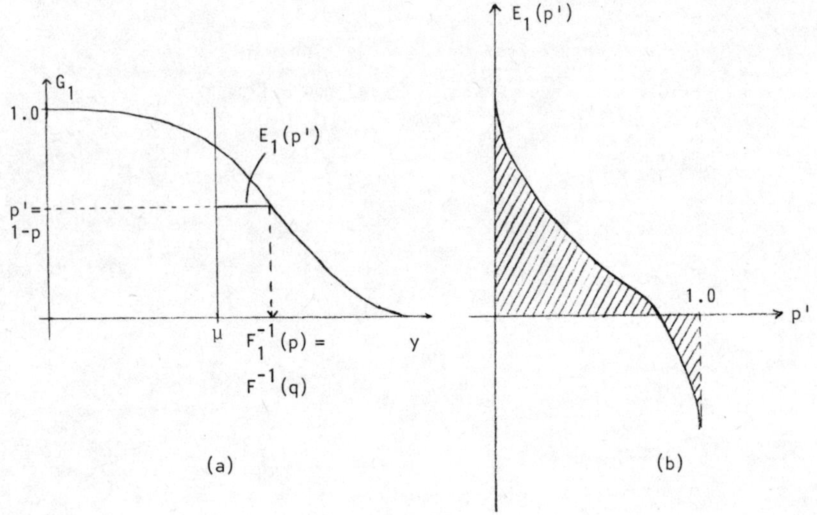

1) Using $\log \mu_g$ as reference will yield the same result as in the y-scale case with respect to the integration.

Since

$$\frac{dE_1(p')}{dp_1'} < \frac{dE(p')}{dp'} < 0 \qquad \text{for } F^{-1}(p) < \mu$$

and

$$\frac{dE(p')}{dp'} < \frac{dE_1(p')}{dp_1'} < 0 \qquad \text{for } \mu < F^{-1}(p),$$

with equality between $\frac{dE_1(p')}{dp_1'}$ and $\frac{dE(p')}{dp'}$ for $\mu = F^{-1}(p)$, and $p' = 1 - F(y)$, $p_1' = 1 - F_1(y)$, the function $E_1(p')$ is more sensitive to "low" incomes ($< \mu$) then $E(p')$ and vice versa for "high" incomes ($> \mu$). These results hold for both the scale cases but the log y-scale case will press more upon the "low" incomes and the y-scale more on the "high" incomes.

This points out $E_1(p')$ as a possible tool (at least graphical) for analyzing the income inequality when our concern are the lower-income groups.

Both the functions $E_1(p')$ and $E(p')$ consist of the difference between the standardized income ($= \tau(\cdot)$) of the income distribution in consideration and the standardized income ($= 1$) of the EGAL distribution. Giving weights to the differences (depending on $p' = 1 - p$) and integrating over p' we obtain the following measures of inequality (dropping the prim's and letting $w(p)$ be a function of $p = F(y)$):

(i) y-scale: $$I(y)_1 = \int_0^1 w(p)E_1(p)dp_1 =$$

$$= \mu \int_0^1 w(q)[\tau(q)-1]dF_1[F^{-1}(q)] =$$

$$= \mu \int_0^1 w(p)\tau(p)[\tau(p)-1]dp \qquad (7.54\,a)$$

$$I(y)_2 = \int_0^1 w(p)E(P)dp =$$

$$= \mu \int_0^1 w(p)[\tau(p)-1]dp \qquad (7.54\,b)$$

(ii) log y-scale: $$I_{log}(y)_1 = \int_0^1 w(p)E_1(p)dp_1 =$$

$$= \int_0^1 w(p)\tau(p)\log\tau(p)dp \qquad (7.54\,c)$$

$$I_{log}(y)_2 = \int_0^1 w(p)E(p)dp =$$

$$= \int_0^1 w(p)\log\tau(p)dp \qquad (7.54\,d)$$

The measure $I(y)_2$ of (7.54b) is an *absolute*-invariant (AI-) *measure*, i.e. a measure that is invariant under a constant addition to incomes (cf. ch. 4) and the measures $I_{log}(y)_1$ and $I_{log}(y)_2$ of (7.54c and d) are *relative*-invariant (RI-) *measures*, i.e. measures that are invariant under a proportional addition to incomes (homogeneous of degree zero), cf. ch. 4.

$I(y)_1$ will be a non-invariant (NI-) measure (cf. e.g. sec. 7.4 below) since it will be neither invariant to constant nor proportional addition to incomes.

Dividing the absolute measure $I^a(y)_2$ (a for absolute) with the arithmetic mean μ we obtain a relative measure denoted by $I^r(y)_2$, i.e.

$$I^r(y) = \mu^{-1} I^a(y)_2.$$

Measures of these types are special cases of the general family of measures discussed in sec. 7.4.

The above discussion of using a distribution comparative function in inequality judgement will be extended in ch. 12 to the case of comparison of two distributions simultaneously.

7.4 GENERAL DEFINITION OF MEASURES AND CLASSES OF MEASURES

There are several approaches to the definition of a general measure of inequality (or equality) in incomes. One way is to join the social welfare approach and base the measure on a well-defined social welfare function (SWF) or a class of SWF's. (Cf. ch. 6 and ch. 4). The axiomatic approach is another way of getting one or several measures: determine the criteria that an appropriate measure should fulfill and then find the possible functional form of the class of measures that could be used.

We will adopt neither of these approaches in this section. Instead *we will show that nearly all measures of inequality (and equality) that have been proposed in the literature are related to each other through a general definition* given below. The main purpose of this is to go over the most common measures and to see whether or not they fulfill the criteria given in ch. 4. The *relative-invariant (RI-) measures* are defined in accordance to the ordinary (or generalized) Lorenz-curve (LC-) diagram and the *absolute-invariant (AI-) measures* to an LC-diagram where the axes are not normalized to the [0,1]-interval[1]. The *compromise inequality (CI-) measures* [2] (or equality measures) are pairs of RI- and AI-measures that are simply interlinked to each other through $\mu RI = AI$ or $AI/\mu = RI$, where RI and AI are the same measure defined in relative and absolute terms, respectively (see the definition below)[3]. *Non-invariant (NI-) measures* are measures having neither the RI-property nor the AI-property.

1) Cf. fig. 4.2.

2) The name compromise is suggested by Blackorby and Donaldson [1980], cf. also Kolm [1976b].

3) μ is the arithmetic mean income but could be substituted by some other "characteristic" income.

By a slight generalization of the definition of an inequality measure given by Bartels [1977 - p. 12] so that it also includes equality measures we receive our first step towards the general definition of an inequality (equality) measure. By partial integration we then have a special case of the general one. In connection with the general definition we will discuss which conditions have to be imposed on the measures (or their weight functions) for the criteria in ch. 4 to hold. The discussion is summarized on pp. 234-236.

Sec. 7.4.1 is devoted to slope difference (SD) measures, sec 7.4.2 to log slope difference (LSD) measures, sec. 7.4.3 to exponential slope difference (ESD) measures. Some other measures are discussed in sec. 7.4.4. The meanings of SD, LSD and ESD are given below.

Inequality and equality measures are determined by the choice of a reference distribution: inequality measures by using a reference distribution as those discussed in ch. 1, especially the EGAL-distribution (cf. criterion EGAL of sec. 4.2) and equality measures by using a non-egality distribution, especially the CON-distribution (cf. criterion CON of sec. 4.2), see the introduction to this chapter. Determining the equality measure for the EGAL-distribution and subtracting the equality measure for the distribution in question gives us a corresponding inequality measure.

The definition of an inequality (equality) measure proposed by Bartels [1977 - p. 12], cf. the introduction to this chapter, could be written in terms of a Lorenz diagram as

$$I = \int_0^1 V(p)[L_r(p) - L(p)]dp, \qquad (7.55)$$

where the difference between the LC of the reference distribution, $L_r(p)$, and LC $L(p)$ of the actual distribution is weighted with a differentiable preference function $V(p)$.

Letting the reference distribution be the EGAL i.e. $L_r(p) = p$, we have an inequality measure, viz.

$$I = \int_0^1 V(p)[p - L(p)]dp, \qquad (7.56)$$

i.e. a weighted area between the LC and the diagonal line[1], cf. Mehran [1976].

Some inequality measures, using the definition (7.56), are given in table 7.4 with their monotone preference functions which are also depicted in figure 7.14a.

The LC's $L(p)$ and $L_r(p)$ in (7.55) are assumed to be continuously differentiable in p and convex to p. The derivatives of $L(p)$ and $L_r(p)$ with respect to p are written as $\tau(p) = F^{-1}(p)/\mu = dL(p)/dp \geq 0$ and $\tau_r(p) = dL_r(p)/dp \geq 0$, cf. definition 7.3. Instead of defining the measure of inequality (equality) in terms of a "weighted Lorenz area" we could define it in terms of weighted differences between the slopes of the tangents of the actual income distribution $\tau(p)$, and the slopes of the tangents of the reference distribution, $\tau_r(p)$, i.e. in terms of weighted differences between relative incomes.

Let a weight function $W(p)$ be continuously differentiable with $dW(p) = V(p)dp$. By partial integration of (7.55) we then have[2]

$$I = \int_0^1 V(p)[L_r(p) - L(p)]dp = \int_0^1 W(p)[\tau(p) - \tau_r(p)]dp \qquad (7.57)$$

i.e. a measure of inequality (equality) in terms of "relative incomes"[3].
Various weight functions are depicted in figure 7.14b, cf. also table 7.4.

1) Amato's [1948] dispersion measure is $C=\int_0^1 V^*(p)u(p)dp=\int_0^1 V^*(p)(\frac{1-p}{p})v(p)dp = \int_0^1 V(p)(p-L(p))dp$, where $u(p)=(\mu-\mu_L(p))/\mu$ and $v(p)=(\mu_U(p)-\mu)/\mu$, $\mu_L(p)$ and $\mu_U(p)$ are defined by (7.9) and (7.10), resp.

2) A necessary condition for this is that $\{W(p)[p-L(p)]\}_0^1 = 0$.

3) Cf. Schutz [1951] and Rosenbluth[1951].

Letting W(p) be independent of proportional addition to incomes, we obtain a set of RI-measures. If the reference distribution is the EGAL, i.e. $L_r(p) = p$ and $\tau_r(p) = 1$, we have the special case of an inequality measure proposed by Giaccardi [1950][1], viz.

$$I = \int_0^1 W(p)[\tau(p) - 1]dp \tag{7.58}$$

Giaccardi discussed both monotone decreasing and increasing weight functions W(p), as those defining the Gini coefficient (twice the Lorenzarea), and the measures proposed by Bonferroni and De Vergottini (cf. table 7.4). The same definition (7.58) is also given by Piesch [1975- pp.130] and Mehran [1976][2] and will be a special case of our general definition given below.

In the case of (7.58) we could transform the weight function W(p) into a constraint function, C(p).

$$C(p) = W(p) - \int_0^1 W(p)dp, \tag{7.59a}$$

with $\int_0^1 C(p)dp = 0$. (7.58) will by this definition (cf. also Giaccardi [1950], Piesch [1975] and Mehran [1976]) be written as

$$I = \int_0^1 C(p)\tau(p)dp. \tag{7.59b}$$

See table 7.4 for some measures with various C(p) and figure 7.15c for these constraint functions depicted. The constraint definition of an inequality measure is not in accordance with our general definition and we will only discuss it occasionally and rather impose that a weight function W(p) should <u>not</u> be a constraint function.

1) Giaccardi defined his class of measures in the discrete case. He also discussed criteria to be imposed on inequality measures.

2) Mehran only requires W(p) to be nondecreasing.

Figure 7.14 (a) Some preference functions (cf. (7.56)) given in relation to the Lorenz area. The preference functions give weights to the Lorenz area.

(c) Some constraint functions (cf. (7.59b)) given in relation to the Lorenz Curve. The constraint functions give weights to relative incomes (i.e. the slope of the tangent to the Lorenz Curve).

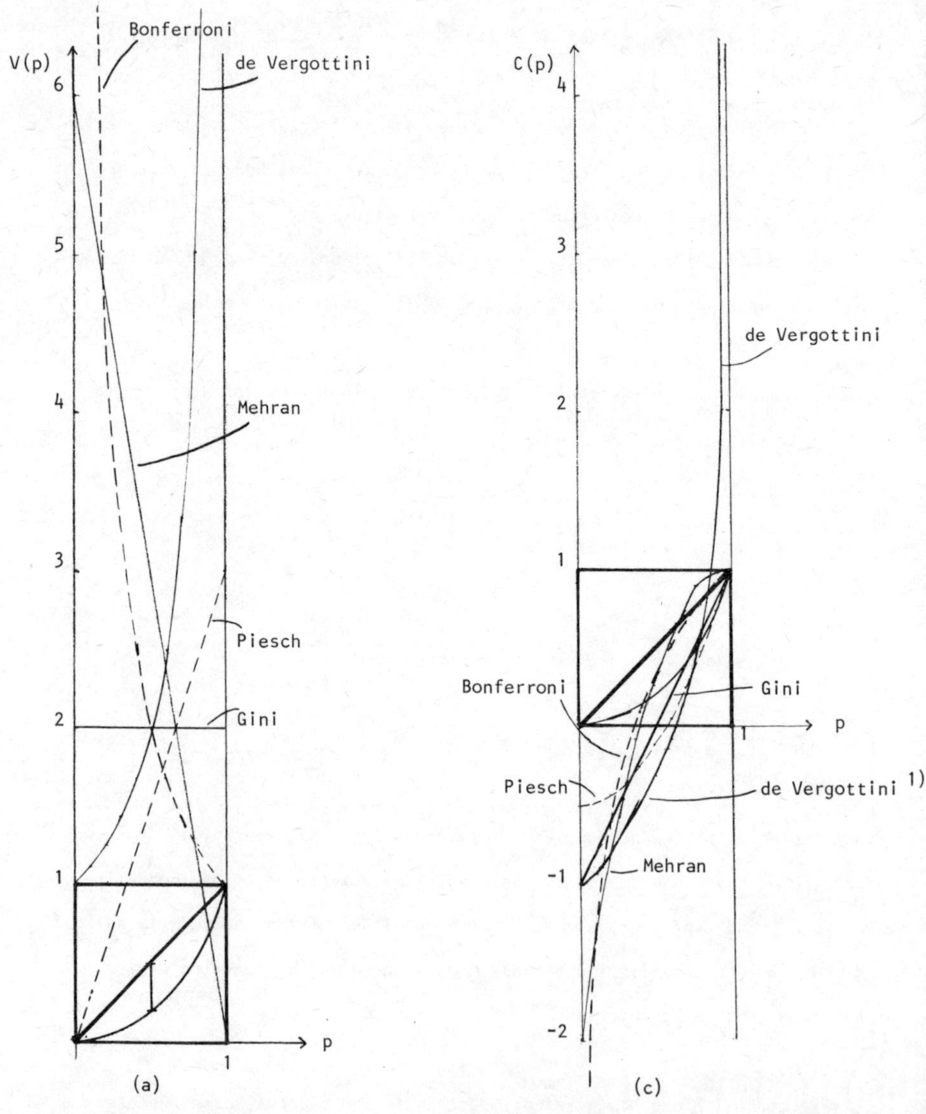

1) See table 7.4 for sufficient condition on L(p)

Figure 7.14, cont. (b) Some weight functions (cf. (7.59)) given in relation to (i) the Lorenz Curve and (ii) the difference between relative incomes (the slope, $\tau(p)$, of the tangent of the Lorenz Curve and the slope of the egalitarian line, $\tau_r(p) = 1$).

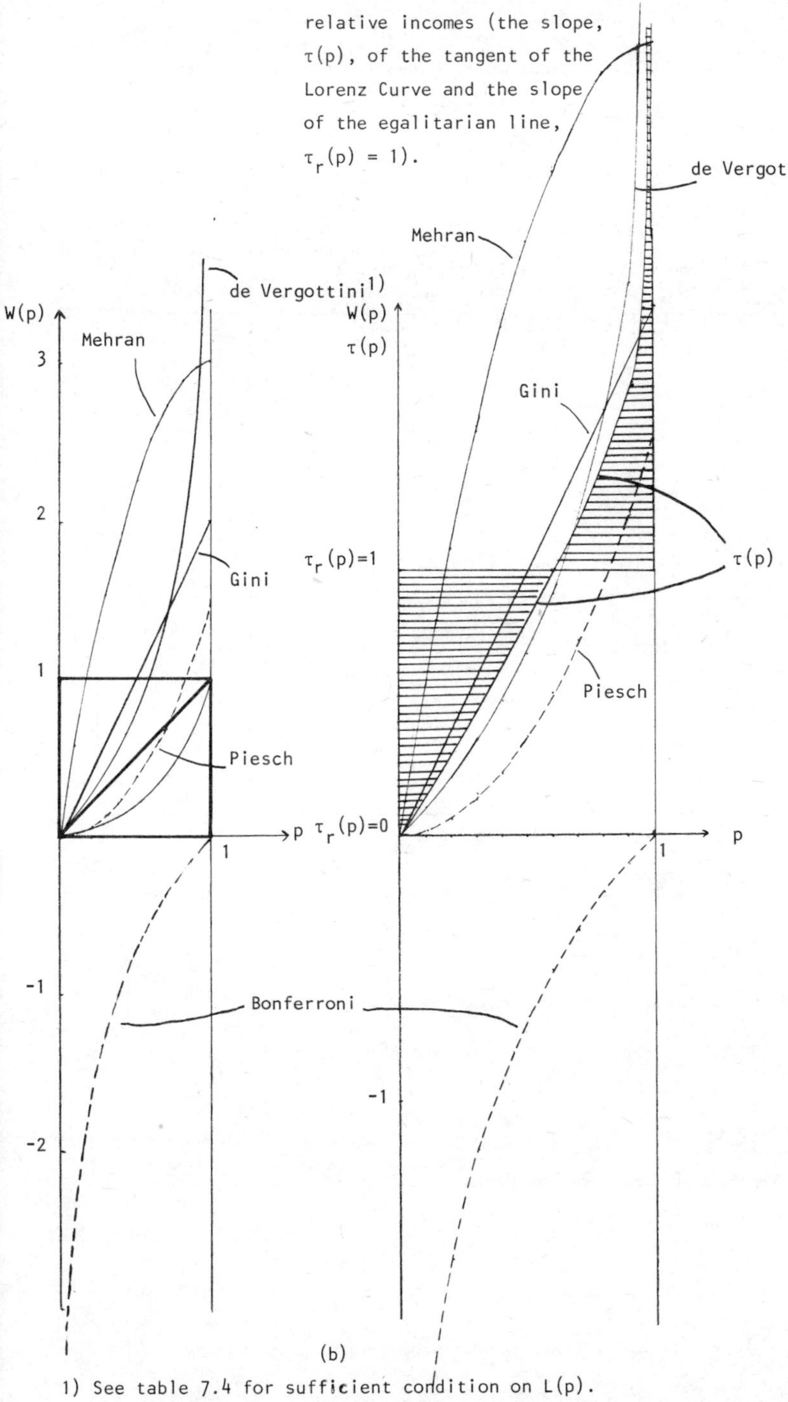

(b)

1) See table 7.4 for sufficient condition on L(p).

Table 7.4 Some inequality measures and their preference, weight and constraint functions. The inequality measures are defined by $I = \int_0^1 V(p)[p - L(p)]dp = \int_0^1 W(p)[\tau(p) - 1]dp = \int_0^1 C(p)\tau(p)dp.$

Measure	Preference function $V(p)=W'(p)$	Weight function $W(p)$	Constraint function $C(p)$	$W''(p)=V'(p)$
Gini	$2 > 0$	$2p$	$2p - 1$	0
Mehran	$6(1-p) > 0$	$3p(2-p)$	$1 - 3[1-p]^2$	$-6 < 0$
Piesch	$3p > 0$	$\frac{3}{2} p^2$	$\frac{1}{2}(3p^2-1)$	$3 > 0$
Bonferroni	$\frac{1}{p} > 0$	$\log p$	$\log p + 1$	$-\frac{1}{p^2} < 0$
De Vergottini	$\frac{1}{1-p} > 0$	$\log \frac{1}{1-p}$ 1)	$\log \frac{1}{1-p} - 1$ 1)	$\frac{1}{(1-p)^2} > 0$

Gastwirth [1975] considered a general measure of dispersion defined by $\int_0^1 \{h[F^{-1}(p)] - h(\mu)\}dp$, where $h[F^{-1}(p)]$ is a convex function with $h(o) = 0$.

A class of RI-measures is defined by

$$\int_0^1 \{\frac{h[F^{-1}(p)] - h(\mu)}{h(\mu)}\} dp$$

The same class of measures, assuming concavity in h, was also discusses by, e.g. Aigner and Heins [1967], Atkinson [1970] and Bentzel [1970] in the framework of utility.

1) A sufficient condition on $L(p)$ for $W(p)(p-L(p)) \to 0$ is that $L(p) = p + o\{1/\log(\frac{1}{1-p})\}$ when $p \to 1$.

The general definition of an inequality (equality) measure

The definition of an inequality (equality) measure proposed by (7.57) is now generalized. Instead of considering a weighted slope difference, $\tau(p) - \tau_r(p)$, we will consider a weighted difference function of power η and give the index power η. Moreover we will consider generalized reference functions $L_r(p)$ and $\tau_r(p) = L_r'(p)$ which need not come from a distribution. Hence $\tau_r(p)$ is not restricted to be positive.

Definition 7.5 A general measure of inequality (equality) is given by

$$I(Y;j,\eta) = \{\int_0^1 W(p) \cdot D[c\tau_j(p),\ c\tau_r(p)]^\eta dp\}^{1/\eta},\ \eta \neq 0 \tag{7.60a}$$

$$\text{Log } I(Y;j,0) = \omega(1)^{-1} \int_0^1 W(p) \text{ Log } D[c\tau_j(p); c\tau_r(p)]dp,\ \eta = 0 \tag{7.60b}$$

$$\text{with } \omega(1) = \int_0^1 W(p)dp \neq 0$$

c is a quantity that can distinguish <u>some</u> measures into RI- and AI-measures and $\tau_j(p)$ is the slope of the tangent to the generalized LC $L_j(p), j=1,2,\ldots,$ of (7.24).

The measures are usually defined in terms of the ordinary LC, i.e. with j=1, and we write $I(Y;1,\eta) = I(Y;\eta)$ and $\text{Log } I(Y;1,0) = \text{Log } I(Y;0)$, respectively. The quantity c can distinguish relative (RI-) and absolute (AI-) measures. In some cases the measures will be non-invariant (NI), independent of c. If $c = \pm 1$ we usually have RI-measures and if $c = \pm\mu$ usually AI-measures. The negative sign is only discussed in connection with the ESD-class below.

Three classes of difference functions will divide the general measure into three subclasses (j = 1):

1. THE SLOPE DIFFERENCE CLASS (the SD-class)

$$D[c\tau(p),\ c\tau_r(p)] = c[\tau(p) - \tau_r(p)] \qquad (7.61a)$$

2. THE LOG-SLOPE DIFFERENCE CLASS (the LSD-class):

$$D[c\tau(p),\ c\tau_r(p)] = \text{Log}\ \ \tau(p) - \text{Log}\ \ \tau_r(p) \qquad (7.61b)$$

3. THE EXPONENTIAL-SLOPE DIFFERENCE CLASS (the ESD-class):

$$D[c\tau(p),\ c\tau_r(p)] = e^{c[\tau(p)-\tau_r(p)]} \qquad (7.61c)$$

The weight function, W(p), is assumed to be independent of proportional addition to incomes and to be a non-constraint function, i.e. $\omega(1) = \int_0^1 W(p)dp \neq 0$. In some cases $\omega(1)$ is assumed to be positive. As mentioned before we assume W(p) to be continuously differentiable.
$L_r(p)$ is now assumed to be a reference function which need not come from a distribution.Hence $\tau_r(p) = L_r'(p)$ is not restricted to be positive.

Measures of inequality (or equality) that we are concerned with are in the form of (7.60) or some simple transformation such as

$$\text{Log I} \quad \text{and} \quad e^{I}$$

The main division of the measures into the three subclasses and according to inequality vs equality and RI-measures vs AI-measures is given in the measure schedule below. The domain of the power η, discussed in the following, and frequently used values of c are given within the cells together with the difference function according to the class definition. In the table we have only considered the EGAL case of $\tau_r(p) = 1, 0 \leq p \leq 1$ and the case of $\tau_r(p) = \beta, 0 \leq p < 1$ and $\beta \leq 0$ except in the LSD-class where $0 < \beta < 1$. $\beta = 0$ corresponds to the CON distribution

SUBCLASSES	INEQUALITY, $\tau_r(p) = 1$	EQUALITY, $\tau_r(p) = \beta$
the SD-class	$D(\cdot,\cdot) = c(\tau(p) - 1)$ $\eta \geq 1$, integer $c = 1 \Rightarrow$ RI-measures $c = \mu \Rightarrow$ AI-measures	$D(\cdot,\cdot) = c(\tau(p) - \beta), \beta \leq 0$ $\eta < 1$ NI-measures if $\beta = 0 \Rightarrow$ $c = 1 \Rightarrow$ RI-measures $c = \mu \Rightarrow$ AI-measures $\eta = 0 \Rightarrow W(p) \neq \alpha\tau(p)^q, \alpha > 0$ $q \geq 1$
the LSD-class	$D(\cdot,\cdot) = \log\tau(p)$ $\eta \geq 1$, integer[1)] independent of c Restriction of RI[2)]: if $\eta \geq 1$, odd $\Rightarrow$ $W(p) = \alpha\tau(p)^q$, $\alpha > 0, q \geq 1$	$D(\cdot,\cdot) = \log\tau(p) - \log\beta$, $0 < \beta < 1$ $\eta = 1$
the ESD-class	$D(\cdot,\cdot) = e^{c\{\tau(p) - 1\}}$ $\eta \geq 0$ $c = \pm 1 \Rightarrow$ RI-measures $c = \pm\mu \Rightarrow$ AI-measures	$D(\cdot,\cdot) = e^{c\{\tau(p) - \beta\}}$ $\beta < 0$. if $\beta = 0$ and $\eta \leq 0$: $c = \pm 1 \Rightarrow$ RI-measures $c = \pm \mu \Rightarrow$ AI-measures

1) If $\eta < 0$ we have inequality measures when $W(p)$ is not equal to a general function of $\tau(p)$ and $W(1) < \infty$. In the sequel we only consider the case when $\eta \geq 1$ and integer, since measures proposed in the literature have this property

2) In general if $W(p) = U(\tau(p))$ the following should hold: $\lim_{x\to 0} U(x)[\log x]^\eta = 0$ and $\lim_{x\to 0} U(\frac{1}{x})x[\log \frac{1}{x}]^\eta > 0$ or $\lim_{x\to 0} U(x)[\log x]^\eta > 0$ and $\lim_{x\to 0} U(\frac{1}{x})x[\log \frac{1}{x}]^\eta = 0$. In the sequel we only consider $U(\tau(p)) = \alpha\tau(p)^q$, $\alpha > 0$ and $q \geq 1$ which yields

$$\lim_{x\to 0} \alpha x^q[\log x]^\eta = 0 \text{ and } \lim_{x\to 0} \alpha x^{-q+1}[\log \frac{1}{x}]^\eta = \infty.$$

Since the scope of this book is concerned with inequality we have to transform the equality measures to obtain what we desire. The main features are as follow: Calculate the value of the equality measure for the EGAL distribution, i.e. let $\tau_r(p) = 1$, $0 \leq p \leq 1$. Take this value (or some simple transformation) and subtract the equality measure (or some simple transformation). The measure obtained by this procedure is an inequality measure. To distinguish inequality and equality measures we denote them I_I and I_E, respectively.
The choice of a prospective transformation is discussed in connection with the discussion of lower and upper bounds of the measures.

Upper and lower bounds for I_I

A desired property of an inequality measure is that it should equal zero when the distribution equals the EGAL (cf. criteria EGAL of sec. 4.2 and MININ of sec. 4.4) and that it should be greater that zero for a distribution deviating from the EGAL. Another property is that it should not be greater than one (criterion MAXNORM of sec. 4.8), where on is obtained when we have the CON distribution, i.e. one i.r.u. receives all incomes and the others zero income[1].

The two criteria tell us that $0 \leq I_I \leq 1$, where I_I is an inequality measure, is a desired property[1]. To see whether this is attained or not we make the following definitions of the two reference distributions:

1) For the RI-measures. In the case of AI-measures the equivalent property is that the upper bound should be μ, the arithmetic mean.

(i) the EGAL distribution:

$$\tau(p) = 1, \; 0 \leq p \leq 1 \tag{7.63}$$

(ii) the CON distribution:

a small proportion of "the population", dp, receives some income $T < \infty$, and

$$\tau(p) = \begin{cases} 0 & 0 \leq p \leq 1-dp \\ 1/dp & 1-dp < p \leq 1. \end{cases} \tag{7.64}$$

The upper bound of I_I is obtained when we let dp tend to zero. In some cases we allow $\tau(p) = \varepsilon$ for $0 \leq p \leq 1-dp$ and take the limit of I_I when $\varepsilon \to 0$,

Using these definitions, the restriction on the weight function W(p) that it is not a constraint function, i.e. $\omega(1) = \int_0^1 W(p)dp \neq 0$, and the desired properties of the inequality measures (to equal zero for the EGAL distribution and to be greater than zero for a non-EGAL distribution) we obtain the various domains of the power η, cf. the last table.

In table 7.5 we have put the lower and upper bounds together within brackets for the three subclasses of measures. We have also entered suitable transformations.

In all cases, except the original defined inequality measures of the SD-class, we impose that $\omega(1) = \int_0^1 W(p)dp > 0$; in the SD-class of original I_I only $\omega(1) \neq 0$. If $W(p) = k > 0$ in the ESD-class the upper bounds of these measures vanish when $\eta = 0$. Further, if we define W(p) so that $\omega(1) = 1$ it follows that the inequality measures are special cases of the SD-measures. However

Table 7.5 Lower and upper bounds of the measures of inequality.

SUB-CLASSES	INEQUALITY MEASURES, I_I $\tau_r(p) = 1$	INEQUALITY MEASURES FROM TRANSFORMED EQUALITY MEASURES, (I_E) $\tau_r(p) \leq 0$ in LSD: $0 < \tau_r(p) < 1$
the SD-class	$I_I = c\{\int_0^1 W(p)[\tau(p)-1]^\eta dp\}^{1/\eta}$, $\eta \geq 1$ <u>η=1</u>: $[0, c[W(1)-\omega(1)]]$ <u>η≥2</u>: $[0,\infty[$	$\tau_r(p) = ($ $I_E = c\{\int_0^1 W(p)\tau(p)^\eta dp\}^{1/\eta}$, $\eta < 1$, $\eta \neq 0$ $\log I_E = \omega(1)^{-1} \int_0^1 W(p) \mathrm{Log}[c\tau(p)]dp$, $\eta = 0$ <u>η<1</u>: $I_I = c[\omega(1)]^{1/\eta} - I_E : [0, c(\omega(1))^{1/\eta}]$ <u>η=0</u>: (i) $I_I = \log c - \log : I_E$: $[0,\infty[$ (ii) $I_I = c - I_E$: $[0,c]$
the LSD-class	$I_I = \{\int_0^1 W(p)[\log \tau(p)]^\eta dp\}^{1/\eta}$, $\eta \geq 1$ <u>η=1,3,...</u> $\Rightarrow W(p) = \alpha\tau(p)^q$: $[0,\infty[$ $\alpha > 0$, $q \geq 1$ <u>η=2,4,...</u>: $[0,\infty[$	$\tau_r(p) = \beta$ $I_E = \int_0^1 W(p) \log \tau(p)\beta^{-1} dp$ $\eta = 1$, $0 < \beta < 1$ $I_I = \omega(1) \log \beta^{-1} - I_E$: $[0,\infty[$ Note: $W(p) \neq \alpha\tau(p)^q$, $\alpha > 0$, $q \geq 1$
the ESD-class	$I_I = \{\int_0^1 W(p) e^{c[\tau(p)-1]\eta} dp\}^{1/\eta}$, $\eta > 0$ $\log I_I = c\omega(1)^{-1} \int_0^1 W(p)[\tau(p)-1]dp$, $\eta = 0$ <u>η>0</u>: (i) $I_I : [\omega(1)^{1/\eta}, e^{-c}\omega(1)^{1/\eta}]$ (ii) $\log I_I$: $c = -1, -\mu : [\log \omega(1)^{1/\eta}, -c + \log \omega(1)^{1/\eta}]$ $c = 1, \mu : [\log \omega(1)^{1/\eta}, \infty[$ <u>η=0</u>: $[0, c(W(1)\omega(1)^{-1}-1)]$ special case of the SD-class	$\tau_r(p) = 0$ $I_E = \{\int_0^1 W(p) e^{c\tau(p)\eta} dp\}^{1/\eta}$, $\eta < 0$ $\log I_E = c\omega(1)^{-1} \int_0^1 W(p)\tau(p)dp$, $\eta = 0$ <u>η<0</u>: (i) $I_I = e^c\omega(1)^{1/\eta} - I_E$ (ii) $I_I = c + \log\omega(1)^{1/\eta} - \log I_E$ $c = -1, -\mu$: (i) $[0, e^c\omega(1)^{1/\eta}]$ (ii) $[0,\infty[$ $c = 1, \mu$: (i) $[0, (e^c-1)\omega(1)^{1/\eta}]$ (ii) $[0,c]$ <u>η=0</u>: (i) $I_I = c - \log I_E : [0, c(1-W(1)\omega(1)^{-1}$ (ii) $I_I = e^c - I_E : [0, e^c - e^{c[W(1)\omega(1)^{-1}]}]$

the measures I_E and $\log I_E$ of the ESD-class with $\eta = 0$ are not equality measures, in the sense we use, when $\omega(1) = 1$. We will therefore omit these cases in the sequel.

The quantity c is restricted to being positive in the SD and LSD-classes. If $\omega(1) = 1$ and $c < 0$ transformation (ii) of the inequality measures of the ESD-class will define the measures at the [0,c] interval, otherwise ($c > 0$) the measures will be defined at the $[0,\infty]$ interval. If $c > 0$ and we use transformation (ii) of the transformed equality measures they will also be defined at the [0,1]-interval ($c < 0 \Rightarrow I_I \in [0,\infty[$).

For the inequality measures given in table 7.4 the lower and upper bounds will equal, using table 7.5,

$$[0,\ W(1) - \omega(1)]$$

where $\omega(1) = \int_0^1 W(p)dp$.

The upper bound, $W(1) - \omega(1)$, equals by definition the value of the constraint function $C(p)$, cf. (7.59a), in $p = 1$. As can be verified, cf. also fig. 7.14 (c), all measures have the upper bound equal to one, except the measure of De Vergottini which equals infinity.

The discussion, so far, has been to obtain domains on the power η for our measures, and it has been based on the discussion, given in ch. 4, that the value of an inequality measure indicating the EGAL distribution (equal incomes) should be zero and that the value should be greater than zero when the income distribution deviates from the EGAL. According to the discussion in ch. 4, the maximum value of an inequality measure should be obtained when the CON distribution is at hand. According to the criterion RANGE it is desired that the value of a RI-measure is at the [0,1]-interval (AI-measures: $[0,\mu]$). The choice of a non-negative value can be disputed, but it is in line with our intrinsic feeling[1)] how a measure should be defined (cf. statistical dispersion measures). Now we shall turn our attention to the weight function W(p). As before we impose the condition of homogeneity of degree zero, i.e. independence of proportional addition/subtraction in incomes. In the SD-class of pure inequality measures we assume $\omega(1) = \int_0^1 W(p)dp \neq 0$ and in the other cases that $\omega(1) > 0$. This means that W(p) is not a constraint function. The weight function W(p) that we will consider here can be (i) a positive constant, (ii) a pure p-function (a function of relative ranks, i.e. of the c.d.f.) or (iii) a pure $\tau(p)$-function[2)] (a function of relative incomes).

What other conditions can be imposed on the weight function? If we look back at the criteria discussed in ch. 4 we see that one criterion that could be used is the TRANSF (i.e. the principle of transfer): from a fixed income distribution we take a certain amount from a poor i.r.u. and give it to some rich i.r.u. By such a non-egalitarian transfer (n.e.t.) the inequality should increase. We could use the theory of a mean preserving spread (cf. sec. 4.2) to examine this, but since we only seek conditions to impose on W(p) we do not need all this[3)]. Instead we will make a minimum definition of the TRANSF: we only assume an infinitesimal non-egalitarian transfer (INET) which does not change the relative ranks of the "givers" and the "receivers" (c.f. rank preserving transfer; Kakwani [1980b - p. 72]).

1) The choice can also rest on statements such as the following by Yntema [1933 - p. 424]: "... coefficients having a definite finite limits, 0 and 1 preferably, are desirable since such limits aid in attaching significance to the numerical value of a coeffient for any particular distribution."

2) The corresponding measure is labelled self-weighted by Piesch [1975-p.133].

3) If W(p) is a pure p-function and we use the theory of a mean preserving spread we will get into straits since the c.d.f. after the n.e.t. will depend on the relative positions of the "givers" and the "receivers" after the n.e.t and also the positions of the i.r.u.'s in between the "givers" before and after, and the "receivers" before and after.

By this definition (cf. Mehran [1976]) we seek what condition(s) we have to impose on W(p) in order to ensure that an INET will increase the value of the inequality measure. If the INET definition is somewhat strengthened we will get further conditions to be imposed on W(p).

Minimum definitions of principle of transfers

Definition 7.6: The principle of an infinitesimal non-egalitarian transfer (INET).

Consider an infinitesimal transfer $\lambda > 0$ from an infinitesimal part, dp, of the population at the p:th fractile of the distribution to i.r.u.'s at the (p+h)th fractile, $0 \leq p < p+h \leq 1$. Performing such a transfer and leaving other things the same, including the relative ranks of the "givers" and the "receivers", should increase inequality. This holds for every p and h. (Cf. criterion TRANSF of sec. 4.2).

To get conditions on W(p) we will proceed as follows: consider the difference between the measure after an INET and the measure before. This is the total INET-effect $T = T(\lambda,p,h)$, which by the definition 7.6 must be greater than zero, i.e. $T > 0$ and $\lim_{\lambda \to 0} T = 0$. The condition $T > 0$ implies an equivalent condition on the change in the measure taken without the η:th root. The limit $(\lambda/\mu \to 0)$ of this change divided by λ/μ gives us necessary and/or sufficient conditions to impose on W(p) for fulfillment of INET by the measure.

To simplify our discussion we recognize the fact that what we require is only "a minimum" definition of a TRANSF.

We discuss this procedure in the SD-class in some detail and then we proceed to discuss the other two classes more briefly. The reference slope for the inequality measures is set equal to one ($\tau_r(p)=1$) and for the equality measures equal to zero ($\tau_r(p)=0$), except for the LSD-class where $\tau_r(p)=\beta, 0<\beta<1$. In the SD- and ESD-classes $\beta > 0$ indicates inequality measures ($\beta \geq 1$ in the LSD-class) and $\beta \leq 0$ equality measures ($0<\beta<1$ in the LSD-class).

1. THE SD-CLASS

1a Inequality measures, $\eta \geq 1$, integer.

We write $cI^{1/\eta} = c\{\int_0^1 W(p)[\tau(p) - 1]^\eta dp\}^{1/\eta}$, where $c = 1, \mu$.

The total effect T of an INET can be written as

$$T = c\{I + dI\}^{1/\eta} - cI^{1/\eta} > 0 \tag{7.64}$$

where

$$\begin{aligned} dI &= \{W(p+h)[\tau(p+h)+ \frac{\lambda}{\mu} -1]^\eta - W(p+h)[\tau(p+h)-1]^\eta - W(p)[\tau(p)-1]^\eta + \\ &+ W(p)\ [\tau(p) - \frac{\lambda}{\mu} - 1]^\eta\ \}\ dp > 0, \end{aligned} \tag{7.65}$$

and the last inequality is equivalent to (7.64).

The implications of an INET are given by (7.65) and dividing it by λ/μ and letting $\lambda/\mu \to 0$ gives us useful conditions on W(p). Before doing this calculation we have to recognize the special cases of the weight function W(p) as mentioned before. If W(p) is a constant function or a function of relative ranks (i.e. a p-function) it will be independent of infinitesimal changes in λ (the INET definition is rank preserving) but if $W(p) = U(\tau(p))$ is a "self-weighted" function (cf. Piesch [1975-p.133] i.e. explicity dependent on $\tau(p)$, we have to take $U'_\tau(\tau(p))$ into consideration. Hence we have the following necessary and sufficient conditions for the fulfillment of INET:

(*i*) $W(p) = k > 0$, constant

$$\eta k dp \, \{[\tau(p+h)-1]^{\eta-1} - [\tau(p)-1]^{\eta-1}\} > 0 \qquad (7.66)$$

(*ii*) W(p) is a function of relative ranks

$$\eta dp \, \{W(p+h) \, [\tau(p+h)-1]^{\eta-1} - W(p)[\tau(p)-1]^{\eta-1}\} > 0 \qquad (7.67)$$

(*iii*) W(p) is a function of relative incomes

$$dp \, \{U'_\tau \, (\tau(p+h))[\tau(p+h)-1]^{\eta} + U(\tau(p+h))\eta[\tau(p+h)-1]^{\eta-1} - U'_\tau(\tau(p))[\tau(p)-1]^{\eta}$$
$$- U(\tau(p))\eta[\tau(p)-1]^{\eta-1}\} > 0 \qquad (7.68)$$

The measure with a constant weight function is always identical to zero when $\eta=1$. A necessary and sufficient condition (NSC) for the fulfillment of INET when the weight function is in terms of relative ranks and $\eta=1$ is given by (7.67). The condition is $W(p+h) - W(p) > 0$, i.e. a sufficient condition for this to hold is that $W'(p) > 0$. Some illustrative examples of this kind are given in table 7.4. The corresponding SC in case (*iii*) is given by (7.71) below with $\eta = 1$ and the inequality ($\geq$) changed for a strict inequality (>). The criterion is not in general fulfilled, cf. the discussion below.

If $\eta \geq 2$ the criterion is always fulfilled when the weight function is constant. Sufficient conditions (SC) for case (*ii*) are obtained by a simple rearrangement of (7.67):

$$\left[\frac{\tau(p+h)-1}{\tau(p)-1}\right]^{\eta-1} > \frac{W(p)}{W(p+h)} \tag{7.69}$$

Since $\tau(p)-1$ and $\tau(p+h)-1$ can be negative the right hand expression of (7.69) is always greater than one if $\eta \geq 3$ and odd or if $\eta \geq 2$ and even if $\tau(p)$ and $\tau(p+h)$ are both less (greater) than one. In other words, if $\eta \geq 3$ and odd, a SC for the fulfillment of INET is that $W'(p) > 0$. If $\eta \geq 2$ and even, a sufficient condition is that $W'(p) > 0$ and that the transfer procedure takes place on the same side of the arithmetic mean income.

The rearrangement, equivalent to (7.69), of (7.68) is

$$\left[\frac{\tau(p+h)-1}{\tau(p)-1}\right]^{\eta-1} > \frac{U'[\tau(p)]\,[\tau(p)-1] + \eta\, U(\tau(p))}{U'(\tau(p+h))\,[\tau(p+h)-1] + \eta U(\tau(p+h))} \tag{7.70}$$

The right hand expression of (7.70) is greater than one if, as above, $\eta \geq 3$ and odd or $\eta \geq 2$, even and the nominator and the denominator have the same sign. If this is fulfilled a SC for the fulfillment of INET is

$$U(\tau(p+h))\,[\tau(p+h)-1] - U'(\tau(p))\,[\tau(p)-1] \geq (-\eta)\{U(\tau(p+h) - U(\tau(p)\} \tag{7.71}$$

and if we let h tend towards zero we obtain

$$U''[\tau(p)]\,[\tau(p)-1] \geq -\,(\eta+1)U'(\tau(p))^{1)} \qquad (7.72)$$

which clearly shows the dependence of on which side of the arithmetic mean income the transfer procedure takes place. INET will not, of course, in general be fulfilled if the transfer takes place from $\tau(p) < 1$ to $\tau(p+h) > 1$. It will only occur if $U'' = 0$ and $U' > 0$, i.e. if $U(\tau(p)) = a+b\tau(p)$, $b > 0$.

1b. Inequality measures transformed from equality measures, $\eta < 1$.

1b.i $\eta = -a < 0$ $(a > 0)$.

We write $I_I = c\omega(1)^{1/\eta} - cI^{1/\eta}$, where $\omega(1) = \int_0^1 W(p)dp \geq 1$ and

$$I = \int_0^1 W(p)[\tau(p)]^\eta \, dp$$

The total effect T of an INET can be written as

$$T = c\omega(1)^{1/\eta} - c\{I + dI\}^{1/\eta} - c\omega(1)^{1/\eta} - cI^{1/\eta} > 0 \qquad (7.73)$$

where

$$dI = \{W(p+h)[\tau(p+h) + \tfrac{\lambda}{\mu}]^\eta - W(p+h)\,\tau(p+h)^\eta - W(p)\tau(p)^\eta + W(p)[\tau(p) - \tfrac{\lambda}{\mu}]^\eta\}\,dp > 0 \qquad (7.74)$$

and the last inequality follows from (7.73) and the fact that $\eta < 0$.

---

1) A necessary and sufficient condition if $\eta = 1$ ($\geq$ is then changed for $>$).

The implications of an INET is hence, as above, given by (7.74) when λ/μ tends towards zero.

In the case of a constant weight function the NSC (when $\lambda/\mu \to 0$, $\tau(p+h)^{a+1} > \tau(p)^{a+1}$, $a = -\eta$) is always fulfilled. The NSC for case *(ii)* is

$$[\frac{\tau(p+h)}{\tau(p)}]^{a+1} > \frac{W(p+h)}{W(p)}$$ and from this an SC is that $W'(p) < 0$.

The corresponding NSC in case *(iii)* is

$$[\frac{\tau(p+h)}{\tau(p)}]^{a} > \frac{aU(\tau(p+h))\tau(p+h)^{-1} - U'(\tau(p+h))}{aU(\tau(p))\tau(p)^{-1} - U'(\tau(p))} \qquad (7.75)$$

and a SC is

$$U'(\tau(p+h)) - U'(\tau(p)) > a\ \{\frac{U(\tau(p+h))}{\tau(p+h)} - \frac{U(\tau(p))}{\tau(p)}\}$$

which yields, when $\tau^*(h) = \tau(p+h) - \tau(p)$ tends towards zero

$$U''(\tau(p)) > a\ \{\frac{U'(\tau(p))}{\tau(p)} - \frac{U(\tau(p))}{\tau(p)^2}\} \qquad (7.76)$$

The last inequality holds if, e.g. $U > 0$, $U' < 0$ and $U'' \geq 0$.

1b.ii $0 < \eta < 1$

INET is always fulfilled when $W(p)$ is a positive constant, and when $W(p)$ is a function of relative ranks an SC is that $W'(p) < 0$. The NSC, corresponding to (7.75) is

$$\left[\frac{\tau(p+h)}{\tau(p)}\right]^{\eta} > \frac{\eta\ U(\tau(p+h)) + U'(\tau(p+h))\ \tau(p+h)}{\eta\ U(\tau(p)) + U'(\tau(p))\ \tau(p)}$$

and an SC is $U''(\tau(p)) + \eta\ U'(\tau(p))\ \tau(p)^{-1} < 0$.

1b.iii $\eta = 0$.

We write $I_I = \log c - I_E$, where $c = 1, \mu$ and $I_E = \omega(I)^{-1} \int_0^1 W(p) \log [\tau(p)]dp$ where $W(p) \neq \alpha\ \tau(p)^q$, $\alpha > 0$, $q \geq 1$.

The total effect T, corresponding to (7.73) is $T = dI_E < 0$, where

$$dI_E = \omega(I)^{-1} \{W(p+h) \log c[\tau(p+h) + \frac{\lambda}{\mu}] - W(p+h) \log c\ \tau(p+h) -$$
$$- W(p) \log c\tau(p) + W(p) \log c\ [\tau(p) - \frac{\lambda}{\mu}]\}\ dp < 0.$$

The NSC's are

(*i*) $W(p) = k > 0$: $\tau(p+h) > \tau(p)$ which is always fulfilled

(*ii*) $W(p)$, a funciton of relative ranks: $\frac{\tau(p+h)}{\tau(p)} > \frac{W(p+h)}{W(p)}$

(*iii*) $W(p) = U(\tau(p)) \neq \alpha\tau(p)$, $\alpha > 0$:

$$U(\tau(p+h))\tau(p+h)^{-1} - U(\tau(p))\ \tau(p)^{-1} > - \{U'(\tau(p+h)) \log c\ \tau(p+h) -$$
$$- U'(\tau(p)) \log c\ \tau(p)\} \qquad (7.77)$$

In case (*ii*) an SC is that $W'(p) < 0$ and in case (*iii*) an NSC is

$$\frac{U(\tau(p))}{\tau(p)^2} < 2\frac{U'(\tau(p))}{\tau(p)} + U''(\tau(p)) \log c\tau(p),\ U(\tau(p)) \neq \alpha\ \tau(p),$$
$$\alpha > 0. \qquad (7.78)$$

The same results are obtained when we consider, e.g. the transformation

$$I_I = c - e^{I_E}.$$

2. THE LSD-CLASS

$I^{1/\eta} = \{\int_0^1 W(p)[\log\tau(p)]^\eta dp\}^{1/\eta}$ is the inequality measure with $\eta \geq 1$ and integer. The measures are RI-measures. If $\eta \geq 1$ and odd we impose that $W(p) = U(\tau(p)) = \alpha\tau(p)^q$, $\alpha>0, q\geq 1$, cf. table 7.5. The NSC for the fulfillment of INET is

$$\{\frac{\tau(p+h)}{\tau(p)}\}^{q-1}[\log\tau(p+h)]^{\eta-1}\{q\log\tau(p+h)+\eta\} > [\log\tau(p)]^{\eta-1}\{q\log\tau(p)+\eta\}$$

which is not in general fulfilled. If $q=1$ and $\eta=1$ we have $\log\tau(p+h)>\log\tau(p)$ which is always fulfilled.

When $\eta \geq 2$ and an even integer and $W(p) \neq U(\tau(p))$ the NSC for the fulfillment of INET is

$$\frac{W(p+h)}{W(p)}\{\log\tau(p+h)\}^{\eta-1} > \{\log\tau(p)\}^{\eta-1}\frac{\tau(p+h)}{\tau(p)}.$$

It is easily seen that it depends on i) the weight function $W(p)$ and ii) on the relative incomes $\tau(\cdot)$. INET is not in general fulfilled. A corresponding condition for the case $W(p) = U(\tau(p))$ can easily be obtained. From this it can be seen that INET is not in general fulfilled.

The inequality measures from transformed equality measures are here only defined for $\eta = 1$ and we have $I_I = \omega(1)\log\beta^{-1} - \int_0^1 W(p)\log\{\tau(p)\beta^{-1}\}dp$, where $0 < \beta < 1$. INET is not in general fulfilled.

3. THE ESD-CLASS

3a Inequality measures, $\eta > 0$.

$$I^{1/\eta} = \{\int_0^1 W(p)e^{c(\tau(p)-1)\eta}dp\}^{1/\eta} \text{ and } c = -1, -\mu \text{ or } 1, \mu.$$

For a constant weight function the criterion is always fulfilled.

If the weight function is a function of relative ranks then an SC is $W'(p) \gtrless 0$ for $c \gtrless 0$.

In the case of relative income weights an NSC is given by

$$e^{\Phi c\eta\,(\tau(p+h) - \tau(p))} > \{\frac{\Phi[U'(\tau(p)) + c\eta U(\tau(p))]}{\Phi[U'(\tau(p+h))+c\eta U(\tau(p+h))]}\},$$

where $\Phi = \begin{cases} -1 \text{ if } c < 0 \\ 1 \text{ if } c > 0 \end{cases}$. From this we have the following SC:

$U''(\tau(p)) > (-c\eta)U'(\tau(p))$, which holds if, e.g. $U'' \geq 0$ and $U' \gtrless 0$ for $c \gtrless 0$.

3b. Inequality measures transformed from equality measures, $\eta < 0$

$$I_I = e^c\,\omega(1)^{1/\eta} - I^{1/\eta}, \text{ where } I = \int_0^1 W(p)e^{c\eta\tau(p)}dp, \ c = -1, -\mu \text{ or } 1, \mu.$$

The criterion of INET is always fulfilled when $W(p) = k > 0$, k constant. An SC in the case of relative rank weights is $W'(p) \gtrless 0$ for $c \lessgtr 0$ and an SC for the case of relative income weights is

$U''(\tau(p)) > (-c\eta)U'(\tau(p))$, which holds if, e.g. $U'' \geq 0$ and $U' \lessgtr 0$ for $c \gtrless 0$.

The discussion above is summarized in table 7.6 for the SD- and ESD-classes.

Table 7.6 Sufficient conditions (SC) imposed on the weight function $W(p)$ for the measures of inequality to fulfill the minimum definition of the principle of transfers (INET, definition 7.6). For the LSD class, see the text.
(1a), (1b), (3c) and (3b) refers to the paragraphs in the text.

Class	W(p)	Inequality measures	Inequality measures transformed from equality measures
		$\eta \geq 1$, integer, $c=1, \mu$ (1a)	$\eta<1$, $c=1, \mu$ (1b)
	(*i*) $W(p)=k>0$, constant	always fulfilled when $\eta \geq 2$	always fulfilled
S	(*ii*) $W(p)$, function of relative ranks	$\eta=1$ SC: $W'(p)>0$ $\eta \geq 3$, odd SC: $W'(p)>0$ $\eta \geq 2$ even not in general, if the transfer procedure takes place on one side of μ then a SC is $W'(p)>0$.	$\eta<1$ SC: $W'(p)<0$
D	(*iii*) $W(p)=U(\tau(p))$, function of relative incomes	see the text SC: (7.70)	see the text $0<\eta<1$: SC: $U''(\tau(p))<0$, $U'(\tau(p))<0$ $\eta=0$, $U(\tau(p)) \neq \alpha\tau(p)^q$, $\alpha > 0$, $q \geq 1$ SC: see (7.78) $\eta<0$ SC: $U(\tau(p))>0$, $U'(\tau(p))<0$, $U''(\tau(p)) \geq 0$
		$\eta>0$, $c=-1.1, -\mu, \mu$ (3a)	$\eta<0$, $c=1.1, -\mu, \mu$ (3b)
	(*i*) $W(p)=k>0$, constant	always fulfilled	always fulfilled
E	(*ii*) $W(p)$, function of relative ranks	$c<0$ SC: $W'(p)<0$ $c>0$ SC: $W'(p)>0$	$c<0$ SC: $W'(p)>0$ $c>0$ SC: $W'(p)<0$
S D	(*iii*) $W(p)=U(\tau(p))$, function of relative incomes	see the text SC: $U''(\tau(p))+c\eta U'(\tau(p))>0$	see the text SC: $U''(\tau(p))+c\eta U'(\tau(p)) > 0$

The criterion of INET (TRANSF, cf. sec. 4.2) only states that an infinitesimal transfer should increase income inequality and does not make any distinction between transfers occurring among the poor or among the rich i.r.u.'s. Atkinson [1970 - p.257-258] noticed that the effect of a n.e.t. on the coefficient of variation[1)] was proportional to $\tau(p+h) - \tau(p)$, i.e. the income difference between the "receiver" and the "giver", but that it was independent on the income level. He suggested that this was a shortcoming of this measure.

Kolm [1976b - p.87] stated that we "... value more such a transfer between persons with given income difference if these incomes are lower than if they are higher.", i.e. if $\tau(p+h) - \tau(p) = \tau(p+h_1 + k) - \tau(p+h_1)$, $0 \leq p < p+h < 1$ and $0 \leq p < p+h_1 \leq p+h_1+k \leq 1$, then the transfer from the "giver" with income $\tau(p)$ should result in a greater increase than the same transfer amount taken from $\tau(p+h_1)$. This strengthening of the TRANSF is labelled "the principle of diminishing transfer" (DIMTRANSF) by Kolm. As seen above the strengthening of the TRANSF made by Kolm stipulates a constant income distance between the "giver" and the "receiver". Cowell [1977 - pp. 59] generalized the distance concept between the "giver" and the "receiver" to a distance function $d = g(s_1) - g(s_2), s_1 > s_2$. Cowell discussed the case when the argument of g is defined as income share.

1) cf. also, e.g. Sen [1973 - p.32] and Love and Wolfson [1976 - p.60].

A generalized distance function such as d would include the DIMTRANSF-definition made by Mehran [1976 - p.808] and "the principle of relatively diminishing transfers" introduced by Kolm [1976 - p.87]. Mehran defined the distance in terms of relative ranks, $g(s_1) = p+h$ and $g(s_2) = p$, $0 \leq p < p+h \leq 1$, i.e. d=h, the relative rank difference between the "giver" and the "receiver". Kolm's principle states that g is defined as a log-income, i.e. $\log\tau(p+h) - \log\tau(p) = \log\tau(p+k+h_1) - \log\tau(p+k)$ or in anti-logarithmic terms that $\tau(p+h)/\tau(p) = \tau(p+k+h_1)/\tau(p+k)$.

In accordance with the definition of an INET we make the following definition:

Definition 7.7: The principle of a diminishing INET effect (DINET).

Compare one INET (definition 7.6) from the population at the pth percentile of the distribution and one from the population at the (p+k)th percentile, $0 \leq p < p+k < p+k+h_1 \leq 1$, $0 \leq p < p+h < 1$. The total effect, T, of the **INET** among "the poor" is greater than a corresponding INET effect among "the rich" i.e.

$$T(\lambda, p, h) > T(\lambda, p+k, h_1) \qquad (7.79)$$

By (7.79) we stipulate that the transfer amount is the same, positive and infinitesimal ($\lambda > 0$). By the discussion above we can distinguish at least three variants depending on the distance functions:

(*i*) $DINET_p$: $T(\lambda, p, h) > T(\lambda, p+k, h_1)$ if $h=h_1$ (7.80a)

i.e. the relative rank difference between the "receivers" and the "givers" is constant (cf. Mehran [1976 - p.808]).

(*ii*) $DINET_\tau$ $T(\lambda, p, h) > T(\lambda, p+k, h_1)$ if $\tau(p+h) - \tau(p) =$

$$= \tau(p+k+h_1) - \tau(p+k) = \tau^*(h), \qquad (7.80b)$$

i.e. the (relative) income difference between the "receivers" and the "givers" is constant (cf. e.g. Kolm [1976b - p.87]).

(*iii*) $DINET_{\log\tau}$ $T(\lambda, p, h) > T(\lambda, p+k, h_1)$ if

$$\log \frac{\tau(p+h)}{\tau(p)} = \log \frac{\tau(p+k+h_1)}{\tau(p+k)} = \log r, \qquad (7.80c)$$

i.e. the difference of (relative) logarithmic incomes between the "receivers" and the "givers" is constant (cf. Kolm [1976b - p.87]).

The order of the three variants of DINET, (*i*) - (*iii*) above, is arbitrary and has nothing to do with our judging of the strength of the three definitions. Instead we are satisfied if one of the three DINET's is fulfilled and the procedure to seek conditions to impose on the weight function is as in the case of the INET. The results are given in table 7.7.

$DINET_p$ is fulfilled by the original inequality measures in the SD-class when $\eta = 1$ and $W'(p) > 0$ and $W''(p) < 0$. Only Mehran's and Bonferroni's measures in table 7.4 fulfill this criterion. In other words, if we consider a weighted Lorenz area as a measure of inequality the preference function $V(p) = W'(p)$ should be positive with $V'(p) = W''(p) < 0$.

Table 7.7 Sufficient conditions (SC) imposed on the weight function W(p) for the measures of inequality to fulfill the minimum definition of the principle of diminishing INET (DINET). $DINET_p$ considers the (relative) rank difference as constant, $DINET_\tau$ the (relative) income difference as constant. Since the INET has to be realized for the fulfillment of DINET the conditions below includes the conditions imposed on INET.

Class	W(p)	Inequality measures	Inequality measures from transformed equality measures
		$\eta \geq 1$, integer, c=1, μ	$\eta \leq 1$, c=1, μ
	(*i*) $W(p)=k>0$, constant	never fulfilled	$\underline{DINET_\tau}$: always fulfilled
	(*ii*) W(p), function of relative ranks	$\eta=1$ $\underline{DINET_p}$ SC: $W'(p)>0$, $W''(p)<0$ $\eta \geq 2$ not in general, depends on the density function	$\eta \leq 1$ not in general, depends on the density function
S D	(*iii*) $W(p)=U(\tau(p))$, function of relative incomes	not in general but if $\eta=1$: $\underline{DINET_\tau}$ SC: $U'''(\tau(p))[\tau(p)-1]+3U''(\tau(p))<0$	$0<\eta<1$ $\underline{DINET_\tau}$: SC: $U(\tau(p))>0$, $U'(\tau(p))<0$, $U''(\tau(p))>0$, $U'''(\tau(p))>0$ $\eta=0$ not in general, depends on the transfer procedure in relation to μ. $\eta<0$ $\underline{DINET_\tau}$: SC: $U(\tau(p))>0$, $U'(\tau(p))<0$, $U''(\tau(p))>0$, $U'''(\tau(p))<0$

LSD		$\eta \geq 1$, c=1	
L	(*i*) W(p)=k>0, constant	$\eta \geq 2$, even: not in general, depends on the transfer procedure in relation to μ.	$\eta=1$ DINET is not fulfilled
S	(*ii*) W(p), function of relative ranks	$\eta \geq 2$, even: not in general, depends on the density function	
D	(*iii*) $W(p)=U(\tau(p))=\tau(p)$ function of relative incomes	$\eta=1$: $\underline{DINET}_{\tau}$: always fulfilled $\eta \geq 3$, odd: not in general, depends on the transfer procedure in relation to μ.	
ESD		$\eta>0$, $c=-1, 1, -\mu, \mu$	$\eta<0$, $c=-1, 1, -\mu, \mu$
	(*i*) W(p)=k>0, constant	$\underline{DINET}_{\tau}$: always fullfilled when c<0.	$\underline{DINET}_{\tau}$: always fulfilled when c>0
	(*ii*) W(p), function of relative ranks	not in general, depends on the density function	not in general, depends on the density function
	(*iii*) $W(p)=U(\tau(p))$, function of relative incomes	$\underline{DINET}_{\tau}$: SC: $U'''(\tau(p))+3c\eta U''(\tau(p))+3(c\eta)^2 U'(\tau(p))+(c\eta)^3 U(\tau(p))<0$ for c>0 SC: $U'''(\tau(p))+2c\eta U''(\tau(p))+(c\eta)^2 U'(\tau(p))<0$ for c<0	$\underline{DINET}_{\tau}$: SC: $U'''(\tau(p))+2c\eta U''(\tau(p))+(c\eta)^2 U'(\tau(p))<0$ for c>0 SC: $U'''(\tau(p))+3c\eta U''(\tau(p))+3(c\eta)^2 U'(\tau(p))+(c\eta)^3 U(\tau(p))<0$ for c < 0

$DINET_\tau$ is always fulfilled when W(p) is a positive constant of the transformed equality measures in the SD-class (with W(p) = 1 we have the Atkinson-Kolm measure). When $\eta > 0$ and $c < 0$ ($\eta < 0$ and $c > 0$) $DINET_\tau$ is always fulfilled for a positive constant weight function when the measures belong to the original inequality measures [1] (transformed equality measures) of the ESD class. In the LSD class $DINET_\tau$ is only fulfilled when $\eta=1$ and $U(\tau(p)) = \tau(p)$.[2] $DINET_\tau$ could also be fulfilled when the weight function is equal to $U(\tau(p))$, a function of relative incomes, in the SD and the ESD classes. Necessary and/or sufficient conditions for the fulfillment of $DINET_\tau$ in this case are given in table 7.7. $DINET_{\log\tau}$ is not fulfilled by any of the measures discussed here.

What have we achieved by this discussion? The following paragraphs will summarize the results:

(1) We started with a quite general definition of inequality (equality) measures (definition 7.5) and restricted our discussion to three distinct subclasses: SD, LSD and ESD. As reference distributions we used the EGAL and the CON to obtain inequality and equality measures, respectively i.e. $L_r(p) = p$ or βp and $L_r'(p) = \tau_r(p) = 1$ or β, where $\beta \leq 0$ in the SD and ESD classes ($0 < \beta < 1$ in the LSD class).

---

[1] Kolm's [1976a] leftist measure.

[2] Theil's 1st measure, cf. sec. 7.3.2.

(2) We assumed the measures to equal zero for the EGAL distribution. The inequality (equality) measures should increase (decrease) with "increasing deviation" from the EGAL distribution. The equality measures were transformed to corresponding inequality measures (cf. table 7.5). It was also stated that the inequality measures could be defined at the (0,1)-interval in the case of *RI*-measures (and at the (0,μ)-interval in the case of *AI*-measures).

(3) By (1) and (2) we obtained domains for the power η in the three subclasses. This restricted the measures further, see table 7.5.

(4) The next step in our search for available measures was to impose restrictions on the weight function W(p). Three families of weight functions were examined: (*i*) a positive constant, (*ii*) a function of relative ranks and (*iii*) a function of relative incomes. We used the principle of an infinitesimal non-egalitarian transfer (INET), definition 7.6, to get necessary and/or sufficient conditions on W(p). By this we saw that some of the families failed to follow INET, see table 7.6.

(5) To get further restrictions on W(p) the principle of an INET was strengthened: the principle of a diminishing INET (DINET), definition 7.7. See table 7.7 for necessary and/or sufficient conditions to be imposed on W(p) for the fulfillment of DINET.

The principal purpose of making these procedures has been, as mentioned before, to see the relationships between measures that have been proposed in the literature. Proposed measures are discussed in subsequent sections. A second purpose of the above procedures has been to obtain rules which should erase less appropriate measures. The decomposability of the measures could be used to restrict the measures further. It is usually proposed that a suitable inequality measure should be additively decomposable.[1)] The decomposability will be discussed at length in ch. 9. It will be seen there that DINET in some cases can be too strong and that in those cases we are satisfied with INET.

---

1) See, e.g. Bourguignon [1979], Cowell [1980] and Shorrocks [1980a].

7.4.1 THE SD CLASS

In the slope difference (SD) class we consider inequality measures through defining the "reference slope" to equal one, $\tau_r(p) = 1$, and equality measures by $\tau_r(p) = -\xi/\mu$, where $\xi \geq 0$. We define the measures in the SD class by

- inequality measures

$$I_I(Y;\ \eta) = \{\int_0^1 W(p)[c(\tau(p)-1)]^{\eta}dp\}^{1/\eta}\quad ,\eta \geq 1 \text{ integer} \tag{7.81a}$$

- equality measures

$$I_E(Y;\ \eta) = \{\int_0^1 W(p)[c(\tau(p)+\frac{\xi}{\mu})]^{\eta}dp\}^{1/\eta},\quad \eta < 1,\ \eta \neq 0 \tag{7.81b}$$

$$\log I_E\ (Y\,;\,0) = \omega(1)^{-1}\int_0^1 W(p)\log c(\tau(p)+\frac{\xi}{\mu})dp,\quad \eta = 0 \tag{7.81c}$$

It is easily seen that the inequality measures belong to the compromise inequality (*CI*-measures, i.e. multiplying a *RI*-measure, I^r, with the arithmetic mean, μ, gives us the corresponding *AI*-measure, $I^a = \mu I^r$, and vice vera ($I^r = \mu^{-1}I^a$). The equality measures can be transformed to inequality measures as is shown in table 7.5. When $\eta < 1$ ($\neq 0$) we use $I_I = c\omega(1)^{1/\eta} - I_E$ and when $\eta = 0$ we can use either $I_I = \log c - \log I_E$ or $I_I = c - I_E$, where the last transformation is bounding I_I at the [0,c]-interval. Note that when $\eta = 0$ we assume $W(p)=U(\tau(p))\neq\alpha\tau(p)^q, \alpha>0$ and $q \geq 1$. The transformed equality measures are in general neither RI- nor AI-measures.

A. Some inequality measures defined by (7.81a) (summarized in table 7.8).

$W(p) = 1$

The coefficient of variation,[1] V, is one of the measures, with constant weight function ($W(p) = 1$), that has been widely used and discussed, see e.g. Dalton [1920], Atkinson [1970], Sen [1973], Kolm [1976b] and Cowell [1977]. Yntema [1933] used it in comparison with seven other measures. He also considered the normalized equivalent[2] to V which he labelled "the coefficient of variation referred to $\sqrt{\mu_2}$", V_N, where μ_2 is the second moment about zero. V_N is in terms of V written as $V/\sqrt{V^2 + 1}$. It fulfills INET but not DINET[3].

V_N is used by e.g. Bartels [1977 - p.19] and the squared normalized coefficient of variation, V_N^2, by e.g. Champernowne [1973 - p.791] and Bartels [1977 - p.19].[4]

The squared coefficient of variation, $V^2 = \sigma^2/\mu$, (σ^2 = the variance), has an interpretation in terms of relative expected depression. The following lemma is given by Kakwani [1980b - p.86][5]:

---

1) Karl Pearson's coefficient of variation, see Kendall and Stuart [1977 - vol. 1, p.48].

2) $V \in [0,\infty[$ and its normalized equivalent $\in [0,1]$

3) Note that μ_2 will increase with $2\mu^2 (\tau(p+h) - \tau(p))$ by an INET.

4) As an alternative to both V and V_N Yntema [1933 - p.433] proposed $1 - \mu/\sqrt{\mu_2}$.

5) We have expressed the lemma in terms of the variance instead of V as Kakwani [1980b - p.86, lemma 5.12].

Kakwani's interpretation of the variance

> If, in any pairwise comparison, a person with lower income suffers some depression proportional to the square of the difference in incomes[1], the average of all such depressions in all possible pairwise comparisons equals the variance. The CON-depression equals μ^2 and is obtained when one i.r.u. receives all incomes.

The squared coefficient of variation is by this interpretation expressed as E (Kakwani depression) / {CON depression}, where E(·) is the expectation operator . The expected "Kakwani depression conditioned by the poorest" equals μ_2 and hence E (Kakwani depression) / E (Kakwani depression | 0) = $= V^2/ (V^2 + 1) = V_N^2$. The effect of an INET on V is proportional to the income difference between the "receiver" and the "giver" (see e.g. Dalton [1920 - p.352], Atkinson [1970 - p.255], Sen [1973 - p.28], Love and Wolfson [1976 - p.60], Cowell [1977 - p.30] and Kakwani [1980b - p.87]). The independence of the income level when performing an INET (the failure of DINET$_\tau$) has been what has given V the most critisism[2].

V is an R*I*-measure and the corresponding A*I*-measure is the standard deviation.

Bartels [1977 - p.20] used the square root of the second moment about $F^{-1}(1)$, i.e. the maximum income, (SMAX) and the normalized equivalent (SMAXN) as measures of inequality. A relative variant is obtained by

---

1) The expected suffered depression by a person with income y equals E (Kakwani depression | x) = $\int_x^\infty (y-x)^2 dF(y)$.

2) Sen [1973 - p.28] also questioned the squaring which is done in V.

dividing SMAX with μ. They all fulfill INET, but fail to fulfill $DINET_\tau$. SMAX equals the square root of the variance plus the squared distance between the maximum income and the arithmetic mean income and hence we can write the relative SMAX as $\{V^2 + (\tau(1) - 1)^2\}^{1/2}$.

W(P) is a function of relative ranks.

The Gini coefficient, the mean difference and related measures.

As is seen by table 7.8 the Lorenz area (LA), the Gini coefficient (R) and the relative and absolute mean difference (G_r and G, resp.) are proportional to each other through: $R = 2LA$, $G_r = 4LA$ and $G = 2\mu R = 4\mu LA = \mu G_r$.

The mean difference G was discussed in the theory of errors of observations in the late nineteenth century by e.g. v. Andrae [1872] and Helmert [1876] (see also v. Bortkiewicz [1930 - pp. 10-11] and David [1968] for reviews of G). It was proposed as a measure of dispersion by Gini [1912], after whom it is usually named (Gini's mean difference). Gini [1914] showed the relation $R = G/2\mu$ (= 2LA) and denoted it the concentration ratio, since it can be interpreted as the ratio between the observed Lorenz area and the maximum Lorenz area (= $^1/_2$) . Various ways of writing these measures by using the above relations are given in table 7.2[1]. The measures follow INET ($W'(p) > 0$) but fail to follow $DINET_p$ ($W''(p) = 0$). The effect of an INET is proportional to the relative rank difference between the "receiver" and the "giver". If we consider the income difference between the "giver" and the "receiver" as constant and the distribution as a typical unimodal distribution then these measures attach more weight to an INET near the mode of the distribution than at the tails (cf. Atkinson [1970 - p.256] and Kakwani [1980b - pp. 72-73]). The measures, by themselves, are most sensitive to extreme incomes (see Bartels

---

1) A generalized Gini is proposed in Blackorby and Donaldson [1980 - pp. 116-117] by John Weymark. This is defined as

$$I = \int_0^1 (h(p)-1)\tau(p)dp, \text{ where } h(p) = W(p)-\omega(1)+1 \text{ and } \omega(1) = \int_0^1 W(p)dp \neq 0.$$

In the case of the ordinary Gini coefficient $h(p) = W(p) = 2p$. This "generalized Gini" is nothing else than the constraint measure (7.59b) discussed by Giaccardi [1950], Piesch [1975] and Mehran [1976].

[1977 - p. 27 and 36]). This is, perhaps, easiest seen by considering the constraint version of the Gini coefficient, $R=\int_0^1 C(p)\,\tau(p)\,dp$ with $C(p) = (2p-1)$. The constraint function, which is depicted in figure 7.14(c), gives zero weight to incomes equal to $\mu(\tau(p)=1)$ and the weights -1 and +1 to the lowest and the highest incomes, respectively.

If we compare two income distributions with the same arithmetic mean income and one distribution Lorenz dominates the other then the measures discussed above, i.e. LA, R and G_r, (both *RI*- and *AI*-measures) for the Lorenz dominating distribution will have lower values than the measures computed for the other distribution.

The Gini coefficient R is the most widely used measure to analyze the size distribution of income (and wealth). The formal way of writing R can be made in several ways as seen by table 7.2 and using R = 2LA. Three ways of looking at R are

$$R = \frac{1}{2\mu}\int_0^\infty\int_0^\infty |y-x|\,dF(x)\,dF(y) = \tag{7.82a}$$

$$= 2\int_0^\infty F(y)\,dF_1(y) \;-1 \tag{7.82b}$$

$$= \frac{1}{\mu}\int_0^\infty\int_0^\infty |y-x|\cdot|F(y)-F(x)|\;dF(x)\,dF(y). \tag{7.82c}$$

In (7.82b) $F_1(y)$ the 1st m.d.f. is defined by (7.1) and in table 7.2 the corresponding expression is written in terms of L(p) as defined by (7.5). By (7.82b) it is easy to establish the identity between (7.82a) and (7.82c). The last expression, (7.82c), is identical to the normalized equivalent to the rank-order weighted mean difference proposed by Bartels [1977 - pp. 23-24].

The Gini coefficient can be interpreted directly from the formal definition (7.82a) and (7.82c). However, Sen [1973 - p.33] and Pyatt [1976 - p.244][1] interpreted (7.82a) in terms of relative expected "suffering from depression" and of expected gain from "a statistical game", respectively (see also Kakwani [1980b - pp. 70-71]):

Sen's interpretation of (7.82a): "relative expected depression".

In any pairwise comparison of incomes, the individual with lower income may suffer from depression when he discovers that his income is the lower one. If it is assumed that this depression is proportional to the difference in incomes, the average (or the mathematical expectation) of all such depressions (Sen depressions) in all pairwise comparisons equal $G/2$, where G is the mean deviation. R is interpreted as the expected Sen depression of the whole population relative to the maximum expected depression (=E (Sen depression | individual with income = 0)[2]), i.e.
$R = E$ (Sen depression) / E_{max} (Sen depression).

Pyatt's interpretation of (7.82a): "relative expected gain from a statistical game".

For one individual with income x we select at random any income y from the population. If the selected income is greater than the actual income of the individual ($y > x$) then he can retain the selected value, otherwise he retains his actual income. All individuals, apart from the richest, would have a mathematical expectation of gaining from it.[3] If all

---

1) Cf. also Pyatt [1980].

2) E (Sen depression | the poorest) = E_{max} (Sen depression)

3) $E(\text{gain} \mid x) = \int_x^\infty (y-x)\, dF(y)$.

expected gains over the whole population are averaged we obtain E (gain) = = G/2. The maximum gain, E_{max}(gain), equals the arithmetic mean income and hence the Gini coefficient can be interpreted as E(gain)/E_{max}(gain).

Similar interpretations can be made from the formulation (7.82c). As an example, in Sen's version we can let the expected suffering from depression for an individual with income x equal E(Bartels depression | x) = $\int_x^\infty (y-x)(F(y) - F(x))\,dF(y)$. Taking the average over all individuals we obtain E(Bartels depression) = μLA, where LA is the Lorenz area and hence the Gini coefficient $R = \frac{E(\text{Bartel depression})}{\frac{1}{2}\mu}$ can be interpreted as

$$\frac{E\ (\text{Bartels depression})}{E(\text{relative rank})\cdot E_{max}\ (\text{Sen depression})}\ ^{1)}.$$

The maximum expected depression equals the expected depression of the poorest (x = 0 and F(0) = 0) and can be written as E_{max} (Bartels depression) = $\mu \frac{1}{2}$ (R+1) where R is the Gini coefficient. The ratio between E (Bartels depression) and E_{max}(Bartels depression) is R/(R+1) = LA/(LA + $\frac{1}{2}$) i.e. the ratio between the Lorenz area and the area situated over the Lorenz Curve in a Lorenz diagram. By this it follows that the Gini coefficient can be written as E (Bartels depression) / (E_{max}(Bartels depression) - E(Bartels depression)).[2)]

---

1) E (relative rank) $= \int_0^\infty F(y)\,dF(y) = 1/2$

2) E_{max}(Sen depression) = 2{E_{max} (Bartels depression) - E(Bartels depression)}.

Another way of interpreting the Gini coefficient is the following extreme interpretation: For a given population, with arithmetic mean income μ, we have observed R. This can be interpreted so that R% of the population have zero-incomes and (1-R)% have $\mu(1-R)^{-1}$-incomes. As an example let R = 0,25 and $\mu = 75000$. By the above definition we interpret this so that 25% of the population have 0-incomes and 75% have an income equal to 100000.

As we have seen there are many ways of interpreting and formulating the Gini coefficient and this manifoldness is reflected in the countless number of published papers on the coefficient. Its welfare implications have been discussed by e.g. Atkinson [1970], Newbery [1970], Sheshinski [1972], Dasgupta, Sen and Starrett [1973], Rothschild and Stiglitz [1973], Sen [1973] and Kakwani [1980b]. One disadvantage of R, discovered in the literature is the inconvenience of decomposition. As we will see in ch. 9 there are various ways of decomposing the measure by subgroups of the population. We will also find that it is not additively decomposable. Is this a disadvantage? We do not wholly and entirely agree that this is a disadvantage, but we leave the discussion to ch. 9. On the other hand the Gini coefficient has one advantage: it is possible to decompose it by income components (see sec 9.3).

<u>Mehran's measure</u> (see Mehran [1976]) is a measure constructed to fulfill $DINET_p$. Consider a constraint function $C(p) = a+b(1-p)^c$ with the following properties $C'(p) > 0$, $C''(p) < 0$, $\int_0^1 C(p)dp = 0$ and $C(1) = 1$. By this we have the solution $C(p) = 1-3(1-p)^2$, and hence $W(p)=3p(2-p)$, cf. table 7.4, with $\omega(1) = 2$. If the measure is interpreted in terms of

a weighted Lorenz area the preference function is $V(p) = 6(1-p)$. The measure, labelled M, can be rewritten in various ways, e.g.

$$M = \int_0^1 (6p-3p^2)\ [\tau(p)-1]\ dp = \qquad (7.83a)$$

$$= 3R - \{3\int_0^\infty F(y)dF_1(y) - 1\} = \qquad (7.83b)$$

$$= \frac{2}{\mu}\int_0^\infty \int_0^y (y-x)[1-F(x)]dF(x)dF(y) = \qquad (7.83c)$$

$$= \frac{2}{\mu}\int_0^\infty \int_0^y (y-x)[\tfrac{3}{2}-F(y)]\ dF(x)dF(y).^{1)} \qquad (7.83d)$$

M can be interpreted in terms of suffering from depression (cf. Sen's interpretation of the Gini coefficient). An individual with income x is compared with an individual with higher income y. Suppose that he suffers from depression when he finds his income lower.[2)] Assume that this depression equals $2(y-x)(1-F(x))$, i.e. he suffers not only by the amount of income difference but also twice his relative rank position as regards the richest individual. On the average he would suffer

$$E(\text{Mehran depression}|x) = 2\int_x^\infty (y-x)(1-F(x))\ dF(x),$$

and the expected suffering from depression in the whole population equals

$$E(\text{Mehran depression}) = \mu M/2,$$

1) An alternative way of writing M is to weight (7.83c) and (7.83d) together with weights adding up to one (not necessarily weights at the [0,1]-interval).

2) If y was lower than x then the individual would not suffer from depression, i.e. the depression is zero.

where μ = E(Mehran depression | 0) = E_{max} (Mehran depression)[1]. In other words we can write Mehran's measure as

$$M = \frac{E(\text{Mehran depression})}{E(\text{relative rank}) \cdot E_{max}(\text{Mehran depression})}$$

The main difference between the Gini coefficient and Mehran's measure in terms of suffering from depressions is that the relative rank of the individual with income x, $F(x)$, is compared with the relative rank of the individual with income y and the richest, respectively.

Piesch' measure [1975 - p.131], P, is an example of a square p-function, αp^2, $\alpha > 0$, where the condition on the constraint function C(1) = 1 is fulfilled, i.e. $P \in [0,1]$. The measure fulfills INET but not $DINET_p$. Piesch [1975 - p.131] also discusses power functions, $W(p) = \alpha p^m$, $\alpha > 0$ and m > 1 which by using C(1) = 1 leads to $W(p) = \frac{m+1}{m} p^m$

The other two p-function measures, Bonferroni's measure and de Vergottini's measure, have been discussed by Giaccardi [1950][2] and Piesch [1975 - pp. 121, 132]. Only Bonferroni's measure fulfills $DINET_p$ and is defined at the [0,1]-interval.

---

1) E_{max}(Sen depression) = E_{max}(Mehran depression)

2) Giaccardi makes reference to papers by Bonferroni in 1930 and by de Vergottini in 1940.

<u>$W(p) = U(\tau(p))$ is a function of relative incomes</u>

If $\eta=1$ and $U(\tau(p)) = \tau(p)$ we obtain the squared coefficient of variation, V^2 $(c=1)$ and its NI-equivalent σ^2/μ $(c=\mu)$. See the discussion above about V. If, on the other hand, $U(\tau(p)) = \log \tau(p)$ and $c=1$, we obtain the sum of Theil's measure (see Theil [1967 - pp. 99 and 125-127])[1], cf. (7.50b). Using the sufficient condition (7.72) shows that INET is fulfilled and using the necessary and sufficient condition given in table 7.7 also shows that $DINET_\tau$ is fulfilled.

Our general inequality measure defined by (7.60a) is made in terms of the generalized Lorenz Curve $L_j(p)$. Using this definition with "Gini-weights", $(W(p) = 2p)$ and $c=1$ we have the jth power Gini coefficient which is

$$\int_0^1 2p(\tau_j(p)-1)dp = (2\mu_j)^{-1}\int_0^\infty\int_0^\infty | y^j - x^j | dF(x)dF(y) = \int_0^1 2\,[p-L_j(p)]\,dp$$

This is only given as a curiosity and we will not consider it any further.

Our RI-measures are defined in terms of weighted differences of the slopes of the tangents to two Lorenz Curves. This can be visualized in a slope diagram, c.f. Schultz [1951] and Rosenbluth [1951].[2] If $\eta = 1$ we can transform the measures, as shown before, to weighted Lorenz areas. For the examples with weights equal to a function of relative ranks see table 7.4 and figure 7.14a. Both V^2 and $T_1 + T_2$ can be interpreted as weighted Lorenz areas:

---

1) Theil's measure is constructed within information theory. For a discussion of entropy and redundance measure from information theory see e.g. Theil [1967], Hart [1971], [1975 - pp. 426-427], [1978], Piesch [1975 - pp. 162-168], Cowell [1977 - pp. 55-62] and Kakwani [1980b - pp. 88-90].

2) See figure 7.14.

Table 7.8 Some inequality measures belonging to the SD class, defined by (7.81a).
$\tau_r(p)$ is the slope of the tangent to the reference distribution, c is a quantity discussed earlier
DINET is a stronger version of INET ("the principle of transfers").

$\tau_r(p)$	η power	W(p) weight function	c	RI/AI	Measure	Notes and alternative ways of expressing the measure	Range	INET/DINET	The measure gives highest weight to
$\tau(1)<\infty$	2	1	1	RI	the square root of the second moment about $\tau(1) < \infty$	the relative SMAX, cf. Bartels [1977 - p.20]	$[0, \infty[$	INET	no specific level
			μ	AI	the square root of the second moment about $\tau^{-1}(1) < \infty$	SMAX in Bartels 1977 - p.20	$[0, \infty[$	INET	"-"[1)]
			$\tau(1)^{-1}$	RI	the normalized square root of the second moment about $\tau(1) < \infty$	SMAXN in Bartels [1977 - p.20]	$[0, 1]$	INET	"-"[1)]
1	2	1	1	RI	the coefficient of variation	$V=\sigma/\mu$, σ = the standard deviation	$[0, \infty[$	INET	high incomes
			μ	AI	the standard deviation	σ	$[0, \infty[$	INET	high incomes
			$\mu/\sqrt{\mu_2}$	RI	the normalized coefficient of variation	$\sigma/\sqrt{\mu_2}=(1-\mu^2/\mu_2)^{1/2}=V/\sqrt{V^2+1}$ cf. Yntema [1933]	$[0, 1]$	INET	high incomes
	1	p	1	RI	Lorenz area	see table 7.2; $\frac{1}{2}$ R, R=Gini coefficient	$[0, \frac{1}{2}]$	INET	extreme incomes
			μ	AI	absolute Lorenz area		$[0, \frac{1}{2}\mu]$	INET	extreme incomes
		2p	1	RI	Gini coefficient	R twice the Lorenz area, cf. table 7.2	$[0, 1]$	INET	extreme incomes
			μ	AI	absolute Gini coefficient	Ra see Blackorby and Donaldson	$[0, \mu]$	INET	extreme incomes
		4p	1	RI	relative mean difference	$\mu^{-1}G$, cf. table 7.2	$[0, 2]$	INET	extreme incomes
			μ	AI	absolute mean	G	$[0, 2\mu]$	INET	extreme incomes

		$3p(2-p)$	1	*RI*	Mehran's measure	M, see the text	[0, 1]	$DINET_p$	low incomes
			μ	*AI*	Mehran's absolute measure	Ma	[0, μ]	$DINET_p$	low incomes
		$\frac{3}{2}p^2$	1	*RI*	Piesch' measure	P	[0, 1]	INET	high incomes
			μ	*AI*	Piesch' absolute measure	P_a	[0, μ]	INET	high incomes
		$\ell og\ p$	1	*RI*	Bonferroni's measure	B	[0, 1]	$DINET_p$	low incomes
			μ	*AI*	Bonferroni's absolute measure	Ba	[0, 1]	$DINET_p$	low incomes
		$\ell og(1-p)^{-1}$	1	*RI*	de Vergottini's measure	dV	[0, ∞[	INET	high incomes
			μ	*AI*	de Vergottini's absolute measure	dVa	[0, ∞[	INET	high incomes
		$\tau(p)$	1	*RI*	squared coefficient of variation	$V^2=\sigma^2/\mu_2$	[0, ∞[	INET	high incomes
			μ	*NI*	absolute squared coefficient of variation	$\mu V^2=\sigma^2/\mu$	[0, ∞[	INET	high incomes
	1	$\ell og\ \tau(p)$	1	*RI*	the sum of Theil's	$T_1+T_2= \ell og\frac{\mu_{gw}}{\mu} + \ell og\ \frac{\mu}{\mu_g}$	[0, ∞[	$DINET_\tau$	low incomes
			μ	*NI*	the absolute sum of Theil's measure	$\mu(T_1+T_2)$	[0, ∞[	$DINET_\tau$	low incomes

1) Bartels [1977 - p. 35] assumed these measures to give highest weight to low incomes. If we write

$$I = \int_0^{Y_{max}} H(y)\,y\,dF(y)$$

then the weight function is H(y). In the case of the SMAX-measures this function can be written in several ways. At least one of these ways gives highest weight to low incomes and at least one gives highest weight to high incomes.

$$V^2 = \int_0^1 (\mu f(F^{-1}(p))^{-1}[p - L(p)]dp = \int_0^1 L''(p)\ [p - L(p)]dp$$

$$T_1 + T_2 = \int_0^1 (F^{-1}(p) \cdot f[F^{-1}(p)])^{-1}\ [p - L(p)]\ dp.$$

If $\eta \geq 2$ we consider a redefined weight function $W^*(p) = W(p)\ [\tau(p)-1]^{\eta-1}$ and the corresponding preference function $V^*(p) = W^{*\prime}(p) = W'(p)[\tau(p)-1]^{\eta-1} + (\eta-1)W(p)[\tau(p)-1]^{\eta-2}L''(p)$, where $L''(p)\ \frac{1}{\mu f[F^{-1}(p)]}$ and hence the RI-measures can be written as

$$\int_0^1 V^*(p)[p - L(p)]\ dp.$$

B. Some inequality measures defined from transformed equality measures defined by (7.81b and c). (Summarized in table 7.9)

The definitions given by (7.81b) and (7.81c) are made with reference to the Lorenz Curve $L_r(p)$ with the slope of the tangents to the LC equal to $\tau_r(p) = -\frac{\xi}{\mu}$, $\xi \geq 0$.

This equals a reference "Lorenz Curve" situated below the Lorenz diagram. This straight line starts at (0,0) and ends at $(1,-\frac{\xi}{\mu})$.

The rules for the fulfillment of INET and DINET are not altered when we consider this reference slope instead of $\tau_r(p) = 0$.

$W(p) = 1$

Kolm's centrist measures, see Kolm [1976a,b], are obtained when $\xi \geq 0, \eta = 1-\varepsilon$, $\varepsilon > 0$, $\neq 1$ and $c = \mu$. If $c = 1$ the measures will be labelled μ-modified centrist measures. They are non-invariant measures when $\xi > 0$.

They obviously obey both INET and DINET$_\tau$, cf. tables 7.6 and 7.7 and are discussed at length in ch. 6.[1]

When $\eta=0$ ($\varepsilon=1$) we can defined two alternative measures (or transformations), viz.

$$I_I = \log\left[\left(1+\frac{\xi}{\mu}\right)\right] - \int_0^1 \log\left[\left(\tau(p)+{}^{\xi}/_{\mu}\right)\right]dp, \quad \in [0,\infty[\,, \tag{7.84a}$$

and

$$I_I = c\left(1+\frac{\xi}{\mu}\right) - \exp\left\{\int_0^1 \log\left[c\left(\tau(p)+{}^{\xi}/_{\mu}\right)\right] dp\right\}, \quad \in [0,c] \tag{7.84b}$$

where (7.84a) is labelled the extended Theil measures. When $\xi > 0$ the measures are NI-measures.

If ξ is set to equal zero ($\eta=1-\varepsilon<1$) we obtain Atkinson's measure, see Atkinson [1970], which is labelled the rightist measure by Kolm [1976a, b]. See the discussion in ch. 6. When $\eta=0$ ($\varepsilon=1$) we have two measures corresponding to (7.84a) and (7.84b). Atkinson's measure is an RI-measure.

Atkinson's measure (7.84a), when $\eta=0$ ($\varepsilon=1$), is equal to Theil's 2nd measure,[2] $\log \frac{\mu}{\mu_g}$,[3] see Theil [1967 - pp. 125-127], and (7.84b) can be written as $c(1 - \frac{\mu_g}{\mu})$, which is with c=1 the RI-measure proposed by Champernowne [1973]. see sec. 7.1.3.

---

1) When ε tends towards infinity more and more weight is given to the lowest incomes. In the limit case we only consider the poorest, see theorem 4 by Hardy, Littlewood and Polya [1934 - p.15]. This special case of Atkinsons measure, $c(1-\tau(0))$, is labelled "the maximin index" by Blackorby, Donaldson and Auersperg [1978, p. 6 and p. 9].

2) It is also labelled the Cobb-Douglas index by Blackorby and Donaldson [1976].

3) If the incomes are defined at $[0,\infty[$, then T_2 has the range $[0,\infty[$, but if the incomes are defined at $[1,\infty[$, which is the usual solution when handling log-incomes, the upper bound equals $\log \mu$.

As is shown by Kolm [1976a - p. 436] his centrist measure tends to an inequality measure in the ESD-class (Kolm's leftist measure) when ξ and ε (=1-η) tend towards infinity and the ratio $\frac{\varepsilon}{\xi} = \frac{1-\eta}{\xi}$ tends towards a finite value which equals α, see below.

Table 7.9 Some inequality measures from transformed equality measures belonging to the SD-class. The equality measures are defined by (7.81b) and (7.81c). $\tau_r(p)$ is the slope of the tangent to the reference distribution. c=1 gives RI-measures. DINET is a stronger version of INET ("the principle of transfers").

$\tau_r(p)$	W(p) weight function	η	c	RI/AI	Measure	Notes and alternative ways of expressing the measures	Range	INET/ DINET	The measures gives highest weight to
0	1	$1-\varepsilon$ $\varepsilon>0$ $\varepsilon\neq 1$	1	RI	Kolm's relative rightist measure=Atkinson's measure	$\xi = 0$	[0,1]	$DINET_\tau$	low incomes, the higher ε the more weight on low incomes
		0 $\varepsilon=1$	1	RI	Champernowne's measure	Ch, the exponential transformation	[0,1]	$DINET_\tau$	low incomes
			1	RI	Theil's 2nd measure	T_2	$[0,\infty[$ [1]	$DINET_\tau$	low incomes [2]

[1] When the incomes are defined at $[0,\infty[$,otherwise, if the incomes are defined at $[1,\infty[$, $T_2 \in [0,\log\mu]$

[2] Theil's 2nd measure gives highest weight to zero incomes ($y \in [0,\infty[$), but if y $[1,\infty[$ the weight for y=1 is $\mu^{-1}\log\mu$ ($\mu^{-1}\log\mu \to 1$ when $\mu \to \infty$) and then the weight decreases and is negative until $y=\mu$, where the weight equals zero (the lowest weight equals $\mu^{-1}\log\mu - e^{-1}$). The maximum weight when $y>\mu$ is obtained when $y \to \infty$ and this maximum weight equals $\mu^{-1}\log\mu$ (e.g. if $\mu = 50000$ then the maximum weight equals 0.000216 when $y>\mu$). Since the weights are negligible we can state that T_2 has no specific 'level of sensitivity'.

7.4.2 THE LSD CLASS

In the logarithmic slope difference (LSD) class we only consider inequality measures, with reference Lorenz Curve $L_r(p) = p$, i.e. $\tau_r(p) = 1$ defined by

$$I_I(y;\eta) = \{\int_0^1 W(p)[\log \tau(p)]^\eta \, dp\}^{1/\eta}, \quad \eta \geq 1 \text{ integer} \qquad (7.85)$$

if $\eta \geq 1$, odd, we consider $W(p) = U(\tau(p)) = \alpha\tau(p)^q$,

$$\alpha > 0, \; q \geq 1$$

if $\eta \geq 2$, even, we consider general $W(p)$

The domain of η and the use of $W(p) = U(\tau(p)) = \alpha\tau(p)^q$ if $\eta \geq 1$ and odd depend on our definition of an inequality measure: a measure should have a non-negative value for a given income distribution. We could also define an inequality measure by defining an appropriate equality preference slope, $\tau_r(p) = \beta$, such that $0 < \beta < 1$. This measure we only define for $\eta = 1$, cf. table 7.5.

<u>$W(p) = 1$</u>

<u>The quasi-standard deviation</u>, σ_q (or the logarithmic standard deviation, cf. e.g. Atkinson [1970 - p.252], Sen [1973 - pp. 28-29] and Cowell [1977 - p.30]) is defined by letting $\eta = 2$. σ_q does not in general follow INET, see the earlier discussion about INET (see also Dasgupta, Sen and Starrett [1973 - p.187], Sen [1973 - p.32] and Cowell [1977 - p.31].

The sum of the squared Theil's 2nd measure, T_2^2, and σ_q^2 equals the variance of logarithmic incomes, $\sigma_{\log}^2$ defined by [1)]

$$\sigma_{\log}^2 = \int_0^1 \{\log \frac{\mu}{\mu_g} - \tau(p)\}^2 \, dp.$$

This is not an inequality measure in our sense.

If we let $\tau_r(p) = \mu_g/\mu$ [2)] in the LSD-class then $\sigma_{\log}^2$ would look like an equality measure but this will contradict the earlier discussion, e.g. that $\eta = 1$ only and that $\tau_r(p)$ will be affected by an INET which is not prefered. One other thing that discards $\sigma_{\log}^2$ as an inequality measure is that if the income domain is $]\varepsilon,\infty[$ then $\sigma_{\log}$ has the range $[0,\infty[$ when the lower income tends towards zero. On the other hand if ε tends towards one $\sigma_{\log}$ equals zero in the case of CON ! All these bring out $\sigma_{\log}$ as an undesirable inequality measure --- the sum of two inequality measures is <u>not</u> an inequality measure in our sense.

<u>$U(\tau(p)) = \tau(p)$</u>

<u>Theil's 1st measure</u>, $T_1 = \log \frac{\mu_{gw}}{\mu}$, is defined by $\eta = 1$ and was introduced as a measure of inequality from information theory by Theil [1967 - p.99]. $\log \mu_{gw}$ can be interpreted as the logarithm of a weighted geometrical mean or the logarithm of the geometrical mean of the 1st m.d.f., i.e. $\log \mu_{gw} = \int_0^\infty \frac{y}{\mu} \log y \, dF(y) = \int_0^\infty \log y \, dF_1(y)$, see the discussion by Hart [1971 - p.79], [1975 - p. 427] and [1978 - table 2]. By the discussion of INET/DINET it is shown that it fulfills DINET_τ.

---

1) $\sigma_{\log}^2$ does not in general fulfill INET, see also the discussion in Creedy [1977a].

2) see (7.61b).

Table 7.10 Some inequality measures belonging to the LSD-class, defined by (7.85).
$\tau_r(p)$ is the slope of the tangents to the reference distribution. *AI*-measures are *RI*-measures.
DINET is a stronger version of INET ("the principle of transfers").

$\tau_r(p)$	W(p) weight function	η	c	*RI*/ *AI*	Measure	Notes and alternative ways of expressing the measure	Range	INET/ DINET	The measure gives highest weight to
1	1	2	-	*RI*	The quasi-standard deviation	σ_q	$[0,\infty[$ 2)	-	low incomes
	$\tau(p)$	1	-	*RI*	Theil's 1st measure	$T_1 = \ell og \frac{\mu_{gw}}{\mu}$, see the text	$[0,\infty[$ 1)	DINET_τ	extreme incomes 3)

1) If the incomes are defined at $[0, \infty[$, otherwise, if the incomes are defined at $[1, \infty[$, $T_2 \in [0, \ell og\ \mu]$.

2) For incomes defined both at $[0, \infty[$ and $[1, \infty[$.

3) If $y \in [0,\infty[$ T_1 actually gives higher weight to sero incomes than high ($< \infty$) incomes; if $y \in [1, \infty[$ T_1 gives highest weight to high incomes.

7.4.3 THE ESD CLASS

In the exponential slope difference (ESD) class we consider inequality measures through defining the "reference slope" to equal one, $\tau_r(p) = 1$, and equality measures by $\tau_r(p) = 0$. The measures are

- inequality measures

$$I_I(Y;\eta) = \{ \int_0^1 W(p)\, e^{c(\tau(p)-1)\}\eta}\, dp\}^{1/\eta}, \quad \eta > 0. \tag{7.86a}$$

- equality measures

$$I_E(Y;\eta) = \{ \int_0^1 W(p)\, e^{c\tau(p)\eta}\, dp\}^{1/\eta}, \quad \eta < 0. \tag{7.86b}$$

c homogeneous of degree zero ⇒ *RI*-measures

c homogeneous of degree one ⇒ *AI*-measures

In table 7.5 we gave the following transformations of the measures (7.86a) and (7.86b):

- inequality measures

$$(i)\quad I_I = I_I(Y;\eta), \qquad I_I \in [\omega(1)^{1/\eta},\ e^{-c}\,\omega(1)^{1/\eta}] \tag{7.86a}$$

$$(ii)\quad I_I = \log I_I(Y;\eta), \qquad I_I \in \begin{cases} [\log\omega(1)^{1/\eta},\ -c+\log\omega(1)^{1/\eta}] & \text{if } c < 0 \\ [\log\omega(1)^{1/\eta},\ \infty[& \text{if } c > 0 \end{cases} \tag{7.86c}$$

- equality measures

$$(i)\quad I_I = e^{c}\omega(1)^{1/\eta} - I_E, \qquad I_I \in \begin{cases} [0,\ e^{c}\omega(1)^{1/\eta}] & \text{if } c < 0 \\ [0,\ (e^{c}-1)\omega(1)^{1/\eta}] & \text{if } c > 0 \end{cases} \tag{7.86d}$$

$$(ii)\quad I_I = c+\log\omega(1)^{1/\eta} - \log I_E, \qquad I_I \in \begin{cases} [0,\ \infty[& \text{if } c < 0 \\ [0,c] & \text{if } c > 0 \end{cases} \tag{7.86e}$$

The measure (7.86a) is an inequality measure if $c < 0$ when we consider the case $\omega(1) = 1$, which is only a matter of definition. The transformation, given by (7.86c), defines the inequality measures at $[0, -c]$ when $c < 0$ and at $[0, \infty[$ when $c > 0$ $(\omega(1) = 1)$. Both cases show that we should choose $c < 0$, i.e. $c = -1$ for an *RI*-measure and $c = -\mu$ for an *AI*-measure (this is for (7.86b) also in accordance with the previous discussion about eligible bounds for the measures). In the case of transformed equality measures we choose transformation (*ii*) and $c > 0$ since these measures have the range $[0,c]$.

If $c = -u < 0$ and $\eta = \alpha > 0$ in (7.86c) and $c = u > 0$ and $\eta = -\alpha < 0$ in (7.86e) with $\omega(1)=1$ then the inequality measures and the transformed equality measures are identical.With $c = -1$ in (7.86c) and $c=1$ in (7.86e) the measures equal $K_c^r(\alpha) = 1 + \frac{1}{\alpha} \log\{\int_0^1 e^{-\alpha\tau(p)} dp\}$ and are labelled Kolm's relative leftist measures.Letting $c=-\mu$ in (7.86c) and $c=\mu$ in (7.86e) we have the corresponding AI-measures.These measures are not CI-measures.Kolm[1976b-p.83] assumed α to be mean dependent,i.e.$\alpha = \alpha(\mu)$,and by this definition it is possibl to construct CI-measures.(7.86a) and (7.86b) are either RI- or AI-measures, depending on the choice of c,but not CI-measures.

As stated in sec. 7.4.1 and as shown by Kolm [1976a - p. 436] (7.86c), with $\eta > 0$, $c < 0$ and $W(p) = 1$, the limiting case of Kolm's centrist measure when ξ and $\varepsilon = 1-\eta$ tends to infinity as $\frac{\varepsilon}{\xi} = \frac{1-\eta}{\xi}$ tends towards $\alpha(<\infty)$. This measure is labelled the leftist measure and Kolm denotes $\eta = \alpha$.[1)] The measure gives highest weights to low incomes. Incomes below the arithmetic mean income (μ) obtain weights greater than one (incomes higher than μ obtains weights lower than one). The higher $\eta = \alpha$ is, the higher weights are given to low incomes.

---

1) Blackorby, Donaldson and Auersperg [1978 - p.9] and Blackorby and Donaldson [1980 - p.116] label Kolm's leftist measure the Kolm-Pollak index, since Pollak [1971] established the form of utility functions being additively separable and homothetic to minus infinity.

Table 7.11 Some inequality measures belonging to the ESD-class, defined by (7.86a).
$\tau_r(p)$ is the slope of the tangent to the reference distribution. c = -1 is an *RI*- preferring quantity.
DINET is a stronger version of INET ("the principle of transfers").

$\tau_r(p)$	W(p) Weight function	η	c	*RI*/*AI*	MEASURE	Notes and alternative ways of expressing the measure	RANGE	INET/DINET	The measures gives highest weight to
1	1	$\alpha > o$	-1	*RI*	Kolm's relative leftist measure	(7.86c) (7.86e) with $\alpha < 0$ and c = 1.	[0,1]	$DINET_\tau$	low incomes

7.4.4 OTHER MEASURES

When our general family of measures was discussed we imposed on the weight function that it should be continuously differentiable. Instead of this restrictive assumption we may impose that the weight function is only continuous[1).]

This implies that even level parameters can be classified into the general measure.[2)]

As examples of such measures consider the SD-class of ordinary inequality measures with $\eta = 1$. Having a weight function (constant score function, see Mehran [1976 - p. 806]), equal to 0 at $p = 0$, 1 at $0 < p < 1$ and 2 at $p = 1$ we obtain $c(\tau(1) - \tau(0))$, i.e. with $c = 1$ the standardized (or relative) range and with $c = \mu$ the range, see sec. 7.1.2. On the other hand if $W(p)$ is a "step score function" (see Mehran [1976 - p. 806]) equal to

$$W(p) = \begin{cases} -1 & \text{if } p \leq p_\mu \\ 1 & \text{if } p > p_\mu \end{cases}$$

we have the relative ($c = 1$) or the absolute ($c = \mu$) mean deviation. This measure can be written as

$$c\frac{\delta_\mu}{\mu} = 2c[F(\mu) - F_1(\mu)] = \tag{7.87a}$$

$$= 2c\{(-1)\int_0^{p_\mu}(\tau(p)-1)\,dp + \int_{p_\mu}^{1}(\tau(p)-1)dp\} = \tag{7.87b}$$

$$= \frac{c}{\mu}\int_0^\infty |y-\mu|dF(y) \tag{7.87c}$$

---

1) Mehran [1976 - p.806] imposed the corresponding constraint function to be nondecreasing and continuous.

2) Mehran [1976 - p.805] labelled his constraint function a "score function".

The mean deviation (δ_μ) as a measure of inequality was introduced by Bortkiewicz (see Bortkiewicz [1930 - p.16]) in 1898 and the relative mean deviation was proposed by Bresciani-Turroni [1910] and by Ricci in 1916 (see Bortkiewicz [1930 - p.17] and Piesch [1975 - p. 54]). Ricci also defined the maximum equalization ratio,[1] MER, which equals $\frac{\delta_\mu}{2\mu}$ (see Yntema [1933 - p. 425 footnote 1] and Piesch [1975 - p.54, footnote 2]).

Both $\frac{\delta_\mu}{\mu}$ and $\frac{\delta_\mu}{2\mu}$ were suggested as measures by Schutz [1951 - p.111] (see also Rosenbluth [1951]). The relative mean deviation has also been proposed by e.g. Kuznetz [1957, 1959] (with data in grouped form) and Morrison [1978]. These measures have the following ranges :

the mean deviation, $\delta\mu$:	[0,2]
the relative mean deviation, $\frac{\delta\mu}{\mu}$:	[0,2]
MER = $\delta\mu/2\mu$:	[0,1]

The interpretation of MER is clear and simple: if we divide the population into two groups, one with incomes less than or equal to the arithmetic mean income μ and one with incomes greater than μ, then the maximum equalization percentage (100 MER) represents the percentage of the total income that should be transferred from the group of i.r.u.'s with incomes greater than μ to the other group so that all i.r.u.'s get the same income.

---

1) 100 times MER gives the maximum equalization percentage, a name which was introduced in Swedish by Lindahl in 1946, see Bentzel [1953 - p.197] for reference.

The MER can easily be interpreted in a Lorenz diagram as the maximum discrepancy between the egalitarian line and the Lorenz Curve, denoted by $A(p_\mu)$ in fig. 7.4, see e.g. Bortkiewicz [1930 - p.17 and fig. 3].[1)] Bortkiewicz [1930 - p.18] also showed that the relative mean difference, $G_r = 2R$, is always greater than the relative mean deviation, $\frac{\delta\mu}{\mu}$. In fact, he showed that G_r can be bounded by MER. The interval, here given for the Gini coefficient $R = G_r/2$, is

$$R \in [\text{MER}, \text{MER}\ (2-\text{MER})]$$ [2)]

The absolute and relative mean deviation and the MER do not in general fulfill INET. It is only sensitive to transfers if the transfer crosses the arithmetic mean income. For a discussion of this/ these measure(s) see e.g. Atkinson [1970], Sen [1973], Piesch [1975], Cowell [1977] and Kakwani [1980b]. More general deviation measures δ_ξ (instead of $\xi = \mu$) are discussed by Piesch [1975 - pp. 58-63].

<u>The length of the Lorenz Curve, λ</u>

Kakwani [1980b - pp.83-85] proposed a "new inequality measure", viz.

$$\lambda^* = \frac{\lambda - \sqrt{2}}{2 - \sqrt{2}}, \qquad \lambda^* \in [0, 1], \tag{7.88}$$

---

1) It is also shown by Bortkiewicz [1930 - p.17 and fig. 3] that the area of the triangle with the sides defined by the egalitarian line and the straight lines between (0,0) and $(p_\mu, L(p_\mu))$ and $(p_\mu, L(p_\mu))$ and (1,1), resp., equals the MER.

2) For a two-points distribution, see Bortkiewicz [1930 - p. 64-72] and Piesch [1975 - pp. 57-58], with the two possible values $\mu_L(p_\mu)$ and $\mu_U(p_\mu)$ (see (7.9) and (7.10)) with probabilities p_μ and $(1-p_\mu)$, resp., is R = MER.

where λ is the length of the Lorenz Curve defined by

$$\lambda = \int_0^1 \sqrt{\tau(p)^2 + 1}\ dp^{1)}, \qquad \lambda \in [\sqrt{2}, 2]. \tag{7.89}$$

As mentioned in the discussion of indicators of the LC, sec. 7.2.2, λ was proposed by Taguchi [1968 - p. 112] and λ^* by Piesch [1975 - pp. 99-100] as a dispersion indicator of the LC.

λ^* is a RI-measure and follows $DINET_\tau$. ~~It~~ attaches higher weight to transfers at the lower end than at the middle and upper ends of the distribution (lemma 5.11 by Kakwani [1980b - p.84]).Regarding the income distribution the measure λ^* attaches highest weight to low incomes.[2)]

An example of Bartel's GWD measure: Gastwirth's index

Bartel's [1977 - p.23] proposed a general class of inequality measures using absolute differences between all possible pairs of values of the income variable Y. The measure, labelled the generalized weighted difference indicator (GWD), was defined as

$$I = \{ \int_0^\infty \int_0^\infty |y-x|^\eta\ W(y,x)\ dF(y)\ dF(x) \}^{1/\eta}, \quad \eta \geq 1.$$

Some of these measures are included in our general family, e.g. if $W(y,x) = 1$ and $\eta = 1$ we obtain the absolute mean difference (see sec. 7.4.1) and if $W(y,x) = 1$ and $\eta = 2$ we obtain $\sqrt{2\sigma^2}$, i.e. the square root

---

1) λ can also be defined as $\lambda = \int_0^1 \sec\theta(p)\, dp$, where θ is the angle between the tangent to the LC in the point (p, L(p)) and the p-axis.

2) λ^* can be rewritten as $\int_0^1 K(p)\,\tau(p)\,dp$, where $K(p) = [\csc\theta(p) - \sqrt{2}]/ /(2-\sqrt{2})$, csc is the cosecant and $\theta(p)$ is defined in footnote 1) above. When p increases from zero to one, $\theta(p)$ increases from zero to $\pi/2$ and $\csc\theta(p)$ decreases from infinity to one.

of the double variance (see also Kendal and Stuart [1977 - vol. 1, p.48]). Bartel's proposed one measure with $W(y,x) = |F(y) - F(x)|$ which he labelled the rank-order weighted mean difference (RWMD), but this is nothing else but the absolute Gini coefficient.

Another measure in the GWD-family is the income weighted mean difference (IWMD), see Bartels [1977 - p.23], which is defined with $\eta = 1$ and $W(y,x) = (y+x)^{-1}$. This measure was proposed by Gastwirth [1973] and equals

$$IWMD = \int_0^\infty \int_0^\infty \frac{|y-x|}{y+x} \, dF(x) \, dF(y).$$

It is not an inequality measure in our sense since it vanishes both for the EGAL and the CON[1] distributions. Between these extreme distributions it takes positive values. If we e.g. consider a two-point distribution with possible values a and b, $b > a$, with probabilities p and q, respectively ($p+q = 1$), then it equals[2] $2pq\,(\frac{b-a}{b+a})$. Its maximum is obtained for $a = 0$ ($b = \mu/q$) and $p = q = 0.5$ which yields $IWMD = 0.5$.[3] The disadvantage of this measure is the confusion in the interpretation of one or two values on it and since it is not an inequality measure in our sense we will not discuss it any further.

---

1) Using $\lim_{a \to 0} \frac{a-a}{a+a} = 0$

2) or $IWMD = 2pq\,(\frac{b-\mu}{b(p-q)+\mu})$, $b > \mu = pa + qb$

3) The maximum of IWMD depends on the distribution, e.g. if we have a three point distribution with possible income values 0,1 and c with equal probabilities then IWMD has an upper bound at 5/9 (obtained when $c \to \infty$).

8. THE LORENZ CURVE AND PRACTICAL CALCULATIONS

In the last chapter we made a review of the Lorenz Curve and related topics. We also introduced a general measure of inequality. The discussion was partly made in the continuous case and partly in the discrete case.

This chapter starts with a discussion of the Lorenz Curve in the discrete case (section 8.1).The discussion is then extended to weighted Lorenz areas and the computation of inequality values is illustrated by a simple example.
Next is the effect of a rank preserving transfer discussed and the problem of intersecting Lorenz Curves is illustrated by an example.

Section 8.2 defines, in the discrete case, the general measure of inequality corresponding to that of sec.7.4 and discusses some measures.

Section 8.3 discusses various methods of obtaining lower and upper bounds on some measures when data is given in grouped form.
Data from Finland and Sweden given in chapter 2 is used for illustration.

8.1 THE LORENZ CURVE AND THE LORENZ AREA IN THE DISCRETE CASE

The population is assumed to consist of N i.r.u.'s, with incomes $Y_1, \ldots, Y_N$. The arithmetic mean income $\mu = N^{-1} \sum_{i=1}^{N} Y_i$. By the notation $Y_{(i)}$ we mean the corresponding rank-ordered income, i.e. $Y_{(1)} \leq Y_{(2)} \leq \ldots \leq Y_{(N)}$. The c.d.f. $F(Y_i)$ and the 1st m.d.f. $F_1(Y_i)$ is defined by

$$F(Y_i) = \frac{i}{N} \qquad i = 1, 2, \ldots, N$$

$$F_1(Y_i) = \frac{S_i}{N\mu} = (N\mu)^{-1} \sum_{j=1}^{i} Y_{(j)} = N^{-1} \sum_{j=1}^{i} \tau_j,$$

where $S_i = \sum_{j=1}^{i} Y_{(j)}$ and $\tau_j = Y_{(j)}/\mu$. The corresponding frequency and 1st moment frequency function is $f_i = \frac{1}{N}$ and $f_{1i} = \frac{Y_{(i)}}{N\mu}$, resp.

If $N < \infty$, the Lorenz Curve defined by the (N+1) points $(F(y_o), F_1(Y_o)) = (0,0)$ and $(F(Y_i), F_1(Y_i))$, $i=1, 2, \ldots, N, ((F(Y_N), (F_1(Y_N)) = (1,1))$ is a polygon graph as in figure 8.1 where N=4.

To illustrate the construction of the discrete Lorenz Curve (LC) and the determination of the Lorenz area (LA) we take the following simple example.

Example 8.1a Let the population consist of N=4 i.r.u.'s with incomes 1, 2, 3, 4. Hence $\mu = 2.5$ and $N\mu = 10$. The c.d.f. and the 1st m.d.f. is given by:

rank-order, i:	1	2	3	4
$F(Y_i)$:	1/4	2/4	3/4	1
$F_1(Y_i)$:	1/10	3/10	6/10	1
$A(F(Y_i))$:	6/40	8/40	6/40	0

The LC is now, see figure 8.1, defined by the straight lines connecting the points $(F(Y_{i-i}), F_1(Y_{i-i})$ and $(F(Y_i), F_1(Y_i))$, $i = 0, 1, \ldots, N$ where $(F(Y_o), F_1(Y_o)) =$ $= (0,0)$ and $(F(Y_N), F_1(Y_n)) = (1,1)$.

The Lorenz area (LA) can now be written in several ways. Alternative expressions are given in table 8.1. The LA for the EGAL distribution equals zero, i.e. $LA_{EGAL} = 0$, and the LA for the CON distribution equals $\frac{1}{2}(1-\frac{1}{N})$, which clearly depends on N. In our example above LA_{CON} equals 3/8. A 'normalized' LA can be defined by $LA^* = \frac{N}{N-1} LA$ and hence LA and LA* are defined at $[0, \frac{1}{2}(1 - \frac{1}{N})]$ and $[0, \frac{1}{2}]$, resp.

LA can e.g. be expressed in the following ways, c.f. table 8.1,

$$LA = \frac{1}{2} \sum_{i=1}^{N} f_{1i} \; (F(Y_i) + F(Y_{i-1})) - \frac{1}{2} = \tag{8.1a}$$

$$= \frac{1}{2} - \frac{1}{2} \sum_{i=1}^{N} f_i \; (F_1(Y_i) + F_1(Y_{i-1})) = \tag{8.1b}$$

$$= \frac{1}{N} \sum_{i=1}^{N-1} A\,(F(Y_i)) = \frac{1}{N} \sum_{i=1}^{N-1} \{ F(Y_i) - F_1(Y_i) \} \tag{8.2}$$

Expression (8.1a) can be intepreted as the sum of the area parts

$$f_{1i} \; \frac{F(Y_i) + F(Y_{i-1})}{2}$$

Figure 8.1 Interpretations of some expressions for the Lorenz area. The expressions (8.1a) and (8.1b) are interpreted in figure 8.1a and expression (8.2) is interpreted in figure 8.1b.

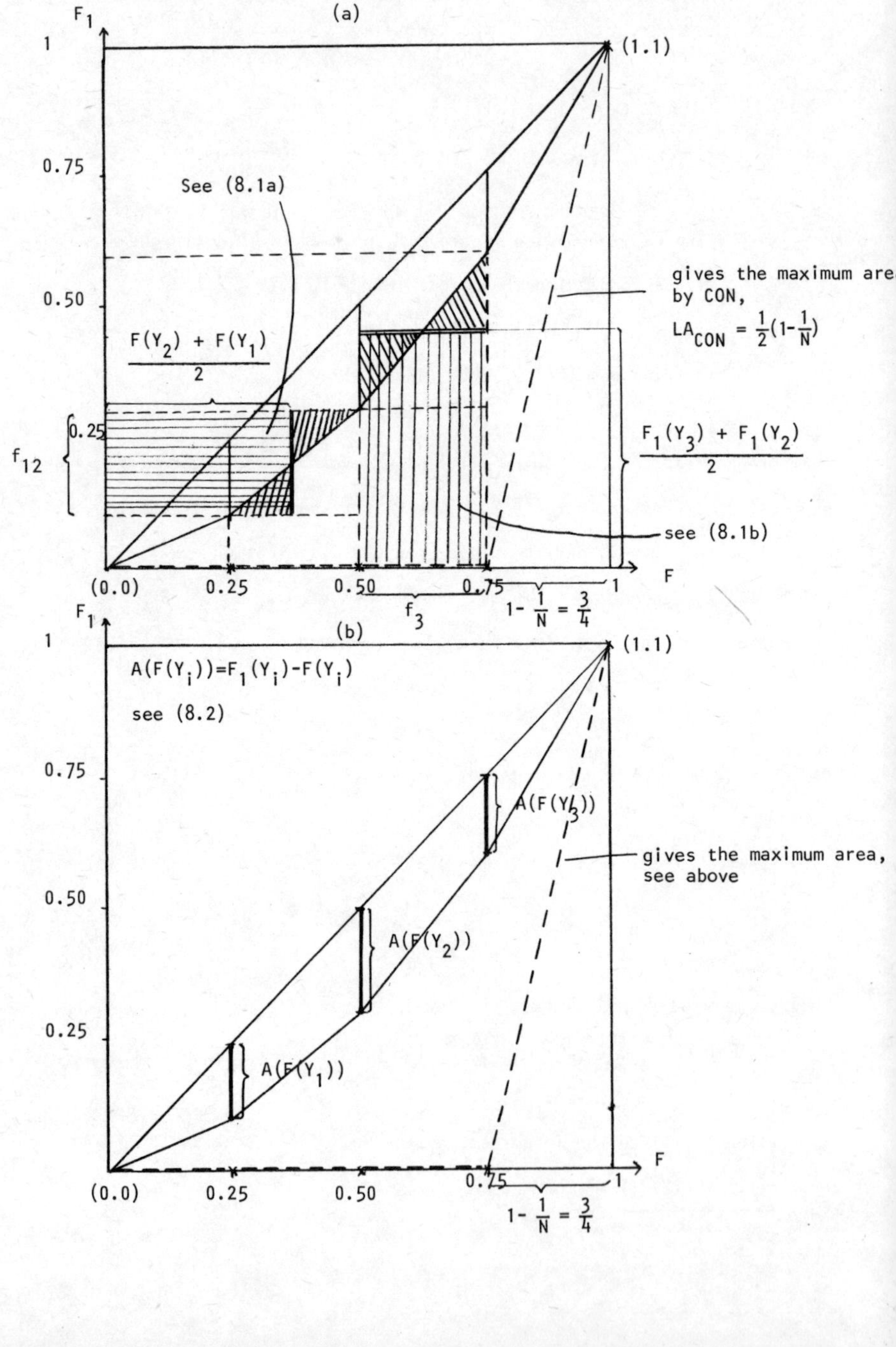

Table 8.1 Alternative ways of expressing the Lorenz area (LA) in the discrete case.

$LA \in [0, \frac{1}{2}(1 - \frac{1}{N})]$	
$LA = \frac{1}{4N^2\mu} \sum_{i=1}^{N} \sum_{j=1}^{N} \mid Y_j - Y_i \mid =$	$\mid a-b \mid = a+b - 2 \min (a, b)$
$= \frac{1}{2} - \frac{1}{2N^2\mu} \sum_{i=1}^{N} \sum_{j=1}^{N} \min (Y_i, Y_j) =$	
$= \frac{1}{2} - \frac{1}{2N} - \frac{1}{N^2\mu} \sum_{i=1}^{N} (N-i+1) Y_{(i)}$	$Y_{(1)} \leq Y_{(2)} \leq \dots \leq Y_{(N)}$
$= \frac{1}{N^2\mu} \sum_{i=1}^{N} iY_{(i)} - \frac{1}{2} (\frac{N+1}{N}) =$	
$= \frac{Cov(i, Y_{(i)})}{N\mu} = Cov(F(Y_i), \tau_i) =$	$F(Y_i) = \frac{i}{N}, \tau_i = \frac{Y_{(i)}}{\mu}$
$= \frac{1}{N^2\mu} \sum_{i=1}^{N} \sum_{j=1}^{N} \mid Y_i - Y_j \mid \cdot \mid F(Y_i) - F(Y_j) \mid =$	
$= \frac{1}{N} \sum_{i=1}^{N-1} A(F(Y_i)) = \frac{1}{N} \sum_{i=1}^{N-1} (F(Y_i) - F_1(Y_i)) =$	The arithmetic mean of differences $A(F(Y_i))$, see figure 8.1b.
$= \frac{1}{2} \sum_{i=1}^{N} f_{1i} (F(Y_i) + F(Y_{i-1})) - \frac{1}{2} =$	see figure 8.1a $\quad F(Y_i)+F(Y_{i-1})=\frac{2i-1}{N}$
$= \frac{1}{2} - \frac{1}{2} \sum_{i=1}^{N} f_i (F_1(Y_i) + F_1(Y_{i-1})) =$	
$= \frac{1}{2} \sum_{i>j} (f_j f_{1i} - f_i f_{1j}) = \frac{1}{2N} \sum_{i>j} (f_{1i} - f_{1j}) =$	$f_i = \frac{1}{N}$
$= \frac{1}{2} \sum_{i=1}^{N} (\frac{i-1}{N}) f_{1i} - \frac{1}{2} \sum_{i=1}^{N} (\frac{N-i}{N}) f_{1i}$	
$LA^* = \frac{N}{N-1} LA \quad \in [0, \frac{1}{2}]$	
$LA^* = \frac{N}{N-1} LA =$	LA, see above
$= \frac{1}{2} \frac{\sum_{i=1}^{N-1} A(F(Y_i))}{\sum_{i=1}^{N-1} F(Y_i)} = \frac{1}{2} \frac{\sum_{i=1}^{N-1} (F(Y_i) - F_1(Y_i))}{\sum_{i=1}^{N-1} (F(Y_i))} =$	
$= \frac{1}{2} \frac{\sum_{i=1}^{N-1} \{(1-F_1(Y_i)) - (1-F(Y_i))\}}{\sum_{i=1}^{N-1} (1-F(Y_i))} =$	$\sum_{i=1}^{N-1} F(Y_i) = \sum_{i=1}^{N-1} (1-F(Y_i)) = \frac{N-1}{2}$
$= \frac{1}{N-1} \sum_{i=1}^{N-1} (F(Y_i) - F_1(Y_i)) = \frac{1}{N-1} \sum_{i=1}^{N-1} \{(1-F_1(Y_i)) - (1-F(Y_i))\}$	

minus the area above the diagonal line (= $^1/2$) and expression (8.1b) as the area below the diagonal line (= $^1/2$) minus the sum of the area parts

$$f_i\left\{\frac{F_i(Y_i) + F_i(Y_{i-1})}{2}\right\},$$ see figure 8.1a.

However, expression (8.2) gives perhaps a simpler interpretation in the Lorenz diagram, see figure 8.1b. It is the arithmetic mean of the N differences $A(F(Y_i)) = F(Y_i) - F_1(Y_i)$ where $A(F(Y_N)) = 0$. Hence the 'normalized' equivalent

$$LA^* = \frac{N}{N-1} LA = \frac{1}{N-1} \sum_{i=1}^{N=1} (F(Y_i) - F_i(Y_i))$$

is perhaps intuitively more appealing as an "arithmetic mean" definition.

Example 8.1b In the example above the differences $A(F(y_i))$ are given and these sum up to $^{20}/40 = ^1/2$ and hence the Lorenz area equals

$$LA = \frac{1}{4} \cdot \frac{1}{2} = \frac{1}{8} \quad , \quad LA \in [0, ^3/_8]$$

$$LA^* = \frac{4}{3} \cdot \frac{1}{8} = \frac{1}{6} \quad , \quad LA^* \in [0, ^1/2]$$

Weighted Lorenz Area

As a measure of inequality, corresponding to the earlier definition (7.56), we use a weighted arithmetic mean of differences $A(F(Y_i))$ defined by

$$I^*(Y,N) = \frac{1}{N-1} \sum_{i=1}^{N-1} V(F(Y_i)) \cdot \{F(Y_i) - F_1(Y_i)\} =$$

$$= \frac{1}{N-1} \sum_{i=1}^{N-1} V(F(Y_i)) \cdot A(F(Y_i)). \qquad (8.3)$$

Having a constant preference (weight) function $V(F(Y_i))$, cf. sec. 7.4, equal to 2 gives us the wellknown Gini coefficient, $R^* \in [0,1]$

Since the Gini coefficient equals twice the Lorenz area we have

$$R = 2LA \quad \in [0, 1-\frac{1}{N}] \qquad \text{and } R^* = 2LA^* \in [0,\ 1],$$

where LA and LA* are given in table 8.1.

Gini [1914] defined the concentration ratio (= the Gini coefficient) as the ratio between the actual Lorenz area and the Lorenz area of the CON distribution. It is easily seen that this equals R* since

$$R^* = \frac{LA^*}{LA^*_{CON}} = \frac{LA}{{}^1/_2} =$$

$$= \frac{LA}{LA_{CON}} = \frac{N}{N-1}\, 2LA = 2LA^*$$

The measures defined by Mehran, Piesch, Bonferroni and de Vergottini in table 7.4 can be written as below, where the measures with a * are defined as (8.3). On the other hand the measures without a * are defined as $I = \frac{N-1}{N} I^*$.

Measure	$V(F(Y_i))$	$\sum_{i=1}^{N-1} V(F(Y_i))$	Definition and interval
GINI	2	2(N-1)	$R = 2LA \quad \in [0,\ 1-\frac{1}{N}]$
			$R^* = \frac{N}{N-1} R \in [0,\ 1]$
MEHRAN	$6(1-F(Y_i)) =$		$M = \frac{6}{N} \sum_{i=1}^{N-1} (1-\frac{i}{N})\, A(F(Y_i)) \in [0,\ 1-\frac{1}{N^2}] =$
	$= \frac{6(N-i)}{N}$	$\frac{11(N-1)}{2}$	$= [0,\ (1-\frac{1}{N})\ (1+\frac{1}{N})]$
			$M^* = \frac{N}{N-1} M \in [0,\ 1+\frac{1}{N}]$

Measure	$V(F(Y_i))$	$\sum_{i=1}^{N-1} V(F(Y_i))$	Definition and interval
PIESCH	$3F(Y_i)$	$\frac{3(N-1)}{2}$	$P = \frac{3}{N} \sum_{i=1}^{N-1} (\frac{i}{N})\, A(F(Y_i)) \in [0,(1-\frac{1}{N})(1-\frac{1}{2N})]$
			$P^* = \frac{N}{N-1} P \quad \in [0,\ 1-\frac{1}{2N}]$
BONFERRONI[1]	$F(Y_i)^{-1}$	$N \sum_{i=1}^{N-1} \frac{1}{i}$ [2]	$B = \frac{1}{N} \sum_{i=1}^{N-1} (\frac{N}{i})\, A(F(Y_i)) \in [0,\ 1-\frac{1}{N}]$
			$B^* = \frac{N}{N-1} B \quad \in [0,\ 1]$
de VERGOTTINI[1]	$(1-F(Y_i))^{-1}$	$N \sum_{i=1}^{N-1} \frac{1}{(N-i)}$ [3]	$dV = \frac{1}{N} \sum_{i=1}^{N-1} (\frac{N}{N-i})\, A(F(Y_i)) \in [0,\ \sum_{j=2}^{N} j^{-1}]$ [4]
			$dV^* = \frac{N}{N-1} dV \in [0,\ \frac{N}{N-1} \sum_{j=2}^{N} j^{-1}]$ [4]

Example 8.1c: The measures, defined above, are calculated for the previous example and is given below together with the possible range of the measures when N = 4.

Gini	$R = {}^1/_4$	$R \in [0,\ {}^3/_4]$
	$R^* = {}^1/_3$	$R^* \in [0,\ 1]$
Mehran	$M = {}^3/_8$	$M \in [0,\ {}^{15}/_4]$
	$M^* = {}^1/_2$	$M^* \in [0,\ {}^5/_4]$

---

1) cf. e.g. Piesch [1975, p.121 and p.123]

2) e.g. if N = 4, $N\Sigma i^{-1} = 7^1/3$

3) e.g. if N = 4, $N\Sigma(N-i)^{-1} = 7^1/3$

4) The upper bounds of dV and dV* are not finite when N tends towards infinity, since $\int_2^\infty x^{-1} dx = [\log x]_2^\infty = \infty$

Piesch	$P = {}^{3}/_{16}$	$P \in [0, {}^{21}/_{32}]$
	$P^* = {}^{1}/_{4}$	$P^* \in [0, {}^{7}/_{8}]$
Bonferroni	$B = {}^{3}/_{10}$	$B \in [0, {}^{3}/_{4}]$
	$B^* = {}^{4}/_{10}$	$B^* \in [0, 1]$
de Vergottini	$dV = {}^{3}/_{10}$	$dV \in [0, {}^{19}/_{3}]$
	$dV^* = {}^{4}/_{10}$	$dV^* \in [0, {}^{22}/_{3}]$

The numerical identities between Bonferroni's measures and de Vergottini's measures depend on the symmetry in $A(F(Y_i))$ and the symmetry in i^{-1} and $(N-i)^{-1}$.

The RI-measures defined by (7.58) can be written as[1)]

$$I(Y,N) = \frac{1}{N}\sum_{i=1}^{N} W\,(F(Y_i))\left[\frac{Y_{(i)}}{\mu} - 1\right] = \frac{1}{N}\sum_{i=1}^{N} W\,(F(Y_i))[\tau_{(i)} - 1] \qquad (8.4a)$$

$$= \sum_{i=1}^{N} C\,(F(Y_i))\,\frac{Y_{(i)}}{N\mu} = \frac{1}{N}\sum_{i=1}^{N} C\,(F(Y_i))\,\tau_{(i)} \qquad (8.4b)$$

where $C\,(F(Y_i)) = W\,(F(Y_i)) - \frac{1}{N}\sum_{i=1}^{N} W(F(Y_i))$, and $I^*(Y,N) = \frac{N}{N-1}\,I(Y,N)$, where $I^*(Y,N)$ corresponds to (8.3).

The weight functions $W(F(Y_i))$ and the constraint function $C(F(Y_i))$ for the measures given above can be obtained from $I(Y,N) = \frac{N-1}{N}I^*(Y,N)$, where $I^*(Y,N)$ is (8.3). The corresponding preference functions are taken from the above scheme. The measures R, M, B, B and dV are rewritten in table 8.2.

1) The $W(\cdot)$-function and the corresponding $C(\cdot)$-function are obtained on the basis of the $V(\cdot)$-function. If we instead (cf. sec.10.2) had defined the measures according to (8.4a) with a function $W(\cdot)$, similar to those in sec. 7.4, we would have obtained different preference functions $V(\cdot)$.

Table 8.2 The measures by Gini, Mehran, Piesch, Bonferroni and de Vertottini written as i) weighted slope differences using a weight function $W(F(Y_i)) = W({}^i/_N)$, see (8.4a) and ii) weighted slopes using a constraint function $C(F(Y_i)) = C({}^i/_N)$.

Measure		$W(F(Y_i)) = W(\frac{i}{N})$	$C(F(Y_i)) = C(\frac{i}{N})$
Gini	R	$2\frac{i}{N}$	$\frac{2i-N-1}{N}$
Mehran	M	$6\frac{i}{N}\ (1+\frac{1}{2N}) - 3(\frac{i}{N})^2$	$6\frac{i}{N}\ (1+\frac{1}{2N}) - 3(\frac{i}{N})^2 - \frac{(N+1)(2N+1)}{N^2}$
Piesch	P	$\frac{3i(i-1)}{2N^2}$	$\frac{3i(i-1)}{2N^2} - \frac{(N-1)(N+1)}{2N^2}$
Bonferroni	B	$-\sum_{j=i}^{N} \frac{1}{j}$	$1 - \sum_{j=i}^{N} \frac{1}{j}$
de Vergottini	dV	$-\sum_{j=i}^{N-1} \frac{1}{N-j}$, if $i = N$ then $\sum_{j=i}^{N-1} \frac{1}{N-j} = 0$	$\sum_{j=2}^{N} \frac{1}{j} - \sum_{j=1}^{N-1} \frac{1}{N-j}$

The effect of a rank preserving transfer

Let us perform a rank preserving transfer (cf. criterion TRANSF, sec. 4.2 and the definition of INET, sec. 7.4) and see what the effect will be on the Lorenz Curve.

We take an amount δ from the poor i.r.u. with income $Y_{(p)}$, $Y_{(p-1)} < Y_{(p)} - \delta$, $Y_{(1)} \leq Y_{(2)} \leq \dots \leq Y_{(N)}$, and give this amount to the rich i.r.u. with income $Y_{(r)}$, $Y_{(r)} + \delta < Y_{(r+1)}$. The effect on the Lorenz area is written as $T_{LA} = LA_{after} - LA_{before}$ and equals

$$T_{LA} = \frac{\delta}{N^2\mu}(r-p) > 0.$$

T_{LA} depends on the size of the transfer amount δ, which is small, and on the size of the rank difference.

If we are interested in the effect on the measures above we could e.g. use the constraint definitions given by (8.4b) which show that T equals

$$T = \frac{\delta}{N\mu}[c(r/_N) - c(p/_N)].$$

For the various measures above we have the following effects of rank preserving transfers.

Gini: $$T_R = \frac{2\delta}{N^2\mu}(r-p)$$

Mehran: $$T_M = \frac{3\delta}{N^3\mu}(r-p)\,[(2N+1) - (r+p)]$$

Piesch: $$T_P = \frac{3\delta}{2N^3\mu}(r-p)\,[r+p-1] \qquad 1 \leq \dots \leq p < \dots < r \leq \dots \leq N$$

Bonferroni: $T_B = \frac{\delta}{N\mu} \sum_{j=p}^{r-1} \frac{1}{j}$

de Vergottini: $T_{dV} = \frac{\delta}{N\mu} \sum_{j=p}^{r-1} \frac{1}{N-j}$

As is seen by these expressions only Mehran's and Bonferroni's measures fulfill the stronger criterion "$DINET_p$" (see sec.7.4) and give more weights to transfers among the poor. Piesch's and de Vergottini's measures give more weights to transfers among the rich and Gini's measure equal weights to every part. See the discussion in sec. 7.4.

On the problem of intersecting Lorenz Curves

Very often when we compare two or more Lorenz Curves we are unable to use the criterion of Lorenz domination (LDOM, sec 4.2) to rank the income distributions according to their intrinsic equality (or inequality) since two LC's intersect. Assume that we have two LC's, labelled LC_1 and LC_2, intersecting once and with equally sized Lorenz areas.

Since the Lorenz areas are equal the corresponding Gini coefficients, R_1 and R_2, fail to rank the two income distributions since $R_1 = R_2$. We could instead use some other measure (or measures) which gives more weight to some parts of the distribution. Since our concern with the i.r.u.'s is often focused on the i.r.u.'s with low incomes we could adopt a measure which focuses on low incomes.

Example 8.2 Assume two populations of sizes $N_1 = N_2 = 4$ and equal arithmetic mean income $\mu_1 = \mu_2 = 5$. The c.d.f.'s ($F(Y_i)_1$ and $F(Y_i)_2$) and the 1st m.d.f.'s ($F_1(Y_i)_1$ and $F_1(Y_i)_2$) of the two populations are given below with their difference functions $A_1(F(Y_i))$ and $A_2(F(Y_i))$:

Population 1 with Lorenz Curve LC_1

rank order, i:	1	2	3	4
$F(Y_i)_1$:	$^1/_4$	$^2/_4$	$^3/_4$	1
$F_1(Y_i)_1$:	$^1/_{20}$	$^5/_{20}$	$^{12}/_{20}$	1
$A_1(F(Y_i))$:	$^4/_{20}$	$^5/_{20}$	$^3/_{20}$	0

Population 2 with Lorenz Curve LC_2

rank order, i:	1	2	3	4
$F(Y_i)_2$:	$^1/_4$	$^2/_4$	$^3/_4$	1
$F_1(Y_i)_2$:	$^2/_{20}$	$^5/_{20}$	$^{11}/_{20}$	1
$A_2(F(Y_i))$:	$^3/_{20}$	$^5/_{20}$	$^4/_{20}$	0

The two LC's, LC_1 and LC_2, intersect at the point $(\frac{2}{4}, \frac{5}{20})$ see figure 8.2 and the Lorenz areas are equal: $LA_1 = LA_2 = \frac{3}{20}$ and $LA_1^* = LA_2^* = \frac{4}{20}$.

The measures discussed before are calculated below for the two populations.

	Population 1	Population 2
Gini:	$R_1 = \frac{3}{10}$	$R_2 = \frac{3}{10}$
	$R_1^* = \frac{4}{10}$	$R_2^* = \frac{4}{10}$
Mehran:	$M_1 = \frac{75}{160}$	$M_2 = \frac{69}{160}$
	$M_1^* = \frac{25}{40}$	$M_2^* = \frac{23}{40}$
Piesch:	$P_1 = \frac{69}{320}$	$P_2 = \frac{75}{320}$
	$P_1^* = \frac{23}{80}$	$P_2^* = \frac{25}{80}$
Bonferroni:	$B_1 = \frac{45}{120}$	$B_2 = \frac{41}{120}$
	$B_1^* = \frac{45}{90}$	$B_2^* = \frac{41}{90}$
de Vergottini:	$dV_1 = \frac{41}{120}$	$dV_2 = \frac{45}{120}$
	$dV_1^* = \frac{41}{90}$	$dV_2^* = \frac{45}{90}$

Figure 8.2 Illustration of intersecting Lorenz Curves, LC_1 and LC_2, causing equal Lorenz areas.

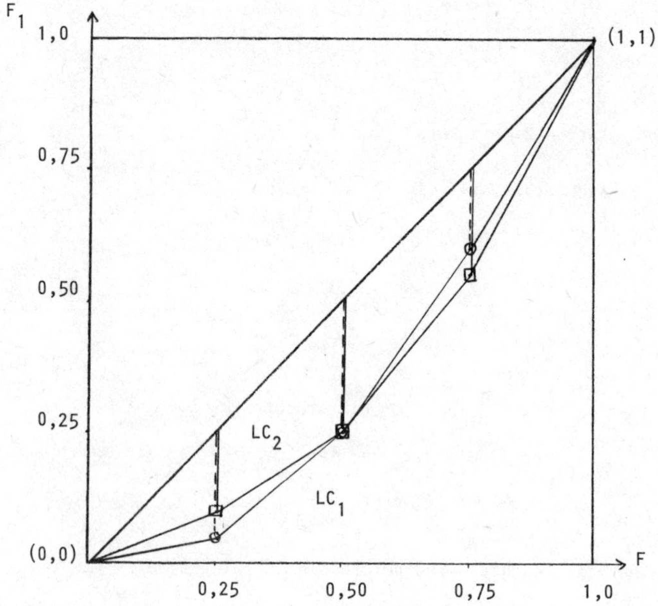

As is seen above the Gini coefficient, R, ranks the two distributions equal (R = 2LA). Mehran's and Bonferroni's measures rank income distribution 2 as more equal than distribution 1 and the reversed ranking is obtained when using Piesch's and de Vergottini's measures. If we are mainly interested in low incomes we should use either Mehran's or Bonferroni's measure (cf. sec. 7.4.1 and table 7.8).

Note the values of Bonferroni's and de Vergottini's measures, which are reversed between the populations. This is so because of the symmetry in their weight-systems and the symmetry in the $A_j(F(Y_i))$, i = 1, 2, 3 and j=1, 2.

8.2 MEASURES OF INEQUALITY

The measure of inequality defined by (8.3), $I^*(Y,N)$, was rewritten by (8.4a)[1]. In accordance with the generalization of (7.57) in sec. 7.4 we now define the following general measure of power η.

Definition 8.1 A general measure of inequality (equality) is given by

$$I(Y,N,\eta) = \{\frac{1}{N}\sum_{i=1}^{N} W(F(Y_i))\ D\ [c\tau_2,\ c\tau_{ri}]^{\eta}\}^{1/\eta}$$

$\eta \neq 0$ (8.5a)

$$\ell og\ I(Y,N,0) = \frac{1}{\omega(1)N}\sum_{i=1}^{N} W(F(Y_i))\ \ell og\ D\ [c\tau_i,\ c\tau_{ri}],$$

$\eta = 0$ (8.5b)

where $\omega(1) = \frac{1}{N}\sum_{i=1}^{N} W(F(Y_i)) \neq 0$

c is a quantity that can be relative/absolute preferring and

$\tau_i = \frac{Y_{(i)}}{\mu}$, where

$Y_{(1)} \leq Y_{(2)} \leq \dots \leq Y_{(N)}$.

The definition is defined in terms of the ordinary LC, c.f. Def. 7.5, and is divided by N and not N-1 as in $I^*(Y,N)$ of sec. 8.1.

We now make a brief review of the three classes defined in sec. 7.4 and the measures discussed in sections 7.4.1 to 7.4.3.

---

1) To be exact it was $I(Y,N) = \frac{N-1}{N} I^*(Y,N)$ that was rewritten in (8.4a).

The principal inequality measures are defined with a reference slope equal to one, i.e. $\tau_{ri} = 1$, $\forall i$, and the equality measures with a reference slope equal to zero, i.e. $\tau_{ri} = 0$, $\forall i$.

<u>The slope difference class (SD)</u>: $D(.,.) = c\ (\tau_i - \tau_{ri})$

With a constant weight function equal to one, $W(F(Y_i)) = 1\ \forall i$, and $c = 1$ ($\tau_{ri} = 1$) we have the coefficient of variation defined as $V = \sigma/\mu$ where σ is equal to $(N^{-1} \sum_{i=1}^{N} (Y_i - \mu)^2)^{1/2}$, i.e. the standard deviation. Related measures are obtained as in table 7.8.

With a weight function of relative ranks, i.e. of $F(Y_i) = \frac{i}{N}$, we have for $\eta = 1$ and $c = 1$ the measures defined and discussed in sec. 8.1 and with a weight function of τ_i's we have e.g. the squared coefficient of variation V^2 ($W = \tau_i$) and the sum of Theil's measures $T_1 + T_2$ ($W = \ell og\tau_i$), see table 7.8.

The inequality measures transformed from equality measures with $\tau_{ri} = -\xi/\mu$ $\eta = 1 - \varepsilon$, $c = 1$, and $W(F(Y_i)) = 1$ are Kolm's μ-modified centrist measures $K_c^m\ (\xi, \varepsilon), \xi > 0$ and $\varepsilon > 0$. With $\xi = 0$ we obtain Atkinson's measure (Kolm's relative rightist measure $A(\varepsilon) = K_c^m\ (0,\varepsilon)$). See table 7.9 and sec. 7.4.1. Kolm's μ-modified centrist measures can be written as

$$K_c^m\ (\xi, \varepsilon) = (1 + \xi/\mu) - \{\frac{1}{N} \sum_{i=1}^{N} (\tau_1 + \frac{\xi}{\mu})^{1-\varepsilon}\}^{1/(1-\varepsilon)}, \ \varepsilon \neq 1 \qquad (8.6a)$$

and

$$K_{ce}^m(\xi, 0) = (1 + \xi/\mu) - \exp\{\frac{1}{N} \sum_{i=1}^{N} \ell og\ (\tau_i + \xi/\mu)\}, \ \varepsilon = 1 \qquad (8.6b)$$

or

$$K^{m}_{\ell og} (\xi, 0) = \log (1+\xi/\mu) - \frac{1}{N} \sum_{i=1}^{N} \log(\tau_i + \xi/\mu), \; \varepsilon = 1 \qquad (8.6c)$$

With $\xi = 0$ (8.6b) equals the Atkinson-Champarnowne's measure (Ch) and (8.6c) Theil's 2nd measure, see sec. 7.4.1.

The log-slope difference class (LSD): $D(\cdot,\cdot) = \log \tau_i - \log \tau_{ri}$. With a constant weight function equal to one, $\tau_{ri} = 1$ and $\eta = 2$ we have for c = 1 the quasi-standard deviation, i.e. $\sigma_q = (N^{-1} \sum_{i=1}^{N} (\log\tau_i)^2)^{1/2}$

Theil's 1st measure is obtained by a weight function equal to τ_i and $\eta = 1$ and c = 1, i.e.

$$T_1 = \frac{1}{N} \sum_{i=1}^{N} \tau_i \log \tau_i = \frac{1}{N\mu} \sum_{i=1}^{N} Y_i \log Y_i - \log \mu = \log \mu_{gW} - \log \mu,$$

where μ_{gW} is a weighted geometrical mean, see sec. 7.4.2.

The exponential-slope difference class (ESD): $D(\cdot,\cdot) = e^{c(\tau_i - \tau_{ri})}$

Kolm's relative leftist measure is defined by letting $\tau_r(p) = 1$, $W(F(Y_i)) = 1$, c = - 1 and $\eta = \alpha > 0$, i.e.

$$I = \left(\frac{1}{N} \sum_{i=1}^{N} e^{\alpha(1 - \tau_i)} \right)^{1/\alpha},$$

or by the transformation, see Kolm [1976a, b],

$$K^{r}_{\ell}(\alpha) = \log I = \frac{1}{\alpha} \log [\frac{1}{N} \sum_{i=1}^{N} e^{\alpha(1-\tau_i)}] = 1 + \frac{1}{\alpha} \log [\frac{1}{N} \sum_{i=1}^{N} e^{-\alpha\tau_1}],$$

where the last expression is the inequality measure transformed from an equality measure, cf. sec. 7.4.3.

Lower and upper bounds and an example

The lower and upper bounds for some measures are given in table 8.3. The upper bounds depend in general on the population size, N, but when N tends to infinity most of the upper bounds tend towards 1, in some cases towards infinity. If the upper bound of a measure depends on N we can divide it with its upper bound (if N is finite) to receive a measure defined at the [0, I]-interval, otherwise we can divide the measure, I, by one plus itself, i.e. $I/(I+1)$. When I tends towards infinity $I/(I+1)$ tends towards one (cf. Champernowne [1974]).

As we have seen in sec. 7.4.1 σ,V and RSMAX (the relative SMAX) are closely interrelated through RSMAX = $\sqrt{V^2 + \mu^{-2} (Y_{max} - \mu)^2}$. Hence, if we compare two distributions of incomes with an equal coefficient of variation and mean income the values of RSMAX only depend on the size of squared deviation between the mean income and the maximum income. The highest inequality measured by RSMAX will in this case be obtained by the distribution with the highest maximum income, cf. the example below.

The normalized SMAX (SMAXN) is by Bartels [1977, p.20] defined as (cf. sec. 7.4.1) $SMAX/(Y_{max} \sqrt{(N-1)/N})$. In the following we have divided the SMAX by its 'CON-value' to obtain SMAXN, i.e. $SMAXN^2 = SMAX/\mu^2 \, N(N-1)$.

To illustrate the various measures given in table 8.3 we use example 8.2 of sec. 8.1.

Table 8.3 Lower and Upper bounds for some measures of inequality. The bounds for the measures given by Gini, Mehran, Piesch, Bonferroni and de Vergottini are given in sec. 8.1.

Class	Measure	Lower bound	Upper bound	Notes	Upper bound when $N \to \infty$
	• Standard deviation, σ	0	$\mu \sqrt{N-1}$		∞
S	• Coefficient of variation, V	0	$\sqrt{N-1}$		∞
	• $V/\sqrt{V^2+1}$	0	$\sqrt{1-{}^1/_N}$		1
D	• RSMAX	0	$\sqrt{N(N-1)}$	The relative SMAX, cf. sec. 7.4.1.	∞
	• SMAXN	0	1	The normalized SMAX = RSMAX/ $\sqrt{N(N-1)}$	1
	• Kolm's μ-modified centrist measure $K_c^m(\xi,\varepsilon)$	0	$(1+\frac{\xi}{\mu}) - \frac{1}{\mu}\{\frac{1}{N}[(N-1)\xi^{1-\varepsilon}+(N\mu+\xi)^{1-\varepsilon}]\}^{1/(1-\varepsilon)}$	$\varepsilon \neq 1,\ \xi > 0$	1
	Atkinson's measure, $A(\varepsilon) = K_c^m(0, \varepsilon)$	0	$1 - ({}^1/_N)^{\varepsilon/(1-\varepsilon)}$	$0 < \varepsilon < 1$	1
		0	1	$\varepsilon > 1$	1
	T_2, Theil's 2nd measures	0	$\ell og(1+\frac{\xi}{\mu})-(1-\frac{1}{N})\ell og\,\frac{\xi}{\mu} - \frac{1}{N}\,\ell og(\frac{N\mu+\xi}{\mu})$	$\xi > 0$ } $\varepsilon = 1$	1
		0	∞	$\xi = 0$ } $\varepsilon = 1$	1
	Champernowne's measures	0	$(1+\frac{\xi}{\mu}) - \frac{\xi}{\mu}\,(1+\frac{N\mu}{\xi})^{1/N}$	$\xi > 0$ } $\varepsilon = 1$	1
		0	1	$\xi = 0$ } $\varepsilon = 1$	1
L	• The quasi standard deviation, σ_q	0	∞	if $Y \in [0,\infty[$	∞
S		0	$[(1-\frac{1}{N})(\ell og\ \mu)^2+\frac{1}{N}[\ell og(N(1-\frac{1}{\mu})+\frac{1}{\mu})]^2]^{1/2}$	if $Y \in [1,\infty[$	$\ell og\ \mu$
D	• T_1, Theil's 1st measure	0	$\sqrt{\ell og\ N}$	if $Y \in [0,\infty[$	∞
		0	$[1-\frac{1}{\mu}+\frac{1}{N}]\ell og[N(\mu-1)+1] - \ell og\ \mu$	if $Y \in [1,\infty[$	∞
E	• Kolm's relative leftist measure	1	$e\{1-\frac{1}{N}+\frac{1}{N}e^{-\alpha N}\}^{1/\alpha}$	measure $[\frac{1}{N}\Sigma e^{\alpha(1-Y_i/\mu)}]^{1/\alpha},\ \alpha > 0$	e
S					
D		0	$1+\frac{1}{\alpha}\,\ell og\ [1-\frac{1}{N}+\frac{1}{N}e^{-\alpha N}]$	the ℓog-variant, $K_\ell^r(\alpha)$	

Example 8.2 cont. In sec. 8.1 we considered an example with two intersecting Lorenz Curves (LC's). The distances between the egalitarian line and the LC's, $A_j(F(Y_i))$, i = 1, 2, 3 and j=1, 2, were symmetrical. Both populations have the size $N_j=4$ and the arithmetic mean income $\mu_j=5$, j=1, 2. The population values are (note: the incomes are not explicitly given in sec. 8.1):

Pop. 1: 1, 4, 7, 8 Pop. 2: 2, 3, 6, 9

The geometrical mean incomes, μ_{gj}, j=1, 2, are $\mu_{g1} \approx 3.868673$ and $\mu_{g2} \approx 4.242641$. The inequalities in the two distributions are given for some measures in table 8.4 together with the upper bound of each measure. The lower bounds are always zero except for the original ESD-class measure whose lower bound is one (the *log*-variant, cf. Kolm [1976a, b], has the lower bound zero). Note that σ, V and $V/\sqrt{V^2+1}$ give equal inequalities to the two distributions, resp., and that RSMAX (the relative SMAX) and SMAXN (the normalized SMAX) give higher inequalities to distribtion 2. As we have seen in sec. 7.4.1 this is only the effect of the squared deviation between the maximum income and the arithmetic mean income, e.g. RSMAX can be written as $\sqrt{V^2 + \mu^{-2}(Y_{max} - \mu)^2}$, where V and μ are equal in the two distributions.

Atkinson's measure has the upper bound one if $\varepsilon > 1$ but if $0 < \varepsilon < 1$ the upper bound clearly depends on the population size (and ε) through the relation $1 - N^{-\varepsilon/(1-\varepsilon)}$ (cf. table 8.3). The upper bound of the *log*-variant of the ESD-class measure (Kolm's relative leftist measure) depends also on the population size (and α) through $1 + \alpha^{-1} \log [1-N^{-1}+N^{-1}e^{-\alpha N}]$, where the second term is always less than or equal to zero and hence the maximum upper bound is one. This bound is obtained either if N tends towards infinity (fixed $\alpha > 0$) or if α tends towards infinity (fixed $N > 2$).

Example 8.2 cont. Let us summarize the results of example 8.2. As we have seen some measures cannot rank the two distributions (on cardinal level), on the other hand, some measures rank the two distributions but give different weights to various parts of the distribution. The results are given in the following table where I_j, j=1, 2, denote an arbitrary inequality measure.

Measures (RI-measures)	The measure gives highest weights to
$I_1 > I_2$	
Mehran's measure, M	Low incomes
Bonferroni's measure, B	" "
Atkinson's measure, $A(\varepsilon)$	" "
Theil's 2nd measure, T_2	" " 1)
Champerowne's measure, Ch	" "
The quasi standard deviation, s_q	" "
Theil's 1st measure, T_1	High incomes 2)
Kolm's relative leftist measure, (K, $\log$ K)	Low incomes
$I_1 = I_2$	
Gini coefficient, R	Extreme incomes
Coefficient of variation, V	High incomes
$I_1 < I_2$	
Piesch's measure, P	High incomes
de Vergottini's measure, dV	" "
RSMAX (SMAXN)	——

1) If $Y \in [0,\infty[$ T_2 gives highest weight to zero incomes, if $Y \in [1,\infty[$ T_2 has no clear level of sensitivity. This can be seen by writing $T_2 = \frac{1}{N}\Sigma[\mu^{-1} \log \mu - Y_i^{-1} \log Y_i]\, Y_i$.

2) If $Y_i \in [1,\infty[$; if $Y \in [0,\infty[$ then T_1 gives highest weight to extreme incomes and especially to zero incomes. This can be seen by writing $T_1 = \frac{1}{N\mu}\Sigma[\log \frac{Y_i}{\mu}]\, Y_i$.

Table 8.4 Inequality in the populations given in example 8.2 measured by some inequality measures. The upper bound of each measure is also given ($N_1 = N_2 = 4$, $\mu_1 = \mu_2 = 5$). If nothing else is stated the lower bounds are equal to zero. See also example 8.2 in sec. 8.1.

Class	Measure	Population 1	Population 2	Upper bound
	• the standard deviation, σ	$\sqrt{7.5} \approx 2.738613$	$\sqrt{7.5} \approx 2.738613$	$\sqrt{75} \approx 8.660254$
	• the coefficient of variation,	$\sqrt{1.5} \approx 1.224745$	$\sqrt{1.5} \approx 1.224745$	$\sqrt{3} \approx 1.732051$
	• $V/\sqrt{V^2+1}$	$\sqrt{6/13} \approx 0.679366$	$\sqrt{6/13} \approx 0.679366$	$\sqrt{3/4} \approx 0.866025$
S	• RSMAX	$\sqrt{0.66} \approx 0.812404$	$\sqrt{0.94} \approx 0.969536$	$\sqrt{12} \approx 3.464102$
D	• SMAXN	$\sqrt{0.055} \approx 0.234521$	$\sqrt{0.078} \approx 0.279801$	1
	• Kolm's relative rightist measure ($\xi = 0$):			
	Atkinson's measure $\varepsilon = 0.5$	0.102354	0.076413	$3/4$
	$\varepsilon = 1.5$	0.357387	0.220431	1
	$\varepsilon = 2.0$	0.472941	0.280000	1
	$\varepsilon = 5.0$	0.717479	0.460898	1
	$\varepsilon = 10.0$	0.766694	0.534720	1
	-"- $\varepsilon = 1$: T_2 (Theil's 2nd measure)	0.256526	0.164252	∞
	-"- $\varepsilon = 1$: Champernowne's measure	0.226265	0.151472	1
L	• the quasi standard deviation, s_q	0.862294	0.621641	∞ if $Y \in [0, \infty[$ 1,5222210 if $Y \in [1, \infty[$
S	• T_1 (Theil's 1st measure)	0.180666	0.150948	$\sqrt{\log 4} \approx 1.177410$ if $Y \in [0, \infty[$ 1,365436 if $Y \in [1, \infty[$
D				
E	• Kolm's relative leftist measure, K:			
S	$\alpha = 0,01$ K	1.001502	1.001500	[1, 1.015011]
	$\alpha = 0,01$ $\log$ K	0.001501	0.001499	0.148994
D	$\alpha = 1$ K	1.166519	1.134811	[1, 2.051158]
	$\alpha = 1$ $\log$ K	0.154024	0.126466	0.718405
	$\alpha = 5$ K	1.704213	1.474428	[1, 2.566296]
	$\alpha = 5$ $\log$ K	0.533104	0.388270	0.942464
	$\alpha = 10$ K	1.937927	1.606556	[1, 2.641196]
	$\alpha = 10$ $\log$ K	0.661619	0.474093	0.971232

8.3 CALCULATIONS FROM GROUPED DATA

Usually most of the published and accessible data on incomes is presented and published in a condensed form, i.e. in various groups as income intervals or deciles. If we want to calculate one or more inequality measures we have to calculate estimates by using the grouped data. This can be made by assumptions regarding the within-group variation, i.e. by means of a specification of within group probability density functions or by some interpolations and extrapolation methods, see e.g. Bortkiewicz [1930], Wold [1935], Brittain [1962], Kakwani and Podder [1973], Gastwirth and Glauberman [1976], Eklind [1978] and Kakwani [1980b]. Cf. also ch. 5.

The basic idea of our approach is to obtain lower and upper bounds for the inequality of a continuous distribution avoiding both curve fitting and traditional interpolation or extrapolation methods.

Let the incomes be defined at the [a,b]-interval and ordered. Income data are condensed into k mutually exclusive groups with group boundaries $]a_{i=1}, a_i]$, $i=0, 1, \ldots, k$, $a_o = a \geq o$ and $a_k = b \leq \infty$

Usually the grouping procedure is made by the data producer or the data publisher. The way of grouping (i.e. the choice of income intervals or fractiles) does not in general follow any mathematical/statistical rules but a tradition. If the purpose of the grouping is to calculate inequality measures you can find optimal methods for grouping in a paper by Aghevli and Mehran [1981].

To obtain the lower and upper bounds ($I_L \leq I \leq I_U$), we have to make assumptions regarding the within group inequality (cf. the next chapter). The lower bounds are obtained by the assumption of zero inequality within each group, i.e. all incomes within a group are equal to the arithmetic group mean income. The upper bounds are obtained by the assumption of maximum inequality within each group, subject to the condition that the arithmetic group mean incomes are unchanged.

These assumptions are possible to use on a specific inequality measure <u>only</u> if the principle of transfer (TRANSF of sec. 4.2 and INET of sec. 7.4) is fulfilled (cf. Love and Wolfson [1976 - pp. 69-70]. The possibility and simplicity of the calculations are closely related to the decomposibility of the inequality measures, cf. the next chapter.

For the measures defined as weighted Lorenz areas (see e.g. sec. 8.1) upper bounds can be derived without any other knowledge than the points on the Lorenz Curve. Two methods are given and illustrated for the Gini coefficient.

8.3.1 LOWER BOUNDS, $I_L \leq I$

Assumption 8.1: All incomes *within* group i, i=1, 2, ..., k, equal the arithmetic group mean income, μ_i.

From grouped data we can only get k-1 points on the Lorenz Curve L(p), except (0,0) and (1,1). The Lorenz Curve given by Assumption 8.1 is the curve given by the straight lines connecting the points $(p_o\ L(p_o)) = (0,0)$ and $(p_1, L(p_1))$, $(p_1, L(p_1))$ and $(p_2, L(p_2))$, ..., $(p_{i-1}, L(p_{i-1}))$ and $(p_i, L(p_i))$, ..., $(p_{k-1}, L(p_{k-1}))$ and $(p_k, L(p_k)) = (1,1)$. This is illustrated in figure 8.3. Note that $p_i = F(a_i)$.

For the SD-class measures with a weight function of relative ranks, see sec. 7.4 and sec. 8.1, i.e. the Gini coefficient and the measures by Mehran, Piesch, Bonferroni and de Vergottini[1], the lower bounds are given by

$$I_L = \sum_{i=1}^{k} \int_{p_{i-1}}^{p_i} V(p)\ [p-L(p_{\mu_i})\ ]\ dp, \qquad (8.7)$$

where $L(p\mu_i) = L(p_{i-1}) + t_i\ (p-p_{i-1})$ and $t_i = [L(p_i) - L(p_{i-1})]\ /[p_i - p_{i-1}] = \frac{\mu_i}{\mu}$ is the slope of the line joining the two adjacent points $(p_{i-1}, L(p_{i-1}))$ and $(p_i, L(p_i))$, i=1, 2, ..., k ($t_1 = L(p_1)/p_1$ and $t_k = (1 - L(p_{k-1}))/(1-p_{k-1})$).

(8.7) can be rewritten as

$$I_L = \sum_{i=1}^{k} (1-t_i) \int_{p_{i-1}}^{p_i} V(p)pdp - \sum_{i=1}^{k} (L(p_{i-1})-t_i p_{i-1}) \int_{p_{i-1}}^{p_i} V(p)dp, \qquad (8.8)$$

where the V(p)'s are given in table 7.4.

---

1) All these measures follow the principle of transfers, cf. table 7.8.

Table 8.5 Lower bounds for some measures defined as weighted Lorenz areas, when data are given in grouped forms.

Measure	Lower bound
Gini, R_L	$\sum_{i=1}^{k-1} (p_i - L(p_i))(p_{i+1} - p_{i-1})$
Mehran, M_L	$\sum_{i=1}^{k-1} (p_i - L(p_i))(p_{i+1} - p_{i-1}) \{3-(p_{i+1}+p_i+p_{i-1})\}$
Piesch, P_L	$\frac{1}{2} \sum_{i=1}^{k-1} (p_i - L(p_i))(p_{i+1} - p_{i-1}) \{p_{i+1}+p_i+p_{i-1}\}$
Bonferroni, B_L	$\sum_{i=1}^{k-1} (p_i - L(p_i)) \{p_{i+1} \frac{\ell og p_{i+1} - \ell og\, p_i}{p_{i+1} - p_i} - p_{i-1} \frac{\ell og\, p_i - \ell og\, p_{i-1}}{p_i - p_{i-1}}\}$
de Vergottini, dV_L	$\sum_{i=1}^{k-1} (p_i - L(p_i))\{[\frac{1-p_{i+1}}{p_{i+1}-p_i}]\ell og\, [\frac{1-p_{i+1}}{1-p_i}] - [\frac{1-p_{i-1}}{p_i-p_{i-1}}]\ \ell og\, [\frac{1-p_i}{1-p_{i-1}}]\}$ $x \log x \to 0$ when $x \to 0$

Table 8.5, cont.

Special case: equally sized groups, $L(p_i) = L_i$
$\frac{k-1}{k} - \frac{2}{k}\sum_{i=1}^{k-1} L_i$ deciles: $R_L = 0{,}9 - 0{,}2 \sum_{i=1}^{9} L_i$
$\frac{(k^2-1)}{k^2} - \frac{6}{k}\sum_{i=1}^{k-1} L_i + \frac{6}{k^2}\sum_{i=1}^{k-1} iL_i$ deciles: $M_L = 0{,}99 - 0{,}6 \sum_{i=1}^{9} L_i + 0.06 \sum_{i=1}^{9} iL_i$
$\frac{(k-1)\ (2k-1)}{2k^2} - \frac{3}{k^2}\sum_{i=1}^{k-1} iL_i$ deciles: $P_L = 0.855 - 0.03 \sum_{i=1}^{9} iL_i$
$(k-1)\ \ell og\ [\frac{k}{k-1}] + \sum_{i=2}^{k-1} \{i\ \ell og\ [\frac{i^2}{i^2-1}] - \ell og\ [\frac{i+1}{i-1}]\}\ L_i$ deciles: $9\ \ell og\ (\frac{10}{9}) + \sum_{i=2}^{9} \{i\ \ell og\ [\frac{i^2}{i^2-1}] - \ell og\ [\frac{i+1}{i-1}]\}\ L_i$
$\ell og\ k + (\ell og\ 4)\ L_{k-1} + \sum_{i=1}^{k-2} \{k - i+1)\ \ell og\ (k-i+1) + (k-i-1)\ \ell og\ (k-i-1) - 2(k-i)\ \ell og\ (k-i)\}L_i$ deciles: $\ell og\ 10 + (\ell og\ 4)\ L_9 + \sum_{i=1}^{8} \{(11-i)\ \ell og(11-i) + (9-i)\ \ell og\ (9-i) - 2(10-i)\ \ell og\ (10-i)\}L_i$

The lower bound for the Gini coefficient, R_L, is given by $V(p) = 2$ and after some algebraic manipulations we have

$$R_L = \sum_{i=1}^{k-1} (p_i - L(p_i))(p_{i+1} - p_{i-1}) = \sum_{i=1}^{k-1} A(p_i)(p_{i+1} - p_{i-1}) \quad (8.9)$$

$$= p_{k-1} - \sum_{i=1}^{k-1} L(p_i)(p_{i+1} - p_{i-1})^{1)}. \quad (8.10)$$

If data are grouped into equally sized groups, e.g. in deciles (k=10), R_L can be simplified into ($p_{i+1} - p_{i-1} = {}^2/_k$)

$$R_L = \frac{2}{k} \sum_{i=1}^{k-1} A(p_i) \quad (8.11)$$

which equals the Gini coefficient from ungrouped data defined by (8.3) with $V(F(Y_i)) = 2$, cf. also table (8.1). (8.11) can be rewritten as

$$R_L = \frac{k-1}{k} - \frac{2}{k} \sum_{i=1}^{k-1} L(p_i),$$ i.e. if k=10 then R_L equals $0.9-0.2 \sum_{i=1}^{9} L(p_i)$.

In a similar way we can write the lower bounds of the measures by Mehran (M_L), Piesch (P_L), Bonferroni (B_L) and de Vergottini (dV_L), see table 8.5. To receive lower bounds of the other measures discussed before we have to use the decomposition formulas which are given in the next chapter. A measure is decomposed into a within term and a rest term, consisting of a between and an acrossterm (see the next chapter). The within term is a weighted sum of the inequalities within each group, but since by Assumption 8.1 these group inequalities equal zero we only have to make use of the rest terms. For the measures discussed earlier in this chapter the lower bounds are given in table 8.6.[2)]

---

1) R_L also can be written as $1 - \sum_{i=0}^{k-1} (p_{i+1} - p_i)(L(p_i)+L(p_{i-1}))$ cf. e.g. Gastwirth [1972] and Mehran [1975].

2) The measures given in table 8.6 follow the principle of transfers. Since the quasi standard deviation, σ_{qL}, does not fulfill the principle of transfers we can not determine an appropriate lower bound for this measure.

Figure 8.3 The geometrical construction of lower and upper bounds on measures defined as weighted Lorenz areas, see the text for discussion.

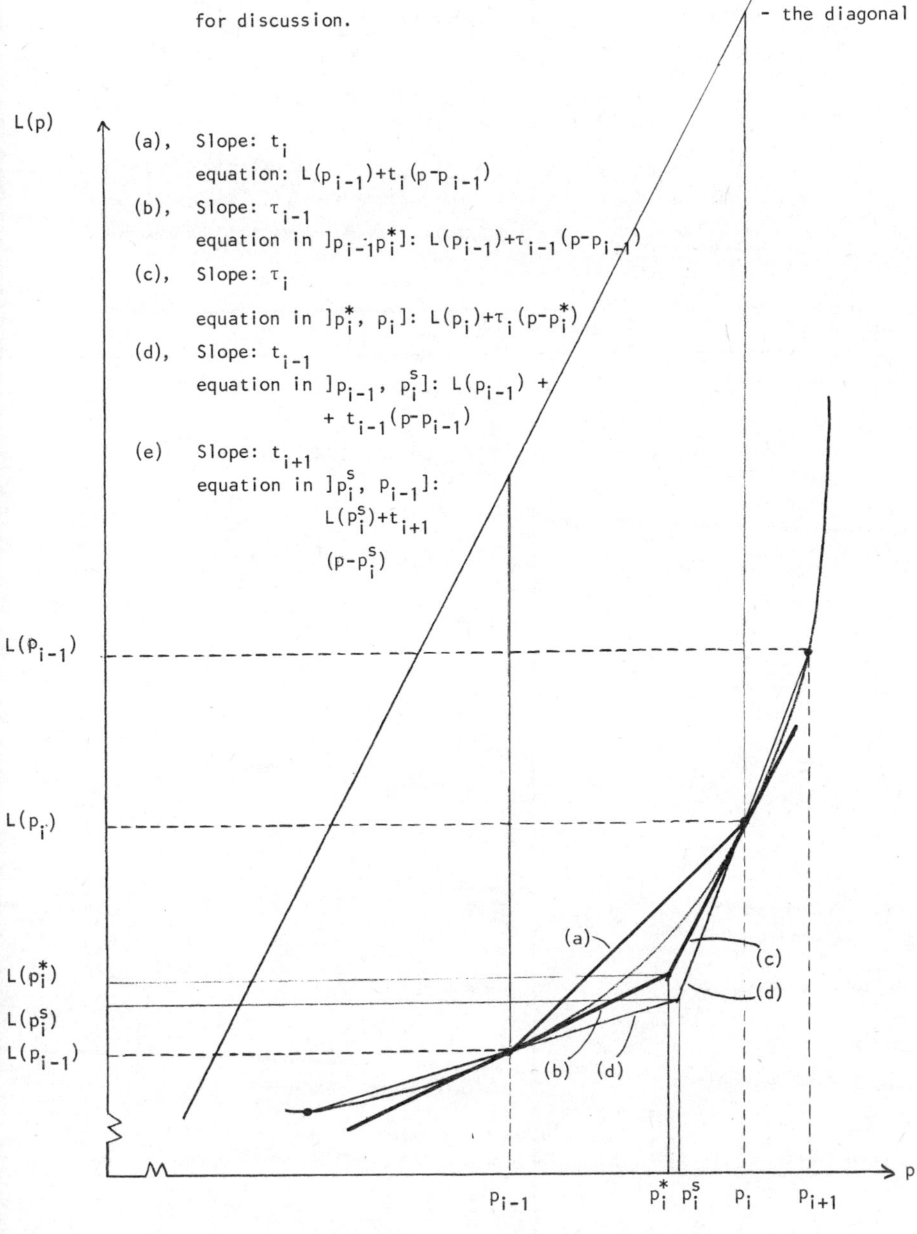

Table 8.6 Lower bounds for some measures, defined by the general measure of inequality, when data are given in grouped forms. All measures fulfill the principle of transfers.
In the table we have used Lorenz Curve terms, i.e. P_i, $L(P_i)$ and $t_i = \frac{L(P_i) - L(P_{i-1})}{P_i - P_{i-1}} = \frac{\mu_i}{\mu}$ is the slope of the line joining the two adjacent points $(P_{i-1}, L(P_{i-1}))$. For the standard deviation, RSMAX and Kolm's relative centrist measure we also need information about the overall arithmetic mean income and the maximum income.

Measure	Lower bound
• the standard deviation, σ_L	$\mu\{\sum_{i=1}^{k} t_i\ [L(P_i) - L(P_{i-1})] - 1\}^{1/2}$
• the coefficient of variation, $V_L = \mu^{-1}\sigma_L$	$\{\sum_{i=1}^{k} t_i\ [L(P_i) - L(P_{i-1})] - 1\}^{1/2}$
$V_L / \sqrt{V_L^2 + 1}$	$\{\sum_{i=1}^{k} t_i[L(P_i)-L(P_{i-1})]-1\}/\{\sum_{i=1}^{k} t_i[L(P_i)-L(p_{i-1})]\}^{1/2}$
• $RSMAX_L$	$\{V_L^2 + \mu^{-2}\ (Y_{max} - \mu)^2\}^{1/2}$
• Kolm's μ-modified centrist measure $K_{cL}^m(\xi,\varepsilon)$	$(1 + \frac{\xi}{\mu}) - \{\sum_{i=1}^{k} (P_i - P_{i-1})[t_i + \frac{\xi}{\mu}]^{1-\varepsilon}\}^{1/(1-\varepsilon)}$
Atkinson's measure $A_L\ (\varepsilon) = K_{cL}^r(0,\varepsilon)$	$1 - \{\sum_{i=1}^{k} (P_i - P_{i-1})\ t_i^{1-\varepsilon}\}^{1/(1-\varepsilon)}$
• Theil's 2nd measure, T_{2L}	$\sum_{i=1}^{k} (P_i - P_{i-1})\ \ell og\ t_i^{-1}$
• Champernowne's measure, Ch_L	$1 - e^{-T_{2L}}$
• Theil's 1st measure, T_{1L}	$\sum_{i=1}^{k} (L(p_i)-L(p_{i-1})\ \ell og\ t_i$
• Kolm's relative leftist measure, $K_{\ell L}^r(\alpha)$	$1 + \frac{1}{\alpha}\ \ell og\ [\sum_{i=1}^{k} (P_i - P_{i-1}]\ e^{-\alpha t_i}]$

8.3.2 UPPER BOUNDS, $I_U \geq I$

When calculating an upper bound for a specific inequality measure we will in general have to have knowledge about the arithmetic mean income within each group (μ_i, i=1, 2, ..., k) and the group boundaries a_{i-1} and and a_i, i=1, 2, ..., k. When we calculated the lower bounds we made use of Assumption 8.1, in which we assumed the within group inequality to be minimum, i.e. all i.r.u.'s within group i receive equal income (= μ_i). In Assumption 8.2 below we assume that within group inequality is maximum, subject to the condition that μ_i is unchanged and that the incomes that the i.r.u.'s receive are either a_{i-1} or a_i, i.e. one of the group interval boundaries.

Assumption 8.2 The incomes within group i, i=1, 2, ..., k, equal either the lower group boundary, a_{i-1} or the upper group boundary, subject to the condition that the arithmetic mean income μ_i is unchanged.

Before making use of this assumption we will briefly consider two methods of computing upper bounds for the Gini coefficient where we only need to know the grouping points, (p_i, $L(p_i)$), i=1, 2, ..., k-1, on the Lorenz Curve. The first method was proposed by Mehran [1975] and the second is labelled the secant method.

Upper bound on the Gini coefficient without knowledge of a_{i-1} and a_i

Mehran's maximization method.

t_i is the slope of the line joining the two adjacent points (p_{i-1}, $L(p_{i-1})$) and (p_i, $L(p_i)$) as defined in sec. 8.3.1 and τ_i is the unknown slope of the tangent to the Lorenz Curve through the point (p_i $L(p_i)$). The two lines with slopes τ_{i-1} and τ_i resp. intersect in the unknown point $(p_i^*, L(p_i^*))$, c.f. figure 8.3. The slope τ_i can be written as

$$\tau_i = \frac{L(p_i) - L(p_i^*)}{p_i - p_i^*} = \frac{L(p_{i+1}^*) - L(p_i)}{p_{i+1}^* - p_i} \tag{8.11}$$

and

$$0 = \tau_o \leq t_1 \leq \tau_1 \leq t_2 \leq \tau_2 \leq \ldots \leq t_k \leq \tau_k = \infty \tag{8.12}$$

The upper bound, R_U, can be written as $R_U = R_L + \Delta_R^*$, where R_L is the lower bound given by (8.9) and Δ_R^* is the Gini grouping factor.

The grouping factor Δ_R^* is the sum of k partial grouping factors Δ_{Ri}^*, defined by

$$\Delta_{Ri}^* = 2 \int_{p_{i-1}}^{p_i^*} \{L(p_{\mu i}) - L(p_{i-1}, \tau_{i-1})\}\, dp + 2 \int_{*\, i}^{i} \{L(p_{\ddot{\mu} i}) - L(p_i^*, \tau_i)\} dp \tag{8.13}$$

where $L(p_{\mu i}) = L(p_{i-1}) + t_i (p - p_{i-1})$ is the equation of the line joining $(p_{i-1}, L(p_{i-1}))$ and $(p_i, L(p_i))$. $L(p_{i-1}, \tau_{i-1}) = L(p_{i-1}) + \tau_{i-1} (p - p_{i-1})$ and $L(p_i^*, \tau_i) = L(p_i^*) + \tau_i (p - p_i^*)$ are the equations of the lines with slopes equal to τ_{i-1} and τ_i, respectively (cf. figure 8.3). After some algebraic manipulations Δ_{Ri}^* can be rewritten in such a way that Δ_R^* equals[1)]

$$\Delta_R^* = \sum_{i=1}^{k} \Delta_{Ri}^* = \sum_{i=1}^{k} ({}_{i} - {}_{i-1})^2 \frac{(\tau_i - t_i)(t_i - \tau_{i-1})}{(\tau_i - \tau_{i-1})} \tag{8.14}$$

---

1) Δ_{Ri}^* can also be calculated geometrically.

where, as stated above, the τ_i's are unknown. The principal aim of the method is to maximize Δ_R^* with respect to τ_i. Setting the partial derivates, $\delta\Delta_R^*/\delta\tau_i$, equal to zero gives the unique solution τ_i^*. This solution equals the first expression in (8.11) where p_i^* and $L(p_i^*)$ are obtained iteratively by

$$\begin{aligned} &p_i^* = 2p_i - p_{i+1}^*,\ p_k^* = 1 \\ & && i=1, 2, \ldots, k-1 \qquad (8.15) \\ &L(p_i^*) = 2L(p_{i-1}) - L(p_{i-1}^*),\ L(p_i^*) = 0 \end{aligned}$$

The solution to the maximization problem, subject to the inequality constraints (8.12), is given by[1)]

$$\tau_i = \begin{cases} t_i & \text{if } t_i > \tau_i^* \\ \tau_i^* & \text{if } t_i \leq \tau_i^* \leq t_{i+1} \\ t_{i+1} & \text{if } \tau_i^* > t_{i+1} \end{cases}$$

The Secant method.

Another upper bound for the Gini coefficient, $R_U = R_L + \Delta_{RS}$, where Δ_{RS} is in general slightly greater than Δ_R^* , can be calculated using the secant method. The line joining the points $(p_{i-2}, L(p_{i-2}))$ and $(p_{i-1}, L(p_{i-1}))$ and the line joining the points $(p_i, L(p_i))$ and $(p_{i+1}, L(p_{i-1}))$ intersect in a point $(p_i^s, L(p_i^s))$, see figure 8.3. By strict convexity of the Lorenz Curve (LC), the LC between the points $(p_{i-1}, L(p_{i-1})$ and $(p_i, L(p_i))$ will be situated straight above the two lines intersecting in $(p_i^s, L(p_i^s))$[2)].

---

1) If these are equally sized groups, e.g. in deciles, the solution is $\tau_i = t_{k-2[\frac{1}{2}(k-i+1)]+1}$, $i=1, 2, \ldots, k-1$, where $[i]$ denotes the largest integer less than or equal to i.

2) By convexity of the LC the LC will be situated above or on the two lines intersecting in $(P_i^s, L(P_i^s))$.

If we denote the area of the triangle, given by $(p_{i-1}, L(p_{i-1}))$, $(p_i, L(p_i))$ and $(p_i^s, L(p_i^s))$, by Δ_{Ri}^s the grouping factor can be written as

$$\Delta_{RS} = \sum_{i=1}^{k} \Delta_{Ri}^s = \sum_{i=1}^{k} (p_i - p_{i-1})^2 \frac{(t_{i+1}-t_i)(t_i-t_{i-1})}{(t_{i+1}-t_{i-1})},$$

where $t_o = 0$ and $t_{k+1} = \infty$.

By the secant method we can also receive upper bounds, I_U, for the measures by Mehran, Piesch, Bonferroni and de Vergottini. These upper bounds can not be given in as simple a form as the upper bound on the Gini coefficient, $R_U = R_L + \Delta_{RS}$, since $W(p) = \int_o^p V(p)\,dp$ is not linear for these cases.[1)]
If we write $I_U = \sum_{i=1}^{k} I_{Ui}$ we have I_{Ui} as

$$I_{Ui} = \int_{i-1}^{p_i^s} V(p)\{p - L(p_{s1i})\}\,dp + \int_{s_i}^{i} V(p)\{p - L(p_{s2i})\}\,dp,$$

where $L(p_{s1i}) = L(p_{i-1}) + t_{i-1}\,(p-p_{i-1})$ is the equation of the line between the points $(p_{i-1}, L(p_{i-1}))$ and $(p_i^s, L(p_i^s))$, $L(p_i^s) + t_{i+1}\,(p-p_i^s)$ is the equation of the line between the points $(p_i^s, L(p_i^s))$ and $(p_i, L(p_i))$ and $p_i^s = \{(t_{i+1} - t_i)p_i - (t_i - t_{i-1})\,p_{i-1}\}/(t_{i+1} - t_{i-1})$,
$L(p_i^s) = \{t_{i+1}\,t_{i-1}\,(p_i - p_{i-1}) + (t_{i+1}\,L(p_{i-1}) - t_{i-1}L(p_i))\}/(t_{i+1}-t_{i-1})$.

Upper bounds with knowledge of a_{i-1} and a_i

Under Assumption 8.2 we maximize the within group inequality, subject to the condition that the arithmetic mean income, μ_i, is unchanged. This maximum is achieved if the proportion λ_i, $0 < \lambda_i < 1$, of the i.r.u.'s

---

1) This is also reflected in the problem of decomposing these measures.

receive the lower bound income, a_{i-1}[1], and the proportion $(1-\lambda_i)$ receive the upper bound income a_i, i.e. $\lambda_i a_{i-1} + (1-\lambda_i)a_i = \lambda_i$. This implies that

$$\lambda_i = \frac{a_i - \mu_i}{a_i - a_{i-1}} = \frac{\tau_i - t_i}{\tau_i - \tau_{i-1}}$$

and (8.16)

$$(1-\lambda_i) = \frac{\mu_i - a_{i-1}}{a_i - a_{i-1}} = \frac{t_i - \tau_{i-1}}{\tau_i - \tau_{i-1}},$$

where τ_i is the slope of the tangent through $(p_i, L(p_i))$ on the Lorenz curve, defined by (8.11) and t_i is the slope of the line joining the two adjacent points $(p_{i-1}, L(p_{i-1}))$ and $(p_i, L(p_i))$. The two tangents through $(p_{i-1}, L(p_{i-1}))$ and $(p_i, L(p_i))$, respectively, intersect in a point $(p_i^*, L(p_i^*))$, where $p_i^* = \lambda_i p_i + (1-\lambda_i)p_{i-1}$ and $L(p_i) = L(p_{i-1}) + \tau_{i-1}\lambda_i (p_i - p_{i-1})$, see figure 8.3.

The upper bounds for the measures defined as weighted Lorenz areas can be written as $I_U = I_L + \Delta^*$, where Δ^* is a grouping factor, cf. the discussion above. The grouping factor within group i, Δ_i^* $(\Delta^* = \sum_{i=1}^{k} \Delta_i^*)$, is defined by

$$\Delta_i^* = (1-\lambda_i)(\tau_i - \tau_{i-1}) \int_{p_{i-1}}^{p_i^*} V(p)(p-p_{i-1})dp + \lambda_i(\tau_i - \tau_{i-1}) \int_{p_i^*}^{p_i} V(p)(p_i - p)dp$$

(8.17)

---

1) To be exact the lower bound of group i is $a_{i-1} + \varepsilon$, $\varepsilon>0$, and the tangent to the slope in the corresponding point on the Lorenz Curve is $\tau_{i-1} + \varepsilon/\mu$. Since this slope is greater than τ_{i-1} the grouping factor Δ_i^*, see below, using τ_{i-1} is greater than the grouping factor using $\tau_{i-1} + \varepsilon/\mu$. This maximizes Δ_i.

For the Gini coefficient, i.e. $V(P) = 2$, the grouping factor Δ^*_{Ri} equals, after some algebraic manipulations[1],

$$\Delta^*_{Ri} = \sum_{i=1}^{k} (p_i - p_{i-1})^2 \lambda_i(1-\lambda_i)(\tau_i - \tau_{i-1}) =$$
$$= \sum_{i-1}^{k} (p_i - p_{i-1})^2 \frac{(\tau_i - t_i)(t_i - \tau_{i-1})}{(\tau_i - \tau_{i-1})} =$$
$$= \frac{1}{\mu} \sum_{i=1}^{k} (p_i - p_{i-1})^2 \frac{(a_i - \mu_i)(\mu_i - a_{i-1})}{(a_i - a_{i-1})},$$

where the second expression is (of course) identical with Δ^*_{Ri} in (8.14). The upper bounds for the measures by Mehran, Piesch, Bonferroni and de Vergottini can also be found by choosing the appropriate V(p):s. As stated above, in the discussion of the secant method, the grouping factors of these measures are not explicitly given in as simple forms as Δ^*_{Ri}, which is due to the fact of the non-linearity of $V(p)p$ in (8.17). However, we can get upper bounds directly, through using the discussion of calculating lower bounds. The interval $]p_{i-1}, p_i]$ is hence subdivided by p^*_i, $p_{i-1} < p^*_i < p_i$, into two mutually exclusive intervals and the upper bounds are written as

$$I_U = \int_{p_{i-1}}^{p^*_i} V(p)[p-(L(p_{i-1})+\tau_{i-1}(p-p_{i-1})]dp + \int_{p^*_i}^{p_i} V(p)[p-(L(p_i)+\tau_i(p-p^*_i))]dp.$$

Alternatively one may choose the formulas given in table 8.5 and exchange p_{i-1}, p_i, p_{i+1} for p_{i-1}, p^*_i, p_i and p^*_i, p_i, p^*_{i+1}, respectively, i.e. we get two sums, one for intervals $]p_{i-1}, p^*_i]$ and one for intervals $]p^*_i, p_i]$.

---

1) $\Delta^*_{R1} = p_1^2(\tau_1 - t_1)\dfrac{t_1}{\tau_1}$ and $\Delta^*_{Rk} = (1 - p_{k-1})^2(t_k - \tau_{k-1})$ when $\tau_k \to \infty$

Discussions of upper bounds under Assumption 8.2 are given for the Gini coefficient by Gastwirth [1971b], [1972]. Gastwirth [1972] also gives a sharper upper bound R_U. If the density function is decreasing within group i, then we can calculate a grouping factor Δ_i^d that is sharper than Δ_i^*, i.e. we have $\Delta_i^d < \Delta_i^*$.

Bounds for measures of the form $\int h(x)dF(x)$, where $h(x)$ is convex and $F(x)$ is concave, are discussed in Gastwirth [1975] and Gastwirth and Krieger [1975] (the form of the measure also includes Gastwirth's family of inequality measures, see sec. 7.4).

Note that the upper bound of group i, a_i, equals the lower bound of group i+1. If, instead, the upper bound of group i equals a_i - 0,5, the lower bound of group i+1 equals a_i+0,5 and the Gini grouping factor equals Δ_{Ri}^{**} then the difference between the Gini grouping factors equals $\Delta_{Ri}^* - \Delta_{Ri}^{**} = (2\mu)^{-1} \sum_{i=1}^{k} (p_i - p_{i-1})^2 - \frac{1}{4\mu} \sum_{i=1}^{k} (p_i - p_{i-1})^2 (a_i - a_{i-1})^{-1}$.

The upper bounds for the measures defined from our general definition and discussed earlier are found by the relation $I_u = f(I_L, \Delta)$, where I_L equals the lower bound, cf. table 8.4, and was calculated under Assumption 8.1 which assumes zero inequality within each group, i.e. $\Delta = 0$. Under Assumption 8.2 we maximize the within group inequality, i.e. Δ. The upper bounds, for which the lower bounds are given in table 8.6, are given in table 8.7.

See also the next chapter for useful formulas when data are grouped.

Table 8.7 Upper bounds for some measures, defined by the general measure of inequality, when data are given in grouped forms. All measures fulfill the principle of transfers.

In the table we have used Lorenz Curve terms, i.e. p_i, $t_i = \frac{\mu_i}{\mu}$ and $\tau_i = \frac{a_i}{\mu}$

For the standard deviation, RSMAX, Kolm's relative centrist measure and Theil's 1st measure we also need information about the overall arithmetic mean income and the maximum income.

The corresponding lower bounds, I_L, are given in table 8.6.

Measure	Upper bound
• The standard deviation, σ_U	$\{\sigma_L^2+\mu^2 \sum_{i=1}^{k} (p_i-p_{i-1})(\tau_i-t_i)(t_i-\tau_{i-1})\}^{1/2}$
• The coefficient of variation, V_U	$\{V_L^2+ \sum_{i=1}^{k} (p_i-p_{i-1})(\tau_i-t_i)(t_i-\tau_{i-1})\}^{1/2}$
$V_U/\sqrt{V_U^2+1}$	V_U, see above
• $RSMAX_U$	$\{V_U^2 + \mu^{-2}(Y_{max} - \mu)\}^{1/2}$
• Kolm's μ-modified centrist measure $K_{cU}^m(\xi,\varepsilon)$	$(1+\frac{\xi}{\mu})- \{\sum_{i=1}^{k}(p_i-p_{i-1}) [\lambda_i(\tau_{i-1}+\frac{\xi}{\mu})^{1-\varepsilon}+(1-\lambda_i)(\tau_i+\frac{\xi}{\mu})^{1-\varepsilon}]\}^{1/(1-\varepsilon)}$
Atkinson's measure $A_U(\varepsilon) = K_{cU}^r(0,\varepsilon)$	$1-\{\sum_{i=1}^{k} (p_i-p_{i-1})[\lambda_i\tau_{i-1}^{1-\varepsilon}+ (1-\lambda_i)\tau_i^{1-\varepsilon}]\}^{1/(1-$
• Theil's 2nd measure, T_{2U}	$\sum_{i=1}^{k} (p_i-p_{i-1}) [\lambda_i \log \tau_{i-1}^{-1}+(1- \lambda_i) \log \tau_i^{-1}]$, $a_o > 0$
• Champernowne's measure, Ch_U	$1-e^{-T_{2U}}$
• Theil's 1st measure, T_{1U}	$\sum_{i=1}^{k} (p_i-p_{i-1}) \{\lambda_i \tau_{i-1} \log \tau_{i-1}+(1-\lambda_i)\tau_i \log \tau_i\}$, $a_k < \infty$
• Kolm's relative leftist measure, $K_{\ell U}^r(\alpha)$	$1+\frac{1}{\alpha} \log \sum_{i=1}^{k} (p_i-p_{i-1})[\lambda_i e^{-\alpha\tau_{i-1}} + (1-\lambda_i)e^{-\alpha\tau_i}]$

Table 8.8 Lower and upper bounds for available income in Finland, 1971, and Sweden, 1972. Data are given in chapter 2. (table 2.1)
The lower bound of the first class is set equal to one, i.e. a_o=1.
The maximum income in Finland is assumed to equal 500 000 FIM.
L.B.= lower bound, U.B.= upper bound.

Measure	Finland		Sweden	
	L.B.	U.B.	L.B.	U.B.
Gini	0.3236	0.326325	0.3162	0.324034
Mehrans method	-	0.326334	-	0.324054
Secant method	-	0.3283	-	0.3291
Piesch	0.2588	0.2623	0.2493	0.2586
Mehran	0.4531	0.4544	0.4500	0.4548
Bonferroni	0.4494	0.4566	0.4451	0.4647
de Vergottini	0.5797	0.7097	0.5290	0.6683
V^2	0.3637	1.3137	0.3213	0.6584
T_1	0.1701	0.2344	0.1594	0.2169
T_2	0.1869	0.3402	0.1834	0.5723
Ch	0.1704	0.2884	0.1675	0.4358
Atkinson, ε=				
0.5	0.0849	0.1033	0.0821	0.1139
1.2	0.2043	0.4427	0.2021	0.7168
1.5	0.2543	0.8822	0.2535	0.9818
1.8	0.3027	0.9879	0.3035	0.9979
2.0	0.3338	0.9956	0.3356	0.9991
Kolm, α=				
0.01	0.0013	0.0056	0.0016	0.0032
1.0	0.1465	0.1550	0.1398	0.1578
2.0	0.2468	0.2517	0.2433	0.2602
5.0	0.4238	0.4405	0.4281	0.4800

9. DECOMPOSITIONS

In the last few chapters we have discussed various measures that will sum up the inequality of an actual, specific distribution of income. During the last few decades many studies on income inequality have searched for the determinants of inequality within a country and attempted to measure the contribution of various components in total inequality. One method of analysis that can be used is decompositions of the measures of inequality.

Two general types of decompositions can be found:

(*i*) *functional decomposition by income-determining characteristics (subgroups)*

the general question is: how much of total inequality is attributable to variability in income-determinant 1 (subgroup 1), how much to variability in income-determinant 2 (subgroup 2), etc., and how much to between (across) group inequality?

(*ii*) *functional decomposition by income sources*

the general question is: how much of total inequality is attributable to income from labour, from capital, from negative and positive transfers, etc.?

The value of these decompositions is stated in Fields [1979a - p. 438][1]: "The value of these decompositions is that they gauge the relative importance of various sources and sectors in respect to overall inequality, and thereby direct our attention to potentially fruitful areas of research."

---

1) Fields distinguishes between three general types of decomposition. His third type involves an unexplained component, see Fields [1979a - p.439].

It is the household (or the family) as an i.r.u. concept that is usually the most interesting i.r.u. definition when analyzing the income inequality. Let us therefore look at some factors that determine the income of a household. These factors can be roughly divided into four groups:

(1) *Household characteristics*

These factors depend on the composition of individuals and their personal characteristics weighted together and also very much on the definition of the concepts that is used.

Personal characteristics are e.g. IQ, differences in ability to work, family socio-economic background (and the possession of property of the family), years of schooling (see Atkinson [1975 - ch.5.4]) and age. Combinations of some personal characteristics will determine the socio-economic group that an individual can be classified into (e.g., type of work and/or type of education).

What about household characteristics?
Of course, the classification of a household into a specific socio-economic group or into an age-group will depend on the classification of a 'head of the household'. This classification will also lead to classification of the household into 'years of education'. On the other hand there are also other typical household characteristics, such as the number of household members and the composition of household members.

The extent to which these factors determine inequality is analyzed mainly by decomposition (*i*).

(2) *State of the market, scarcity and marginal productivity*

Factors that belong to this group are e.g. (see Baumol and Blinder [1979 - p.564],

(a) differences in intensity of work

(b) compensating wage differentials

(c) risk-taking by investing money in some uncertain venture.

These are mainly analyzed by decomposition (*i*).

(3) *Political, economic and administrative power in the society*

Political power may, according to Pen [1978], be separated into exerting groups such as government, pressure groups, political parties, voters, etc. and the impact on income distribution is twofold:

(a) distortion of the primary distribution of incomes by wage policy, price policy and monetary policy

(b) redistribution by the budget and social security funds.

The influence of economic power (Pen [1978]) on income distribution can be separated into two important parts, namely power exerted by

(a) labour unions

(b) 'profits'.

Factors belonging to this group (e.g. the negative and positive transfers) are set up by the society to reduce the income differences between households in available income.

The extent to which these factors determine inequality is analyzed mainly be decomposition (*ii*).

(4) *Luck and other stochastic factors*

Factors belonging to this group are (cf. Stiglitz [1978]), e.g.

(a) occupational luck

(b) investment luck and

(c) accidents and illness.

These factors can hardly be analyzed by using the above decompositions.

Some of the factors that determine the inequality of an income distribution can be seen as 'democratic' (see Paglin [1975]) in the sense that they affect all people (households). One such factor is 'age' (age of the head of the household) and another one is 'the number of household members'. The factors can also be divided into (a) compensatory (choice-related) and (b) non-compensatory (opportunity-related) differences (see ch. 1 and Söderström [1981]). The democratic factors above will, with this terminology, be compensatory. The intrinsic effect of compensatory differences may therefore be excluded from the income distribution. This leads us to use a new reference distribution, deviating from the EGAL (the egalitarian), when analyzing the inequality. As soon as we have determined the reference distribution the general measure of sec. 7.4 and sec. 8.2 can be used. It is important to note the fact that using a new reference distribution does not mean that we can measure the deviation of individual incomes from the reference incomes (above: compensatory incomes) determining the reference distribution. The discussion in this chapter will nevertheless use the EGAL distribution as the reference.

Comparisons of income inequality can be made either between countries (one or more years) or within a country for two or more years. Demographic characteristics, such as the proportion of households classified as farmers, entrepreneurs, workers etc., frequently vary between countries or change with time. If we subdivide the household by such characteristics and if the inequality within each subpopulation is zero but the income varies with the subpopulations, then the intrinsic inequality within the whole population depends on these demographic characteristics. If we want to analyze the inequality within various countries (or within a country, for two or more years) without the effects of some demographic characteristics we can use one country (or one year) as a reference base. The other countries (years) are then standardised according to the demographic factors within the reference country. Other standardizations can also be made.

To simplify the decompositions they will partly be made in the continuous case, i.e. with a continuous income variable $Y = F^{-1}(p)$[1], with a continuous differentiable c.d.f. $F(y)$ and 1 st. m.d.f. $F_1(y)$. The expected value of Y is assumed to be non-zero and finite, $E(Y) = \mu$. The income variable is assumed either non-negative or non-positive to allow both positive incomes and negative incomes (taxes). In both cases will the slope of the tangent to the Lorenz Curve (LC) at the

1) $F^{-1}(p) = \inf_y \{y|F(y) \geq p\}$, $0 \leq p \leq 1$, see sec. 7.1.1.

point (p, L(p)), $\tau(p) = \frac{F^{-1}(p)}{\mu}$ (i.e. the relative income), is positive. The value space of $Y = F^{-1}(p)$ can be extended to the whole real axis, cf. Wold [1935], if $\mu \neq 0$. The upper bound of e.g. the Gini coefficient is then greater than one. This extention can, of course, not be used for measures that involve $\log \tau(p)$.

Some notations to be used

Let the population be divided into k mutually exclusive subgroups (subpopulations). The jth group, j = 1,2 ..k, has the c.d.f. $F(y)_j$, 1 st m.d.f. $F_1(y)_j$ and $E_j(Y) = \mu_j < \infty$, $\mu_j \neq 0$.

Disaggregation of the c.d.f. F(y) gives

$$F(y) = \sum_{j=1}^{k} f_j \; F(y)_j, \tag{9.1}$$

where $f_j \geq 0$, $\sum_{j=1}^{k} f_j = 1$ and

$$\mu = \sum_{j=1}^{k} f_j \mu_j. \tag{9.2}$$

Disaggregation of the 1st. m.d.f. $F_1(y)$ gives

$$F_1(y) = \sum_{j=1}^{k} f_{1j} F_1(y)_j, \tag{9.3}$$

where $f_{1j} = f_j \mu_j / \mu$ and $\sum_{j=1}^{k} f_{1j} = 1$ (follows from (9.2)).

f_j equals the share of i.r.u.'s in subgroup j, and $f_{1j} = f_j \mu_j / \mu$ equals the income share that is held by the i.r.u.'s in subgroup j, j=1,2, ..., k.

Let the total income Y_t be composed of k additive income sources, either non-negative with $\mu_j > 0$ or non-positive with $\mu_j < 0$:

$$Y_t = \sum_{j=1}^{k} Y_j . \tag{9.4}$$

and

$$\mu_t = \sum_{j=1}^{k} \mu_j , \tag{9.5}$$

where $\mu_j = E(Y_j) < \infty$, $\mu_j \neq 0$.

We define

$$q_j = \mu_j / \mu_t \ , \quad j = 1,2,...,k, \ t\text{=total income.} \tag{9.6}$$

Sec. 9.1 deals with decompositions of inequality measures by subgroups (subpopulations). These subgroups are either divided according to some household characteristics (subgroups), i.e. decomposition of type (*i*) above. The decomposition by income source (*ii*) is dealt with in sec. 9.2 and standardization methods in sec. 9.3.

9.1 DECOMPOSITION BY SUBGROUPS

The frequently most desired property of an inequality measure is that it is additively decomposable, i.e. the inequality measure can be expressed as the sum of a '*within-group*' inequality term and a '*between-group*' inequality term. The within-group term is a weighted sum of the subgroup inequality values and the between-group term is some function of the arithmetic mean incomes, μ_j, j=1, 1,..., k. See e.g. Bourguignon [1979] and Shorrocks [1980a].

By using the assumptions that the inequality measure, I, is continuous, has continuous second derivatives, follows SYM, REPLIC and PROPORTION (criteria of ch. 4) $I \geq 0$ (equality if and only if criterion EGAL of ch. 4 holds) and that there exist a set of coefficients $W_j(\mu, N)$ such that $I = \sum_{j=1}^{k} W_j(\mu, N)\, I_j + I_B$ [1)], where W_j is a function of μ and the number of i.r.u.'s in the population, I_j is the within-group inequality in group j, j=1, 2, .., k, and I_B is the between-group inequality term defined above, Shorrocks [1980a - p. 622] has shown that there exists a one-parameter (c) family of inequality measures that is additively decomposable. The family is

(*i*) $$I_c(y) = \frac{1}{N} \frac{1}{c(c-1)} \sum_{i=1}^{N} \{\tau_i^{\,c} - 1\},\ c \neq 0,1$$

(*ii*) $$I_o(y) = -\frac{1}{N} \sum_{i=1}^{N} \log \tau_i,\ c = 0$$

(*iii*) $$I_1(y) = \frac{1}{N} \sum_{i=1}^{N} \tau_i \log \tau_i,\ c = 1$$

1) This is the form of an additively decomposable inequality measure.

where $\tau_i = y_i/\mu$. (*ii*) equals T_2, Theil's 2nd measure, (*iii*) equals T_1, Theil's 1st measure and (*i*) with c=2 equals the square of the coefficient of variation. The same results were given by Bourguignon [1979]. Cowell [1980] discussed the structure of additive inequality measures by assuming PARSYM instead of SYM (see the criteria in ch. 4).

The between-group term is a function of the within-group arithmetic means[1)] μ_j and it mearuses, in some sense the subgroups relative positions on the real axis (the income axis). Frequently it measures the μ_js deviation from the overall arithmetic mean income μ, cf. with analysis of variance where the total sum of squares, $SST = \sum_{i=1}^{N} (y_i - \mu)^2$, is decomposed into a sum of squares within groups, SSW, and a sum of squares between groups, SSB, where $SSW = \sum_{j=1}^{k} \sum_{i=1}^{N_j} (\eta_{ji} - \mu_j)^2$, $SSB = \sum_{j=1}^{k} N_j(\mu_j - \mu)^2$ and N_j is the number of i.r.u.'s in group j.

We will see below that there exist measures where the 'between-group' term is not a funciton of the arithmetic group means but a function of paired comparisons of incomes, where the pair of incomes is taken from group j and l, respektively, $j \neq l$, j, l = 1, 2, ., k. We designate this decomposition term *across-group* inequality (cf. Mehran [1975b - p. 146]. Hence, the across-group term measures the deviation between i.r.u.'s from different groups including their intrinsic within-group inequality. One example of an inequality measure that has this decomposition property is the Gini coefficient.

An inequality measure that is decomposed into the sum of a within-group term and an across-group term is not additively decomposable in the sense that is given by the above definition. Is it a disadvantage to have measures that are within / across decomposable? We do not think so,

1) In some cases the geometrical means.

since the across-group term includes information about the positions of 'individual' incomes on the income axis and not merely the arithmetic group means.[1)]

If, for purposes of analysis, it is seen as a disadvantage not to have a between-group term in the decomposition formula this can be introduced and the residual, i.e. the difference between the across-group term and the between-group term, can be regarded as an *interaction* term, cf. Mehran [1975b - pp. 147-148].

1) See also Blackorby, Donaldson and Auersperg [1978 - pp 20-21].

9.1.1 ONE-WAY DECOMPOSITION

In this section we will decompose some measures of inequality according to one classification variable (one economic sector variable or one income determinant characteristic). For simplicity, as stated before, the decompositions are mainly done in the continuous case but we also give the corresponding discrete formulas.

We begin with the Lorenz Curve (LC) associated measures and then continue with the other measures discussed earlier (ch. 7 and 8).

A. LC associated measures

The decomposition of the Gini coefficient, R, (and thus of the absolute mean difference, $G = 2\mu R$) has for many years been one of the favourite topics in the literature of inequality decomposition. The non-simplicity of decomposing R is reflected by many authors, see e.g. the non-additivity discussed by Garvy [1952 - p. 38] and the non-additive decomposability discussed by Theil [1967 - p. 123]. The various suggestions of decomposition formulas for R given in the literature are shown to originate from one single decomposition formula and this is a within/across decomposition. The discussion ends with an example.

A first step towards a decomposition of R was made by Bortkiewicz [1930 - pp. 72-88]. He decomposed the absolute mean difference $G(= 2\mu R)$ into two non-overlapping groups (a lower and an upper income-group):

$$G = f_\ell^2 \, G_\ell + f^2_u \, G_u + 2 f_\ell f_u G_{\ell u} \qquad (9.7)$$

where G_ℓ, G_u and $G_{\ell u}$ are the within lower income-group, within upper income-group and the across group absolute mean difference. f_ℓ and f_u are the population shares.

Dividing (9.7) by μ and letting μ_ℓ and μ_u denote the arithmetic group means (cf. (7.9) and (7.10)) we get the decomposition made by Mendershausen [1946], i.e.

$$R = f_\ell \, F_{1\ell} \, R_\ell = f_u \, f_{1u} \, R_u + (f_\ell \, f_{1u} - f_u \, f_{1\ell}) \qquad (9.8)$$

where f_{1j}, j=l, u, are the income share defined by $f_{1j} = f_j \mu_j / \mu$. The across-group term $f_\ell \, f_{1u} - f_u \, f_{1\ell}$ was expressed as $\frac{N_\ell N_u}{N^2} \left(\frac{\mu_u - \mu_\ell}{\mu}\right)$ in the discrete case by Mendershausen [1946 - p. 167].

If we assume $R_\ell = R_u = 0$ the across-group term is identical with twice the last but one expression among the LA (Lorenz Area) expressions in table 8.1 when only two groups are considered. The decomposition by G (and hence R) into mutually exclusive income intervals was extended to the case of, say, k intervals by Taguchi [1968 - p. 123]. Koo, Quan and Rasche [1981] also proposed an identical decomposition and computations of weighted Lorenz area ratios from accumulated income intervals.

(9.2) is a special case of the more general one which follows:

To obtain the principal decomposition of the Gini coefficient we use the following formula of R:

$$R = \frac{1}{\mu} \int F(y) \, [1 - F(y)] dy$$

which is given for LA $= \frac{1}{2}$ R in table 7.2 (ef. also Bortkiewicz [1930 - p. 81]). Using (9.1) and the fact that the population shares sum up to one, $\sum_{j=1}^{k} f_j = 1$ we have (cf. Mehran [1975b])

$$R = \frac{1}{\mu}\int_0^\infty F(y)\,\{1-F(y)\}dy = \frac{1}{\mu}\int_0^\infty \{\sum_{j=1}^{k} f_j\; F(y)_j\}\{\sum_{j=1}^{k} f_j(1-F(y)_j)\}dy =$$

$$= \frac{1}{\mu}\sum_{j=1}^{k} f_j^{\,2}\int_0^\infty F(y)_j\,(1-F(y)_j\}dy +$$

$$+ \frac{1}{\mu}\sum\sum_{i<j} f_i f_j \int_0^\infty \{F(y)_i\;[1-F(y)_j] + F(y)_j\;[1-F(y)_i]\}\,dy.$$

This can be written as

$$R = \sum_{j=1}^{k} f_j\, f_{1j}\, R_{jj} + \sum\sum_{i<j} \frac{1}{\mu}\, f_i\, f_j\, R^*_{ij} \qquad (9.9)$$

where $R_{jj} = \frac{1}{\mu_j}\int_0^\infty F(y)_j\,\{1-F(y)_j\}\,dy$ is the Gini coefficient within group j

and $R^*_{ij} = \int_0^\infty \{F(y)_i\;[1-F(y)_j] + F(y)_j\;[1-F(y)_i]\}\,dy$ is an across-like Gini coefficient.

By definition $R = (2\mu)^{-1}G = (2\mu)^{-1}\,E\,(|X - Y|)$, where $E\,(|X - Y|)$ is the expected value of absolute income differences of all pairs, X and Y, of the same distribution (cf. table 7.2) and using the same notation $R_{jj} = (2\mu_j)^{-1}\,E(|X_j - Y_j|)$, where the subscript j, j = 1, 2, .., k, stands for subgroup j.

The Gini coefficient across subgroups i and j can be defined by

$$R_{ij} = (\mu_i + \mu_j)^{-1}\,E(|Y_i - Y_j|) =$$

$$= (\mu_i + \mu_j)^{-1}\,R^*_{ij}, \qquad (9.10)$$

where $E(|Y_i - Y_j|)$ is the expected value of absolute income differences of all pairs, Y_i and Y_j, one taken from subgroup i and one from subgroup j, and R_{ij}* is defined by (9.9).

The following properties hold for R_{ij}, cf. Mehran [1975b - pp. 146-147]:

(*i*) symmetry: $R_{ij} = R_{ji}$

(*ii*) identical distributions: $R_{ij} = R_{jj}$ if $F(y)_i = F(y)_j$
(or $R_{ij} = R_{ii}$)

(*iii*) $0 \leq R_{ij} \leq 1$,

where by (9.9) and (9.10)

$$R_{ij}=(\mu_i + \mu_j)^{-1}\int_0^\infty \{F(y)_i\ [1-F(y)_j]+ F(y)_j\ [1-F(y)_i]\}\ dy$$

using (9.10) we can rewrite (9.9) as

$$R = \sum_{j=1}^{k} f_j\ f_{1j}\ R_{jj} + \sum\sum_{i<j} (f_i\ f_{1j} + f_j\ f_{1i})R_{ij} =$$

$$= \sum_{j=1}^{k} f_j\ f_{1j}\ R_{jj} + \sum\sum_{i \neq j} f_i\ f_{1j}\ R_{ij}, \qquad (9.11)$$

which is our principal decomposition of R and it can also be written as $R = R_W + R_A$, i.e. a within and across decomposition, where $R_W = \sum_{j=1}^{k} f_j\ f_{1j}\ R_{jj}$.

Another way of rewriting (9.9) is as follows:

$$R = \sum_{j=1}^{k} f_j \; f_{1j} \; R_{jj} + \sum\sum_{i<j} \{f_i \; f_{1j} \; R^r_{ij} + f_j \; f_{1i} \; R^r_{ji}\} =$$

$$= \sum_{j=1}^{k} f_j \; f_{1j} \; R_{jj} + \sum\sum_{i \neq j} f_i \; f_{1j} \; R^r_{ij}, \qquad (9.12)$$

where $R^r_{ij} = \frac{1}{\mu_j} \int_0^\infty F(y)_i (1-F(y)_j) \, dy$ [1] and this can be thought of a one-direction Gini across from subgroup j to i (R_{ij} above can in the same way be thought of as a double-direction Gini across).

The last across group term in (9.12) can be written as

$$\sum_{j=1}^{k} R_{(i)j} = \sum_{j=1}^{k} \{\sum_{\substack{j=1 \\ i \neq j}}^{k} f_i \; f_{1j} \; R^r_{ij}\}, \qquad (9.13)$$

where $R_{(i)j}$ can be thought of as a one-direction Gini across from subgroup j to the other k-1 groups.

Obviously $\sum_{j=i}^{k} f_j \; f_{1j} < 1$ and $k < \sum_{j=1}^{k} [f_j \; f_{1j} + 1] < k+1$. This fact made Soltow [1960] propose a reformulation of $R = \sum_{j=1}^{k} f_j \; f_{1j} \; R_{jj} + \sum_{j=1}^{k} R_{(i)j}$ (from (9.12) and (9.13)) as

$$R = \sum_{j=1}^{k} f_j \; f_{1j} \; R_{jj} + \sum_{j=1}^{k} \omega_j \; R^s_{(i)j}, \qquad (9.14)$$

where $R^s_{(i)j} = w_j^{-1} \; R_{(i)j}$ and $\omega_j = \frac{1}{2} [f_j \; (1-f_{1j}) + f_{1j} \; (1-f_j)]$. The total weights $f_j \; f_{1j} + \omega_j$ now add up to 1.

We have earlier discussed the within/across decomposition versus within/between decomposition. An argumentation against the within/across decomposition is given by Mehran [1975b - pp 147-148]: "It can be argued that when one compares the inequality between distributions, one usually thinks of a certain measure of relative dispersion of

---

1) $\mu_i R^r_{ji} + \mu_j R^r_{ij} = (\mu_i + \mu_j) R_{ij}$ and $R^r_{ij} = \frac{\mu_i}{\mu_j} R^r_{ji} + (1 - \frac{\mu_i}{\mu_j})$

their means independently of the extent of inequality within the distributions. On this basis the decomposition across/within would be inadequate since the concept of inequality across distributions is implicitly related to the inequality within distributions."

If the relation between the across-group term and the within-group term is taken as a disadvantage we can, as stated before, introduce a between-group term. Such a term is a function of the arithmetic means, μ_j, and is frequently obtained as the measure of inequality computed when the within group inequalities equal zero under the constraint of unaffected arithmetic mean incomes, i.e. all i.r.u.'s within group j are assumed to have income equal to μ_j, j = 1,2, .., k.

By definition of R we have the between-group inequality defined as

$$R_B = (2\mu)^{-1} \sum_{j=1}^{k} \sum_{j=1}^{k} f_i \; f_j \; | \mu_i - \mu_j | = \mu^{-1} \sum\sum_{i<j} f_i \; f_j \; |\mu_i - \mu_j| =$$

$$= \sum\sum_{i \neq j} f_i \; f_{1j} \; \frac{|\mu_i - \mu_j|}{\mu_i + \mu_j} \qquad (9.15)$$

To receive R from the sum of R_W and R_B, the within-group and between-group terms, we have to introduce a residual, or an interaction term (cf. Mehran [1975b -p.148]), $R_I = R_A - R_B$. R_I can by use of (9.10), (9.11) and (9.15) be written as

$$R_I = R_A - R_B =$$

$$= \sum\sum_{i \neq j} \frac{f_i \; f_{1j}}{\mu_i + \mu_j} \{R^x_{ij} - |\mu_i - \mu_j|\} = \sum\sum_{i \neq j} \frac{f_i f_{1j}}{\mu_i + \mu_j} \{E\;(|Y_i - Y_j|) - |\mu_i - \mu_j|\} =$$

$$= \sum_{i \neq j}\sum f_i \, f_{1j} \, \{R_{ij} - \frac{|\mu_i - \mu_j|}{\mu_i + \mu_j}\}. \tag{9.16}$$

The interaction between group i and j $(\mu_i + \mu_j)^{-1}$ $\{E(|Y_i - Y_j|) - |\mu_i - \mu_j|\}$, given by (9.16) can be interpreted as a measure of the extent of income domination of one group over the other, apart from the absolute difference between their arithmetic mean incomes.

It can be seen that

$$0 \leq R_I \leq \max \{R_{ii}, R_{jj}\},$$

where the two extreme cases are obtained when (cf Mehran [1975b - p.148])

(i) The incomes in one group, e.g. group i, completely dominate over the incomes of the other group, i.e. $Y_i > Y_j$, where Y_i stands for the incomes in group i. This implies that $E(|Y_i - Y_j|) = |\mu_i - \mu_j|$, and hence $R_I = 0$, which follows from (9.16).

(ii) Neither group dominates over the other in such a way that $F(y)_i = F(y)_j$. From the definition of $E(Y_i - Y_j|)$, (9.10) it hence follows that $R^x_{ij} = 2R^x_{ii} = 2R^x_{jj}$ and $\mu_i = \mu_j$. In this case the maximum R_I equals $\max \{R_{ii}, R_{jj}\}$.

If the subgroups are defined as mutually exclusive income intervals then $R_I = 0$ (by (i)) and this gives the income interval decomposition (using (9.15))

$$R = \sum_{j=1}^{k} f_j \, f_{1j} \, R_{jj} + \sum_{i \neq j}\sum f_i \, f_{1j} \, \frac{|\mu_i - \mu_j|}{\mu_i + \mu_j} =$$

$$= \sum_{j=1}^{k} f_j \, f_{1j} \, R_{jj} + \mu^{-1} \sum\sum_{i<j} f_i \, f_j \, |\mu_i - \mu_j|.$$

This is the decomposition of R corresponding to that of the absolute mean difference G given by Taguchi. [1965 - p.123] (see also Nelson [1977 - p.497]). Letting k = 2 we have the special case given by Bortkiewicz and Mendershausen[1)] as discussed earlier. The decomposition (9.11) corresponding to G was also given by Piesch [1975 - p.212]. Bhattacharya and Mahalanobis [1967 - p.10] decomposed G as (we write it in terms of R)

$$R = R'_W + R_B = R_W + R_I + R_B$$

where $R'_W = R_W + R_I$ (given by (9.11) and (9.16), respectively) is a within-group like term, including the interaction term, and R_B (given by (9.15)) is the between-group term. The same decomposition, $R = R_W + R_B + R_I$, was also given by Pyatt [1976 - p.252], Pyatt's decomposition was made in terms of expected gains (cf. sec. 7.4.1). The decomposition $R = R_W + R_I + R_B$ was also given implicitly by Love and Wolfram [1976 - p.67].

<u>Rao's decomposition</u>

Rao [1969] used the fact that $\sum_{j=1}^{k} f_{1j} = 1$ to decompose R. Putting $f_{1j} = 1 - \sum_{i \neq j} f_{1i}$ into the within term in (9.9) we obtain

$$\sum_{j=1}^{k} f_i \, f_{1j} \, R_{jj} = \sum_{j=1}^{k} f_j \, R_{jj} - \sum\sum_{i \neq j} f_i \, f_{1j} \, R_{jj}. \qquad (9.17)$$

The decomposition (9.9) will, with the use of (9.17), be equal to

---

1) cf. also Pyatt [1980].

$$R = \sum_{j=1}^{k} f_j R_{jj} + \sum\sum_{i<j} \{f_i f_{1j} (R^r_{ij} - R_{ii}) + f_j f_{1i} (R^r_{ji} - R_{jj}\} \tag{9.18}$$

where R^r_{ij} is defined in (9.12).

(9.18) is the decomposition proposed by Rao, where the first term is interpreted as a within term and the second as an across term (in Rao's terminology: "a term depending on the inter sub-population differences ...").

The term within brackets in the across term can be written as

$$\frac{1}{\mu} \int_0^\infty \frac{(\mu_j F(y)_i - \mu_i F(y)_j)^2 - (\mu_j F(y)_i - \mu_i F(y)_j)(\mu_j - \mu_i)}{\mu_i \mu_j} dy.$$

<u>Piesch's and Mangahas' decomposition</u>

The decomposition formula proposed by Piesch [1975 - p.208] and Mangahas [1975 - p.10][1)] is similar to that suggested by Rao. The difference lies in that Piesch (and Mangahas) used the fact that $\sum_{j=1}^{k} f_j = 1$, i.e. substituting $f_j = 1 - \sum_{i \neq j} f_i$ into (9.9) yields

$$R = \sum_{j=1}^{k} f_{1j} R_{jj} + \sum\sum_{i<j} \frac{f_i f_j}{\mu} \int_0^\infty [F(y)_j - F(y)_i]^2 dy. \tag{9.19}$$

Piesch also showed that R must lie in the following interval $\min_j R_{jj}$ + (across-term in (9.19)) $\leq R \leq \max_j R_{jj}$ + (across-term in (9.19)).

1) Cf. also Fields [1979a - p.441].

In the discrete case with a population of N i.r.u's and k subgroups of N_j i.r.u's, respectively, $N = \sum_{j=1}^{k} N_j$, the decomposition given by (9.9) can be written as

$$R = \sum_{j=1}^{k} f_i \, f_{1j} \, R_{jj} + \sum_{i<j}\sum \frac{1}{\mu} f_i \, f_j \, R^x_{ij}$$

where
$$R^x_{ij} = \{\frac{2}{N_i N_j} \sum_{\ell=1}^{N_i+N_j} \ell_j \, Y_{\ell|i} - \mu_i\} + \{\frac{2}{N_i N_j} \sum_{\ell=1}^{N_i+N_j} \ell_i \, Y_{\ell|j} - \mu_j\} =$$
$$= \frac{2}{N_i N_j} \left[\sum_{\ell=1}^{N_i+N_j} (\ell_i \, Y_{\ell|j} + \ell_j \, Y_{\ell|i})\right] - (\mu_i + \mu_j) \qquad (9.20)$$

In R^x_{ij} we arrange the N_i+N_j incomes in ascending order and define ℓ_i as *the rank-order in subgroup i* of the element belonging to the i:th subgroup *which is either* equal to the ℓ:th element in the aggregated group consisting of N_i+N_j elements <u>or</u> if the ℓ:th element ($\ell = 1, 2, \ldots, N_i+N_j$) belongs to the j:th group as the rankorder of the element in subgroup i which is nearest to the ℓ:th element (for illustration, see the example below). $Y_{\ell|i}$ is defined as

$$Y_{\ell|i} = \begin{cases} Y_\ell \text{ if } Y_\ell \text{ belongs to the i:th subgroup} \\ 0 \text{ if } Y_\ell \text{ belongs to the j:th subgroup} \end{cases}$$

The Gini coefficient across subgroups i and j is defined as (9.10), i.e.
$$R_{ij} = \frac{2}{N_i N_j (\mu_i + \mu_j)} \sum_{\ell=1}^{N_i+N_j} (\ell_i \, Y_{\ell|j} + \ell_j \, Y_{\ell|i}) - 1 \qquad (9.21)$$

If we want to introduce a between-group term (and hence an interaction term) we use (9.15) and (9.16).

Example 9.1 Decomposition of the Gini coefficient.

We consider a population of N=4 i.r.u's with incomes 1, 2, 3 and 4, i.e. $\mu = 2.5$ and $R = \frac{1}{4}$ ($R = \frac{2}{N^2\mu} \sum_{i=1}^{N} iy_{(i)} - (\frac{N+1}{N})$

where $Y_{(1)} \leq Y_{(2)} \leq \cdots \leq Y_{(N)}$)

Subgroup 1: y: 1,3 . $\mu_1 = 2$, $N_1 = 2$, $f_1 = \frac{1}{2}$, $f_{11} = \frac{4}{10}$

" 1: y: 2,4 $\mu_2 = 3$, $N_2 = 2$, $f_2 = \frac{1}{2}$ $f_{12} = \frac{6}{10}$

Using R above we obtain

$R_{11} = \frac{1}{4}$ and $R_{22} = \frac{1}{6}$

To obtain R^{x}_{12} we consider the following arrangement

Subgroup number	Y income	$\ell_1 \times Y_{\ell\|2}$	$\ell_2 \times Y_{\ell\|1}$
1	1	1 x 0	0 x 1
2	2	1 x 2	1 x 0
1	3	2 x 0	1 x 3
2	4	2 x 4	2 x 0
	Σ	10	3

where ℓ_i and $Y_{\ell|i}$, i = 1,2, are defined above.

We now have

$$R^{x}_{12} = \frac{2}{2\cdot 2}(10+3) - (2+3) = \frac{13}{2} - 5 = \frac{3}{2}^{1)},$$

and the total across group inequality is

$$R_A = \frac{1}{\mu} f_1 f_2 R^{x}_{12} = \frac{3}{20}.$$

---

1) R_{12} equals $\frac{3}{10}$.

The within-group term $R_W = \sum_{j=1}^{2} f_j \; f_{1j} \; R_{jj}$ equals

$$R_W = \frac{1}{2} \cdot \frac{4}{10} \cdot \frac{1}{4} + \frac{1}{2} \cdot \frac{6}{10} \cdot \frac{1}{6} = \frac{2}{20}$$

and hence we have $R_W + R_A = \frac{2}{20} + \frac{3}{20} = \frac{1}{4}$.

Introducing a between-group term we obtain

$$R_B = \frac{\frac{1}{2} \cdot \frac{1}{2}}{2.5} \quad |2-3| = \frac{1}{10} \quad \text{and hence } R_I = R_A - R_B = \frac{1}{20}$$

which yields

$$R = R_W + R_B + R_I = \frac{2}{20} + \frac{1}{10} + \frac{1}{20} = \frac{1}{4}.$$

Table 9.1 One-way decomposition by subgroups of the Gini coefficient, R.
f_j = the population share in group j, f_{1j} = the income share in group j.

R =	Notes
$R_W + R_A$, where $R_W = \sum_{j=1}^{k} f_j f_{1j} R_{jj}$ within-group term $R_A = \sum\sum_{i \neq j} f_i f_{1j} R_{ij}$ across-group term	(9.11) or (9.9) (see also (9.21)) Mehran [1975b]
$R_W + R_B + R_I$, where $R_B = \sum\sum_{i \neq j} f_i f_{1j} \frac{\lvert \mu_i - \mu_j \rvert}{\mu_i + \mu_j}$ between-group term $R_I = R_A - R_B$ interaction term	(9.15) (9.16) Mehran [1975b] Bhattacharya and Mahalanobis [1967] Piesch [1975] Pyatt [1976] Love and Wolfson [1976]
$R_W + R_B$ $R_I = 0$	Subgroups = mutually exclusive income intervals Taguchi [1968], see also Bortkiewicz [1931], Mendershausen [1946], Nelson [1977].
$R'_W + R'_A$, where $R'_W = \sum_{j=1}^{k} f_j R_{jj}$ $R'_A = \sum\sum_{i<j} f_i f_{1j} (R^r_{ij} - R_{ii}) + f_j f_{1i}(R^r_{ji} - R_{jj})$	population weighted decomposition by Rao [1969] (9.18)
$R''_W + R''_A$, where $R''_W = \sum_{j=1}^{k} f_{1j} R_{jj}$ $R''_A = \sum\sum_{i<j} \frac{f_i f_j}{\mu} \int_0^\infty [F(y)_j - F(y)_i]^2 dy$	income weighted decomposition by Piesch [1975], Mangahas [1975] (9.19)
$R_W + R'''_A$, where $R'''_A = \sum_{j=1}^{k} \omega_j R^s_{(i)j}$	(9.14), Soltow [1960], $\sum_{j=1}^{k} (f_j f_{1j} + \omega_j) = 1$

The decompositions of Mehran's and Piesch's measures are not as 'simple' as the decomposition of the Gini coefficient. We have noticed a reflection of this during the discussion of upper bounds of these measures from grouped data in sec. 8.3.2.

Mehran's measure, M, can be written as $M = \int_0^1 (6\,p-3\,p^2)\ (\tau(p)-1)\ dp =$ $= 3R - 2P$, where R is the Gini coefficient and P is Piesch measure. If we could decompose Piesch measure in a similar way as R then we would have the decomposition of M immediately. To decompose P we could either use $P = \frac{3}{2}\int_0^\infty F(y)^2\ dF_1(y) - \frac{1}{2}$ or $P = \frac{3}{2\mu}\int_0^\infty F(y)^2(1-F(y))\ dy - \frac{1}{2}$[1). We use the first expression and (9.1) and (9.3) and obtain

$$P = \sum_{j=1}^{k} f_{1j}\ f_j^{\ 2}\ P_{jj} + \sum_{i \neq j}\sum f_{1j}\ f_i^{\ 2} P_{ij} + \sum_{j=1}^{k}\sum_{i<h}\sum f_{1j}\ f_i\ f_h P_{ih,j} + \varepsilon_p,$$

where $P_{jj} = \frac{3}{2}\int_0^\infty F(y)_j^{\ 2} d\ F_1(y)_j - \frac{1}{2}$ is the within group j Piesch measure,

$P_{ij} = \frac{3}{2}\int_0^\infty F(y)_i^{\ 2}\ dF_1(y)_j - \frac{1}{2}$ is the 'across' group i and j Piesch measure,

$P_{ih,j} = \frac{3}{2}\int_0^\infty F(y)_i\ F(y)_h\ dF_1\ (y)_j - \frac{1}{2}$ is the 'across' groups i, h and j, Piesch measure,

$\varepsilon_p = \sum_{j=1}^{k}\ \sum_{i=1}^{k}\ \sum_{h=1}^{k} f_{1j}\ f_i\ f_h - \frac{1}{2}$ is a Piesch residual.

The awkwardness of this decomposition is obvious and of course the same is true for Mehran's measure. We will therefore suggest that these measures should not be used for decomposition analysis. Bonferroni's and de

1) By this and the fact that $R = \frac{1}{\mu}\int_0^\infty F(y)[1-F(y)]dy$ we can write $M = \frac{1}{2} + \frac{3}{\mu}\int_0^\infty F(y)[1-F(y)]^2\ dy.$

Vergottini's measures are not decomposable by subgroups because of the logarithmic expressions (see e.g. sec. 7.4).

B. Some other measures

The measures discussed here are identical to the measures discussed in sec. 8.2.

SD-class

The LC associated measures are discussed above.

The *variance*, σ^2 is easily decomposed into a within-group and a between-group term (σ^2 is the only absolute invariant (AI)-measures we discuss here), $\sigma^2 = \sigma_W^2 + \sigma_B^2$ where $\sigma_W^2 = \sum_{j=1}^{k} f_j \sigma_j^2$ and $\sigma_B^2 = \sum_{j=1}^{k} f_j \ (\mu_j - \mu)^2$.

The *squared coefficient of variation*, V^2, belongs to the class of additively decomposable inequality measures discussed by Shorrocks [1980a - p.622], see also Bourguignon [1979 -p.918]. The decomposition of V^2 is also discussed by e.g. Rosenbluth [1951-p.937], Theil [1967 - pp.[124-125], Piesch [1975-p.215] and Bartels [1977 - p.43].

V^2 can be written as $V^2 = V_W^2 + V_B^2$, where $V_W^2 = \sum_{j=1}^{k} q_j \ V_j^2$ and

$$V_B^2 = \sum_{j=1}^{k} f_j \ (\frac{\mu_j}{\mu} - 1)^2 = \sum_{j=1}^{k} q_j - 1 \quad \text{and} \quad q_j = f_{1j} \frac{\mu_j}{\mu} = f_j (\frac{\mu_j}{\mu})^2$$

The sum of the weights in the within-group term is greater than one,

$\sum_{j=1}^{k} q_j = 1 + \sum_{j=1}^{k} f_j \ (\frac{\mu_j}{\mu} - 1)^2 = 1 + V_B^2 > 1$, cf. Theil [1967 - p.125] and

Piesch [1975 - p.215], i.e. the sum of the weights in the within-group term is dependent on the between-group term. This is considered by Theil [1967 - p. 125] and Shorrocks [1980a - p. 624] as a disadvantage of this measure, "... because one should prefer a measure for which the within-set components, including their weights, are independent of the between-set component".

$V^2/(V^2+1)$ can not be decomposed into within- and between (across) group terms.

Bartels [1977 - p.20] *RSMAX*^{2} and *SMAXN*^{2} can also be decomposed into within and between group terms.

$RSMAX^2 = RSMAX_W^2 + RSMAX_B^2$ and $SMAXN^2 = SMAXN_W^2 + SMAXN_B^2$, where

$$RSMAX_W^2 = \sum_{j=1}^{k} q_j \; RSMAX_j^2 \;, \quad RSMAX_B^2 = \sum_{j=1}^{k} f_j \left(\frac{Y_{max} - Y_{jmax}}{\mu}\right)\left(\frac{Y_{max} + Y_{jmax} - 2\mu}{\mu}\right)$$

and $q_j = f_{1j} \frac{\mu_j}{\mu}$, see above, and $SMAXN_W^2 = \sum_j q_j \; SMAXN_j^2$ and $SMAXN_B^2 =$

$$= \sum_{j=1}^{k} f_j \left(\frac{Y_{max} - Y_{jmax}}{N\mu}\right)\left(\frac{Y_{max} + Y_{jmax} - 2\mu}{(N-1)\mu}\right)^{1)}$$

Kolm's μ-modified centrist measure, $K_c^m(\xi,\varepsilon)$, $\xi > 0$, is not additively decomposable in the sense of the definition given earlier. $K_c^m(\xi,\varepsilon)$ can be decomposed as

$$K_c^m(\xi,\varepsilon) = 1 + \frac{\xi}{\mu} - \{ \sum_{j=1}^{k} F_{1j} \left(\frac{\mu_i}{\mu}\right)^{-\varepsilon} [1 + \frac{\xi}{\mu_j} - K_c^m(\xi,\varepsilon)_j]^{1-} \}^{1/1-\varepsilon}$$

---

1) We have here used the formulation of SMAXN given in sec. 8.2.

This measure is, in Bourguignon's [1979 - p. 903 and p. 918] terms aggregative. Aggregativity is a general property which implies that a measure can be written as a function of the within-group inequalities and only these inequalities and their aggregate characteristics μ_j and N_j are necessary; N_j equals the number of i.r.u's within group j.

Letting $\xi = 0$ in $K_c^m(\xi,\varepsilon)$ we obtain *Atkinson's measure*, $A(\varepsilon) = K_c^m(0,\varepsilon)$, which is 'aggregative' and can be written as

$$A(\varepsilon) = 1 - \{ \sum_{j=1}^{k} f_{1j} \left(\frac{\mu_j}{\mu}\right)^{-\varepsilon} [1 - A(\varepsilon)_j]^{1-\varepsilon}\}^{1/1-\varepsilon},$$

see. e.g. Jakobsson and Normann [1974 - p.105] and Blackorby, Donaldson and Auersperg [1978 - p.19].

If we let ε tend towards zero in $K_c^m(\xi,\varepsilon)$ we have a measure which for $\xi = 0$ equals T_2, *Theil's 2nd measure*, and this measure is additively decomposable

$$K_{clog}^m(\xi, 0) = \sum_{j=1}^{k} f_j K_{clog}^m(\xi, 0)_j + \sum_{j=1}^{k} f_j \log \left[\frac{\mu + \xi}{\mu_j + \xi}\right], \xi > 0,$$

and letting $\xi = 0$ we obtain T_2, Theil's 2nd measure, i.e.

$$T_2 = \sum_{j=1}^{k} f_j T_{2j} + \sum_{j=1}^{k} f_j \log \left(\frac{\mu}{\mu_j}\right).$$

This is given by Theil [1967 - p.125], Bourguignon [1979 - p.912], Shorrock [1980a - p.622] and Cowell [1980 - p.530]. By the definition given by Bourguignon T_2 is the only 'population weighted' additively decomposable inequality measure. T_2 belongs, as said before, to the class proposed by Shorrock.

The transformation of K_c^m $(\xi, 0)$ given by (7.84c), which is $K_{ce}^m(\xi,0) = 1+\frac{\xi}{\mu} - \exp\{\int_0^\infty \ell og\ [\frac{y+\xi}{\mu}]\ dF(y)\}$ is aggregative in a multiplicative way and can be decomposed as

$$K_{ce}^m(\xi,\ 0) = 1 + \frac{\xi}{\mu} - \prod_{j=1}^{k} \{ \frac{\mu_j}{\mu} [1 + \frac{\xi}{\mu_j} - K_{ce}^m\ (\xi,\ 0)_j]\}^{f_j}$$

and letting $\varepsilon = 0$ we have *Champernowne's measure*, see sec. 7.4.1, i.e.

$$K_{ce}^m(0,0) = 1 - \prod_{j=1}^{k} \{ \frac{\mu_j}{\mu} [1 - K_{ce}^m\ (0,0)_j]\}^{fj},$$

where $K_{ce}^m\ (0,0) =- 1\frac{\mu_g}{\mu}$

LSD-class

The *quasi-variance*[1], σ_q^2, is within/between decomposable. It can be written as

$$\sigma_q^2 = \sum_{j=1}^{k} f_j\ \sigma^2_{qj} + \sum_{j=1}^{k} f_j\ (\ell og\ \frac{\mu_j}{\mu})\ (\ell og\ \frac{\mu_g}{\mu\mu_j}^2).$$

Theil's 1st measure, T_1, is by the definition given by Bourguignon the only 'income weighted' additively decomposable measure. It can be written as

$$T_1 = \sum_{j=1}^{k} f_{1j}\ T_{1j} + \sum_{j=1}^{k} f_{1j}\ \ell og\ \frac{\mu_j}{\mu}$$

The decomposition is given by e.g. Theil [1967 - p.93], [1972 - p.100], Bourguignon [1979 - p.915], Shorrock [1980a - p.622] and Cowell [1980 - p.530].

1) The log variance $\sigma^2_{\ell og}$ can be written as $\sigma^2_{\ell og} = \sum_{j=1}^{k} f_j\ \sigma^2_{\ell og\ j} + \sum_{j=1}^{k} f_j\ (\ell og\ \frac{\mu_{gj}}{\mu_g})^2$.

ESD-class

Kolm's relative leftist measure, $K^r_\ell(\alpha)$ has not the aggregativity property. It can be written in the following way (cf. Blackorby, Donaldson and Auersperg [1978 - p.16].

$$K^r_\ell(\alpha) = 1 + \frac{1}{\alpha}\,\ell og \int_0^\infty e^{-\alpha y/\mu} dF(y) =$$

$$= 1 + \frac{1}{\alpha}\,\ell og \{ \sum_{j=1}^{k} f_j \, e^{-\alpha\,[1-T(\alpha)_j]} \} = \frac{1}{\alpha}\,\ell og \{ \sum_{j=1}^{k} f_j \, e^{\alpha T(\alpha)_j} \}$$

where

$T(\alpha)_j = 1 + \frac{1}{\alpha}\,\ell og \int_0^\infty e^{-\alpha y/\mu} dF(y)_j$ and the difference between $T(\alpha)_j$ and $K^r_\ell(\alpha)_j$ is that μ_j has been replaced by μ.

Other measures

The maximum equalization ratio, MER, see sec. 7.4.4, is not an inequality measure by our definition. A decomposition proposal of MER is given in Piesch [1975 - pp. 214-215] and Nygård and Sandström [1980 - p.127 and pp. 232-235].

9.1.2 ON SOME GENERALIZATIONS

The measures that are decomposable by one factor (one-way decomposition) can also be decomposed by m factors, $m \geq 2$ (m-way decompositions).[1)] As examples, the variance and squared coefficient of variation can be decomposed according to the analysis of variance (ANOVA). A decomposition of Theil's 1st measure (T_1) in the case of $m = 2$ is e.g. given by Fishlow [1972 - p.395], see also Fields [1979a - p.442] for a review. In the same manner as before, the Gini coefficient can be decomposed by m groups (cf. Mehran [1975b - pp. 148-149]) as (for m = 2)

$$R = \sum_{j=1}^{k} \sum_{h=1}^{k} f_{jh}\, f_{1jh}\, R_{jh} + \sum_{(jh)\neq(d\ell)} \sum f_{jh}\, f_{1d\ell}\, R^{r}_{(jh)\,(d\ell)},$$

which corresponds to (9.12) where $j, d = 1,2 .., k$ and $h,\ell = 1, 2, .., g$ are indices for the two characteristics, respectively, and $R_{jh} = \frac{1}{\mu_{jh}} \int_{o}^{\infty} F(y)_{jh}\{1-F(y)_{jh}\}\, dy$ and $R^{r}_{(jh)(d\ell)} = \frac{1}{\mu_{d\ell}} \int_{o}^{\infty} F(y)_{jh}\, \{1-F(y)_{d\ell}\}\, dy$. The number of terms in the within-group term is kg and in the between-group term kg(kg-1). Other formulations are possible, cf. the one-way decomposition of R.

Soltow [1960] made projections of R into the future within a country (he used formula (9.14)). To make projections of income inequality he made the following simplifying assumption:

1) If m = 2 the households can be cross-classified by e.g. the two characteristics 'sex of the head of the household' (2 groups) and 'type of household' (e.g. socio-economic groups).

The distribution of incomes within and across subpopulations remain constant with respect to a base year, t_o.

Define the projections of the population shares at time t, in group j, as

$$f_{tj} \geq 0,\ j = 1, 2, .., k \text{ and } \sum_{j=1}^{k} f_{tj} = 1,$$

and hence $f_{1tj} = f_{tj} \frac{\mu_j}{\mu}$

As an example we may use the definition (9.11) of the Gini coefficient to project R at time t as

$$R(t) = \sum_{j=1}^{k} f_{tj}\, f_{1tj}\, R(t_o)_{jj} + \sum_{i \neq j}\sum f_{ti}\, f_{1tj}\, R(t_o)_{ij},$$

where $R(t_o)$ is the corresponding Gini coefficient at time t_o. Cf. the standardization method in sec. 9.3.

If in accordance with ch. 1 we can crystallize compensatory factors from a given set of income determining factors we could get a new reference distribution (cf. Paglin [1975]).

An example of an 'ideal' situation in the case of household (disposable/ available) incomes we may assume that all individuals get exactly the same income (per capita income)[1]. The income determining factor may be called 'number of household members'. Let the household be classified into k mutually exclusive classes on this classificatory variable and assume the within-class income to be constant, i.e. the income in

1) Suggestions have been made to put weights on the individuals in a household according to their needs. The use of such weights results in 'standardized' incomes, see e.g. Danziger and Taussig [1979].

In Sweden there have been several attempts of configurations of such weighting schemes: one example is the scheme suggested by the Central Bureau of Statistics (Stockholm, Sweden): 1 adult: 1.0,2 adults: 2.7,1 child: 0.5,2 children: 0.9,3 children: 1.2.

class j is μ_j, j = 1, ..., k. The k classes are arranged in ascending order according to their mean income.

As an example we may depict the Gini coefficient by twice the corresponding Lorenz area in a LC-diagram. The new reference line, which takes the number of household members into consideration, is the broken chain curve[1] (k - 1 points excluding (0,0) and (1,1) in the LC-diagram).

The new 'non-compensatory' Gini coefficient will be

$$R_{nc} = R - R_B = R_W + R_I$$

where R_B is the between Gini coefficient defined in (9.15); R_W and R_I are defined by (9.11) and (9.16), respectively.

The discussion, so far, has been made on the underlying assumption that all i.r.u.'s are treated homogeneously (criterion SYM of sec. 4.2). If we are able to stratify the i.r.u.'s into k mutually exclusive, homogeneous, subgroups (criterion PARSYM of sec 4.2) in such a way that

---

1) Owing to the assumption that incomes are constant within each class (μ_j, j = 1, ..., k) we by-pass the method used by Paglin [1975], who assumed a specific functional form for the LC.

every pair of groups constitutes two non-homogeneous groups we would require that the overall measure of inequality should not equal the ordinary equivalent discussed earlier in this section.

Since the i.r.u.'s within each subgroup are assumed to follow SYM we can calculate the inequality within each subgroup, $I(y)_j$, $j = 1, 2, \ldots,$ k. Assume now that we are able to choose a uniqe PARSYM-weight system $\{u_j\}$, $j = 1, 2, \ldots, k$. Within group j there are N_j i.r.u.'s with incomes y_{ji}, $i = 1, 2, \ldots, N_j$. When considering the PARSYM criterion we weight the incomes with the PARSYM-weights: $z_{ji} = u_j\, y_{ji}$. The arithmetic mean income of subgroup j, under PARSYM, now equals $\mu_{pj} = u_j \mu_j$ and hence the relative incomes within group j equals

$$\tau_{pji} = \frac{u_j y_{ji}}{\mu_{pj}} = \frac{y_{ji}}{\mu_j} = \tau_{ji}, \text{ i.e. criterion SYM is fulfilled.}$$

The within-group term is in general, for a measure written as a within-group term and a between-/across-group term, written as a weighted sum of within-group inequalities with weights defined as a function of f_j and f_{1j}, say $W_j\,(f_j, f_{1j})$. By the introduction of the PARSYM criterion these weights will be different and they will equal $W_j\,(f_j, f^p_{1j})$, where $f^p_{1j} = e_j f_{1j}$, $e_j = u_j \frac{\mu}{\mu_p}$ and

$$\mu_p = \sum_{j=1}^{k} u_j\, f_j\, \mu_j \quad (\mu = \sum_{j=1}^{k} f_j\, \mu_j).$$

The between/across terms will now change. We illustrate this by using the Gini coefficient and Theil's two measures.

Using (9.12) the Gini across term can, under PARSYM,[1] be written as

$$R_A^P = \sum_{i \neq j}\sum f_j \, f_{1j}^P \, R_{ij}^{rP}, \text{ where } f_{1j}^P \text{ is defined as above and } R_{ij}^{rP}$$

equals[2]

$$R_{ij}^{rP} = R_{ij}^{r} + \left(\frac{\mu_i}{\mu_j} - 1\right) \frac{\mu_i}{\mu_j} \int_o^1 (1-F(y)_i) dF_1(y)_j.$$

The between group terms in T_1 and T_2 are under PARSYM[1], equal to

$$T_{1B}^P = \sum_{j=1}^{k} f_{1j}^P \, \ell og \frac{\mu_j}{\mu} + \sum_{j=1}^{k} f_{1j}^P \, \ell og \; e_j$$

and

$$T_{2B}^P = T_{2B} - \sum_{j=1}^{k} f_j \, \ell og \; e_j.$$

Until now we have not put any restrictions on the weights u_j, j=1, 2, ..., k. If we go from criterion PARSYM back to SYM we impose that the formulas given above should equal the earlier formulas. This holds only if $u_j = 1$, j=i, 2, ..., k, under SYM, i.e. if $u_j=1$ then $f_{1j}^P = f_{1j}$, $\mu_p=\mu$, $e_j=1$ and all the formulas are identical with the ordinary equivalent.

According to the above, the sum of the PARSYM should equal the number of subgroups, i.e. $\sum_{j=1}^{k} u_j = k$. The income share weights, f_{1j}, add up to

---

1) by the definition of the weights above

2) R_{ij}^{rP} is defined by using a partial integration variant of R_{ij}^{r}.

one. By this it seems natural to constrain f_{1j}^{P}, j= 1, 2, ..., k, such that $\sum_{j=1}^{k} f_{1j}^{P} = 1$, i.e. $\sum_{j=1}^{k} U_j f_{1j} = \frac{\mu_P}{\mu}$,

which also follows by definition of μ_p.

If the stratification of the population is e.g. due to 'equal productivity' (cf. sec. 4.2) we can use productivity shares, q_j, j=1, 2, ..., k, $\sum_j q_j = 1$, and define $u_j = kq_j$. This is one of many possibilities to aggregate inequalities under PARSYM.

9.2 DECOMPOSITION BY INCOME SOURCES

The second general type of decomposition that was mentioned in the introduction to ch. 9 was the decomposition by income sources. The main occasion for making this type of decomposition is that it is a useful tool to see whether or not an income source (an income factor) affects the inequality of total income.

We assume that the total income (disposable, available) Y_t is the sum of incomes from k different income sources Y_j, j=1, 2, ..., k, i.e. $Y_t = \Sigma Y_j$. The arithmetic total mean income is denoted by μ_t and the aritmetic mean income of source j by μ_j. The income variables Y_j, j=1, 2, ..., k, are either non-negative ($Y_j \geq 0$) or non-positive ($Y_j \leq 0$). By this we ensure the possibility of negative incomes (taxes), cf. the introduction to ch. 9. We also assume μ_t, $\mu_j \neq 0$, j=1, 2, ..., k.

The general question was: of total inequality, how much is attributable to income source 1, to income source 2, etc? This question could be reformulated as: how should we measure the effect of income source j, j=1, 2, ..., k, on the inequality of total income?

As we will see below the effect will be measured by some product moment function. In general we can subdivide the measures that are decomposable by income sources into a function of (*i*) product moment measures on ordinal-interval scale level or a function of (*ii*) product moment measures on interval-interval scale level. In the first case we have product moments of functions of ranks and variates Y_j and in the second case product moments of functions of the variates $Y_t, Y_1, \ldots, Y_k$.

By the assumption of non-negative incomes ($Y_j \geq 0$ and $\mu_j > 0$) and of non-positive incomes ($Y_j \leq 0$ and $\mu_j < 0$) we have from the definition (9.6) that

$$q_j = \mu_j/\mu_t \gtrless 0.$$

If A is an event we can define the random variable I, the indicator of the event A by, cf. sec. 7.2.3,

$$I\{A\} = \begin{cases} 1 & \text{if the event A occurs} \\ 0 & \text{otherwise.} \end{cases}$$

Using this indicator variable I we can now define the c.d.f. and the 1st m.d.f. of the total income by

$$F(y)_t = E[I\{Y_t \leq y\}]$$

and (9.22)

$$F_1(y)_t = E[Y_t \cdot I\{Y_t \leq y\}]/\mu_t.$$

The c.d.f. and the 1st m.d.f. of income source j, j=1,2,...,k, can be defined in a similar way by changing the index t to j.
We now define, using the above indicator variable, the 1st m.d.f. of income source j conditionally on the total income.

Definition 9.1 The conditional c.d.f., $F^*_{1S}(y)_j$, of income source j, j=1,2,...,k, is defined by

$$F^*_{1S}(y)_j = E[Y_j \cdot I\{Y_t \leq y\}]/\mu_j. \tag{9.23}$$

The 1st m.d.f. of the total income can now be written as a weighted sum of conditional 1st m.d.f.'s. This is given by the following proposition.

Proposition 9.1 $F_1(y)_t = \sum_{j=1}^{k} q_j F_{1S}^*(y)_j$,

where q_j is given by (9.6) and $F_{1S}^*(y)_j$ by Definition 9.1.

The proposition follows directly from the above definition.

The measures of inequality in total income that we will decompose by income sources are written as, (cf. e.g. the constraint measures in sec. 7.4).

$$I_t = \int_0^1 C(\cdot)_t \, dF_1(\cdot)_t$$ [1)]

where the function $C(\cdot)_t$ is either a function of "relative ranks" in total income (type (*i*) decomposition by income sources) or a function of "relative ranks" in total income (type (*ii*) decomposition) and $\int_0^1 C(\cdot)_t \, dF(\cdot)_t = 0$, i.e. $C(\cdot)_t$ is a constraint function (according to sec. 7.4).

Proposition 9.2 The measure of inequality of total income I_t is decomposed according to

1) In our earlier notation I can be written as $\int_0^1 C(\cdot)\tau(p)dp$, cf. sec. 7.4. Note also that we write I instead of $I(y)$ in this section.

$$I_t = \sum_{j=1}^{k} q_j I^*_j$$

where $I^*_j = \int C(\cdot)_t \, dF^*_{1S}(\cdot)_j$ is labelled the *pseudo inequality measure* of income source j.

The proposition follows from proposition 9.1.

For every income source j, j=1, 2, ..., k, we can compute the inequality I_j defined as $\int C(\cdot)_j dF_1(\cdot)_j$, and hence we have two measures for every income source: on the one hand we have the ordinary inequality measure, I_j on the other we have the pseudo inequality measure, I^*_j. Loosely speaking this last measure is the inequality of income source j given by the rank-order in total income.

In general $I^*_j \neq I_j$ and hence we can make the following definitions:

Definition 9.2 (a) The *disequalizing effect* of income source j on total income inequality is defined as $(I_j \neq 0)$

$$E_j = \frac{I^*_j}{I_j} \quad , \; j = 1, 2, \ldots, k. \qquad (9.24a)$$

(b) The *factor inequality weights* of income source j is defined as $(I_j \neq 0 \, , \, I_t \neq 0)$

$$FIW_j = q_j E_j \frac{I_j}{I_t} = q_j \frac{I^*_j}{I_t} \quad , \qquad (9.24b)$$

j=1, 2, ..., k,

where $q_j = \mu_j/\mu_t$ is the income share of source j.

E_j is not defined when $I_j = 0$. Since $I_j = 0$ implies that $I^*_j = 0$ we can define the disequalizing effect to equal zero when $I_j = 0$.

By proposition 9.2 we can decompose the inequality of total income, using (9.24a), as

$$I_t = \sum_{j=1}^{k} q_j I^*_j = \sum_{j=1}^{k} q_j E_j I_j \qquad (9.25)$$

i.e. a weighted sum of the inequalities within each income source (with weights that do not in general sum up to one). Dividing (9.25) with I_t we have the results that 100% of inequality can be written as the sum of the FIW_j:s defined in (9.24b), i.e.

$$100\% = \sum_{j=1}^{k} FIW_j .$$

The concept FIW is e.g. used by Fields [1979a - p.441], [1979b - p.329] in the decomposition of the Gini coefficient. For the Gini coefficient, the disequalizing effect E_j is in accordance with sec. 7.2.3, the 'measure of correlation', C, introduced by Blitz and Brittain [1964].

Proposition 9.3 The disequalizing effect, defined by (9.24a) is bounded by

$$-1 \leq E_j \leq 1. \qquad (9.26)$$

A proof in the discrete case is given by Rao [1969].

E_j equals one when either the "relative ranks" are identical in total income and in income source j or the "relative incomes" are identical in total income and in income source j. $E_j = -1$ is obtained when the ordering in income source j is reversed in relation to the ordering in total income. E_j will be interpreted below.

A positive value on E_j would increase the inequality and a negative value (i.e. a negative disequalizing effect = an equalizing effect) would decrease the inequality when $q_j = \mu_j/\mu_t > 0$. On the other hand, if $q_j = \mu_j/\mu_t < 0$, we have the reversed case. This is summarized by the following table.

	disequalizing effect	
	$E_j<0$	$E_j>0$
negative incomes ($q_j<0$)	increase in inequality of total income ($FIW_j>0$)	decrease in inequality of total income ($FIW_j<0$)
positive incomes ($q_j>0$)	decrease in inequality of total income ($FIW_j<0$)	increase in inequality of total income ($FIW_j>0$)

It is readily seen that the sign (+, increase/-, decrease) of the effect of income source j on inequality of total income is given by the sign of $q_j E_j$, j=1, 2, ..., k. Since it is frequently only the taxes that are negative incomes we can study the sign on the E_j to see whether or not income source j is equalizing or disequalizing. In the same manner the sign on the factor inequality weights (FIW_j, j=1, 2, ..., k) determines the equalizing/disequalizing effect of income source j (see the table above).

Shorrock [1980b] showed that under some general assumptions there exists coefficient $a_i(y)$, i=1,2, ..., N and N equals the number of i.r.u.'s such that the contribution of income source j to inequality of total income may be written as $S_j(Y_j,Y_t) = \sum_{i=1}^{k} a_i(Y)Y_{ji}$ where $a_i(y)$ are defined by $I(y)_t = \sum_{i=1}^{N} a_i(y)Y_{ti}$ where t stands for total income. The S_j's are defined by

$$I_t = \sum_{j=1}^{k} S_j(Y_j,Y_t).$$

Shorrock [1980b - p.14] also made tha constraint assumption that

$$\sum_{j=1}^{N} a_i(y) = 0.$$

In our notations S_j corresponds to $q_j I^*_j = q_j E_j I_j = FIW_j I_j$, $a_i(y)$ corresponds up to a multiplicative constant our constraint weights $C(\cdot)_t$.

As we stated earlier the measure of inequality that we decompose by income sources can be subdivided into two groups. The names of these groups of measures are given as a cause of the discrete equivalents. The first group consists of measures that we label functions of product moment measures on ordinal-interval scale level, and the second of measures that we label functions of product moment measures on interval-interval scale level. I_t can be written as

$$\int_0^1 C(\cdot)_t \, dF_1(\cdot)_t,$$

where

$$\int_0^1 C(\cdot)_t \, dF(\cdot)_t = 0.$$

In the first group $C(\cdot)_t$ depends on y only through $F(y)_t$ while in the second group only through y/μ_t $(=\tau(p))$.

Due to the constraint $\int C(\cdot)_t \; dF(\cdot)_t = 0$ we can write (cf. sec. 7.4)

$$C(\cdot)_t = W(\cdot)_t - \omega(\cdot)_t,$$

where $\omega(\cdot)_t = \int_0^\infty W(\cdot)_t \; dF(\cdot)_t$, and using the fact that $\int_0^\infty dF_1(y)_t = 1$ we have

$$I_t = \int_0^\infty \{W(\cdot)_t - \omega(\cdot)_t\} \{y/\mu_t - 1\} \; dF(y)_t = \mathrm{Cov}\;\{W(\cdot)_t, Y_t/\mu_t\}.$$

Similarly we have $I_j = \int\{W(\cdot)_j - \omega(\cdot)_j\}\{y/\mu_j - 1\}dF(y)_j = \mathrm{Cov}\{W(\cdot)_j, Y_j/\mu_j\}$.

By the definition of I^*_j it is readily seen that it can be written as

$$I^*_j = \mathrm{Cov}\;\{W(\cdot)_t, Y_j/\mu_j\},$$

j=1, 2, ..., k.

Applying these notations to E_j defined by (9.24a) we obtain

$$E_j = \frac{\mathrm{Cov}(W(\cdot)_t, Y_j/\mu_j)}{\mathrm{Cov}(W(\cdot)_j, Y_j/\mu_j)} = \frac{\sigma_{W(\cdot)_t}\,\sigma_{Yj/\mu j}\;\rho(W(\cdot)_t, Y_j/\mu_j)}{\sigma_{W(\cdot)_j}\,\sigma_{Yj/\mu j}\;\rho(W(\cdot)_j, Y_j/\mu_j)} =$$

$$= \frac{\sigma_{W(\cdot)_t}}{\sigma_{W(\cdot)_j}} \cdot \frac{\rho(W(\cdot)_t, Y_j/\mu_j)}{\rho(W(\cdot)_j, Y_j/\mu_j)}, \qquad (9.28)$$

cf. the discussion of the Gini coefficient in sec. 7.2.3.

By (9.28) we see that the disequalizing effect E_j can be interpreted as the product of a ratio of standard deviations and a ratio of coefficients of correlations.

If $W(\cdot) = W(F(y))$, i.e. a function of the c.d.f. (in the direct case: relative ranks) then $\sigma_{W(\cdot)_t} = \sigma_{W(\cdot)_j}$ and hence the disequalizing effect equals $E_j = \rho(W(F(y)_t, Y_j/\mu_j) / \rho(W(F(y)_j, Y_j/\mu_j)$. E_j is labelled a relative correlation coefficient by e.g. Fields [1979a - p.440], [1979b - p.328].

In the following we will use simplifying notations. The ratio Y_j/μ_j will be denoted $\tau(p)_j$ and $F(y)_j = p_j$, j = 1,2,...,k,t. The conditional 1st m.d.f. $F^*_{1S}(y)_j$ will in a similar way be denoted $F^*_{1S}(p)_j = E[Y_j \cdot I\{Y_t \leq F^{-1}(p)_t\}]/\mu_j$, where $F^{-1}(p)_t = \inf_y\{y \mid F(y)_t \geq p\}$. A pseudo Lorenz Curve, corresponding to $F^*_{1S}(p)_j$, is denoted $L^*_S(p)_j$, j=1,2,...,k.

The discussion of the disequalizing effect applies [illegible] the Gini coefficient and the measures proposed by Mehran, Piesch, Bonferroni and de Vergottini discussed in sec. 7.4. The disequalizing effects can in these cases be written as

Measure	Disequalizing effect, E_j
Gini, R	$\dfrac{\rho(p_t, \tau(p)_j)}{\rho(p_j, \tau(p)_j)}$
Mehran, M	$\dfrac{\rho(6p_t - 3p_t^2, \tau(p)_j)}{\rho(6p_j - 3p_j^2, \tau(p)_j)} = \dfrac{\rho(2p_t - p_t^2, \tau(p)_j)}{\rho(2p_j - p_j^2, \tau(p)_j)}$
Piesch, P	$\dfrac{\rho(\frac{3}{2} p_t^2, \tau(p)_j)}{\rho(\frac{3}{2} p_j^2, \tau(p)_j)} = \dfrac{\rho(p_t^2, \tau(p)_j)}{\rho(p_j^2, \tau(p)_j)}$
Bonferroni, B	$\dfrac{\rho(\log p_t, \tau(p)_j)}{\rho(\log p_j, \tau(p)_j)}$
de Vergottini, dV	$\dfrac{\rho(\log(1-p_t)^{-1}, \tau(p)_j)}{\rho(\log(1-p_j)^{-1}, \tau(p)_j)}$

The Gini coefficient

Before turning to the second group of measures, i.e. when $W(\cdot)_t = W(\tau(p)_t)_t$, we shall use the Lorenz diagram to interpret the pseudo Gini coefficient, $R^*_j = \int_o^1 (2p-1)\, dF^*_{1S}(p)_j$, and the disequalizing factor E_j.

By the definitions of E_j in (9.24a) and (9.26) it follows that

$$- R_j \leq R^*_j \leq R_j,$$

and hence the Lorenz Curve (LC) corresponding to R^*_j, the pseudo LC $L^*_S(p)_j$, will be situated between $L(p)^-_j$ and $L(p)_j$, where $L(p)_j$ is the LC of the j:th income source and $L(p)^-_j$ is the LC that is obtained by $L(p)^-_j = 1 - L(p')_j$ where $p' = 1 - p$. This is depicted in figure 9.1.a. $L(p)^-_j$ is simply the mirror picture of $L(p)_j$ when $L(p)_j$ has been rotated 180° around the diagonal perpendicular to the diagonal line (cf. sec. 7.2.5). The pseudo LC can be defined as $L^*_S(p)_j = F^*_{1S}(p)_j$ (= $E[\, Y_j \cdot I\{Y_t \leq F^{-1}(p)_t\}]/\mu_j$ cf. (9.23)).

An example on the curves $L(p)_j$, $L(p)^-_j$ and $L^*_S(p)_j$ is depicted in figure 9.1.a.

Figure 9.1 The pesudo Lorenz Curve $L^*_S(p)_j$ and its bounds $L(p)^-_j$ and $L(p)_j$.

(a) Twice the area between $L^*_S(p)_j$ and the diagonal line equals the pseudo Gino coefficient R^*_j. The area segment above the diagonal line contributes with negative sign to R^*_j. The dotted line indicates an example of a pseudo Lorenz Curve having neutral effect ($R^*_j = 0$).

(b) The Gini error, $\varepsilon_{RJ} = R_j - R^*_j$, equals twice the shaded area. j indicates income source j.

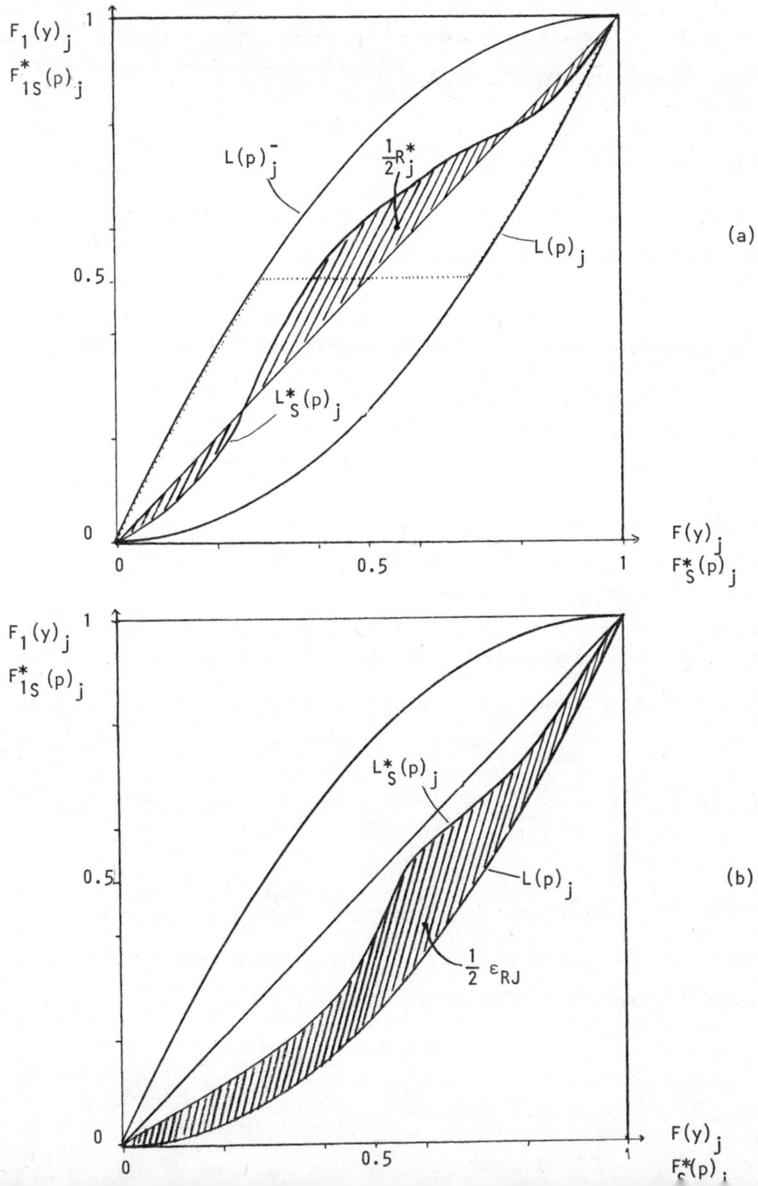

If, for positive incomes, $L^*_S(p)_j$ is completely situated above the diagonal line it will be interpreted so that income source j is *absolutely equalizing* and its effect is measured by E_j. On the other hand, if $L^*_S(p)_j$ is completely situated below the diagonal line it will be interpreted so that income source j is *absolutely disequalizing* and if $L^*_S(p)_j$ follows the diagonal line the effect is said to be *absolutely neutral*. The corresponding interpretation will be reversed for negative incomes.

If $L^*_S(p)_j$ intersects with the diagonal line the effect of income source j on total income inequality can be *equalizing* ($E_j < 0$ for positive incomes), *neutral* ($E_j = 0$) or *disequalizing* ($E_j > 0$ for positive incomes).

The pseudo Gini coefficient, R^*_j, is by definition equal to twice the area between the pseudo LC $L^*_S(p)_j$ and the diagonal line with the area segments above the diagonal line contributing with negative sign. R^*_j given by $L^*_S(p)_j$ in figure 9.1.a is hence (see the depicted curve) negative. On the other hand the pseudo Gini coefficient obtained by the pseudo LC indicated by the dotted line in figure 9.1.a equals zero.

These income sources are equalizing and neutral, respectively. The neutral income source in this example is given by the following conditional c.d.f.

$$F^*_{1S}(y)_j = \begin{cases} 1 - F_1(y)_j & \text{if} \quad F(y)_t \leq 0{,}5 \\ F_1(y)_j & \text{if} \quad F(y)_t > 0{,}5, \end{cases}$$

which gives rise to two cancelling Lorenz area segments. In both this last example and in the case of $L^*_S(p)_j = p$, the diagonal line, $R^*_j = 0$, but as is obvious, the two income sources have different effects on various parts of the size distribution of total income. One is absolutely neutral, i.e. neutral in every part of the distribution, and the other is only neutral, i.e. neutral in the whole distribution. This points out the importance of visualizing the pseudo LC:s and not only of considering the disequalizing effects E_j, $j = 1, 2, \ldots, k$.

$E_j = R^*_j / R_j$ can also be interpreted as the ratio between a pseudo Lorenz area and a Lorenz area. The difference between R_j and R^*_j, $\varepsilon_{Rj} = R_j - R^*_j$, equals twice the area between the LC $L(p)_j$ and the pseudo LC $L^*_S(p)_j$, cf. figure 9.1.b. ε_{Rj} is labelled the Gini error by Fei, Ranis and Kuo [1978 - p. 45], [1979 - p. 336]. Both the disequalizing effect E_j and the relative Gini error, $h_j = \varepsilon_{Rj}/R_j = 1 - E_j$ were introduced by Rao [1969 - p.422]. Blitz and Brittain [1964] labelled E_j a measure of correlation and pointed out that in the extreme cases, i.e. $E_j = \pm 1$, it is identical to Spearman's rank correlation coefficient. See also sec. 7.2.3.

By these notations we can write R, the Gini coefficient as, using (9.25),

$$R = \sum_{j=1}^{k} q_j R^*_j = \sum_{j=1}^{k} q_j E_j R_j = \tag{9.29 a}$$

$$= \sum_{j=1}^{k} q_j \frac{\rho(p_t, \tau(p)_j)}{\rho(p_j, \tau(p)_j)} R_j = \tag{9.29b}$$

$$= \sum_{j=1}^{k} q_j R_j - \sum_{j=1}^{k} q_j h_j R_j = \sum_{j=1}^{k} q_j R_j - \sum_{j=1}^{k} q_j \varepsilon_{Rj} \geq 0 \tag{9.29c}$$

(9.29a) corresponds to the principal decomposition (9.25) (9.29b) when divided by R corresponds to Fields' [1979a - p.441],[1979b - p.329] concept factor inequality weights, (FIW), i.e. we can write

$$FIW_j = q_j \frac{\rho(p_t, \tau(p)_j)}{\rho(p_j, \tau(p)_j)} \cdot \frac{R_j}{R},$$

and the first term in (9.29c) corresponds to a decomposition proposed by Rao [1969 - pp.422-423]. (Rao also proposed (9.29a)), see also Fei, Ranis and Kuo [1978 - p. 48].

Given the inequality within each income source the first term in (9.29c) can be regarded as, the maximum contribution to total income inequality, since if $h_j = 0$ ($\varepsilon_{Rj} = 0$) then the i.r.u.'s within income source j are rank-ordered in exactly the same way as in total income. The second term in (9.29c) can be interpreted[1)] as the sum of weighted deviations between the pseudo LC's and the LC's of each income source; $\varepsilon_{Rj} = R_j - R^*_j$. See figure 9.1.b.

Fei, Ranis and Kuo [1978 - pp. 41-50], [1979 - ch. 10] assumed as a special case income source j to be a linear transformation of total income, $Y_j = \alpha_j + \beta_j Y_t$, j = 1, 2, ..., k, where

$\sum_{j=1}^{k} \alpha_j = 0$ and $\sum_{j=1}^{k} \beta_j = 1$ since $\sum_{j=1}^{k} Y_j = Y_t$. The parameters α_j and β_j

---

1) Rao [1969 - p.423] labelled the term $f_{1j}\, h_j\, R_j$ as 'inequality-adding' when $h_j = 0$ ($\Rightarrow E_j = 1$ and in our notation disequalizing), 'inequality-offsetting' when $h_j = 2$ ($\Rightarrow E_j = -1$, equalizing) and 'neutral' when $h_j = 1$ ($\Rightarrow E_j = 0$).

were approximated by a system of k linear regression coefficients, $\hat{Y}_j = a_j + b_j Y_t$, where[1] $a_j = \mu_j - b_j\mu_t$, $b_j = \mathrm{Cov}(Y_j, Y_t)/\sigma^2_{Y_t}$ and by the relation

$Y_t = \sum_{j=1}^{k} Y_j = \sum_{j=1}^{k} \hat{Y}_j$ it is obvious that $\sum_{j=1}^{k} a_j = 0$

$\sum_{j=1}^{k} b_j = 1$. The estimated $\hat{Y}_j$:s were used to approximate R_j, $j = 1, 2, \ldots, k$ in (9.29c), the income shares are unchanged and we have the following reformulation of the decomposition of R as

$$R = \sum_{j=1}^{k} q_j \hat{R}_j - \sum_{j=1}^{k} q_j \varepsilon_{Rj} - \sum_{j=1}^{k} q_j \theta_j,$$

where $\theta_j = (\hat{R}_j - R_j)$ is a non-linearity error.

Fei, Ranis and Kuo [1978 - pp. 49-50] also proved the following relations:

$$\hat{R}^*_j = (b_j/\ q_j)R \text{ and } \hat{R}_j = \pm\ \hat{R}^*_j$$

where the sign depends on the linear relation between Y_j and Y_t (positive sign if $\beta_j \geq 0$ and negative sign if $\beta_j < 0$), cf. also Fei, Ranis and Kuo [1979 - p.361] and the discussion in sec. 7.2.5. They use

$$\hat{R} = \sum_{j=1}^{k} q_j \hat{R}_j - \sum_{j=1}^{k} q_j \varepsilon_{Rj}$$

as an approximation of R, i.e. assuming linearity. The use of this model when data are in grouped form is discussed by Pyatt, Chen and Fei [1980].

---

1) We assume data from the whole population and not sample data as Fei et al.

A similar discussion on the disequalizing effects E_j for the measures proposed by Mehran, Piesch, Bonferroni and de Vergottini can be made. Notice that these measures weight the various parts of the Lorenz area in different ways.

We now turn to the second group of measures that are decomposed by income sources. These can be written as

$$I_t = \mathrm{Cov}\{W(\tau(p)_t)_t,\ \tau(p)_t\}$$

and by the discussion earlier we have

$$\begin{aligned} I_t &= \mathrm{Cov}\{W(\tau(p)_t)_t,\ \tau(p)_t\} = \\ &= \sum_{j=1}^{k} q_j\ \mathrm{Cov}\{W(\tau(p)_t)_t,\ \tau(p)_j\} = \qquad (9.30) \\ &= \sum_{j=1}^{k} q_j\ E_j\ \mathrm{Cov}\ \{W(\tau(p)_j)_j,\ \tau(p)_j\}, \end{aligned}$$

where the disequalizing effect E_j equals

$$E_j = \frac{\mathrm{Cov}\{W(\tau(p)_t)_t,\ \tau(p)_j\}}{\mathrm{Cov}\{W(\tau(p)_j)_j,\ \tau(p)_j\}} = \frac{\sigma\ W(\tau(p)_t)_t}{\sigma\ W(\tau(p)_j)_j} \cdot \frac{\rho\{W(\tau(p)_t)_t,\ \tau(p)_j\}}{\rho\{W(\tau(p)_j)_j,\ \tau(p)_j\}} \qquad (9.31)$$

In (9.30) $\rho\{W(\tau(p)_j)_j,\ \tau(p)_j\}$ is the Pearson correlation coefficient between $\tau(p)_j$ and $W(\tau(p)_j)_j$, i.e. the correlation coefficient between the relative incomes in income source j and a function of these relative incomes. If the function is linear, i.e. $W(\tau(p)) = \alpha+\beta\tau(p)$, then $\rho\{W(\tau(p)_j)_j,\ \tau(p)_j\} = 1$ and $E_j = \mathrm{Cov}\ (\tau(p)_t,\ \tau(p)_j)/\sigma_j^2$ and hence (9.31) equals

$$\beta V_t^2 = \sum_{j=1}^{k} \frac{\beta}{\mu_t^2} \mathrm{Cov}(Y_t, Y_j), \tag{9.32a}$$

where V_t^2 is the squared coefficient of variation (a *RI*-measure). Since $V_t^2 = \sigma_t^2/\mu_t^2$ we have an *AI*-measure which by using (9.32a) equals

$$\sigma_t^2 = \sum_{j=1}^{k} \mathrm{Cov}(Y_t, Y_j).$$

Turning again to the *RI*-measure V_t^2 (squared coefficient of variation)[1] it is readily seen that this can be written as

$$V_t^2 = \sum_{j=1}^{k} q_j V_{tj}^2 = \tag{9.32b}$$

$$= \sum_{j=1}^{k} q_j E_j V_j^2 \tag{9.32c}$$

where $E_j = V_{tj}^2/V_j^2$ and $V_{tj} = V_j^*$ is the pseudo coefficient of variation, or a coefficient of covariation, between total income and income source j.

Note that σ_t^2 can be written as $\sigma_t^2 = \sum_{j=1}^{k} \sigma_t \sigma_j \rho_{tj}$, where ρ_{tj} is the correlation coefficient between total income and income source j. Dividing both sides by σ_t it is readily shown that the standard deviation σ_t is decomposable as $\sigma_t = \sum_{j=1}^{k} \sigma_j \rho_{tj}$.

V^2 and the measures discussed earlier (R, M, P, B and dV) are the only *RI*-measures that we have discussed earlier (ch. 7 and ch. 8) that are decomposable as (9.25). If we do not use the constraint laid down on $C(\cdot)_t$ we can decompose Bartel's $RSMAX^2$ and $SMAXN^2$, Theil's both measures, σ_q^2

---

1) Layard and Zabalza [1979 - p.135] decomposed V^2 into a within income source term and a between term.

and Kolm's μ-modified centrist and relative leftist measures, including Atkinson measure. As an example, the last measure, $A(\varepsilon)_t$, can be written as

$$A(\varepsilon)_t = 1 - \{\sum_{j=1}^{k} q_j \{1 - A(\varepsilon)_j^*\}^{1-\varepsilon}\}^{1/1-\varepsilon},$$

where $A(\varepsilon)_j^*$ is the pseudo Atkinson measure defined by

$$A(\varepsilon)_j^* = 1 - \{\int_o^1 \tau(p)_j^{-\varepsilon} dF_{1S}^*(p)_j\}^{1/1-\varepsilon}$$

Let us now turn to the discrete case. We illustrate by an example.

In the discrete case the pseudo measures are written as, (cf. sec. 8.1 and sec. 8.2),

$$R_j^* = \frac{2}{N} \sum_{j=1}^{N} \frac{i_t}{N} \frac{Y_{ji}}{\mu_j} - (\frac{N+1}{N}) \tag{9.33a}$$

$$M_j^* = \frac{6}{N} \sum_{j=1}^{N} \{\frac{i_t}{N} (1 + \frac{1}{2N})\} \frac{Y_{ji}}{\mu_j} - \frac{3}{N} \sum_{j=1}^{N} (\frac{i_t}{N})^2 \frac{Y_{ji}}{\mu_j} - \frac{(N+1)(2N+1)}{N^2} \tag{9.33b}$$

$$P_j^* = \frac{3}{2N} \sum_{j=1}^{N} \{\frac{i_t^2 - i_t}{N}\} \frac{Y_{ji}}{\mu_j} - \frac{(N-1)(N+1)}{2N^2} \tag{9.33c}$$

$$B_j^* = \frac{1}{N} \sum_{j=1}^{N} \{1 - \sum_{d=i}^{N} \frac{1}{d}\} \frac{Y_{ji}}{\mu_j} \tag{9.33d}$$

$$dV_j^* = \frac{1}{N} \sum_{j=1}^{N} \{ \sum_{j=2}^{N} \frac{1}{d} - \sum_{d=i}^{N-1} \frac{1}{N-d} \} \frac{Y_{ji}}{\mu_j} \tag{9.33e}$$

$$V_j^{2*} = V_{tj}^2 = \frac{1}{\mu_t \mu_t} \cdot \frac{1}{N} \sum_{j=1}^{N} (Y_{ti} - \mu_t)(Y_{ji} - \mu_j), \tag{9.33f}$$

where $Y_{j1} \leq Y_{j2} \leq \dots \leq Y_{jN}$ are the rank-ordered incomes in income source j, j=1, 2, ..., k, and i_t is the rank-order in total income that i.r.u.

number i in income source j has. This is illustrated by the following example.

Example 9.2 Consider a small population of $N = 5$ persons, having incomes from four different income sources (labor, capital, etc.) and a positive transfer from the government. The sum of the first four income sources are labelled factor income (cf. ch. 1), $Y_F = \sum_{j=1}^{4} Y_j, Y_j > 0$ and $\mu_j > 0$, $j = 1, 2, 3, 4$. From these incomes they have to pay a progressive tax, $Y_{TAX} < 0$ to the government. We use the progressive tax function proposed by Piesch, see sec. 7.2.6, example iv) of taxation functions with $\lambda = 2$. Some of the poorest, according to Y_F receive subsidies from the government, $Y_s > 0$. The total income (disposable income), is then $Y_T = Y_F + Y_{TAX} + Y_S = \sum_{j=1}^{k} Y_j + Y_{TAX} + Y_S$. The incomes are given in table 9.2.

From table 9.2 we have the income "shares" $q_j = \mu_j/\mu$ as

$$q_1 = q_2 = q_3 = \frac{5}{21.62},\quad q_4 = \frac{9.2}{21.62},\quad (q_F = \frac{24.2}{21.62}),\quad q_{TAX} = \frac{-4.56}{21.62}$$

and $q_s = \dfrac{2}{21.62}$.

In table 9.3 we have summarized the results, when using the Gini coefficient, R. The corresponding Lorenz Curves (ordinary and pseudo) are dipicted in the Lorenz diagram in figure 9.2.

Table 9.2 Income data for a population of N=5 persons. The incomes are ranked according to total income, Y_T.

$Y_T = Y_1 + Y_2 + Y_3 + Y_4 + Y_{TAX} + Y_s = Y_F + Y_{TAX} + Y_s$, where the factor income $Y_F = \sum_{j=1}^{4} Y_j > 0$, $Y_i > 0$, $\forall_j$, is the sum of four income sources. $Y_{TAX} < 0$ is the paid tax and $Y_s > 0$ is the subsidies received.

$\tau_j = Y_j/\mu_j$ and rank_j is the rank-order according to income source j, j=1, 2, 3, 4, TAX and s, in τ_j.

$\mu_T = \mu_F + \mu_{TAX} + \mu_s = \sum_{j=1}^{k} \mu_j + \mu_{TAX} + \mu_s$.

	Y_1			Y_2			Y_3			Y_4			$Y_F = \sum_{j=1}^{4}$			Y_{TAX}			Y_s			Y_τ		
rank_T	Y_1	τ_1	rank_1	Y_2	τ_2	rank_2	Y_3	τ_3	rank_3	Y_4	τ_4	rank_4	Y_F	τ_F	rank_F	Y_{TAX}	τ_{TAX}	rank_{TAX}	Y_s	τ_s	rank_s	Y_T	τ_T	rank_τ
1	9	9/5	5	1	1/5	1	9	9/5	5	2	2/9.2	1	21	21/24.2	3	-3.2	$\frac{3.2}{4.58}$	3	2	2/2	3	19.8	$\frac{19.8}{21.62}$	1
2	5	5/5	3	5	5/5	3	1	1/5	1	9	9/9.2	3	20	20/24.2	2	-3.0	$\frac{3.0}{4.58}$	2	3	3/2	4	20	$\frac{20.0}{21.62}$	2
3	3	3/5	2	7	7/5	4	3	3/5	2	5	5/9.2	2	18	18/24.2	1	-2.4	$\frac{2.4}{4.58}$	1	5	5/2	5	20.6	$\frac{20.6}{21.62}$	3
4	7	7/5	4	3	3/5	2	5	5/5	3	13	13/9.2	4	28	28/24.2	4	-5.8	$\frac{5.8}{4.58}$	4	0	0	1.5	22.2	$\frac{22.2}{21.62}$	4
5	1	1/5	1	9	9/5	5	7	7/5	4	17	17/9.2	5	34	34/24.2	5	-8.5	$\frac{8.5}{4.56}$	5	0	0	1.5	25.5	$\frac{25.5}{21.62}$	5
Σ	25	1	-	25	1	-	25	1	-	46	1	-	121	1	-	-22.9	1	-	10	1	-	108.1	1	
	μ_1=5			μ_2=5			μ_3=5			μ_4=9.2			μ_F=24.2			μ_{TAX}= -4.58			μ_s=2			μ_T=21.62		

Table 9.3 The result of decomposing the Gini coefficient.
Data: See table 9.2.
The figures are rounded to four decimals.

Source	q_j	R_j	R_j^*	$E_j=R_j^*/R_j$	FIW_j, %	Source effect
1	0.2313	0.2400	- 0.2240	- 0.9300	- 103.0	absolutely equalizing
2	0.2313	0.2400	+ 0.2240	+ 0.9300	+ 103.0	absolutely disequalizing
3	0.2313	0.2400	0	0	0	neutral
4	0.4255	0.3478	+ 0.2957	+ 0.8500	+ 250.1	absolutely disequalizing
Factor:	1.1193	0.1323	+ 0.1124	+ 0.8500	+ 250.1	absolutely disequalizing
TAX	-0.2118	0.2620	+ 0.2341	+ 0.8900	- 98.6	(Y_{TAX} < 0) absolutely equalizing
SUBSIDIES:	0.0925	0.5200	- 0.2800	- 0.5400	- 51.5	absolutely equalizing
TOTAL:	1	0.0503	-		100	-

Figure 9.2a shows that the Lorenz Curves (LC's) of income sources 1, 2 and 3 are identical. Since the pseudo LC of income source 1 is strictly above the diagonal line and the equivalent curve of income source 2 is strictly below the diagonal line, the effects of these income sources are absolutely equalizing and absolutely disequalizing, respectively, since $Y_j > 0$, $j = 1, 2$. The pseudo LC of income source 3 intersects with the diagonal line and the area segments above and below the diagonal line are identical (to check this, use e.g. (8.3) in sec. 8.1 - cf. with figure 8.1.b), i.e. the effect of this source is neutral.

Figure 9.2 The Lorenz Curves and pseudo Lorenz Curves of example 9.2. See example 9.2.

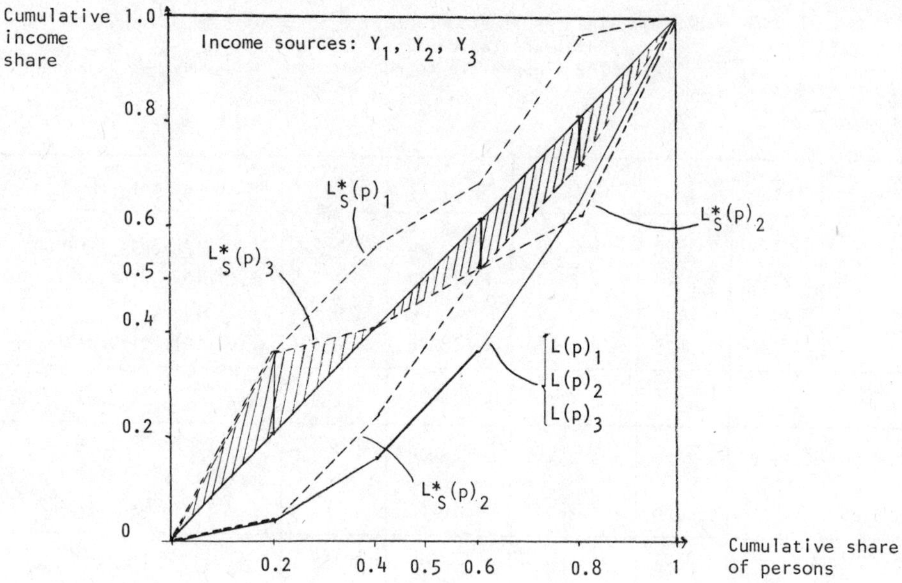

(a)

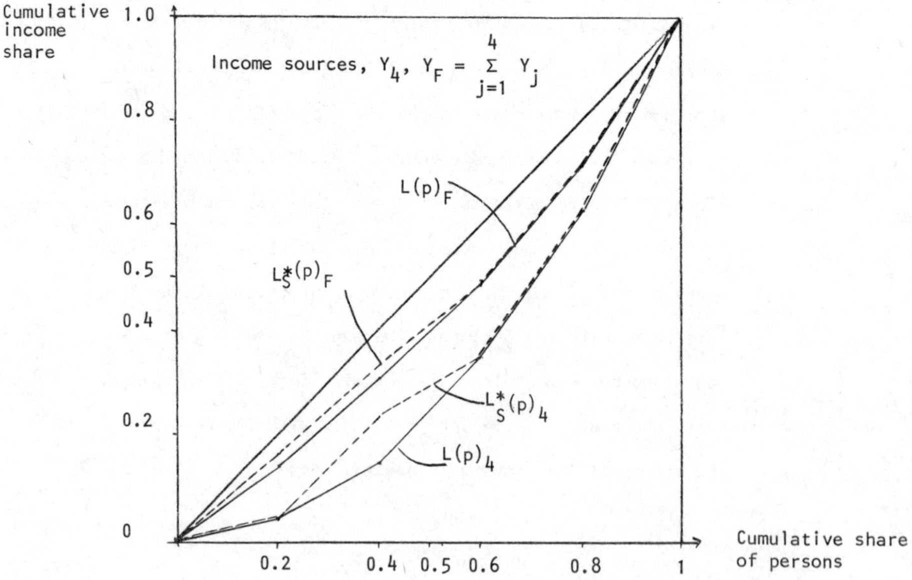

(b)

Figure 9.2 cont.

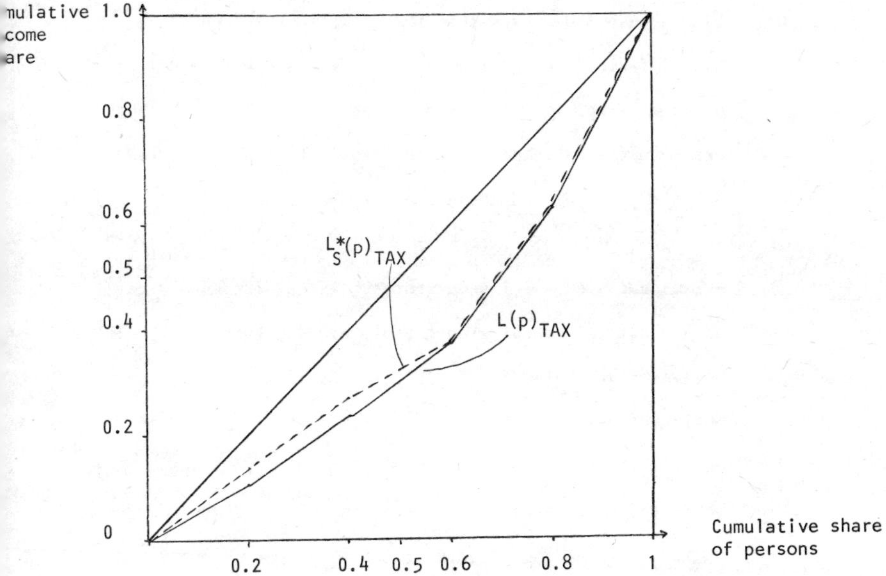

(c)

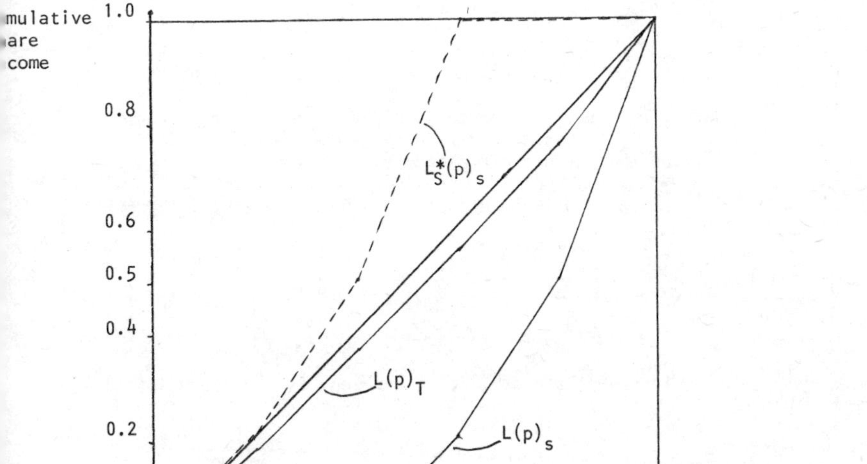

(d)

By figure 9.2.b we see that the effects of income source 4 and of factor income (i.e. $Y_F = \sum_{j=1}^{k} Y_j$) are both absolutely disequalizing. The effects of taxes and subsidies are both absolutely equalizing since the pseudo LC's are situated below ($Y_{TAX} < 0$) and above the diagonal line.

As we have seen, all income sources, except income source 3, were <u>absolutely</u> equalizing or <u>absolutely</u> disequalizing. If we had only studied the numerical effects, table 9.3, we would not have been able to distinguish between equalizing (disequalizing) and absolutely equalizing (disequalizing). This shows the importance of depicting the LC's and the pseudo LC's. Note that the effects of income sources 1 and 2 on total income inequality cancel out each other.

The inequalities within the various income sources using the measures by Mehran, Piesch, Bonferroni and de Vergottini together with the squared coefficient of variation are summarized, together with their pseudo equivalence, in table 9.4. The disequalizing effects are also given in table 9.4. The effects of income sources 1 and 2 on total income inequality cancel out each other as in the case of R above. The Gini coefficient gives the highest weights to extreme incomes (low and high incomes), see sec. 7.4.1 and sec. 8.2, and the effect of income source 3 is neutral, $E_{R3} = R_3^*/R_3 = 0$. Of the other measures, Mehran's and Bonferroni's give the highest weight to low incomes and Piesch's, De Vergottini's and the squared coefficient of variation give the highest weight to high incomes. This is reflected in the effects of income source 3, since this in-

Table 9.4 The results of decomposing the measures by Mehran, Piesch, Bonferroni, de Vergottini and the squared coefficient of variation.

Data: see table 9.2

The figures are rounded to four decimals

Source	q_j	Mehran's measure, M			Piesch's measure, P			Bonferroni's measure, B			de Vergottini's measure, dV			Squared coefficient of variation, V^2		
		M_j	M_j^*	$E_{nj}=M_j^*/M_j$	P_j	P_j^*	$E_{Pj}=P_j^*/P_j$	B_j	B_j^*	$E_{Bj}=B_j^*/B_j$	dV_j	dV_j^*	$E_{dVj}=\frac{dV_j^*}{dV_j}$	V_j^2	V_j^{2*}	$E_{V^2j}=\frac{V_j^{2*}}{V_j^2}$
1	0.2313	0.4800	-0.3456	-0.7200	0.2400	-0.1632	-0.6800	0.4000	-0.3067	-0.7667	0.4000	-0.2933	-0.7333	0.3200	-0.0363	-0.1134
2	0.2313	0.4800	+0.3456	+0.7200	0.2400	+0.1632	+0.6800	0.4000	+0.3067	+0.7667	0.4000	+0.2933	+0.7333	0.3200	+0.0363	+0.1134
3	0.2313	0.4800	-0.0960	-0.2000	0.2400	+0.0480	+0.2000	0.4000	-0.1133	-0.2833	0.4000	+0.0800	+0.2000	0.3200	+0.0167	+0.0522
4	0.4255	0.4904	+0.4278	+0.8723	0.2504	+0.2296	+0.9167	0.4069	+0.3634	+0.8931	0.4174	+0.3884	+0.9306	0.3422	+0.0505	+0.1476
Factor income	1.1193	0.1845	+0.1428	+0.7742	0.1061	+0.0972	+0.9159	0.1519	+0.1147	+0.7552	0.1787	+0.1642	+0.9190	0.0604	+0.0226	+0.3742
Taxes	-0.2118	0.3584	+0.2997	+0.8363	0.2138	+0.2012	+0.9412	0.2949	+0.2425	+0.8223	0.3619	+0.3416	+0.9437	0.2480	+0.0469	+0.1891
Subsidies	0.0925	0.7440	-0.3120	-0.4194	0.4080	-0.2640	-0.6471	0.6083	-0.2333	-0.3836	0.6833	-0.4333	-0.6341	0.9000	-0.0629	-0.0699
Total income	1	0.0675	-	-	0.0419	-	-	0.0554	-	-	0.0713	-	-	0.0096	-	-
Highest weight to		low incomes			high incomes			low incomes			high incomes			high incomes		

Table 9.5 Factor inequality weights, FIW_j, of example 9.2.
The total income inequality is set equal to 100% and the effects of various income sources on total income are given in % summing up to 100. FIW_j is defined by (9.24b).
The figures are rounded.

Source	Factor Inequality Weights, %					
	Mehran M	Bonferroni B	Gini R	Piesch P	de Vergottini dV	Squared coefficient of variation, V^2
1	-118.4	-128.0	-103.0	- 90.0	- 95.1	- 87.8
2	+118.4	+128.0	+103.0	+ 90.0	+ 95.1	+ 87.8
3	- 32.9	- 47.3	0	+ 26.5	+ 25.9	+ 40.3
4	+269.8	+279.1	+250.1	+233.2	+231.8	+224.6
Factor income	+236.9	+231.8	+250.1	+259.7	+257.7	+264.9
Taxes	- 94.1	- 93.1	- 98.6	-101.7	-101.5	-104.0
Subsidies	- 42.8	- 38.7	- 51.5	- 58.0	- 56.2	- 60.9
Total income	100	100	100	100	100	100
Highest weight to	low incomes		extreme incomes	high incomes		

come source is interpreted as equalizing when using Mehran's and Bonferroni's measures ($E_{M3} < 0$, $E_{B3} < 0$) and disequalizing when using the other three measures. These results are perhaps more apparent when we use the factor inequality weights FIW, %) to describe the effects of various income sources on total income, see table 9.5.

The subadditivity property introduced by Kolm, [1976a - p.422 and 1976b - sec. IX], can be expressed in terms of our notations as, cf. (9.29c),

$$I_t \leq \sum_{j=1}^{k} q_j I_j$$

This property is also named "non-increasing inequality under additions of distributions". Kolm discussed the property in the case of his measures.

This book is mainly designed for the static approach of the measurement of income inequality. The decomposition by income sources can be used as a dynamic tool for analyzing changes in the aggregate distribution of incomes over a range of years.

If t_j denotes time (e.g. year), j=1, 2, ..., k, and Y_T is the total income of k years, $Y_T = \sum_{j=1}^{k} Y_{tj}$, then the total income of k years can be decomposed as, cf. (9.25) as

$$I_T = \sum_{j=1}^{k} q_{tj} E_{tj} I_{tj}$$

where E_{tj} can be interpreted as a measure of the mobility among the i.r.u.'s at year t with respect to the total income (income aggregate). A similar approach is used by Kolm [1976b - sec. IX], who discussed the effect of growth on income inequality with respect to 'subadditivity'.

9.3 STANDARDIZATIONS

An income inequality study can be made in several ways. Three principal types can be distinguished:

(*i*) Cross-section study of one country

(*ii*) Time-period study of one country

(*iii*) Inter-country study of two or more countries

In a cross-section study of one country a single inequality value has not much meaning per se but it only measures the deviation of the size distribution of income from a reference distribution, frequently the egalitarian (EGAL) distribution, and it is exceedingly dependent on the measure of inequality chosen. If the population is subdivided into several mutually exclusive subgroups, e.g. socio-economic groups or age groups, we can compare the inequality values of these subgroups to see whether one group has extensively more intrinsic inequality than the others or not. We can also account for the subgroups' contribution to the overall inequality value (cf. sec. 9.1). Usually the arithmetic mean incomes differ between such subgroups. One question that could be justified in such an analysis is "How much would the overall inequality value have been if the mean incomes within each subgroups had been equal, everything else remaining the same?"

The same question could, of course, be asked if we make a time-period study of one year or an inter-country study of two or more countries. But there are also other questions that could be asked concerning these two types of studies. Considering one country over a period of two (or more) years it is obvious that the demographic caracteristics change (a change that is more or less dependent on the time period between the two years). Usually the arithmetic mean incomes also change and hence the relative mean incomes. In an inter-country study this is more obvious since we then have two completely different populations and two different governments and labor markets.

Questions that could be asked in these types of analyses are "How much would the inequality value have been if there had only been changes in

(1) population

(2) mean incomes

(3) both population and mean incomes

(4) inequality within each subgroups?

The method, briefly summarized below, for analyzing questions like those mentioned is standardization, see e.g. Love and Wolfson [1976 - ch. 4]. We use only the Gini coefficient, R, and Theil's two measures, T_1 and T_2, to describe the methodologies, but the generalization to other measures will be obvious. We assume the measures to be relative invariant (RI-)measures, i.e. they fulfil criterion PROPORTION (see ch. 4).

Cross-section standardization

The very first question in the previous section could be reformulated as follows: If the inequalites within each subgroup were unchanged but we had a change in the income scale so that all subgroups received the same arithmetic mean income, what would then the overall inequality value be? This can be analyzed with a cross-section standardization.

We can proceed as follows: if the income variable of subgroup j, j = 1, 2, ..., k, is Y_j with $\mu_j < \infty$ ($\mu_j > 0$), then its standardized equivalent equals $Y_j^s = \frac{\mu}{\mu_j} Y_j$ and $\mu_j^s = \mu$, j = 1. 2, ..., k. The corresponding standardized slope to the tangent to the Lorenz Curve (LC) in subgroup j, j = 1, 2, ..., k, would then be $\tau(p)_j^s = \tau(p)_j$, i.e. not affected.

If a measure $I(y)$ in general is decomposed into $I(y) = I(y)_W + I(y)_I + I(y)_B$, where $I(y)_W$ is the within-group term, $I(y)_I$ is the interaction term and $I(y)_B$ is the between-group term (the interaction term is frequently equal to zero) then the standardized measure equals $I(y)^s = I(y)_W^s + I(y)_I^s$, since by the standardization the between-group term will vanish. The only change in $I(y)_W^s$ and $I(y)_I^s$ is that if it contains income shares f_{1j} then $f_{1j}^s = f_j$ ($f_j^s = f_j$, i.e. the population shares are unchanged).

The cross-section standardized Gini coefficient, R^s, is then,using (9.12), equal to

$$R^s = \sum_{j=1}^{k} f_j^2 R_{jj} + \sum_{i \neq j}\sum f_i f_j R_{ij}^r \qquad (9.34)$$

and Theil's two measures are

$$T_1^s = \sum_{j=1}^{k} f_j T_{1j} \quad \text{and} \quad T_2^s = \sum_{j=1}^{k} f_j T_{2j} \qquad (9.35)$$

In (9.35) we see that the only change is that the between-terms are zero and $f_{1j}^s = f_j$. For the Gini coefficient we had to use (9.12) because of the definition of R_{ij}^{r} which is unchanged by standardization. The only change is $f_{1j}^{s} = f_{j}$.

The change in inequality value is then given by $I(y) - I(y)^{s}/I(y)$ and for the Gini coefficient this is given by

$$\{ \sum_{j=1}^{k} f_j (f_{1j}-f_j) R_{jj} + \sum_{i \neq j}\sum f_i (f_{ij}-f_j) R_{ij}^{r} \}/ R.$$

Note also the equivalence (and different approach) between this method and the method used by Paglin [1975] to receive a new reference distribution (i.e. changing the diagonal line in the Lorenz diagram to a new reference line defined by $\tau_r(p) \neq p$). The Gini coefficient measured by use of a new reference LC is obtained by taking $R^{P} = R_W + R_I$, i.e. we assume the between group term to equal zero (cf. (9.11) and (9.16)). In the above standardization of R we did not make use of R_B but only R_A.

The above standardization could, of course, be generalized to more than one variable cf. Love and Wolfson [1976 - pp.41-43]. See also Theil [1967 - pp. 110-114].

Inter-country and/or Time-period standardization

By question (1) above we could e.g. ask the following: If we are comparing the inequalities of two countries and their populations have been decomposed into equal subgroups (by definition, e.g. socio-economic groups) and if the population shares in country A had been equal to those of country B, what would then the overall inequality value of country A be? Questions like this can be answered if in an inter-country study (time-period study of one country) we use the characteristics of one country (one year) as a standard.

The assumptions we make by questions like (1) - (4) above are

(1) use a standard population share f_j^s,
whiche implies that $f_{1j}^s = f_j^s \frac{\mu_j}{\mu}$, j = 1, 2, ..., k.

$$R^{s1} = \sum_j f_j^s f_{1j}^s R_{jj} + \sum_{i \neq j}\sum f_i^s f_{1j}^s R_{ij}^r \quad \text{(using (9.12))}$$

$$T_1^{s1} = \sum_j f_{1j}^s T_{1j} + \sum_j f_{1j}^s \log \frac{\mu_j}{\mu}$$

$$T_2^{s1} = \sum_j f_j^s T_{2j} + \sum_j f_j^s \log \frac{\mu}{\mu_j}$$

For T_1 see also Theil [1967 - pp.110-114], [1972 - pp.105-106].

(2) use a standard relative mean income, $\frac{\mu_j^s}{\mu^s}$
which implies $f_{1j}^s = f_j \frac{\mu_j^s}{\mu^s}$, j = 1, 2, ..., k. This affects the between (across) group terms.

$$R^{s2} = \sum_j f_j f_{1j}^s R_{jj} + \sum_{i \neq j}\sum f_i f_{1j}^s R_{ij}^r \quad \text{(using (9.12))}$$

$$T_1^{s2} = \sum_j f_{1j}^s T_{1j} + \sum_j f_{1j}^s \log \frac{\mu_j^s}{\mu^s}$$

$$T_2^{s2} = \sum_j f_j T_{2j} + \sum_j f_j \log \frac{\mu^s}{\mu_j^s}$$

(3) use standards f_j^s and $f_{1j}^s = f_j^s \frac{\mu_j^s}{\mu^s}$, j=1, 2, ..., k.

$$R^{s3} = \sum_j f_j^s f_{1j}^s R_{jj} + \sum_{i \neq j}\sum f_i^s f_{1j}^s f_{ij}^r \quad \text{using (9.12))}$$

$$T_1^{s3} = \sum_j f_{1j}^3 T_{1j} + \sum_j f_{1j}^s \log \frac{\mu_j^s}{\mu^s}$$

$$T_2^{s3} = \sum_j f_j^s T_{2j} + \sum_j f_j^s \log \frac{\mu^s}{\mu_j s}$$

(4) use standard within group inequalities $I(y)_j^s$, j=1, 2, ..., k.

$$R^{s4} = \sum_j f_j \, f_{1j} \, R_{jj}^s + \sum_{i \neq j}\sum f_i \, f_{1j} \, R_{ij}^r \qquad \text{(using (9.12))}$$

$$T_1^{s4} = \sum_j f_{1j} \, T_{1j}^s + \sum_j f_{1j} \, \ell og \, \frac{\mu_j}{\mu}$$

$$T_2^{s4} = \sum_j f_j \, T_{2j}^s + \sum_j f_j \, \ell og \, \frac{\mu}{\mu_j}$$

For a discussion and an extention to two or more classification variables, see Love and Wolfson [1976 - pp. 38-41, 43-45].

Approach (1) above is similar to the projection approach proposed by Soltow [1960], cf. sec. 9.1.2.

For a discussion of the effect of changes in the population on e.g. the Gini coefficient see Morley [1981].

10. SAMPLING FOR INEQUALITY

In this chapter we consider some of the problems involved in measuring income inequality on a sample basis, an issue which seems to have escaped rightful attention in the literature of inequality measurement. This want of an appropriate discussion is not merely caused by ignorance, but rather connected with the intractability of the inequality measures with respect to their sampling properties. This intractability will of course also restrict the scope of the present chapter.

10.1 SOME USEFUL LEMMAS

Suppose that the income Y in an infinite population is distributed among the i.r.u's - say individuals - according to the c.d.f F(y), y > 0. The inverse of F(y) will, as before, be denoted $F^{-1}(p)$.

A simple random sample of n individuals is drawn. Let $y_1, y_2, .., y_n$ denote the ordered incomes of the sample, $y_1 \leq y_2 \leq .. \leq y_n$. Our objective is to estimate the inequality of the distribution F(y) as summarized by some specific inequality measure θ belonging to the general family

$$I(Y;j,\eta) = \{\int_0^1 W(p)\, D\big(c\tau_j(p), c\tau_r(p)\big)^{\eta} dp\}^{1/\eta}, \quad \eta \neq 0. \qquad (7.60a)$$

The estimate of θ will be denoted T_n, where n refers to the sample size.

Firstly we note that since the limiting distribution of the estimated measures in many cases may be expected to be normal - this will in fact be our working hypothesis - the power 1/η in (7.60a) is of minor concern. This is an immediate consequence of the following lemma (let $g(\theta) = \theta^{1/\eta}$, where $\theta = \int_0^1 W(p)\, D\big(c\tau_j(p), c\tau_r(p)\big)^{\eta} dp$.[1])

Lemma 10.1 (Rao [1973; p.385]).

Let $\{T_n\}_{n=1,2,..}$ be a sequence of statistics such that

$$n^{\frac{1}{2}}(T_n - \theta) \xrightarrow{L} X \sim N(0, \upsilon^2(\theta)),$$

where $\xrightarrow{L}$ denotes convergence in distribution, and g be a function of a single variable admitting the first derivative g'.

Then

$$n^{\frac{1}{2}}\{g(T_n) - g(\theta)\} \xrightarrow{L} X \sim N(0, v^2(\theta)),$$

1) This lemma may also be applied to the case η = 0 (cf. (7.60b), p.211).

where $v^2(\theta) = \{g'(\theta)\upsilon(\theta)\}^2$.

Moreover, if $g'(\theta)$ and $\upsilon(\theta)$ are continuous, then

$$\frac{n^{\frac{1}{2}}\{g(T_n) - g(\theta)\}}{v(T_n)} = \frac{n^{\frac{1}{2}}\{g(T_n) - g(\theta)\}}{g'(T_n)\upsilon(T_n)} \xrightarrow{L} Z \sim N(0,1).$$

From this it follows that if $0 < \alpha < 1$ and $z_{\alpha/2}$ is the solution of $\Phi(z_{\alpha/2}) - \Phi(-z_{\alpha/2}) = 1 - \alpha$, then

$$\left(g(T_n) - z_{\alpha/2}\, n^{-\frac{1}{2}}\, v(T_n)\ ,\ g(T_n) + z_{\alpha/2}\, n^{-\frac{1}{2}}\, v(T_n)\right)$$

provides an asymptotic similar distribution free confidence interval for $g(\theta)$ with level $1 - \alpha$.

Secondly, we observe that many measures of our general family may be written as

$$I = g(\theta_1, \theta_2), \tag{10.1}$$

where θ_1 and θ_2 denote population characteristics and g is a totally differentiable function. This is for instance the case of the compromise inequality (CI) measures, which are pairs of relative-invariant (RI) and absolute-invariant (AI) measures (cf. section 7.4) interlinked through $RI = AI/\mu$, or (10.1) with $\theta_1 = AI$, $\theta_2 = \mu$, and $g(\theta_1, \theta_2) = \theta_1/\theta_2$, $\theta_2 \neq 0$.
Now, if T_{1n} and T_{2n} denote estimates of θ_1 and θ_2 from a sample of size n, we may take advantage of the following lemma.

Lemma 10.2 (Rao [1973; p.387]).

If $n^{\frac{1}{2}}(T_{1n} - \theta_1)$ and $n^{\frac{1}{2}}(T_{2n} - \theta_2)$ are asymptotically bivariate normally distributed with mean zero and covariance matrix $\Sigma = \{\sigma_{ij}\}_{i=1,2}^{j=1,2}$, then

$$n^{\frac{1}{2}}\{g(T_{1n}, T_{2n}) - g(\theta_1, \theta_2)\}$$

is asymptotically normal with zero mean and variance

$$v^2(\theta_1,\theta_2) = \sigma_{11}\left(\frac{\partial g}{\partial\theta_1}\right)^2 + 2\sigma_{12}\left(\frac{\partial g}{\partial\theta_1}\right)\left(\frac{\partial g}{\partial\theta_2}\right) + \sigma_{22}\left(\frac{\partial g}{\partial\theta_2}\right)^2.$$

Moreover, if all elements of Σ and the partial derivatives $\frac{\partial g}{\partial\theta_i}$ are continuous functions of the parameters θ_1 and θ_2, then

$$\frac{n^{\frac{1}{2}}\{g(T_{1n},T_{2n}) - g(\theta_1,\theta_2)\}}{v(T_{1n},T_{2n})} \xrightarrow{L} Z \sim N(0,1)$$

For the case $g(\theta_1,\theta_2) = \theta_1/\theta_2$ we obtain

$$n^{\frac{1}{2}}(T_{1n}/T_{2n} - \theta_1/\theta_2) \xrightarrow{L} X \sim N(0,\theta_2^{-2}\sigma_{11}-2\theta_1\theta_2^{-3}\sigma_{12}+\theta_1^2\theta_2^{-4}\sigma_{22}).$$

Using the same method as above we may construct an asymptotic similar distribution free confidence interval for $g(\theta_1,\theta_2)$.

Thirdly, we would like to draw attention to two useful results obtained by Shorack [1972] and Sendler [1979]. The first result may be adopted when considering inequality measures which may be written on the form

$$\theta = I(Y) = \int_0^1 R(p)\, F^{-1}(p)\, dp\,, \tag{10.2}$$

where $R(p)$ is a real valued function on $[0,1]$.

In this case it seems reasonable to choose real numbers r_{ni}, $i=1,..,n$, and define a step function

$$R_n(p) = \begin{cases} r_{ni}\,, & \frac{i-1}{n} < p \leq \frac{i}{n}\,, \quad i=1,..,n \\ r_{n1}\,, & p = 0 \end{cases} \tag{10.3}$$

so that $R_n(p)$ lies close to $R(p)$, and try the estimator

$$T_n = \frac{1}{n}\sum_{i=1}^{n} r_{ni}Y_i \tag{10.4}$$

for θ. The following lemma shows that the limiting distribution of T_n is normal under quite general conditions.

Lemma 10.3 (Shorack [1972; Theorem 1], Sendler [1979; Proposition 2]).

Let r_{ni}, i=1,..,n, be real numbers and define $R_n(p)$ according to (10.3).

If the following three conditions hold:

(a) there exists a function R(p), continuous on [0,1], such that $R_n(p)$ converges uniformly towards R(p),[1)]

(b) there are constants A, b_1, b_2 and δ, $\delta > 0$, such that with

$$B(p) = Ap^{-b_1}(1-p)^{-b_2} \qquad 0 < p < 1$$
$$D(p) = Ap^{-\frac{1}{2}+b_1+\delta}(1-p)^{-\frac{1}{2}+b_2+\delta}$$

we have

$|R_n(p)| \leqq B(p)$ for sufficiently large n,

$|R(p)| \leqq B(p)$, and

$F^{-1}(p) \leqq D(p)$,

(c) $\int_0^1 (R_n(p) - R(p))F^{-1}(p)dp = o(n^{-\frac{1}{2}})$,

then

$$n^{\frac{1}{2}}(T_n - \theta) \xrightarrow{L} X \sim N(0, v^2(\theta)),$$

where $v^2(\theta) = \int_0^1\int_0^1 \left(\min(p,q)-pq\right)R(p)R(q)dF^{-1}(p)dF^{-1}(q)$, provided that $0 < v^2(\theta) < \infty$.

Moreover it can be shown (see Sendler [1979]) that if the conditions of lemma 10.3 hold and, additionally, $|R_n(p)|$ and $|R(p)|$ are uniformly bounded, then

$$v^2(T_n) = \sum_{i=1}^{n-1}\sum_{j=1}^{n-1} \left(\min(\tfrac{i}{n},\tfrac{j}{n}) - \tfrac{i}{n}\tfrac{j}{n}\right) r_{ni}\, r_{nj}\, (y_{i+1} - y_i)(y_{j+1} - y_j) \qquad (10.5)$$

1) The condition of continuity and uniform convergence on [0,1] may be relaxed by excluding any set of p's, whose Lebesque-Stieltjes measure given by F^{-1} is zero. See Shorack [1972].

provides a strongly consistent estimate for $v^2(\theta)$. Hence, for given $0 < \alpha < 1$ and $z_{\alpha/2}$ the solution of $\Phi(z_{\alpha/2}) - \Phi(-z_{\alpha/2}) = 1 - \alpha$,

$$\left(T_n - z_{\alpha/2}\, n^{-\frac{1}{2}}\, v(T_n)\ ,\ T_n + z_{\alpha/2}\, n^{-\frac{1}{2}}\, v(T_n)\right)$$

may be taken as an asymptotic similar distribution free confidence interval for θ with confidence level $1 - \alpha$.

A similar result to that of lemma 10.3 holds (see Sendler [1979]) for inequality measures of the ratio form

$$\theta = I(Y) = \frac{\int_0^1 R(p)\, F^{-1}(p)\, dp}{\int_0^1 S(p)\, F^{-1}(p)\, dp}\ , \tag{10.6}$$

where $R(p)$ has the same properties as above and $S(p)$ is a measurable real valued function on $[0,1]$, such that $S(p) \geqq 0$ and the denominator $\int_0^1 S(p)F^{-1}(p)dp$ does not vanish. Now we choose two sets of real numbers, r_{ni} and s_{ni}, $i=1,..,n$, define the step function $R_n(p)$ as in (10.3) and $S_n(p)$ correspondingly as

$$S_n(p) = \begin{cases} s_{ni}\ , & \frac{i-1}{n} < p \leqq \frac{i}{n}\ , \quad i=1,..,n \\ s_{n1}\ , & p = 0 \end{cases} \tag{10.7}$$

so that $R_n(p)$ and $S_n(p)$ are close to $R(p)$ and $S(p)$, respectively. The counterpart to the estimator (10.4) will in this case be

$$T_n = \frac{\frac{1}{n}\sum_{i=1}^{n} r_{ni} y_i}{\frac{1}{n}\sum_{i=1}^{n} s_{ni} y_i} = \frac{\sum_{i=1}^{n} r_{ni} y_i}{\sum_{i=1}^{n} s_{ni} y_i} \tag{10.8}$$

and as a parallel to lemma 10.3 we have

Lemma 10.4 (Sendler [1979; Theorem 1]).

Let r_{ni} and s_{ni}, i=1,..,n, be real numbers. Provided that $s_{ni} \geqq 0$ for every i and $s_{nj} > 0$ for at least one j, define $R_n(p)$ and $S_n(p)$ according to (10.3) and (10.7) respectively.

If the conditions of lemma 10.3 hold for both $R_n(p)$ and $S_n(p)$, i.e. if

(a) there exist functions R(p) and S(p), both continuous on [0,1], such that $R_n(p)$ and $S_n(p)$ converge uniformly towards R(p) and S(p), respectively,[1)]

(b) $|R_n(p)| \leqq B(p)$ and $|S_n(p)| \leqq B(p)$ for sufficiently large n, $|R(p)| \leqq B(p)$ and $|S(p)| \leqq B(p)$, and $F^{-1}(p) \leqq D(p)$, where B(p) and D(p) are defined in lemma 10.3(b),

(c) $\int_0^1 (R_n(p) - R(p))F^{-1}(p)dp = o(n^{-\frac{1}{2}})$ and $\int_0^1 (S_n(p) - S(p))F^{-1}(p)dp = o(n^{-\frac{1}{2}})$,

then

$$n^{\frac{1}{2}}(T_n - \theta) \xrightarrow{L} X \sim N(0, v^2(\theta)),$$

where $v^2(\theta) = \{\int_0^1 S(p)F^{-1}(p)dp\}^{-2} \int_0^1\int_0^1 (\min(p,q)-pq)U(p)U(q)dF^{-1}(p)dF^{-1}(q)$,

$U(p) = R(p) - \theta S(p)$, provided that the limiting variance $v^2(\theta)$ is positive and finite.

Introducing the notations $\mu_S = \int_0^1 S(p)F^{-1}(p)dp$ and $\upsilon^2(\theta) = \int_0^1\int_0^1 (\min(p,q)-pq)U(p)U(q)dF^{-1}(p)dF^{-1}(q)$ we may write $v^2(\theta)$ as $v^2(\theta) = \mu_S^{-2}\upsilon^2(\theta)$.

Provided uniform boundedness of the R- ans S-functions it can, as above, be seen that

1) See note 1) to lemma 10.3.

$$m_{sn} = \frac{1}{n} \sum_{i=1}^{n} s_{ni} y_i \text{ , and}$$

$$\upsilon^2(T_n) = \sum_{i=1}^{n-1} \sum_{j=1}^{n-1} \left(\min\left(\frac{i}{n},\frac{j}{n}\right) - \frac{i}{n}\frac{j}{n}\right) U_n\left(\frac{i}{n}\right) U_n\left(\frac{j}{n}\right)(y_{i+1}-y_i)(y_{j+1}-y_j), \tag{10.9}$$

where $U_n(\frac{i}{n}) = R_n(\frac{i}{n}) - T_n S_n(\frac{i}{n}) = r_{ni} - T_n s_{ni}$, may be taken as strongly consistent estimates for μ_S and $\upsilon^2(\theta)$, respectively.

Thus, an asymptotic similar distribution free confidence interval for θ takes the form

$$\left(T_n - z_{\alpha/2} \frac{\upsilon(T_n)}{n^{\frac{1}{2}} m_{sn}} \text{ , } T_n + z_{\alpha/2} \frac{\upsilon(T_n)}{n^{\frac{1}{2}} m_{sn}} \right).$$

10.2 ASYMPTOTIC PROPERTIES OF INEQUALITY ESTIMATES

We will now use the lemmas of the preceeding section in constructing estimators for some members of the general family (7.60a) of inequality measures and in deriving their limiting distributions. We restrict our attention to the ordinary case $j = 1$, i.e. the measures under consideration is of the form

$$I(Y;\eta) = \{\int_0^1 W(p)\, D\big(c\tau(p), c\tau_r(p)\big)^{\eta}\, dp\}^{1/\eta}. \qquad (10.10)$$

Depending on the choice of the D-function the inequality measures belong to the SD-, the LSD-, or the ESD-subclass discussed in chapter 7.

Some measures of the SD-class

We start out by considering the inequality measures of the SD-class with $D(.,.) = c(\tau(p) - 1)$. Taking $\eta = 1$, we obtain for $c = 1$ the RI-measures

$$I(Y) = \int_0^1 W(p)\big(\tau(p) - 1\big)dp = \int_0^1 C(p)\tau(p)dp, \qquad (10.11)$$

and for $c = \mu$ the corresponding AI-measures

$$I(Y) = \int_0^1 W(p)\mu\big(\tau(p) - 1\big)dp = \int_0^1 W(p)\big(F^{-1}(p) - \mu\big)dp = \int_0^1 C(p)F^{-1}(p)dp, \qquad (10.12)$$

where $C(p) = W(p) - \int_0^1 W(p)dp$ is the constrain function of (7.59a). This subset of the SD-class includes e.g. the inequality measures of Gini, Mehran, and Piesch (cf. sec. 7.4). Observing that $\tau(p) = F^{-1}(p)/\mu$ and $\mu = \int_0^1 F^{-1}(p)dp$ it is easily seen that (10.11) and (10.12) in fact correspond to (10.2) and (10.6), respectively, with $R(p) = C(p)$ and $S(p) = F^{-1}(p)$. Lemma 10.3 and lemma 10.4 may thus be used in constructing estimators for these measures and establishing their limiting distributions.

It should be noted that these two lemmas do not in general determine any unique estimator for the inequality measure in question, but rather a set of estimators with an identical limiting distribution.

If we take the weight function $W(p)$ as our point of departure we may substitute $\frac{i}{n}$ for p to obtain $W(\frac{i}{n})$ and derive the corresponding discrete constraint function as $C(\frac{i}{n}) = W(\frac{i}{n}) - \frac{1}{n}\Sigma W(\frac{i}{n})$. Defining the step functions of (10.3) and (10.7) as

$$R_n(p) = \begin{cases} C(\frac{i}{n}) \ , & \frac{i-1}{n} < p \leq \frac{i}{n} \ , \quad i=1,..,n \\ C(\frac{1}{n}) \ , & p = 0 \end{cases}$$

and

$$S_n(p) = \quad 1 \ , \ 0 \leq p \leq 1,$$

the conditions of lemma 10.3 and 10.4 may be checked.

For instance, in the case of the Gini coefficient we have $W(p) = 2p$ and thus $W(\frac{i}{n}) = 2i/n$ and $C(\frac{i}{n}) = R_n(p) = \frac{2i-1}{n} - 1$. The estimators of (10.4) and (10.8) now takes the form

$$T_n = \frac{1}{n} \sum_{i=1}^{n} (\frac{2i-1}{n} - 1)y_i, \text{ and}$$

$$T_n = \frac{\sum_{i=1}^{n} (\frac{2i-1}{n} - 1)y_i}{\sum_{i=1}^{n} y_i},$$

respectively, and it is easily seen that the requirement on the R- and S-functions posed by the lemmas are fulfilled in this case. Hence, the limiting distribution of the estimators is normal and unbiased.

In the same way estimators for the measures of Mehran and Piesch may be constructed. These and the estimator for the Gini coefficient are shown in table 10.1 together with expressions for their asymptotic variances. In the table, and subsequently, the notation m is used for the sample mean,

$$m = m_{1n} = \frac{1}{n} \sum_{i=1}^{n} y_i.$$

Table 10.1. Estimators for the inequality measures of Gini, Mehran, and Piesch.

Measure, θ	Formula	Estimator, T_n
The Gini coefficient, R	$\int_0^1 (2p-1)\tau(p)dp$	$\frac{\Sigma(\frac{2i-1}{n}-1)y_i}{\Sigma y_i} = \frac{2\Sigma i y_i}{n^2 m} - \frac{n+1}{n} = \frac{1}{2n^2 m}\Sigma\Sigma \lvert y_i - y_j \rvert$
The absolute Gini coefficient	$\int_0^1 (2p-1)F^{-1}(p)dp$	$\frac{1}{n}\Sigma(\frac{2i-1}{n}-1)y_i = \frac{1}{n^2}\{2\Sigma i y_i - (n+1)\Sigma y_i\} = \frac{1}{2n^2}\Sigma\Sigma \lvert y_i - y_j \rvert$
Mehran's measure, M	$\int_0^1 \{1 - 3(1-p)^2\}\tau(p)dp$	$\frac{\Sigma\{1 - 3(1-\frac{i}{n})^2 - \frac{3n-1}{n^2}\}y_i}{\Sigma y_i} = \frac{6n\Sigma i y_i - 3\Sigma i^2 y_i}{n^3 m} - \frac{4n^2+3n-1}{2n^2}$
Mehran's absolute measure	$\int_0^1 \{1 - 3(1-p)^2\}F^{-1}(p)dp$	$\frac{1}{n}\Sigma\{1 - 3(1-\frac{i}{n})^2 - \frac{3n-1}{2n^2}\}y_i = \frac{1}{n^3}\{6n\Sigma i y_i - 3\Sigma i^2 y_i - \frac{1}{2}(4n^2+3n-1)\Sigma y_i\}$
Piesch' measure, P	$\int_0^1 \frac{1}{2}(3p^2-1)\tau(p)dp$	$\frac{\Sigma\{\frac{1}{2}(3(\frac{i}{n})^2 - 1) - \frac{3n+1}{4n^2}\}y_i}{\Sigma y_i} = \frac{3\Sigma i^2 y_i}{2n^3 m} - \frac{2n^2+3n+1}{4n^2}$
Piesch' absolute measure	$\int_0^1 \frac{1}{2}(3p^2-1)F^{-1}(p)dp$	$\frac{1}{n}\Sigma\{\frac{1}{2}(3(\frac{i}{n})^2 - 1) - \frac{3n+1}{4n^2}\}y_i = \frac{1}{2n^3}\{3\Sigma i^2 y_i - \frac{1}{2}(2n^2+3n+1)\Sigma y_i\}$

Table 10.1. (cont.) Asymptotic variance of the estimators.[1)]

Measure, θ	Asymptotic variance of $n^{\frac{1}{2}}(T_n - \theta)$
The Gini coefficient, R	$2\mu^{-2}\int_0^1 (1-p)(2p-1-R)\int_0^p q(2q-1-R)dF^{-1}(q)dF^{-1}(p)$
The absolute Gini coefficient	$2\int_0^1 (1-p)(2p-1)\int_0^p q(2q-1)dF^{-1}(q)dF^{-1}(p)$
Mehran´s measure, M	$2\mu^{-2}\int_0^1 (1-p)(3p^2-6p+2+M)\int_0^p q(3q^2-6q+2+M)dF^{-1}(q)dF^{-1}(p)$
Mehrans absolute measure	$2\int_0^1 (1-p)(3p^2-6p+2)\int_0^p q(3q^2-6q+2)dF^{-1}(q)dF^{-1}(p)$
Piesch´ measure, P	$\frac{1}{2}\mu^{-2}\int_0^1 (1-p)(3p^2-1-2P)\int_0^p q(3q^2-1-2P)dF^{-1}(q)dF^{-1}(p)$
Piesch´ absolute measure	$\frac{1}{2}\int_0^1 (1-p)(3p^2-1)\int_0^p q(3q^2-1)dF^{-1}(q)dF^{-1}(p)$

1) .The estimators are asymptotically unbiased and normally distributed.

The limiting variances may be estimated according to (10.5) and (10.9). For the estimator R_n of the Gini coefficient, R, we for instance obtain the expression

$$v^2(R_n) = \sum_{i=1}^{n-1}\sum_{j=1}^{n-1}\left(\min\left(\frac{i}{n},\frac{j}{n}\right)-\frac{i}{n}\frac{j}{n}\right)\left(\frac{2i-1}{n}-1-R_n\right)\left(\frac{2j-1}{n}-1-R_n\right)(y_{i+1}-y_i)(y_{j+1}-y_j).$$

The calculations involved in the estimation of the variance are however very cumbersome, which partly obstructs their application in practice.

Estimators for measures related to the Gini coefficient, viz. the Lorenz area $(W(p)=p)$ and the mean difference $(W(p)=4p)$, and the corresponding limiting variances may readily be derived through obvious modifications of the Gini index estimator.

An unbiased estimator for the absolute mean difference $G = 2\int_0^1 (2p-1)F^{-1}(p)dp = \int_0^\infty\int_0^\infty |x-y|dF(x)dF(y)$ is given by $G_n = \frac{1}{n(n-1)}\sum_{i=1}^{n}\sum_{j=1}^{n}|y_i-y_j|$. For its variance we obtain the expression

$$V(G_n) = \frac{1}{n(n-1)}\{4\sigma^2 - 4(n-2)\int_0^\infty\int_0^\infty\int_0^\infty|x-y||x-z|dF(x)dF(y)dF(z) - 2(2n-3)G^2\},$$ where σ^2 is the population variance. See Nair [1936], Lomnicki [1952], and Kendall and Stuart [1977].An alternative expression for $V(G_n)$ and an unbiased estimate of this magnitude is given in Glasser [1962].

A number of SD-measures, e.g. the standard deviation and the squared coefficient of variation, are closely related to the population variance

$$\sigma^2 = \int_0^\infty (y-\mu)^2 dF(y) = \int_0^1 (F^{-1}(p)-\mu)^2 dp.$$

It is well-known that the sample variance

$s^2 = \frac{1}{n-1}\sum_{i=1}^{n}(y_i-m)^2$, where $m = \frac{1}{n}\sum_{i=1}^{n} y_i$ is the sample mean, provides an unbiased estimate of σ^2. It may further be shown (see e.g. Hansen et.al. [1953]) that the variance of the estimator equals

$V(s^2) = \frac{1}{n}(\beta_4 - \frac{n-3}{n-1})\sigma^4$, where $\beta_4 = \sigma^{-4}\int_0^\infty (y-\mu)^4 dF(y)$ is the Pearson measure of kurtosis, and that the limiting distribution is normal (see e.g. Cramer 1946), i.e.

$$n^{\frac{1}{2}}(s^2 - \sigma^2) \xrightarrow{L} X \sim N(0,(\beta_4 - 1)\sigma^4).$$

From this it follows that lemma 10.1 and lemma 10.2, once it is recognized that $n^{\frac{1}{2}}(m-\mu) \xrightarrow{L} X \sim N(0,\sigma^2)$, may readily be used to obtain asymptotically normally distributed estimators for the variance-related SD-measures and derive the corresponding limiting variances. Examples of such estimators are given in table 10.2.

In comparing the asymptotic variances of the estimators for the four measures related to the coefficient of variation it is easily seen from table 10.2 that the normalized variants have a lower relative variance than the corresponding non-normalized estimators, and that the estimator for the normalized coefficient of variation is associated with the lowest asymptotic rel-variance.

Turning to inequality measures derived from equality measures in the SD-family, we restrict our attention to the measures

$$I(Y;\eta) = c(1+\xi/\mu) - c\ \{\int_0^1 \left(\tau(p) + \xi/\mu\right)^\eta dp\}^{1/\eta}, \quad \eta < 1 \tag{10.13}$$

$$I(Y;0) = c(1+\xi/\mu) - c\exp\{\int_0^1 \log\left(\tau(p) + \xi/\mu\right) dp\}, \tag{10.14}$$

where $c = 1$ or $c = \mu$, including e.g. the rightist and centrist inequality measures of Kolm 1976 .

Introducing the variates $X = (Y+\xi)^\eta$ and $Z = \log(Y+\xi)$ it is readily seen that (10.13) and (10.14) may be rewritten as

$$I(Y;\eta) = c\mu^{-1}\{\mu + \xi - \mu_X^{1/\eta}\} \tag{10.13*}$$

$$I(Y;0) = c\mu^{-1}\{\mu + \xi - \exp(\mu_Z)\} \tag{10.14*}$$

Table 10.2. Estimators for the variance-related SD-measures and their asymptotic variances.[1)]

Measure, θ	Estimator, T_n	Asymptotic variance of $n^{\frac{1}{2}}(T_n - \theta)$
The standard deviation, σ	$s = \left(\frac{1}{n-1} \sum_{i=1}^{n} (y_i - m)^2\right)^{\frac{1}{2}}$	$\frac{1}{4}(\beta_4 - 1)\sigma^2$
The coefficient of variation, $V = \sigma/\mu$	s/m	$V^2\{\frac{1}{4}(\beta_4 - 1) - V\beta_3 + V^2\}$
The squared coefficient of variation, $V^2 = \sigma^2/\mu^2$	s^2/m^2	$4V^4\{\frac{1}{4}(\beta_4 - 1) - V\beta_3 + V^2\}$
The normalized coefficient of variation, $V/(V^2+1)^{\frac{1}{2}}$	$\frac{s/m}{(s^2/m^2 + 1)^{\frac{1}{2}}}$	$\frac{V^2}{V^2+1}(V^2+1)^{-2}\{\frac{1}{4}(\beta_4 - 1) - V\beta_3 + V^2\}$
The squared normalized coefficient of variation, $V^2/(V^2+1)$	$\frac{s^2/m^2}{s^2/m^2 + 1}$	$4\frac{V^4}{(V^2+1)^2}(V^2+1)^{-2}\{\frac{1}{4}(\beta_4 - 1) - V\beta_3 + V^2\}$

1) The estimators are asymptotically unbiased and normally distributed.

In the table the symbol β_k is used for the population magnitude $\beta_k = \sigma^{-k} \int_0^\infty (y-\mu)^k dF(y)$.

with $\mu = E(Y)$, $\mu_X = E(X)$, and $\mu_Z = E(Z)$. The simple estimators

$$m_X = \frac{1}{n}\sum_{i=1}^{n}(y_i + \xi) \quad \text{and} \quad m_Z = \frac{1}{n}\sum_{i=1}^{n}\log(y_i + \xi)$$

provide unbiased and asymptotically normally distributed estimates for μ_X and μ_Z, respectively. Lemma 10.2 may thus be used in obtaining estimators for the measures (10.13) and (10.14) with normal limiting distributions. These are presented in table 10.3.

From the table it is seen that the limiting variance associated with the estimator

$$T_n = 1 - \{\frac{1}{n}\sum_{i=1}^{n}(y_i/m)^{\eta}\}^{1/\eta}, \quad \eta = 1 - \varepsilon,$$

for Atkinson´s inequality measure (or Kolm´s rightist measure),

$$\theta = 1 - \{\int_0^1(\tau(p))^{\eta}dp\}^{1/\eta}, \text{ is } (1-\theta)^2\{V^2 - \frac{2}{\eta}\mu^{-1}\mu_X^{-1}\sigma_{XY} + (\frac{1}{\eta})^2V_X^2\}.$$

In the case $\eta = 0$ an alternative to (10.14) is to define (cf. section 7.4.1) the inequality measure as

$$I(Y;0) = \log\big(c(1+\xi/\mu)\big) - \int_0^1 \log\{c\big(\tau(p)+\xi/\mu\big)\}dp = \quad (10.15)$$

$$= \log(1+\xi/\mu) - \int_0^1 \log\big(\tau(p)+\xi/\mu\big)dp =$$

$$= \log(\mu+\xi) - \mu_Z. \quad (10.15^*)$$

An estimator for this magnitude is also given in table 10.3. For the special case $\xi = 0$ we obtain Theil´s second inequality measure $T_2 = -\int\log\big(\tau(p)\big)dp$ which may be estimated with $-\frac{1}{n}\Sigma\log(y_i/m)$.

Table 10.3. Estimators for some SD-measures of Kolm-type and their asymptotic variances.[1)]

	Measure, θ	Estimator, T_n	Asymptotic variance of $n^{\frac{1}{2}}(T_n - \theta)$
$\eta < 1$	Kolm's centrist measure, $\theta = \mu + \xi - \mu_X^{1/\eta}$	$m + \xi - m_x^{1/\eta} = m + \xi - \{\frac{1}{n}\Sigma(y_i + \xi)^\eta\}^{1/\eta}$	$\sigma^2 - \frac{2}{\eta}\mu_X^{-1+1/\eta}\sigma_{XY} + (\frac{1}{\eta})^2 \mu_X^{2/\eta} V_X^2$
	Kolm's μ-modified centrist measure, $\theta = 1 + \frac{\xi}{\mu} - \mu^{-1}\mu_X^{1/\eta}$	$1 + \frac{\xi}{m} - m^{-1}m_x^{1/\eta} = 1 + \frac{\xi}{m} - \{\frac{1}{n}\Sigma(\frac{y_i}{m} + \frac{\xi}{m})^\eta\}^{1/\eta}$	$\mu^{-2}\{(\xi-\mu_X^{1/\eta})^2 V^2 + \frac{2}{\eta}\mu^{-1}(\xi-\mu_X^{1/\eta})\mu_X^{-1+1/\eta}\sigma_{XY} + (\frac{1}{\eta})^2\mu_X^{2/\eta}V_X^2\}$
$\eta = 0$	Kolm's centrist measure, $\theta = \mu + \xi - \exp(\mu_Z)$	$m + \xi - \exp(m_z) = m + \xi - \exp\{\frac{1}{n}\Sigma\log(y_i + \xi)\}$	$\sigma^2 - 2\exp(\mu_Z)\sigma_{YZ} - \exp(2\mu_Z)\sigma_Z^2$
	Kolm's μ-modified centrist measure, $\theta = 1 + \frac{\xi}{\mu} - \mu^{-1}\exp(\mu_Z)$	$1 + \frac{\xi}{m} - m^{-1}\exp(m_z) = 1 + \frac{\xi}{m} - \exp\{\frac{1}{n}\Sigma\log(\frac{y_i}{m} + \frac{\xi}{m})\}$	$\mu^{-2}\{(\xi-\exp(\mu_Z))^2 V^2 + 2\mu^{-1}(\xi-\exp(\mu_Z))\exp(\mu_Z)\sigma_{YZ} + \exp(2\mu_Z)\sigma_Z^2\}$
	Extended Theil's second measure, $\theta = \log(\mu+\xi) - \mu_Z$	$\log(m + \xi) - m_z = -\frac{1}{n}\Sigma\log\left(\frac{y_i + \xi}{m + \xi}\right)$	$(\mu+\xi)^{-2}\sigma^2 - 2(\mu+\xi)^{-1}\sigma_{YZ} + \sigma_Z^2$

1) The estimators are asymptotically unbiased and normally distributed.

In the table the following symbols are used: $\mu = E(Y)$, $\mu_X = E((Y+\xi)^\eta)$, $\mu_Z = E(\log(Y+\xi))$, $\sigma^2 = V(Y)$, $\sigma_X^2 = V((Y+\xi)^\eta)$,

Some other measures

If the difference function D of (10.10) is defined as $D(.,.) = \log\tau(p) - \log\tau_r(p)$ we obtain the measures of the LSD-class. Choosing $\eta = 1$ and $\tau_r(p) = 1$ we get the inequality measures

$$I(Y) = \int_0^1 W(p) \log\tau(p)\, dp ,$$

including Theil´s first inequality measure ($W(p) = \tau(p)$). Using the transformation $U = Y\log Y$ Theil´s measure may be written as

$$\theta = T_1 = \mu^{-1}\mu_U - \log\mu,$$

where $\mu_U = E(U) = E(Y\log Y)$. The obvious sample estimate of μ_U is $m_u = \frac{1}{n}\Sigma y_i \log y_i$ with a normal limiting distribution. The corresponding sample estimator, based on lemma 10.2, for Theil´s inequality measure is

$$T_n = m^{-1}m_u - \log m = \frac{1}{n}\Sigma\frac{y_i}{m}\log\left(\frac{y_i}{m}\right)$$

and the associated limiting variance of $n^{\frac{1}{2}}(T_n - \theta)$ is given by

$$\mu^{-2}\{(1+\mu^{-1}\mu_U)^2\sigma^2 - 2(1+\mu^{-1}\mu_U)\,\sigma_{YU} + \sigma_U^2\},$$

where $\sigma_U^2 = V(Y\log Y)$ and $\sigma_{YU} = Cov(Y, Y\log Y)$.

Turning to the standard deviation of the log-incomes,

$$\sigma_{\log} = \{\int_0^1 (\log\tau(p) - \log(\mu_g/\mu))^2 dp\}^{\frac{1}{2}},$$

where $\mu_g = \exp\{\int \log y\, dF(y)\}$ is the geometric mean income, we note that the measure is related to the standard deviation of the SD-class. An estimator of $\sigma_{\log}$ is easily derived by an application of the results of the preceding section (cf. table 10.2) to the transformed variate $Z = \log Y$.

The leftist measure of Kolm [1976],

$$I(Y;\eta) = \frac{1}{\eta}\log\{\int_0^\infty \exp(-\eta(y-\mu))dF(y)\} = \mu + \frac{1}{\eta}\log\{\int_0^\infty \exp(-\eta y)dF(y)\},$$

viz. the log-transformation of the ESD-measure (7.86a) with $W(p)=1$ and $c=-\mu$, may be estimated with

$$T_n = \frac{1}{\eta}\log\{\frac{1}{n}\Sigma\exp(-\eta(y_i-m))\} = m + \frac{1}{\eta}\log\{\frac{1}{n}\Sigma\exp(-\eta y_i)\},$$

an asymptotically unbiased and normally distributed estimator. The associated limiting variance equals

$$\sigma^2 + \frac{2}{\eta}\mu_Z^{-1} + (\frac{1}{\eta})^2\mu_Z^{-2}\sigma_Z^2 ,$$

where $\mu_Z = E(\exp(-\eta Y))$ and $\sigma_Z^2 = V(\exp(-\eta Y))$.

For the μ-modification $I(Y;\eta) = 1 + \frac{1}{\eta}\mu^{-1}\{\int\exp(-\eta y)dF(y)\}$ of Kolm's leftist measure the corresponding results are easily derived.

For the mean deviation

$$\delta_\mu = \int_0^\infty |y-\mu|dF(y)$$

Gastwirth [1974] showed that under quite general conditions the sample magnitude

$$d_m = \frac{1}{n}\sum_{i=1}^{n}|y_i - m|$$

provides an asymptotically unbiased estimator with normal limiting distribution. The limiting variance of $n^{\frac{1}{2}}(d_m - \delta_\mu)$ is given by

$$4p_\mu^2\sigma^2 - 4(1-2p_\mu)\int_0^\mu (y-\mu)^2 dF(y) - \delta_\mu^2 ,$$

where $p_\mu = F(\mu)$. If the distribution is symmetric we have $p_\mu = 0.5$ and the limiting variance is reduced to $\sigma^2 - \delta_\mu^2$, which was suggested by Kendall and Stuart [1977; p.255] as an approximation of the limiting variance.

As the limiting covariance between $n^{\frac{1}{2}}(d_m - \delta_\mu)$ and $n^{\frac{1}{2}}(m-\mu)$ equals (see Gastwirth [1974])

$$2\,p_\mu \sigma^2 - 2\int_0^\mu (y-\mu)^2 dF(y)$$

we may use lemma 10.2 in deriving an asymptotically unbiased and normally distributed estimator for the maximum equalization ratio

$$\theta = \delta_\mu/2 = \frac{1}{2\mu}\int_0^\infty |y-\mu|\,dF(y)$$

and deducing its limiting variance. The estimator is readily seen to equal

$$T_n = d_m/2m = \frac{1}{2nm}\Sigma\,|y_i - m|$$

and the associated limiting variance is given by

$$(\theta - p_\mu)^2 V^2 + \mu^{-2}(2\theta + 2p_\mu - 1)\int_0^\mu (y-\mu)^2 dF(y) - \theta^2,$$

which in the case of a symmetric distribution is reduced to $(\theta^2 + \frac{1}{4})\,V^2 - \theta^2$.

10.3 REMARKS ON THE ASYMPTOTIC APPROACH

The estimators given in the preceding section should be familiar to the reader: superficially they are similar to the inequality measures of the discrete case presented in chapter 8, differing from these mainly through the replacement of the population size N with the sample size n. It is not hard to see that the estimators and their asymptotic properties are also valid in the discrete case - with obvious modifications (use of sums instead of integrals) of the expressions for the limiting variances to meet the notion of a discrete distribution - if the sample scheme is simple random sampling with replacement.

At first glance it may in a sample context seem appropriate to base the choice between potentially useful inequality measures on a comparison of the limiting variances of the corresponding sample statistics and prefer measures with smaller associated asymptotic (relative) variability.[1] Although knowledge of the asymptotic variances of the estimators no doubt is of great value, it must be realized that different inequality measures are generally far from perfect substitutes for one another - as should be clear from the discussion in the preceding chapters. A choice between measures based on mainly the associated limiting variances may thus be throughly mistaken. It should also in this context be noted that a comparison of asymptotic variances usually involves intractable mathematical excercises. A simple way to ensure tractability would of course be by imposing some elementary c.d.f F(y) for the population from which the sample is drawn - e.g. a rectangular distribution - but obviously there is not much empirical sense in such a rigid assumption.

1) Cf. the discussion of the measures related to the coefficient of variation in section 10.2.

As a consequence of these considerations we will not stress the asymptotic properties of the measures per se, but rather use them as tools to obtain confidence intervals for the unknown value of the inequality measure of interest using the method sketched in section 10.1.

There are at least three qualifications of the asymptotic approach which properly should be dealt with before any attempt to use asymptotic results in the contruction of confidence intervals should be made.
Firstly, we have to consider the usual objection against any asymptotic theory: it is not clear to what extent the results are applicable for a finite sample size.
Secondly, under the supposition that the asymptotic theory is applicable for a given (sufficiently large) sample size it would be very handy if the variance of sample statistics of interest could be assessed without excessive computational efforts.
Thirdly, it must be realized that most empirical surveys on income differences are based on more complicated designs than simple random sampling, and, moreover, that inequality measurement is only seldom the main reason for carrying out surveys; two facts which must be taken into account when estimating the inequality measure and assessing its sampling error.

Finite sample size

The estimators discussed in section 10.2 were shown to be asymptotically normally distributed with the limiting expected value equal to the population value of the inequality index and asymptotic variance of magnitude n^{-1} times a constant depending on the distribution F(y). The asymptotic results may, as we have noted, be used when pursuing confidence intervals for the inequality measure. The pertinence of this estimation procedure is crucially dependent on how fast the estimators approach their asymtotic behavior. It is clear that, in general, the speed of the convergence towards the limiting normal distribution will be conditioned on the population distribution F(y). There are scarcely any research findings to seize upon in this context, and only some tentative conclusions may be presented here.

To start with we note that under the presuppostition of a symmetrical unimodal c.d.f F(y) the use of the asymptotic results may be reasonable even for small sample sizes, since in this case it may be expected that the bias involved in the estimation is negligible and that the convergence towards a normal distribution is relatively rapid. This is in accordance with the suggestion of Glasser [1962], who studied the absolute mean difference G of a normal population. Referring to Kamat [1953] Glasser states that for $n \geqq 20$ or even smaller, the distribution of the sample mean difference might be reasonably approximated by a normal curve. Under the same assumption of a normal c.d.f F(y) we may also use the guidelines concerning the standard deviation σ given by Hansen et al [1953; p. 136].[1)] These indicate that a sample size of $n = 50$ may be sufficient to ensure an approximately normal distribution of the sample statistic s.

Income distributions in the real world are, however, not even approximately symmetrical, but rather skewed to the right and highly leptokurtic ($\beta_4 >> 3$). With increasing skewness the convergence towards the limiting distribution will be detained. In sampling from a highly skewed distribution the extreme incomes of the upper tail, though rare, have usually considerable effects on the resulting sampling distribution even for moderately large samples. Extreme incomes are only sporadically included in a simple random sample

1) Hansen et al use the relative (asymptotic) standard error of the estimate s as a benchmark suggesting that if the sample size is large enough for this magnitude to fall short of 0.1, the limiting distribution provides a reasonably close approximation for most practical purposes.

of a moderate size, but once occurring they tend to increase the estimate of the inequality measure dramatically. Hence, the sampling distribution will be skewed to the right and a confidence interval $T_n \pm z_{\alpha/2}\{V(T_n)\}^{\frac{1}{2}}$ will tend to fall to the right (left) of the population value θ of the inequality index with a probability exceeding (falling short of) $\alpha/2$.

From this discussion it can be concluded that very large samples may be needed to justify an application of the asymptotic results. As regards the Gini coefficient, the maximum equalization ratio, and Theil´s first inequality measure McDonald and Jensen [1979] found, through the use of Monte Carlo methods, that sample sizes of 1 000 or larger are required to obtain approximately normal sampling distributions if the population is gamma distributed. Using the crude rule of Hansen et al [1953] we conclude that if $\beta_4 = 500$, a not implausible value, more than 12 000 observations would be necessary for a normal approximation of the distribution of the sample standard deviation.[1)]

In Nygård [1981] Monte Carlo methods were used to obtain sampling distributions for the estimates of nine different inequality indexes (the absolute mean difference, the Gini coefficient, the variance, the squared coefficient of variation, Kolm´s centrist measure with $\xi = 0$, Atkinson´s inequality measure, the mean deviation, the maximum equalization ratio, and the log-variance). The samples were drawn from the distribution of household incomes in Finland 1971 (cf. chapter 2), a leptokurtic distribution with $\beta_4 = 485$, and included $n = 500$ and $n = 1\,000$ observations. The resulting sampling distributions for the Gini coefficient, Atkinson´s measure with ε $(= 1-\eta) = 2.0$, the maximum equalization ratio, and the log-variance are reproduced in figure 10.1. All sampling distributions in this study exhibit positive skewness and particularly striking are the ill-conditioned distributions associated with the variance (and the related squared coefficient of variation)

1) Kish [1965; p. 289] refers to an investigation of U.S. incomes showing the kurtosis $\beta_4 = 80\,000$ (!), implying that a normal approximation would require a sample of size $n = 2\,000\,000$.

Figure 10.1 Sampling distributions for estimates of the Gini coefficient, Atkinson's measure ($\varepsilon = 2.0$), the maximum equalization ratio, and the log-variance.
The distributions are based on 1 000 independent samples of size $n = 500$ and $n = 1\,000$.

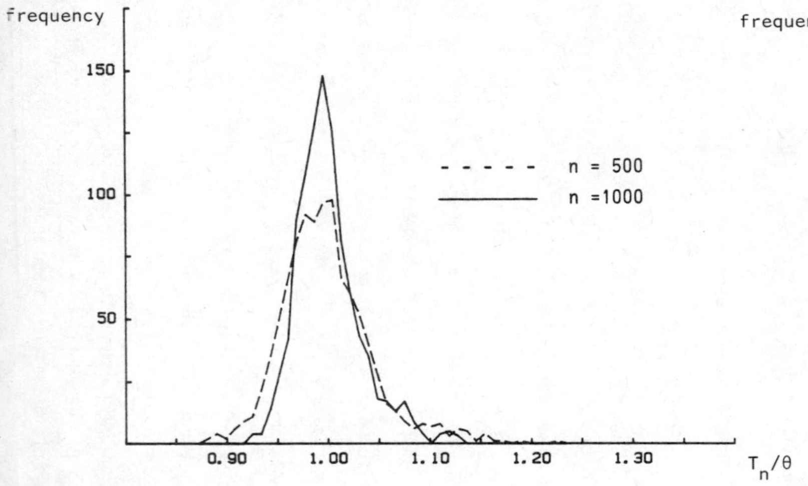

Sample size	n = 500	n = 1 000
Estimates, T_n		
- mean	0.3252	0.3259
- standard deviation	0.0146	0.0106
Population value of the inequality index	$\theta = 0.3258$	

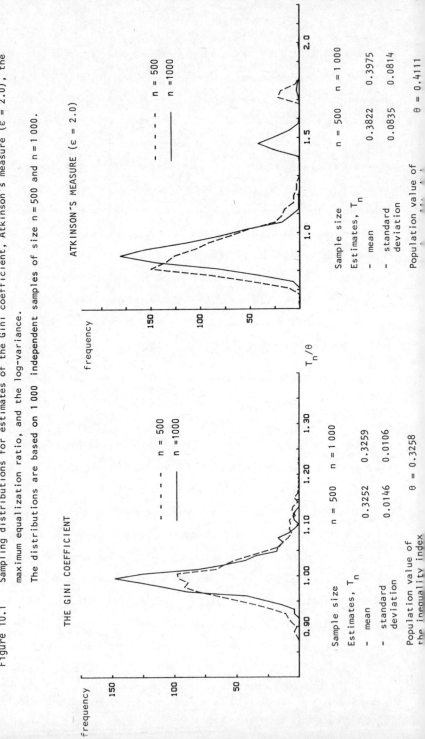

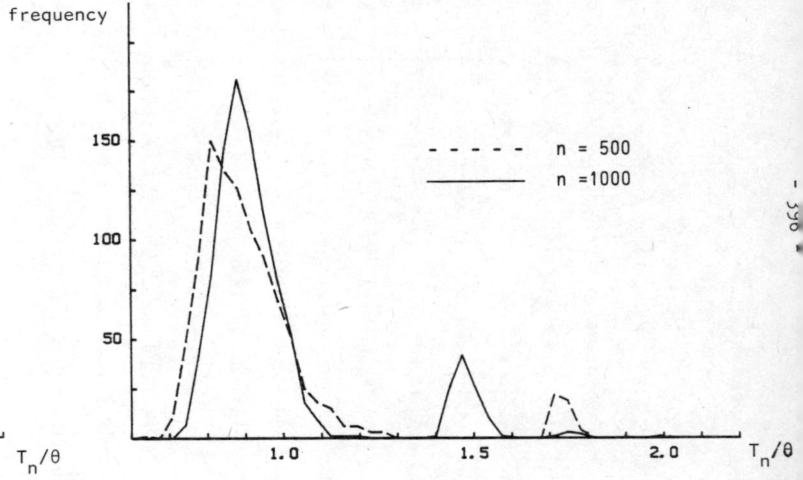

Sample size	n = 500	n = 1 000
Estimates, T_n		
- mean	0.3822	0.3975
- standard deviation	0.0835	0.0814
Population value of	$\theta = 0.4111$	

Figure 10.1 (cont.)

THE MAXIMUM EQUALIZATION RATIO

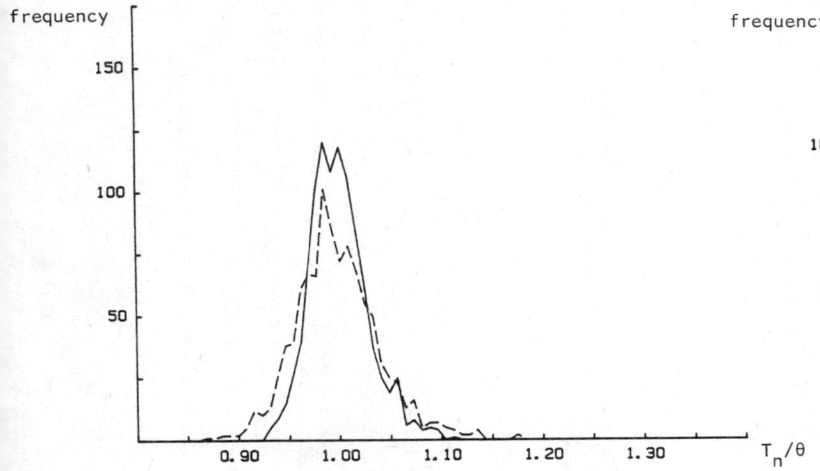

Sample size	n = 500	n = 1 000
Estimates, T_n		
- mean	0.2312	0.2317
- standard deviation	0.0096	0.0066
Population value of the inequality index	θ = 0.2317	

THE LOG-VARIANCE

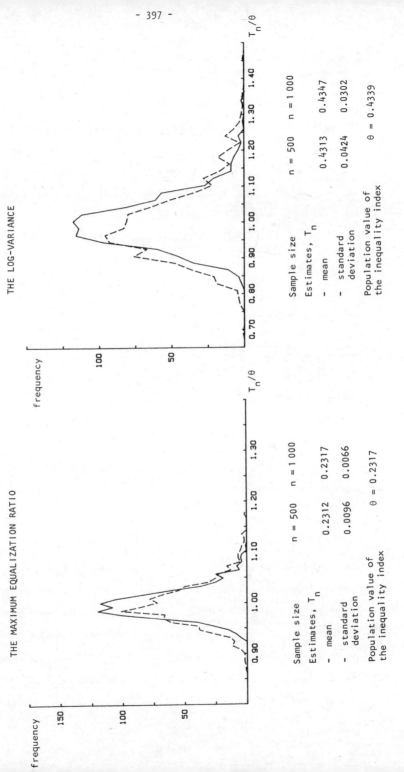

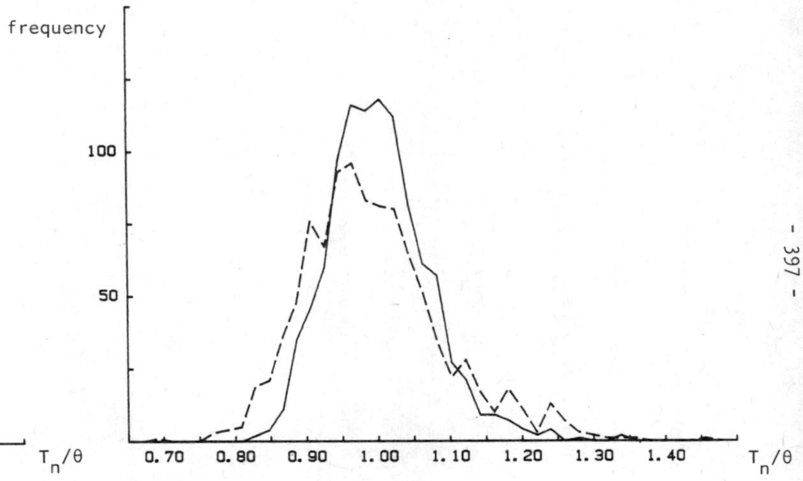

Sample size	n = 500	n = 1 000
Estimates, T_n		
- mean	0.4313	0.4347
- standard deviation	0.0424	0.0302
Population value of the inequality index	θ = 0.4339	

and the Atkinson index (and the related centrist measure of Kolm). For the other five measures studied normal approximations of the sampling distributions may be used for $n = 1\,000$ without any fatal loss of accuracy.
In comparing the relative variability of the four pairs of AI and RI measures the tentative conclusion emerged that the estimators of the RI measures exhibit a lower rel-variance than the corresponding AI estimator. This is coherent with the expectation of a positive covariance between the AI statistics and the sample mean when sampling from a population skewed to the right.

Assessing the variance

Having a large simple random sample the variance associated with an estimate may be computed according to the methods outlined in section 10.1. The computational efforts involved in this are however considerable - just look at formula (10.5) or (10.9) - and hence the researcher is frequently compelled to seek 'quick and easy' alternatives in assessing the variance. In this section we briefly review some calculation methods found in standard textbooks on survey sampling.

Subsampling

Computing labor can be substantially reduced by selecting a random subsample from the original sample and assessing the variance from this. Suppose, for instance, that the asymptotic variance, $v^2(\theta)$, associated with an estimate T_n of the inequality index θ is to be calculated and that $v^2(T_n)$ provides a strongly consistent estimate of $v^2(\theta)$ (cf. lemma 10.3). At our disposal we have a random sample of size $n = 2000$. Instead of using $v^2(T_{2000})$ as an estimate of $v^2(\theta)$ we may select a random subsample of, say, 100 observations

and base the variance estimation on $v^2(T_{100})$.
This method can easily be extended to the case of k independent subsamples: For each subsample we calculate the variance and take the mean of these as our final variance estimate.[1)] Hence, in our illustration we could use $\frac{1}{8}\Sigma v^2(T_{100,i})$ as a final approximation to $v^2(\theta)$, where $v^2(T_{100,i})$, $i = 1,..,8$, denote the estimated variances from 8 independent subsamples, each consisting of 100 observations.
The practability of the subsampling approach is however restricted by the evident fact that the resulting variance estimates may involve considerable bias.

The jackknife method

This method is based on the idea that the variability of a statistic can empirically be quantified by examining how much the statistic changes when observations are erased from the sample. See e.g. Cox and Hinkley [1974].
Let $T_n = T_n(y_1,y_2,..,y_n)$ denote the estimator of interest and define $T_{n-1}^{(i)}$ as the value of the estimate when y_i is deleted from the sample,

$T_{n-1}^{(i)} = T_{n-1}(y_1,..,y_{i-1},y_{i+1},..,y_n)$.

The variance, $V(T_{n-1})$, of the estimate T_{n-1} based on n-1 observations may now be calculated as

$$\hat{V}(T_{n-1}) = \sum_{i=1}^{n} \{T_{n-1}^{(i)} - T_{n-1}^{(.)}\}^2, \qquad (10.16)$$

where $T_{n-1}^{(.)} = \frac{1}{n}\Sigma T_{n-1}^{(i)}$. After a sample size modification we obtain the estimate

$$\hat{V}(T_n) = \frac{n-1}{n}\hat{V}(T_{n-1}) = \frac{n-1}{n}\sum_{i=1}^{n} \{T_{n-1}^{(i)} - T_{n-1}^{(.)}\}^2. \qquad (10.17)$$

1) In the case of the Gini coefficient this reduces the number of computations (additions and multiplications) involved in calculating the variance $v^2(R_N)$ (cf. p. 384) with, approximately, a factor $1 - k^{-2}$, i.e. a split of the sample into two subsamples results in 75 per cent less computational labor.

It can be shown (see Efron and Stein [1981]) that the jackknife estimate of variance (10.16) is nonnegatively biased $E(\hat{V}(T_{n-1})) \geq V(T_{n-1})$, and hence conservative in expectation, for any estimator symmetric in its arguments. The modified estimate (10.17) possesses nice large sample properties (see Thorburn [1975]) and, although it is not generally true that $\hat{V}(T_n)$ is conservative in expectation, $E(\hat{V}(T_n)) \geq V(T_n)$ holds if T_n is included in the family of U-statistics, which is, for example, the case of the absolute mean difference.

The computing labor may further be reduced by using an incomplete version of the jackknife estimator of variance: By sequential deletion of k observations from the original (unordered) sample we compute the statistics

$T_{n-k}^{(i)} = T_{n-k}(y_1,\dots,y_{ik-k},y_{ik+1},\dots,y_n)$.

If $p = n/k$ is an integer we obtain p such estimates of θ with mean $T_{n-k}^{(.)} = \frac{1}{p}\Sigma T_{n-k}^{(i)}$ and $V(T_n)$ may be approximated as

$$\hat{V}(T_n) = \frac{p-1}{p}\sum_{i=1}^{p}\{T_{n-k}^{(i)} - T_{n-k}^{(.)}\}^2.$$

See Thorburn [1975].

More complex sample designs

Most sample surveys on income differences violate the assumption of unrestricted simple random sampling. Operative economic sample designs frequently use stratification and clustering.[1] This naturally affects the reliability of sample statistics, and, more important, an assessment of the sampling variation is restrained by, sometimes formidable, theoretical obstacles.

1) In this context we will ignore the difficulty introduced by sampling without replacement. In practice the sample sizes are usually small in relation to the size of the entire population and the estimation may be carried out without any greater loss of accuracy as if the sample had been selected with replacement. However, if the sampling fraction is high, this difficulty should be properly attended.

Consider for instance the relatively uncomplicated design of stratified element sampling (simple random sampling within strata), in which case the estimation may be carried out largely in line with the decomposition procedures discussed in section 9.1. The sampling error of the 'within-group' estimates of inequality can be calculated according to the methods of simple random sampling. An assessment of the variability of the compound estimate, including an estimate of 'between-group' inequality, is however more exacting, since the 'within-group' and 'between-group' estimates are not independent. With more complex sampling schemes the difficulties involved in estimating the sampling errors increase rapidly.
Essentially the following three alternatives of handling the variability of complex samples are available (see Kish and Frankel [1970]).

(1) To omit computing and presenting standard errors - apparently in waiting for the possible development of the extremely intricate distribution theory needed for a sound treatment of the variability in complex samples.

(2) To compute the standard errors as if a simple random sample had been selected.

(3) To use experimental methods, whose properties are not fully known, in computing the standard errors.

The first alternative, representing current practice, is clearly unsatisfactory. Since more sophisticated sampling schemes, properly used, are more efficient than pure random sampling, it may be argued that the second alternative could be used to obtain upper bounds for the sampling errors. This would indeed be the fact if the sampler really took pains to accomplish good estimates of inequality indexes. In practice, however, the primary aim of income surveys is usually to acquire a reliable picture of the main part of the income distribution. As a consequence of this more extreme incomes, crucial for the estimation of inequality measures, tend to be under-represented in the sample and for this reason the sampling errors of the inequality estimates may well exceed those calculated on the basis of simple random assumptions. Empirical evidence of standard errors exceeding the simple random case is presented in Love and Wolfson [1976].

In complex samples natural estimates of inequality measures are obtained from the sample counterparts to the discrete measures of chapter 8 by giving the raising factor of each income, indicating the number of i.r.u's in the population to which the sample observation corresponds, a frequency interpretation.1) Thus, when considering, say, the (absolute) mean difference we may use the estimate $T_n = \Sigma\Sigma|y_i - y_j|f_i f_j/(\Sigma f_i)^2$, where f_i, $i=1,..,n$, denote the raising factors.
An important point to be noted is that many inequality index estimators of this type may be expected to have normal limiting distributions. In the case of stratified element sampling this follows immediately from an extension of lemma 10.2 (see Rao [1973; p.387]) and the decomposition procedure.

To demonstrate the possibility of basing standard error estimates on experimental methods we will briefly discuss the method of balanced repeated replications (BRR) suggested by Kish and Frankel [1970].
Suppose that the original sample, S, from which the estimate $T = T(S)$ of θ is calculated (omitting for simplicity the subscript n of the estimator) is the compound of two primary equisized independent random selections from each of H strata.2) From the sample S, consisting of H pairs of replicates, we then

1) In stratified element sampling the raising factor simply equals the inverse of the sampling fraction in the stratum from which the observation is drawn.

2) If the sample is selected with stratified element sampling we can artificially obtain a similar initial sample by randomly splitting the observations of each stratum into two equisized groups (see Love and Wolfson [1976]).

select one replicate to represent each stratum and in this way obtain the half-sample S_i. The other H subsamples, one from each stratum, constitute the associated complementary half-sample S_i^*. From the half-samples we calculate the estimates $T_i = T(S_i)$ and $T_i^* = T(S_i^*)$ of θ and form the statistic

$$\hat{T}_i = \frac{1}{2}(T_i + T_i^*).$$

As there are 2^{H-1} distinct pairs of half-samples and associated complements in all, each replicating (except for size) the selection and - through T_i, T_i^*, and $\hat{T}_i$ - the estimation process underlying the estimate T, we may try to quantify the sample variation of T by examining the variability of $\hat{T}_i$ over different half-samples. It is easily seen that $\frac{1}{4}(T_i - T_i^*)^2$ gives an unbiased estimate of the variance of $\hat{T}_i$, and averaging over k repetitions of the process we get the estimator

$$\hat{V}(\hat{T}_i) = \frac{1}{4k} \sum_{j=1}^{k} (T_j - T_j^*)^2 \qquad (10.18)$$

for $V(\hat{T}_i)$. More important, (10.18) may also be expected to yield useful estimates of the variance V(T) itself. The rationale for this is that $\hat{T}_i$ may be used as a close approximation of T - if the estimator is linear we in fact have $\hat{T}_i = T$ for every $i=1,..,2^{H-1}$ - and if $\hat{V}(\hat{T}_i)$ gives precise estimates of $V(\hat{T}_i)$ it should also give reasonable estimates of V(T).
To reduce the number k of repetitions needed to obtain a reliable estimate $\hat{V}(\hat{T}_i)$ Kish and Frankel [1970] suggest the use of orthogonal balancing based on $k = H+1$ repetitions. In the linear case this produces estimates of the variance equal to the estimate obtained from all 2^{H-1} possible repetitions.

The appropriateness of the BRR method is crucially dependent on the stability of the k estimates $\hat{T}_i$, or more precisely on the magnitudes $e_i = \hat{T}_i - T$, $i=1,..,k$, which should always be approximately zero. Before any application of BRR standard errors these magnitudes should be carefully checked.[1)]

1) This involves the calculation of T_i and T_i^*, $i=1,..,k$, which in inself may provide useful information about the distribution of the estimates.

11. WHAT HAVE WE ACHIEVED?

Let us now briefly look back upon the previous examination.
In chapter 1 we set out by declaring that the main purpose of the study is to characterize an income distribution with respect to its inequality. To this end the primary conditions of inequality comparisons were examined and a number of reasonable criteria on an inequality measure were set up (chapters 3-4). In chapters 5-8 a variety of measures were exposed and chapters 9 and 10 dealt with the important topics of decomposition and sampling, respectively. The analysis has been carried out wholly within the statical framework.

So far little has been said about the highly significant issue of the comparative aspect of inequality measurement. For instance, different inequality measures may well result in incompatible rankings of a set of income distributions. If so, which ranking should be regarded as revealing the 'true' inequality preferences of the community in question?

Particularly in the previous parts of the study we have mostly imposed ceteris paribus conditions. One may now ask: Which measure of inequality is the most appealing one under these circumstances ?
Quite naturally no single measure can reflect all aspects of an income distribution, only summarize it to a certain extent. The choice of an appropriate measure is obviously conditioned by the scope of the distributional study in question (cf ch 1), but may nevertheless be facilitated by considering some reasonable criteria that the measure should fulfil. The properties of a number of inequality measures are summarized in table 11.1.

The results of the preceding chapters suggest the following conjectures.

□□ If the main purpose is to compare inequality over **a period** of time within a society or between two or more societies the criteria of chapter 4 are highly significant.

First and foremost it must be recognized that our discussion has been based on the symmetry assumption (SYM of sec. 4.2) and setting this aside will have far-reaching consequences. Since no convenient substitute for the SYM is available, this once again stresses the fact that the i.r.u's must be properly defined so that there is no reason for a differentiated treatment of them.

The part of the distribution which a measure reflects is another aspect not to be neglected when considering different measures. In this context it may be argued that the lower part of the income distribution (low incomes) or at least the extreme parts (low and high incomes) should be our major concern.

A discussion of how different parts of the distribution affect an inequality measure is clearly interlinked with the principle of transfers (TRANSF in sec. 4.2, INET in sec. 7.4). If we wish an inequality measure to be more sensitive to changes among the poor than among the rich we have to seek among measures fulfilling some stronger version of the principle of transfers (DIMTRANSF in sec. 4.8, DINET in sec. 7.4).

As an example we look at measures based on weighted Lorenz areas. The Gini coefficient has a constant weight and hence it does not follow DINET. On the other hand, Mehran´s and Bonferroni´s measures give higher weights to the lower part of the Lorenz area than to the upper. This implies, cf. sec. 7.4, that DINET is fulfilled. In this respect

Table 11.1 A summary of some inequality measures fulfillment of certain criteria. Some measures fulfill the criterion MINNORM, of sec. 4.8, i.e. the lower bound zero is obtained when the EGAL distribution is present. Since LDOM is fulfilled the upper bounds are obtained for the CON distribution. The measures also fulfill the property of infinitesimal non-egalitarian transfer (INET).
All measures below are relative invariant (RI-)measures, i.e. they fulfill criterion PROPORTION but not ADO (cf. sec. 4.3 and 4.8).

Discussions about decomposibility is given in ch. 9 and discussions about the sampling properties is given in ch. 10. For definitions of the measures and details, see e.g. sec. 7.4.

* = the criterion is fulfilled -- = the criterion is not fulfilled

Measures	Criteria: Range	SYM	Principle of transfer	LDOM	REPLIC	Decomposition by: Subgroups into within-term and Between	Across	Income sources	Sampling properties	The measure gives highest weight to
• SD-class										
inequality measures										
RSMAX	[0,∞[	*	INET	*	*	*	--	--	-	--
SMAXN	[0,1]	*	INET	*	*	*	--	--	-	--
Gini, R	[0,1]	*	INET	*	*	--	*	*	sec. 10.2-3	extreme inc.
Mehran, M	[0,1]	*	$DINET_p$	*	*	--	*	*	sec. 10.2	low incomes
Piesch, P	[0,1]	*	INET	*	*	--	*	*	sec. 10.2	high incomes
Bonferroni, B	[0,1]	*	$DINET_p$	*	*	--	--	*	-	low incomes
de Vergottini, dV	[0,∞[	*	INET	*	*	--	--	*	-	high incomes
squared coefficient of variation, V^2	[0,∞[	*	INET	*	*	*	--	*	sec.10.2-3	high incomes
the sum of Theil's measures, T_1+T_2	[0,∞[	*	$DINET_\tau$	*	*	*	--	--	-	low incomes

Measures	Criteria									The measure gives highest weight to
	Range	SYM	Principle of transfer	LDOM	REPLIC	Decomposition by			Sampling properties	
						Subgroups into within-term and		Income sources		
						Between	Across			
transformed equality measure										
Kolm's relative centrist										
$K_c^r(\xi,\varepsilon)$										
$\xi>0, \varepsilon>0, \neq 1$	[0,1]	*	$DINET_\tau$	*	*	--	--	--	sec. 10.2	depends on ε (low incomes if ε high)
$\xi=0, \varepsilon>0, \neq 1$	[0,1]	*	$DINET_\tau$	*	*	--	--	--	sec. 10.2	"
(Atkinson)										
$\varepsilon = 1$										
exponential										
$\xi > 0$	[0,∞[	*	$DINET_\tau$	*	*	--	--	--	sec. 10.2	low incomes
$\xi = 0$	[0,1]	*	$DINET_\tau$	*	*	--	--	--	sec. 10.2	low incomes
(Champernowne's)										
Logarithmic										
$\xi > 0$	$[0, \log(1+\frac{\mu}{\xi})]$	*	$DINET_\tau$	*	*	*	--	--	sec. 10.2	low incomes
$\xi = 0$, T_2	[0,∞[	*	$DINET_\tau$	*	*	*	--	--	sec. 10.2	low incomes
• LSD-class										
inequality measure										
T_1	[0,∞[	*	$DINET_\tau$	*	*	*	--	--	sec. 10.2	extreme incomes
• ESD-class										
Kolm's relative leftist										
$K_\ell^r(\alpha)$	[0,1]	*	$DINET_\tau$	*	*	--	--	--	-	low incomes

they may be preferred to the Gini coefficient.[1)]

On the other hand, if we are most concerned with high incomes the measures of Piesch and de Vergottini may be considered more appropriate.

Other measures like Kolm´s (Atkinson´s) include an optional 'inequality aversion parameter' that may be chosen to direct attention to certain parts of the distribution.

The principle of transfers (or equivalently, Lorenz domination) is the principal criterion of strict inequality rankings. It may therefore be used as a decisive argument when considering different measures. However, one problem which frequently arises is that of intersecting Lorenz curve - in which case the principle of transfers is too weak a measure for determining a proper course of action. Specifically, which income distribution is to be judged as the more equal of two distributions having the same Lorenz areas (Gini coefficients)? In these cases measures like those above, adopting a varying weighting scheme, may prove advantageous.

In this context the additional problems of assessing inequality on a sample basis should not be overlooked.

1) To overcome this "shortcoming" of the Gini coefficient ,R, Hagerbaumer [1977] introduced the minor concentration ratio, MCR, as a complement to the ordinary R.The MCR is a relative "poverty-measure" and related to the extreme interpretation of R given in sec. 7.4.1.

- If the purpose is to analyze the effect of income differences between subpopulations (e.g. between socio-economic groups) we could choose a measure that is easy to decompose. According to sec. 9.1.1 the most attractive ones from the point of view of simplicity are

  The squared coefficient of variation, V^2

  Theil's 1st measure, T_1

  Theil's 2nd measure, T_2

  The quasi-variance, ${}_q^2$

  The first three measures are additively decomposable implying a condition of isolated subgroups, i.e. inequalities across groups are a priori precluded. On the other hand, if the eligible decomposition of an inequality measure should include an across term, then the simplest measure with this property is

  The Gini coefficient, R.

- If the main purpose of the study is to analyze the effect of different income sources on the inequality of the distribution of available income we could choose among the following measures.

Measure		gives highest weight to	definition
Mehran's,	M	low incomes	sec. 9.2
Bonferroni's	B	low incomes	sec. 9.2
Gini coefficient	R	extreme incomes	sec. 9.2
Piesch	P	high incomes	sec. 9.2
de Vergottini	dV	high incomes	sec. 9.2
Squared coefficient of variation	V^2	high incomes	sec. 9.2

It should be noted that the measures listed above are only suggestions - <u>the purpose</u> of the income survey in question is always the main determinant when choosing a proper measure of inequality.

Note also that, according to the earlier discussion, the method of comparing two income distributions is in one way an *indirect method*, since we consider the two distributions separately and compare two values of an inequality **index**.
A more *direct method* would be to study the distributions simultaneously. Two such methods will be discussed in a formal way in the next chapter.

12. SIMULTANEOUS COMPARISON OF INCOME DISTRIBUTIONS

The most frequently used method of comparing income distributions with respect to their inequality is by means of an inequality measure applied on the distributions separately. This method is indirect.

A direct method would be to study the two distributions simultaneously. In this chapter we will discuss in a formal way two such methods, the first involving the Gini-across inequality (cf. sec. 9.1.1) as a simultaneous measure. It will be seen that Dagum's [1980] 'economic distance ratio' is directly related to this. The second method is based on the comparative function proposed by Malmquist [1970].

12.1 THE INEQUALITY ACROSS TWO DISTRIBUTIONS

In sec. 9.1 we decomposed the inequality measures by subgroups into a within-group term and an across/between-group term, where the between group term is a function of the arithmetic mean incomes μ_j, $j = 1,2,\ldots, k$, and the across term measures the deviation 'between' incomes from different groups.

If we consider the income distributions of two populations and decompose the inequality measure of their compound distribution ($I(y)_c$) into a within- and an across-group term, it can be written as

$$I(y)_c = w_1(f_1,f_{11})I(y)_1 + w_2(f_2,f_{12})I(y)_2 + u(f_1,f_2,f_{11},f_{12})I(y)_{12},$$

where the weights w_1, w_2 and u are functions of population and income shares.

By the indirect method, mentioned earlier, we consider whether the difference $I(y)_2 - I(y)_1$ is greater than zero or not[1]. A direct method is to consider the across-inequality $I(y)_{12}$. One measure that has the property of being decomposable into within- and across-group terms is the Gini-coefficient, R, which can be written as

$$R_c = f_1f_{11}R_{11} + f_2f_{12}R_{22} + (f_1f_{12} + f_2f_{11})R_{12} = \qquad \text{(from (9.11))}$$

(12

$$= f_1f_{11}R_{11} + f_2f_{12}R_{22} + (f_1f_{12}R^r_{12} + f_2f_{11}R^r_{21}), \qquad \text{(from (9.12))}$$

1) This is wrongly discussed for the Gini coefficient by Piesch [1975 - pp.51-52 and De Simoni [1967].

where

$$(\mu_1 + \mu_2)R_{12} = \mu_2 R^r_{12} + \mu_1 R^r_{21} = \int_0^\infty \{F(y)_1[1 - F(y)_2] + $$

$$+ F(y)_2[1 - F(y)_1]\}dy \tag{12.2}$$

The ordinary Gini coefficient, R, can be written as

$$R = (2\mu)^{-1} \; E(|Y - X|) = (2\mu)^{-1} \int_0^\infty \int_0^\infty |y - x| dF(x) dF(y),$$

i.e. as a function of the expected value of the absolute difference between two randomly selected incomes, X and Y, from the same distribution. In a similar way we can define the expected value of the absolute income differences between two incomes, Y_1 and Y_2, one randomly selected from population 1 and one from population 2. Denoting this $E(|Y_2 - Y_1|)$ it is readily seen that

$$E(|Y_2 - Y_1|) = \int_0^\infty \int_0^\infty |Y_2 - Y_1| dF(y)_1 dF(y)_2 =$$

$$= \int_0^\infty \{F(y)_1[1 - F(y)_2] + F(y)_2[1 - F(y)_1]\}dy, \tag{12.3}$$

where $F(y)_i$, $i = 1,2$, denotes the c.d.f.'s of population i, i = 1,2. Hence the Gini across-inequality may be written as

$$R_{12} = E(|Y_2 - Y_1|)/(\mu_2+\mu_1) = qR^r_{12}+(1-q)R^r_{21} = q(R^r_{12}-R^r_{21})+R^r_{21}, \tag{12.4}$$

where $q = \mu_2/(\mu_2 + \mu_1)$. This magnitude has the properties (cf. sec. 9.1.1):

(i) symmetry, i.e. $R_{12} = R_{21}$,

(ii) if the distributions are identical, i.e. $F(y)_1 = F(y)_2$, then $R_{11} = R_{22} = R_{12}$ and hence the across inequality equals the inequality within the populations,

(iii) $0 \leq R_{12} \leq 1$,

(iv) if the distributions are non-overlapping then $R_{12} = \frac{\mu_2 - \mu_1}{\mu_2 + \mu_1}$, (assuming $\mu_2 > \mu_1$)

(v) if $F(y)_1$ equals the EGAL-distribution, defined in sec. 7.4, then

$$R_{12} = \left(\frac{\mu_2 - \mu_1}{\mu_2 + \mu_1} \right) + F(\mu_1)_2 - \frac{2\mu_2}{\mu_2 + \mu_1} F_1(\mu_1)_2$$

where we have assumed without loss of generality that $\mu_2 \geq \mu_1$.

If both distributions are EGAL-distributions with equal arithmetic mean incomes, $\mu_1 = \mu_2$, then R_{12} obtains its lower bound zero (property (iii)). On the other hand if $\mu_2 > \mu_1$ then $R_{12} = (\mu_2 - \mu_1)/(\mu_2 + \mu_1)$ (from property (iv)). One possible disadvantage of R_{12} is that it equals $(\mu_2 - \mu_1)/(\mu_2 + \mu_1)$, whenever the distributions are non-overlapping independent of their shape. In accordance with sec. 9.1.1, the inequality across two populations can be subdivided into the sum of a between-population term and an interaction term. The between term is defined by (9.15) as

$$R_{B12} = |\mu_2 - \mu_1| / (\mu_2 + \mu_1)$$

and hence the interaction term equals (cf. (9.16))

$$R_{I12} = (\mu_2 + \mu_1)^{-1} \{E(|Y_2 - Y_1|) - |\mu_2 - \mu_1|\}.$$

This last term measures the degree of how much two distributions overlap. If the distributions are non-overlapping R_{I12} equals zero and hence $R_{12} = R_{B12}$, cf. property (iv) above.

By property (v) we see that if $F(y)_1$ eqúals the EGAL and $\mu_2 = \mu_1$ then $R_{12} = F(\mu_2)_2 - F_1(\mu_2)_2$ = MER, i.e. the maximum equalization ratio of income distribution 2, cf. sec. 7.4.4. The upper bound of R_{12} (property (iii) is obtained when both distributions are equal to the CON (cf. sec. 7.4).Since $(\mu_2 + \mu_1)R_{12}$ equals $\mu_1 R^r_{21} + \mu_2 R^r_{12}$ and $\mu_1 R^r_{21}$, inturn, equals by substitution and partial integration $\mu_2 R^r_{12} - (\mu_2 - \mu_1)$, we can write R_{12} as

$$R_{12} = \frac{2\mu_2}{(\mu_2+\mu_1)} R^r_{21} - \left(\frac{\mu_2-\mu_1}{\mu_2+\mu_1} \right) \qquad (12.5)$$

Dagum [1980] proposed two inequality measures for comparison of income distributions. In the sequel we will show that one of these measures is only a function of the Gini-across, R_{12}.

The two measures were a 'head-count' measure (d_o) and an income inequality measure (d_1), defined under the assumption that $\mu_2 > \mu_1$ 1), by

$$d_o = \int_0^\infty F(y)_1 dF(y)_2 \qquad (12.6a)$$

and

$$d_1 = \mu_2 \int_0^\infty F(y)_1 dF_1(y)_2 - \mu_1 \int_0^\infty F_1(y)_1 dF(y)_2 \qquad (12.6a)$$

Only d_1 takes into account the relative incomes (through $F_1(y)$).

d_1, which is labelled an economic distance by Dagum [1980], can be rewritten as

$$d_1 = \mu_2 \int_0^\infty F(Y)_1 dF_1(y)_2 - \mu_1 \int_0^\infty [1 - F(y)_2] dF_1(y)_1 =$$

$$= \mu_2 R^r_{12} = \frac{1}{2} (\mu_2 + \mu_1) R_{12} + \frac{1}{2} (\mu_2 - \mu_1) \qquad (12.7)$$

where R^r_{12} and R_{12} are defined in sec. 9.1.1 and above.

1) In an earlier paper Dagum [1978] assumed $\tilde{\mu}_2 > \tilde{\mu}_1$, where $\tilde{\mu}_i$, i=1,2,is the median.

An economic distance ratio is defined by Dagum [1980 - p. 1794] as

$$D_1 = \frac{d_1 - \min d_1}{\max d_1 - \min d_1}$$

where $\max d_1$ is the unconditional expectation of the absolute 'mean difference' $E(|Y_2-Y_1|)$ and $\min d_1$ is given when Y_2 and Y_1 are independent and identically distributed. It can be shown that (cf. Dagum [1980 - pp. 1794-1795]) $\max d_1 = E(|Y_2-Y_1|) = (\mu_2+\mu_1) R_{12}$ and $\min d_1 = \max d_1/2$.

Using (12.7) we can now write the economic distance ratio as

$$D_1 = \frac{\mu_2 R^r_{12} - \frac{1}{2}(\mu_2 + \mu_1)R_{12}}{\frac{1}{2}(\mu_2 + \mu_1)R_{12}} = \frac{(\mu_2 - \mu_1)}{(\mu_2 + \mu_1)} R^{-1}_{12}, \qquad (12.8)$$

i.e. given the arithmetic mean incomes, $\mu_2 > \mu_1$, D_1 is completely determined by the Gini-across. By property (iv) above it follows that if the two distributions are non-overlapping ($\mu_2 > \mu_1$) then $D_1 = 1$ and if distribution 1 equals the EGAL then $D_1 = (\mu_2 - \mu_1)/[\mu_2 - \mu_1 + (\mu_2 + \mu_1)F(\mu_1)_2 - 2\mu_2 F_1(\mu_1)_2]$.

12.2 COMPARATIVE FUNCTIONS

The discussion in sec. 7.3 of using a distribution comparative function in inequality judgement will now be extended to the case of simultaneous comparison of two distributions. Having the same notations as in sec. 7.3 and distinguishing the two distributions using subscripts 1 and 2 we can compare their distribution comparative functions:

$$D(p)_2 - D(p)_1 = \{F_1^{-1}(p)_2 - F^{-1}(p)_2\} - \{F_1^{-1}(p)_1 - F^{-1}(p)_1\} =$$

$$= \{\mu_2\tau_1(p)_2 - \mu_1\tau_1(p)_1\} - \{\mu_2\tau(p)_2 - \mu_1\tau(p)_1\} \qquad (12.9a)$$

where $\tau_1(p)_i = F_1^{-1}(p)_i/\mu_i$, $\tau(p)_i = F^{-1}(p)_i/\mu_i$ and $F_1^{-1}(p)_i$ and $F^{-1}(p)$ are defined by (7.3). $F_1^{-1}(p)_i = F^{-1}(q)_i$;$i = 1,2$, where $q > p$, see figures 7.1 and 7.12.

The logarithmic variant is defined by

$$D_{log}(p)_2 - D_{log}(p)_1 = \log \frac{\tau_1(p)_2}{\tau_1(p)_1} - \log \frac{\tau(p)_2}{\tau(p)_1} \qquad (12.9b)$$

Before continuing the discussion we may notice the problem[1] arising from different mean incomes ($\mu_1 \neq \mu_2$ or $\mu_{g1} \neq \mu_{g2}$). The difference between the two distribution comparative functions in (12.9a) is sensitive to shifts in the mean incomes. This sensitiveness is more obvious when the above difference is written as

$$D(p)_2 - D(p)_1 = C_1(p) - C(p).$$

1) Under the assumption of criterion PROPORTION of sec. 4.2.

The right-side expression is a difference between two comparative functions, viz.

$$C_1(p) = \begin{cases} \mu_2\tau_1(p)_2 - \mu_1\tau_1(p)_1 & \text{in y-scale} \\ \log \dfrac{\tau_1(p)_2}{\tau_1(p)_1} + \log \dfrac{\mu_1}{\mu_2} & \text{in log y-scale} \end{cases}$$

and

$$C(p) = \begin{cases} \mu_2\tau(p)_2 - \mu_1\tau(p)_1 & \text{in y-scale} \\ \log \dfrac{\tau(p)_2}{\tau(p)_1} + \log \dfrac{\mu_1}{\mu_2} & \text{in log y-scale} \end{cases}$$

$C(p)$ is the comparative function proposed by Malmquist [1970], (cf. also Esberger and Malmquist [1972] and Cowell [1977]), and $C_1(p)$ is the equivalent comparative function defined on $G_1(y)_i$, $i = 1,2$, $G_1(y)_i = 1 - F_1(y)_i$, cf. sec. 7.3.1.

To circumvent the mean dependence we may inspect the standardized comparative functions, i.e. $C_1(p)$ and $C(p)$ measured over $\tau(p)$ (or $\log \tau(p)$). These *standardized comparative functions* are thus defined as

$$C_{1s}(p) = \begin{cases} \tau_1(p)_2 - \tau_1(p)_1 & \text{in y-scale} \quad (12.10a) \\ \log \dfrac{\tau_1(p)_2}{\tau_1(p)_1} & \text{in log y-scale} \quad (12.10b) \end{cases}$$

and

$$C_s(p) = \begin{cases} \tau(p)_2 - \tau(p)_1 & \text{in y-scale} \quad (12.11a) \\ \log \dfrac{\tau(p)_2}{\tau(p)_1} & \text{in log y-scale} \quad (12.11b) \end{cases}$$

Two comparative functions are outlined in figure 12.1. Their relation to the corresponding Lorenz Curves in figure 12.2 is immediate.

We denote $\tau(p) = \frac{F^{-1}(p)}{\mu}$ by z and consider the complementary c.d.f. and 1st m.d.f. $G(z)$ and $G_1(z)$, cf. sec. 7.1.4.

Both of the comparative functions can be decomposed in terms of *standardized* $E_{1s}(p)$ and $E_s(p)$ respectively, where $E_{1s}(p)$ is defined as $(\tau_1(p) - 1)$ in z-scale and $\log \tau_1(p)$ in log z-scale and $E_s(p)$ as $(\tau(p) - 1)$ in z-scale and $\log \tau(p)$ in log y-scale:

$$C_{1s}(p) = E_{1s}(p)_2 - E_{1s}(p)_1$$

$$C_s(p) = E_s(p)_2 - E_s(p)_1$$

Since the integrals of $E_s(p)_1$ and $E_s(p)_2$ are equal to zero it follows that $G(z)_1$ and $G(z)_2$ must intersect. This is not, in general, true for $G_1(z)_1$ and $G_1(z)_2$.

LOG SCALE

Consider now $G(z)_1$ and $G(z)_2$ on log z-scale (cf. figure 12.1). Absolute equality will be obtained for a distribution $G(z)$ if it follows the vertical line through $z = 1$ and comparing two distributions we will judge distribution 2 as more equal than distribution 1 if

$$\frac{dG(z_2)_2}{d \log z_2} < \frac{dG(z_1)_1}{d \log z_1} \ (< 0), \qquad (12.12)$$

conditional that $p = G(z_2)_2 = G(z_1)_1$, for every p.

(12.12) can be rewritten as $\frac{d \log z_2}{dG(z_2)_2} > \frac{d \log z_1}{dG(z_1)_1}$ which is equal to

$$\frac{dE_s(p)_2}{dp} > \frac{dE_s(p)_1}{dp} \qquad (12.13)$$

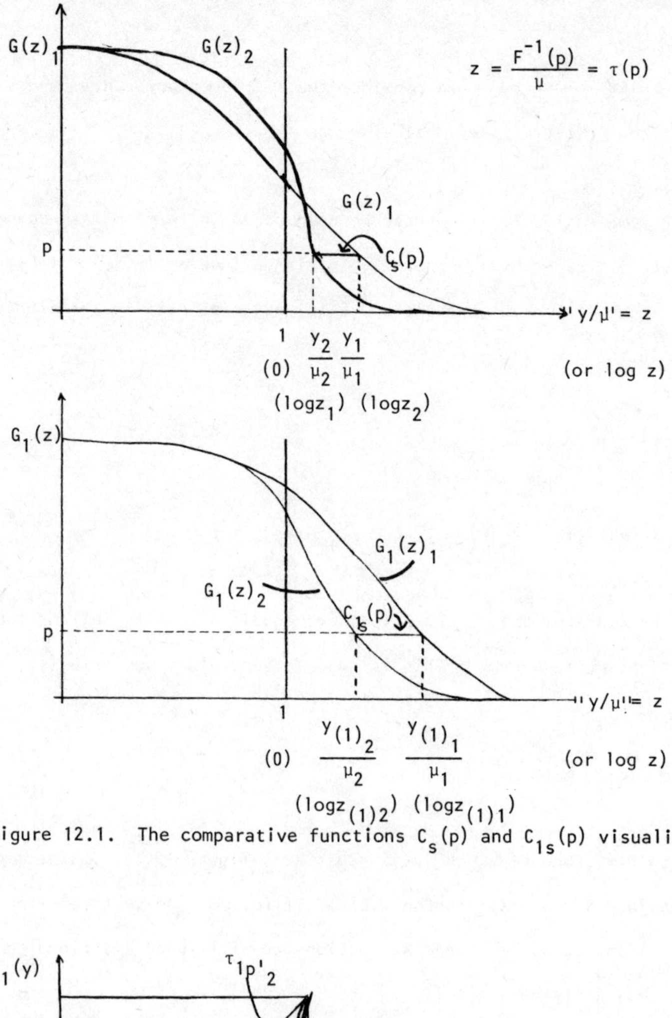

Figure 12.1. The comparative functions $C_s(p)$ and $C_{1s}(p)$ visualized.

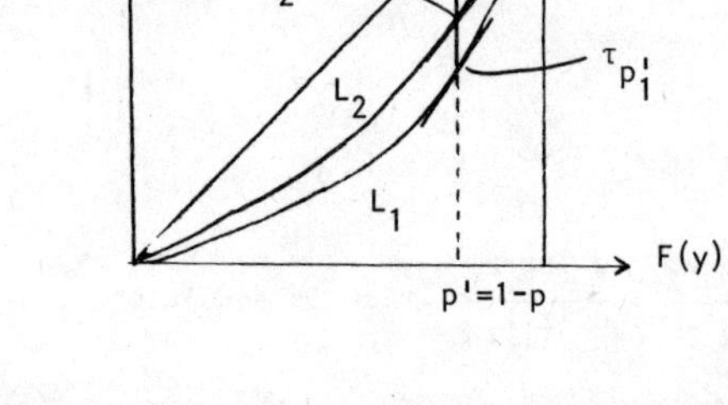

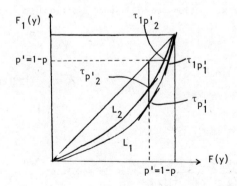

Figure 12.2. The Lorenz curves of income distributions $F(y)_2$ (L_2) and $F(y)_1 (L_1)$. L_2 Lorenz dominates L_1.

The last inequality, (12.13), can be transformed to equal

$$\frac{dC_s(p)}{dp} > 0 \qquad (12.14)$$

If this condition is fulfilled for $0 < p < 1$ then it is equivalent to the earlier statement : distribution 2 is judged as more equal than distribution 1. If $dC_s(p)/dp < 0$ we judge the first distribution as more equal than the second. Condition (12.14) is the standardized equivalent criterion for inequality judgement by Malmquist [1970].

The following relation between $dC_s(p)/dp$ and the corresponding Lorenz curves can be shown to hold (cf. Cowell [1977]):

* $\frac{dC_s(p)}{dp} > 0$ for $0 < p < 1 \Rightarrow$ distribution 2 is Lorenz-dominating over distribution 1

{ $\frac{dC_s(p)}{dp} < 0$ for $0 < p < 1 \Rightarrow$ distribution 1 is Lorenz-dominating over distribution 2}

Hence, if (12.14) is fulfilled, for $0<p<1$, then it implies Lorenz domination. Since the former criterion does not imply (12.14) we judge Lorenz domination as a weaker form of inequality (equality) judgement.

If a relation holds for the standardized comparative function, $C_s(p)$, it will also hold for the non-standardized comparative function, $C(p)$, since the former function can be expressed as the latter and a scale factor.

$$C_s(p) = C(p) - \log \frac{\mu_2}{\mu_1} .$$

If instead of considering $G(z)_1$ and $G(z)_2$ on log z-scale we consider $G_1(z)_1$ and $G_1(z)_2$ on z-scale we obtain the same results as above. On the other hand, if we use log z-scale, the equivalent expression for (12.14) will be (with the same 'equality'-argument as for $G(z)_1$ and $G(z)_2$) $\frac{dC_{1s}(p)}{dp} > 0$. This will not, of course, imply Lorens domination (or partial Lorenz domination) but instead it implies that

$$\int_0^{p'} z^2 dF(z)_1 < \int_0^{p'} z^2 dF(z)_2 .$$

The integral of $C_s(p)$ over the interval [0,1] equals zero $(C_s(p)=E_s(p)_2 - E_s(p)_1)$ when taken in y-scale. The difference between the Gini coefficient of two populations equals by definition

$$R_2 - R_1 = 2 \int_0^1 p\, C_s(p)dp.$$

BIBLIOGRAPHY

AGHEVLI, B.B. and MEHRAN, F. [1981]. Optimal Grouping of Income Distribution Data. JASA, Vol 76, 1981
AIGNER, D.J. and HEINS, A.J. [1967]. A Social Welfare View of the Measurement of Income Inequality. Rev. Income Wealth, Vol 13, 1967
AITCHINSON, J. and BROWN, J.A.C. [1954]. On the Criteria for Descriptions of Income Distribution. Metroeconomica, Vol 6, 1954
— [1957] The Lognormal Distribution. Cambridge University Press, Cambridge, 1957
ALKER, H.R.Jr. [1970]. Measuring Inequality. In 'The Quantitative Analysis of Social Problems', ed. E.R. Tufte, Addison-Wesley Publ Co, Reading, Massachusetts, 1970
ALLEN, R.G.D. [1975]. Index Numbers in Theory and Practice. Aldine Publ Co, Chicago, 1975
AMATO, V. [1948]. Sulla misura della concentrazione del redditi. Revista Italiana di Economia Demografica e Statistica, Vol 2, 1948
ANDRAE, von [1872]. Über die Bestimmung des wahrscheinlichen Fehlers durch die gegebenen Differenzen von m gleich genauen Beobachtungen einer Unbekannten. Astronomische Nachrichten, Bd 79, No 1889, 1872
ARROW, K. [1951, 1963]. Social Choice and Individual Value. Wiley, London, 1951 (2nd ed. 1963)
ATKINSON, A.B. [1970]. On the Measurement of Inequality. J. Econ. Theory, Vol 2, 1970
— [1975]. The Economics of Inequality. Oxford University Press, London, 1975

BARTELS, C.P.A. [1977]. Economic Aspects of Regional Welfare, Income Distribution and Unemployment. Martinus Nijhoff Social Sciences Division, Leiden, 1977
BARTELS, C.P.A. and VRIES, O.M. [1977]. Succint Analytical Descriptions of Income Distributions using Transformation Functions. Econ. Appl., Vol 30, 1977
BAUMOL, W.J. and BLINDER, A.S. [1979]. Economics, Principles and Policy. Harcourt Brace Jovanovich Inc, New York, 1979
BAXTER, M.A. [1980]. Minimum Variance Unbiased Estimation of the Parameters of the Pareto Distribution. Metrika, Vol 27, 1980
BELLETTINI, A. [1954]. Delle relazioni fra alcune constanti statistiche e la curvā di concentrazione. Statistica, Vol 14, 1954
BENTZEL, R. [1953]. Inkomstfördelningen i Sverige. Uppsala, 1953
— [1970]. The Social Significance of Income Distribution Statistics. Rev. Income Wealth, Vol 16, 1970
BHATTACHARYA, N. and MAHALANOBIS, B. [1967]. Regional Disparities in Consumption in India. JASA, Vol 62, 1967
BJERKE, K. [1970]. Income and Wage Distributions — Part I: A Survey of the Literature. Rev. Income Wealth, Vol 16, 1970
BLACKORBY, C. and DONALDSON, D. [1976]. Measures of Equality and their Meaning in Terms of Social Welfare. Discussion Paper No 76—20, Dept. of Economics, Univ. of British Columbia, June 1976
— [1977]. Utility vs Equity: Some Plausible Quasi-Orderings. J. Public Econ., Vol 7, 1977
— [1980]. A Theoretical Treatment of Indices of Absolute Inequality. Int. Econ. Rev., Vol 21, 1980
BLACKORBY, C., DONALDSON, D. and AUERSPERG, M. [1978]. Inequality within and

among Population Subgroups: Ethically Consistent Subindices. Discussion Paper No 78—36, Dept. of Economics, Univ. of British Columbia, October 1978

BLINDER, A.S. [1974]. Towards an Economic Theory of Income Distribution. MIT Press, Cambridge, Massachusetts, 1974

BLITZ, R.C. and BRITTAIN, J.A. [1964]. An Extension of the Lorenz Diagram to the Correlation of two Variables. Metron, Vol 23, 1964

BORTKIEWICZ, L. von [1930]. Die Disparitätsmasse der Einkommenstatistik. XIXe Session de l'institut International de Statistique, Haag, 1930.

BOURGUIGNON, F. [1979]. Decomposable Inequality Measures. Econometrica, Vol 47, 1979

BOWMAN, M.J. [1945]. A Graphical Analysis of Personal Income Distribution in the U.S. Amer. Econ. Rev., Vol 35, 1945

BRESCANI-TURRONI, C. [1910]. Di un indice misuratore della disuguaglianza nella distribuzione della riccezza. Studi in Onore di Biagio Brugi, Palermo, 1910

BRITTAIN, J.A. [1962]. Interpolation of Frequency Distributions of Aggregated Variables and Estimation of the Gini Concentration Measure. Metron, Vol 22, 1962

BROWN, H.P. [1968]. Pay and Profits. A.M. Kelley Publ., New York, 1968

— [1977]. The Inequality of Pay. Oxford University Press, Oxford, 1977

BROWN, J.A.C. [1976]. The Mathematical and Statistical Theory of Income Distribution. In 'The Personal Distribution of Income', ed. A.B. Atkinson, Allen and Unwin, London, 1976

CHAMPERNOWNE, D.G. [1937]. The Theory of Income Distribution. Report to the Oxford Meeting, Sept. 25—29 1936, Econometrica, Vol 5, 1937

— [1952]. The Graduation of Income Distributions. Econometrica, Vol 20, 1952

— [1953]. A Model of Income Distribution. Econ. J., Vol 63, 1953

— [1973]. The Distribution of Income Between Persons. Cambridge University Press, London, 1973

— [1974]. A Comparison of Measures of Inequality of Income Distributions. Econ. J., Vol 84, 1974

COWELL, F.A. [1977]. Measuring Inequality. Philip Allan Publ. Ltd, Oxford, 1977

— [1980]. On the Structure of Additive Inequality Measures. Rev. Econ. Stud., Vol 47, 1980

COX, D.R. and HINKLEY, D.V. [1974]. Theoretical Statistics. Chapman and Hall, London, 1974

CREEDY, J. [1977a]. Pareto and the Distribution of Income. Rev. Income Wealth, Vol 23, 1977

— [1977b]. The Principle of Transfers and the Variance of Logarithms. Oxford Bull. Econ. Statist., Vol 39, 1977

CREEDY, J., HART, P.E. and KLEVMARKEN, N.A. [1981]. Income Mobility in Great Britain and Sweden. In 'The Statics and Dynamics of income', eds. N.A. Klevmarken and J.A. Lybeck, Tieto Ltd, Clevedon, 1981

CRAMÉR, H. [1946]. Mathematical Methods of Statistics. Princeton University Press, Princeton, 1946

CRAMER, J.S. [1973]. Empirical Econometrics. North-Holland Publ. Co, Amsterdam, 1973 (first published in 1969)

DAGUM, C. [1977]. A New Model of Personal Income Distribution: Specification and Estimation. Econ. Appl., Vol 30, 1977

— [1978]. A Measure of Inequality between Income Distributions. Econ. Appl., Vol 31, 1978

— [1980]. Inequality Measures between Income Distributions with Applications. Econometrica, Vol 48, 1980
DALTON, H. [1920]. The Measurement of the Inequality of Income. Econ. J., Vol 30, 1920
DANZIGER, S. and TAUSSIG, M.K. [1979]. The Income Unit and the Anatomy of Income Distribution. Rev. Income Wealth, Vol 25, 1979
DASGUPTA, P., SEN, A. and STARRETT, D. [1973]. Notes on the Measurement of Income Inequality. J. Econ. Theory, Vol 6, 1973
DAVID, H.A. [1968]. Gini's Mean Difference Rediscovered. Biometrika, Vol 55, 1968
DAVIES, D.G. [1980]. Measurement of Tax Progressivity: Comment. Amer. Econ. Rev., Vol 70, 1980
DAVIS, H.T. [1941]. The Analysis of Economic Time Series. The Principia Press Inc, Bloomington, Indiana, 1941
DEBREU, G. [1959]. The Theory of Value. Wiley, New York, 1959
DE SIMONI, S. [1967]. Sulle relazioni tra il rapporto di concentrazione ed una funzione di dissomiglianza nello schema di graduazione. Statistica, Vol 27, 1967
DORFMAN, R. [1979]. A Formula for the Gini Coefficient. Rev. Econ. Statist., Vol 61, 1979

EFRON, B. and STEIN, C. [1981]. The Jackknife Estimate of Variance. Ann. Statist., Vol 9, 1981
ELTETÖ, Ö. and FRIGYES, E. [1968]. New Income Inequality Measures as Efficient Tools for Causal Analysis and Planning. Econometrica, Vol 36, 1968
ESBERGER, S.E. and MALMQUIST, S. [1972]. En statistisk studie av inkomstutvecklingen. Statistiska Centralbyrån och Bostadsstyrelsen, Monografiserie nr 8, Stockholm, 1972

FEI, J.C.H., RANIS, G. and KUO, S.W.Y. [1978]. Growth and the Family Distribution of Income by Factor Components. Quart. J. Econ., Vol 92, 1978
— [1979]. Growth with Equity, The Taiwan Case. Oxford University Press, New York, 1979
FELLMAN, J. [1976]. The Effect of Transformations on Lorenz Curves. Econometrica, Vol 44, 1976
— [1980]. Transformations and Lorenz Curves. Working Papers No 48, Swedish School of Economics and Business Administration, Helsinki, 1980
FIELDS, G.S. [1979a]. Decomposing LDC Inequalities. Oxford Econ. Papers, Vol 31, 1979
— [1979b]. Income Inequality in Urban Columbia: A Decomposition Analysis. Rev. Income Wealth, Vol 25, 1979
FIELDS, G.S. and FEI, J.C.H. [1978]. On Inequality Comparisons. Econometrica, Vol 46, 1978
FRISK, P.R. [1961]. The Graduation of Income Distributions. Econometrica, Vol 29, 1961

GARVY, G. [1952]. Inequality of Income: Causes and Measurement. Studies in Income and Wealth, Vol 15, Conference on Research in Income and Wealth, New York, 1952
GASTWIRTH, J. [1971a]. A General Definition of the Lorenz Curve. Econometrica, Vol 39, 1971
— [1971b]. Robust Estimation of the Gini Index of Income Inequality. Bull. ISI, Vol 44, 1971
— [1972]. The Estimation of the Lorenz Curve and Gini Index. Rev. Econ. Statist., Vol 54, 1972

— [1973]. A New Index of Income Inequality. Contributed Paper, 39th Session of the International Statistical Institute, Wien, 1973

— [1974]. Large Sample Theory of Some Measures of Income Inequality. Econometrica, Vol 42, 1974

— [1975]. The Estimation of a Family of Measures of Economic Inequality. J. Econometrics, Vol 3, 1975

GASTWIRTH, J. and GLAUBERMAN, M. [1976]. The Interpolation of the Lorenz Curve and the Gini Index from Grouped Data. Econometrica, Vol 44, 1976

GASTWIRTH, J. and KRIEGER, A.M. [1975]. On Bounding Moments from Grouped Data. JASA, Vol 70, 1975

GIACCARDI, F. [1950]. Un criterio per la costruzione di indici di conzentrazione. Revista Italiana di Economia Demografica e Statistica, Vol 4, 1950

GIBRAT, R. [1931]. Les Inégalités Economiques. Paris, 1931

— [1957]. On Economic Inequalities. Int. Econ. Papers, Vol 7, 1957, translation of chapters V-VII of Gibrat [1931]

GINI, C. [1909]. Il diverso accrescimento delle classi sociali e la concentrazione della riccezza. Giornale degli Economisti, January 1909

— [1912]. Variabilità e mutabilità. Bologna, 1912

— [1914]. Sulla misura della concentrazione e della variabilita dei caratteri. Atti del R. Istituto Veneto, Bd 73, 1913—14

— [1930]. Sul massimo degli indici de variabilità. Metron, Vol 8, 1930

— [1936]. On the Measurement of Concentration with Special Reference to Income and Wealth. Cowles Commission Research Conference 1936, Colorado College Publications, Colorado Springs, 1936

GLASSER, G.J. [1961]. Relationship between the Mean Difference and Other Measures of Variation. Metron, Vol 21, 1961

— [1962]. Variance Formulas for the Mean Difference and Coefficient of Concentration. JASA, Vol 57, 1962

HAGERBAUMER, J.B. [1977]. The Gini Concentration Ratio and the Minor Concentration Ratio: A Two-Parameter Index of Inequality. Rev. Econ. Statist., Vol 59, 1977

HAINSWORTH, G.B. [1964]. The Lorenz Curve as a General Tool of Economic Analysis. Economic Record, September 1964

HANSEN, M., HURWITZ, W. and MADOW, W. [1953]. Sample Survey Methods and Theory, Vol II, Theory. John Wiley & Sons, New York, 1953

HARDY, G.H., LITTLEWOOD, J.E. and POLYA, G. [1934]. Inequalities. Cambridge, 1934

HART, P.E. [1971]. Entropy and Other Measures of Concentration. J. Royal Statist. Soc., Ser. A, Vol 134, 1971

— [1975]. Moment Distributions in Economics, An Exposition. J. Royal Statist. Soc., Ser. A, Vol 138, 1975

— [1976]. The Dynamics of Earnings, 1963—1973. Econ. J., Vol 86, 1976

— [1978]. Redundant Inequalities. National Institute of Economic and Social Research, Discussion Paper No 18, London, 1978

HELMERT, F.R. [1876]. Die Berechnung des wahrscheinlichen Beobachtungsfehlers aus den ersten Potenzen der Differenzen gleichgenauer direchter Beobachtungen. Astronomische Nachrichten, Bd 88, No 2029, 1876

JAKOBSSON, U. [1976]. On the Measurement of the Degree of Progression. J. Public Econ., Vol 5, 1976

JAKOBSSON, U. and NORMANN, G. [1974]. Inkomstbeskattningen i den ekonomiska

politiken. IUI, Stockholm, 1974
— [1975]. En progressiv skatt i en inflationsekonomi. Ekonomisk Debatt, 1975:8
JOHNSON, H.G. [1973]. The Theory of Income Distribution. Gray-Mills Publ. Ltd, London, 1973

KAKWANI, N.C. [1977]. Applications of Lorenz Curves in Economic Analysis. Econometrica, Vol 45, 1977
— [1980a]. Functional Forms for Estimating the Lorenz Curve: A Reply. Econometrica, Vol 48, 1980
— [1980b]. Income Inequality and Poverty, Methods of Estimation and Policy Applications. Oxford University Press, New York, 1980
— [1980c]. On a Class of Poverty Measures. Econometrica, Vol 48, 1980
KAKWANI, N.C. and PODDER, N. [1973]. On the Estimation of the Lorenz Curve from Grouped Observations. Int. Econ. Rev., Vol 14, 1973
— [1976]. Efficient Estimation of the Lorenz Curve and Associated Inequality Measures from Grouped Observations. Econometrica, Vol 44, 1976
KALECKI, M. [1945]. On the Gibrat Distribution. Econometrica, Vol 13, 1945
KAMAT, A.R. [1953]. The Third Moment of Gini's Mean Difference. Biometrika, Vol 40, 1953
KENDALL, M.G. [1955]. Rank Correlation Methods. Griffin, London, 2nd ed., 1955
KENDALL, M.G. and STUART, A. [1977]. The Advanced Theory of Statistics, Vol 1. Griffin, London, 4th ed., 1977
KIENZLE, E.C. [1980]. Measurement of Tax Progressivity: Comment. Amer. Econ. Rev., Vol 70, 1980
KISH, L. [1965]. Survey Sampling. John Wiley & Sons, New York, 1965
KISH, L. and FRANKEL, M.R. [1970]. Balanced Repeated Replications for Standard Errors. JASA, Vol 65, 1970
KLEIN, L.R. [1962]. An Introduction to Econometrics. Prentice-Hall Inc, Englewood Cliffs, New Jersey, 1962
KLOEK, T. and van DIJK, H.K. [1977]. Further Results on Efficient Estimation of Income Distribution Parameters. Econ. Appl., Vol 30, 1977
KOLM, S.C. [1976a]. Unequal Inequalities I. J. Econ. Theory, Vol 12, 1976
— [1976b]. Unequal Inequalities II. J. Econ. Theory, Vol 12, 1976
KONDOR, Y. [1971]. An Old-New Measure of Income Inequality. Econometrica, Vol 39, 1971
— [1975]. Value Judgements Implied by the Use of Various Measures of Income Inequality. Rev. Income Wealth, Vol 21, 1975
KOO, A.Y.C., QUAN, N.T. and RASCHE, R. [1981]. Identification of the Lorenz Curve by Lorenz Coefficients. Weltwirtschaftliches Archiv, Bd 117, 1981
KRAVIS, I. [1962]. The Structure of Income. University of Pennsylvania, 1962
KRUPP, H-J. [1978]. Transfer Policy and Changes in Income Distribution. In 'Personal Income Distribution', eds. W. Krelle and A.F. Shorrocks, North-Holland Publ. Co, Amsterdam, 1978
KURIEN, C.J. [1977]. The Measurement and Trends of Inequality: Comment. Amer. Econ. Rev., Vol 67, 1977
KUZNETS, S. [1957]. Quantitative Aspects of the Economic Growth of Nations, II: Industrial Distribution of National Product and Labour Force. Economic Development and Cultural Change, Supplement to Vol 5, 1957
— [1959]. Six Lectures on Economic Growth. The Free Press, Glencoe, Illinois, 1959

LAYARD, R. and ZABALZA, A. [1979]. Family Income Distribution: Explanation and Policy Evaluation. J. Political Econ., Vol 87, 1979

LERNER, A.P. [1944]. The Economics of Control. McMillan, London, 1944

LEVINE, D.B. and SINGER, N.M. [1970]. The Mathematical Relation between the Income Distribution and the Measurement of Income Inequality. Econometrica, Vol 38, 1970

LINDERS, F.J. [1929]. Några anmärkningar till inkomststatistiken vid 1920 års folkräkning. Nordisk Statistisk Tidskrift, Bd 8, 1929

LITTLE, I.M.D. [1952]. Social Choice and Individual Values. J. Political Econ., Vol 60, 1952

LOMNICKI, Z.A. [1952]. The Standard Error of Gini's Mean Difference. Ann. Math. Statist., Vol 23, 1952

LORENZ, M.O. [1905]. Methods for Measuring Concentation of Wealth. JASA, New Series No 70, 1905

LOVE, R. and WOLFSON, M.C. [1976]. Income Inequality: Statistical Methodology and Canadian Illustrations. Statistics Canada, Catalogue 13—559 Occasional, March 1976

LYDALL, H.F. [1976]. Theories of the Distribution of Earnings. In 'Personal Distribution of Incomes', ed. A.B. Atkinson, Allen und Unwin, London, 1976

MADDALA, G.S. and SINGH, S.K. [1977]. Estimation Problems in Size Distribution of Incomes. Econ. Appl., Vol 30, 1977

MALMQUIST, S. [1970]. On a Method of Comparing Two Continuous Distribution Functions. Annales, Academiae Regae Scientarum Upsaliensis, Almqvist & Wiksell, Stockholm, 1970

MANDELBROT, B. [1960]. The Pareto-Lévy Law and the Distribution of Income. Int. Econ. Rev., Vol 1, 1960

MANGAHAS, M. [1975]. Income Inequality in the Philippines: A Decomposition Analysis. ILO, Population and Employment, Working Paper No. 12, Geneva, February 1975

MARTIĆ, L. [1970]. A Geometrical Note on New Income Inequality Measures. Econometrica, Vol 38, 1970

MCDONALD, J.B. and JENSEN, B. [1979]. An Analysis of Some Properties of Alternative Measures of Income Inequality Based on the Gamma Distribution Function. JASA, Vol 74, 1979

MEHRAN, F. [1975a]. Bounds on the Gini Index Based on Observed Points of the Lorenz Curve. JASA, Vol 70, 1975

— [1975b]. A Statistical Analysis on Income Inequality Based on a Decomposition of the Gini Index. Proceedings of the 40th Session of ISI, Warsaw, 1975

— [1976]. Linear Measures of Income Inequality. Econometrica, Vol 44, 1976

MENDERHAUSEN, H. [1939]. On the Measurement of the Degree of Inequality of Income Distributions. Cowles Commission for Research in Economics, University of Chicago, 1939

— [1946]. Changes in Income Distribution During the Great Depression. Studies in Income and Wealth, Vol 7, National Bureau of Economic Research, New York, 1946

MICHAL, J. [1978]. Size Distribution of Household Incomes and Earnings in Developed Socialist Countries. In 'Personal Income Distribution', eds. W. Krelle and A.F. Shorrocks, North-Holland Publ. Co, Amsterdam, 1978

MORLEY, S.A. [1981]. The Effect of Changes in the Population on Several Measures of Income Distribution. Amer. Econ. Rev., Vol 71, 1981

MUELLBAUER, J. [1974]. Inequality Measures, Prices and Household Composition. Rev. Econ. Stud., Vol 41, 1974

MUSGROVE, P. [1980]. Income Distribution and the Aggregate Consumption Function. J. Political Econ., Vol 88, 1980

NAIR, U.S. [1936]. The Standard Error of Gini's Mean Difference. Biometrika, Vol 28, 1936

NELSON, E.R. [1977]. The Measurement and Trend of Inequality: Comment. Amer. Econ. Rev., Vol 67, 1977

NEWBERY, D. [1970]. A Theorem on the Measurement of Inequality. J. Econ. Theory, Vol 2, 1970

NICHOLSON, J.L. and BRITTON, A.J.C. [1976]. The Redistribution of Income. In 'Personal Distribution of Income', ed. A.B. Atkinson, Allen and Unwin, London, 1976

NIEHANS, J. [1955]. Eine Messziffer für Betriebsgrössen. Zeitschrift für die gesamte Staatswissenschaft, Bd 111, 1955

NYGÅRD, F. [1981]. Mätning av inkomstjämnhet — en studie av ett statistiskt operationaliseringsproblem. Meddelanden från ekonomisk-statsvetenskapliga fakulteten vid Åbo Akademi, Statistiska Institutionen, Ser. A:163, Turku, 1981

NYGÅRD, F. and SANDSTRÖM, A. [1980]. On the Measurement of Income Inequality: A Review, Part II. Studies Based on International Statistical Data, 2, Department of Statistics, University of Stockholm, Research Report 1980:5

ORD, J.K. [1975]. Statistical Models for Personal Income Distributions. A Modern Course on Statistical Distributions in Scientific Work, Vol 2, D. Reidel Publ. Co, Derdrecht-Holland, 1975

PAGLIN, M. [1975]. The Measurement and Trend of Inequality: A Basic Revision. Amer. Econ. Rev., Vol 65, 1975

PARETO, V. [1896]. La Courbe de la Repartition de la Richesse. Viret-Genton, Lausanne, 1896

— [1897]. Cours d'Economie Politique. Rouge, Lausanne, 1897

PEN, J. [1971]. Income Distribution. Facts, Theories, Policies. Praeger Publ., New York, 1971

— [1978]. The Role of Power in the Distribution of Personal Income: Some Illustrative Numbers. In 'Personal Income Distribution', eds. A. Krelle and A.F. Shorrocks, North-Holland Publ. Co, Amsterdam, 1978

PIESCH, W. [1975]. Statistische Konzentrationsmasse. J.C.B. Mohr (Paul Siebeck), Tübingen, 1975

POLLAK, R.A. [1971]. Additive Utility Functions and Linear Engel Curves. Rev. Econ. Stud., Vol 38, 1971

PRAAG, B. van [1978]. The Perception of Income Inequality. In 'Personal Income Distribution', eds. A. Krelle and A.F. Shorrocks, North-Holland Publ. Co, Amsterdam, 1978

Provisional Guidelines on Statistics of the Distribution of Income, Consumption and Accumulation of Households. United Nations, Dept. of Economic and Social Affairs, Studies in Methods, Series M No. 61, New York, 1977

PYATT, G. [1976]. On the Interpretation and Disaggregation of Gini Coefficients. Econ. J., Vol 86, 1976

— [1980]. Poverty and Welfare Measures Based on the Lorenz Curve. Development Research Center, World Bank, January 1980

PYATT, G., CHEN, C-N. and FEI, J. [1980]. The Distribution of Income by Factor Components. Quart. J. Econ., Vol 94, 1980

RAO, C.R. [1973]. Linear Statistical Inference and Its Applications. John Wiley & Sons, New York, 2nd ed., 1973

RAO, V.M. [1969]. Two Decompositions of the Concentration Ratio. J. Royal Statist. Soc., Ser. A, Vol 132, 1969

RASCHE, R.H., GAFFNEY, J., KOO, A.Y.C. and OBST, N. [1980]. Functional Forms for Estimating the Lorenz Curve. Econometrica, Vol 48, 1980
ROSENBLUTH, G. [1951]. Note on Mr. Schutz's Measure of Income Inequality. Amer. Econ. Rev., Vol 41, 1951
ROTHSCHILD, M. and STIGLITZ, J.E. [1970]. Increasing Risk: I. A Definition. J. Econ. Theory, Vol 2, 1970
— [1973]. Some Further Results on the Measurement of Inequality. J. Econ. Theory, Vol 6, 1973
RUTHERFORD, R.S.G. [1955]. Income Distributions, A New Model. Econometrica, Vol 23, 1955

SAHOTA, G.S. [1978]. Theories of Personal Income Distribution: A Survey. J. Econ. Literature, Vol 16, 1976
SALEM, A.B.Z. and MOUNT, T.D. [1974]. A Convenient Descriptive Model of Income Distribution: The Gamma Density. Econometrica, Vol 42, 1974
SAMUELSON, P.A. and SWAMY, S. [1974]. Invariant Economic Index Numbers and Canonical Duality: Survey and Synthesis. Amer. Econ. Rev., Vol 64, 1974
SCHAICH, E. [1971]. Lorenzfunktion und Gini-koeffizient in kritischer Betrachtung. Jahrb. f. Nationalök. u. Stat., Bd 185, 1971
SCHUTZ, R.R. [1951]. On the Measurement of Income Inequality. Amer. Econ. Rev., Vol 41, 1951
SEN, A. [1970]. Collective Choice and Social Welfare. Holden-Day, San Francisco, 1970
— [1973]. On Economic Inequality. Oxford University Press, Oxford, 1973
— [1976]. Real National Income. Rev. Econ. Stud., Vol 43, 1976
— [1977]. On Weights and Measures: Informational Constraints in Social Welfare Analysis. Econometrica, Vol 45, 1977
— [1978]. Ethical Measurement of Inequality: Some Difficulties. In 'Personal Income Distribution', eds. A. Krelle and A.F. Shorrocks, North-Holland Publ. Co, Amsterdam, 1978
— [1979]. Personal Utilities and Public Judgements: Or What's Wrong with Welfare Economics. Econ. J., Vol 89, 1979
— [1980]. Description as Choice. Oxford Econ. Papers, Vol 32, 1980
SENDLER, W. [1979]. On Statistical Inference In Concentration Measurement. Metrika, Vol 26, 1979
SHESHINSKI, E. [1972]. Relation between a Social Welfare Function and the Gini Index of Income Inequality. J. Econ. Theory, Vol 4, 1972
SHORACK, G.R. [1972]. Functions of Order Statistics. Ann. Math. Statist., Vol 43, 1972
SHORROCKS, A.F. [1976]. Income Mobility and the Markov Assumption. Econ. J., Vol 86, 1976
— [1980a]. The Class of Additively Decomposable Inequality Measures. Econometrica, Vol 48, 1980
— [1980b]. Source Decomposition of Income Distribution. Discussion Paper, London School of Economics, February 1980
SINGH, S.K. and MADDALA, G.S. [1975]. A Stochastic Process for Income Distributions and Tests of Income Distribution Functions. JASA, Proceedings of Business and Economics Section, 1975
— [1976]. A Function for Size Distribution of Income. Econometrica, Vol 44, 1976
SOLTOW, L. [1960]. The Distribution of Income Related to Changes in the Distribution of Education, Age and Occupation. Rev. Econ. Statist., Vol 42, 1960

SPIEGEL, M. [1961]. Theory and Problems of Statistics. Schaum Publ. Co, New York, 1961
STAEHLE, H. [1937]. Short Period Variations in the Distribution of Incomes. Rev. Econ. Statist., Vol 19, 1937
STIGLITZ, J. [1978]. Equality, Taxation and Inheritance. In 'Personal Income Distribution', eds. A. Krelle and A.F. Shorrocks, North-Holland Publ. Co, Amsterdam, 1978
STOIKOV, V. [1975]. How Misleading are Income Distributions? Rev. Income Wealth, Vol 21. 1975
STUART, A. [1954]. The Correlation between Variate-Values and Ranks in Samples from a Continuous Distribution. Brit. J. Statist. Psychology, Vol 7, 1954
SUITS, D.B. [1977]. Measurement of Tax Progressivity. Amer. Econ. Rev., Vol 67, 1977
— [1980]. Measurement of Tax Progressivity: Reply. Amer. Econ. Rev., Vol 70, 1980
SÖDERSTRÖM, L. [1981]. Compensatory and Non-Compensatory Income Differences — A Preliminary Exposition. In 'The Statics and Dynamics of Income', eds. N.A. Klevmarken and J.A. Lybeck, Tieto Ltd, Clevedon, 1981

TAGUCHI, T. [1968]. Concentration-Curve Methods and Structures of Skew Populations. Annals of the Institute of Statistical Mathematics, Vol 20, Tokio, 1968
THEIL, H. [1967]. Economics and Information Theory. Studies in Mathematical and Managerial Economics, Vol 7, North-Holland Publ. Co, Amsterdam, 1967
— [1972]. Statistical Decomposition Analysis. North-Holland Publ. Co., Amsterdam, 1972
— [1975]. Theory and Measurement of Consumer Demand, Vol 1. North-Holland Publ. Co, Amsterdam, 1975
THORBURN, D. [1975]. Large Sample Properties of Jackknife Statistics. University of Lund, 1975
TINBERGEN, J. [1977]. Income Distribution: Second Thoughts. De Economist, Vol 125, 1977
— [1978]. Equitable Income Distribution: Definition, Measurement, Feasibility. In 'Personal Income Distribution', eds. A. Krelle and A.F. Shorrocks, North-Holland Publ. Co, Amsterdam, 1978

VARIAN, H.R. [1979]. Distibutive Justice, Welfare Economics, and the Theory of Fairness. In 'Philosophy and Economic Theory', eds. F. Hahn and M. Hollis, Oxford University Press, Oxford, 1979
VARTIA, Y.O. [1980]. Interpolation of Frequency Curves by Cubic Splines. Department of Statistics, University of Helsinki, Research Report No. 22, November 1980
VARTIA, P.L.I. and VARTIA, Y.O. [1981]. Description of the Income Distribution by the Scaled F Distribution Model. In 'The Statics and Dynamics of Income', eds. N.A. Klevmarken and J.A. Lybeck, Tieto Ltd, Clevedon, 1981

WEIZSÄCKER, C.C. [1978]. Annual Income, Lifetime Income and Other Income Concepts in Measuring Income Distribution. In 'Personal Income Distribution', eds. A. Krelle and A.F. Shorrocks, North-Holland Publ. Co, Amsterdam, 1978
WILES, P. [1978]. Our Shaky Data Base. In 'Personal Income Distribution', eds. A. Krelle and A.F. Shorrocks, North-Holland Publ. Co, Amsterdam, 1978
WOLD, H. [1935]. A Study on the Mean Difference, Concentration Curves and Concentration Ratio. Metron, Vol 12, 1935

YNTEMA, D. [1933]. Measures of the Inequality of the Personal Distribution of Wealth and Income. JASA, Vol 28, 1933
YOUNG, A.A. [1917]. Do the Statistics of the Concentration of Wealth in the United States Mean What They are Assumed to Mean? JASA, Vol 12, 1917

INDEX